W9-AOO-394

Book Markets for Children's Writers™ 2006

Acknowledgments

The editors of this directory appreciate the generous cooperation of our instructor and student contributors and the children's book editors who made clear their policies and practices.

MARNI MCNIFF, Editor

SUSAN TIERNEY, Articles Editor

HEATHER BURNS-DEMELO, Assistant Editor

CLAIRE BROWN, Assistant Editor

SHERRI KEEFE, Assistant Editor

JANINE MANGIAMELE, Assistant Editor

Contributing Writers: Eileen Byrne, Heather Burns-DeMelo, Barbara Cole, Louanne Lang, Pamela Purrone

Cover Art: Joanna Horvath

Contents

Step-by-Step Through the Submissions Process   5

This section offers step-by-step instructions for compiling a submissions package.

Gateway to the Markets   55

Contents (Cont.)

Step-by-Step Through the Submissions Process

Ready, Aim . . . Research and Prepare to Sell

Writers are like archers. Our target is to compose the best possible work and find it a home, a market, a bull's-eye. To be a good archer, we first have to have a strong interest, a passion, for the sport. We acquire the best possible equipment, high-quality bow and arrows, and maintain them well. We practice our aim and technique, and train with a coach if needed. The better these requirements are followed, the more frequently we hit the bull's-eye. Now substitute the following steps and see if the simile holds for your favorite "sport"—writing.

1 - **Target the subject.** Is your topic of personal interest and a subject you feel passionate about? An editor isn't going to be enthusiastic about a book if you're not. What type of research will make it interesting and successful? Children's editors today require first-rate, primary research.

2 - **Target the quality.** Have you done your best writing? Practiced your skills, gone to writers' conferences, taken courses, joined critique groups, or in some way worked at your craft and gained the right "equipment?"

3 - **Target the audience.** Can you see it clearly? What is the age? Reading level? Interest? Voice?

4 - **Target the competition.** Are there other books on comparable subjects? If you're writing in one genre, what else is out there? Do you have a truly different slant to offer?

5 - **Target the market generally.** Is your book to be trade, mass-market, religious, crossover, regional, educational?

6 - **Target the individual publisher and editor.** What is this particular company and editor most interested in, most successful with?

We will take you step-by-step through the process of hitting some of these targets. Only you can work on the quality, but we will coach you through subject, audience, competition, and market objectives and how to reach them. You'll come nearer and nearer to a bull's-eye with every arrow—every manuscript sent flying.

Target the Subject

Whether you're finding new ideas, developing a defined project, or searching for markets for your completed manuscript, you can improve the submission process by taking time to do fundamental research. The first step is to select an idea that interests you, that you believe will appeal to readers as much as it does to you, and then collect information about it.

This idea and research development step is an important first measure toward selling your book. While most editors and successful writers will tell beginners to focus on writing a good book, not on worrying about what's fashionable in the market and what's not—and they're correct—a good book requires authenticity if it's fiction, and accuracy if it's nonfiction. Subject research is essential in composing the best possible manuscript, whether it's historical background for a novel or a text, geographical information on a region or city, updated data for a scientific principle, or even searches for good character names on a census or genealogical site. Finding and refining your idea with research will strengthen your work, and poise it to sell.

Research resources. Writers have a surfeit of research resources today in the Internet quiver. The Web gives writers access to libraries, research studies, museums, associations, businesses, and a seemingly endless supply of miscellaneous sites available through myriad search engines. You can do this research at your local library if you're not set up at home. Look at:

- encyclopedia sites that might provide links to more detailed pages on other sites.
- university libraries online.
- government resources like the Library of Congress, the Smithsonian, NASA.
- museum sites, such as the Metropolitan Museum of Art in

7

New York, the British Museum, and many other world-class museums.

- the sites of smaller, more focused museums, historical sites, even corporations (for that article on sneakers, for example).
- organizations that range from the social to the arts to sports, from the local to the universal.
- journalism and other sites that lead to "experts" for interviews.

Some sites help you to find the existence of material, but you'll need to get it physically from the library or another source. Some sites, however, provide actual content—text, photos, data—online.

Accuracy and annotations. Websites have links to other sites. Follow the trail, the links, and keep clear notes on where you go and what you learn, so you don't lose important resources or unintentionally plagiarize. Narrow in on your topic, and be sure to check and recheck your information against other sources. Take every care with accuracy, since children's editors today require primary research sources and they want precision. Keep a running bibliography; you will need it for your submission package and even if you don't, it's a good idea for back-up and additional research, if it's needed. Be sure to check the _Book Markets for Children's Writers'_ listings for indications of the kind of bibliographical or other research annotations targeted editors require. (See, for example, the bibliography on page 35.)

Fiction and research. Perhaps you're writing fiction and don't believe you need to do research. You might not, but you very well may. Is your story set in a seaside town you recall from childhood? What's the weather like there when your story is set? Are you sure? Do you need inspiration for character names for a contemporary or historical story? Check local newspapers for stories about children of a particular age and time. Remember that "local" has new meaning on the Internet. You can look up _The Columbus Dispatch_ (Ohio) or _The Waterbury Republican_ (Connecticut) or _The Mercury News_ (San Jose, California). Check a genealogy site for names, or for story ideas, or for nonfiction research. Use all your resources, and of course, turn to print, too. Through your local library you have access to networks of other libraries that will help you borrow virtually any book you need.

Internet Research Resources

A list of possible Internet research sites that purports to be comprehensive would take up many pages, but here are broad categories and site examples to start the subject research process.

● **Search engines:** www.google.com and www.dogpile.com are effective search engines because they provide specificity and variety when searching a subject. For a different kind of search, try www.about.com, which offers expert guides to help you navigate through a subject.

● **Government sites:** The U.S. government's sites are a great place to begin research: Look for books, historical archives, photos, and much more at the Library of Congress (www.loc.gov). At NASA (www.nasa.gov), try the Strategic Enterprises sites for space, technology, exploration, earth and physical sciences, and biology. The Smithsonian site (www.smithsonian.org) is divided into Art & Design, History & Culture, Science & Technology. Go to the Government Printing Office (www.access.gpo.gov) and FirstGov (www.firstgov.gov), for everything from government operations to health to mining to special education.

● **Reference sites:** The *Encyclopedia Britannica* (www. britannica.com) site gives brief information on myriad topics, and provides helpful links; a subscriber service allows access to longer articles and more information. The Learning Network's www.infoplease.com is an almanac site with facts on topics from world events to art, architecture, biographies, holiday calendars, weather, health, weights and measures, and much more.

● **Museums:** Large and small museums across the country, and the world, can be indispensable to the writer. Through a search engine, see if local historical societies, for example, have websites. Or try the Metropolitan Museum of Art (www.metmuseum.org), British Museum (www.thebritishmuseum.ac.uk), or try the Virtual Library museums pages (www.icom.org/vlmp) to find museums around the world.

Target the Audience

Developing ideas means not only thought and research about your topic or story, but information about the readers. Audience is the meeting place of idea and market research. Who will read this story? Who is this ultimate market? What grabs the reader?

Experts. Search out "experts" who can help you learn which books kids are reading at which ages, or what parents or educators are reading, if they're your projected audience. Talk to children's librarians and teachers about the kinds of stories and topics currently, or universally, appealing to young readers. Ask them about curriculum needs, especially for nonfiction. Go to bookstores and speak to managers who specialize in children's books. Online, go to library and reading sites, like those for the American Library Association (ALA) and the International Reading Association (IRA).

Developmental stages. Find out what's happening developmentally at a given age, what's being studied at school, what interests spark your audience. Talk to scout leaders, coaches, and music teachers. Observe and talk to the children themselves, especially about books if you can. Go to children's websites to see the topics they cover, and watch television programming and read young people's magazines to learn more about contemporary youth culture. Go to parenting websites to see what problems and joys arise. But remember, you'll need to find your own slants on these subjects—your own way of holding your bow and releasing your arrow.

Age ranges. Use *Book Markets for Children's Writers*: Browse through the listings to look at the ages covered and review the sample titles. Or start with the Category Index (page 556) and look under "preK" or "middle grade" or "young adult," and review the publishers listed. Request their catalogues or visit their websites. Catalogues are generally free upon request with a stamped, self-addressed, 9x12 envelope. Examining the catalogues, in print or online, is a helpful practice even at this stage of research, though it will be essential once you focus in on publishers where you'll target your work. See how many titles are published in what genres, for what age ranges; see what gives you a sense of their subjects and style. What feel do you get for the picture book illustrations, for

Age-Targeting Resources

- **American Library Association (ALA)** and **International Reading Association (IRA):** The lists of books for children compiled by these two organizations will help direct you to age-appropriate writing (www.ala.org and www.reading.org). The ALA also lists "Great Sites!" for children, which helps writers focus in on kids' interests.

- **American Academy of Pediatrics:** Try the AAP's (www.aap.org) You and Your Family page, or the publications page.

- **Bright Futures:** Available on this organization's website (www.brightfutures.org) are downloads of tip sheets on developmental stages, and a variety of resources on juvenile and adolescent health and behavioral development.

- **National Network for Child Care (NNCC):** The website (www.nncc.org) is divided into early childhood, school age, teens, and evaluation, as well as topics such as intellectual, language, emotional/social, and an Ages and Stages series.

- **Search Institute:** This nonprofit's organization (www.search-institute.org) and website highlight 40 developmental assets for children from grades 6 to 12.

Finding Child and Teen Sites

- **KidsClick!:** A librarian-generated list of more than 600 sites for children (http://sunsite.berkeley.edu/KidsClick!). Categories include facts & reference, weird & mysterious, religion & mythology, machines & transportation, and more.

- **The Kids on the Web:** A list of sites compiled since 1994 by the author of *Children and the Internet: A Zen Guide for Parents and Educators* www.zen.org/~brendan/kids.html; ALA-recommended site.

- **Surfing the Net with Kids:** A newspaper columnist's recommendations (www.surfnetkids.com), with current topics, a calendar of interesting events, many topics.

example, if that is what you want to write, and how is the text likely to reflect that? Is this a wide-ranging publisher, or does it fill a niche?

You might need or want to buy a book to advance your research into what a particular segment of children is reading. Amazon.com or Barnesandnoble. com, along with other sites that help you buy books or locate out-of-print titles, have become one of a writer's best friends. Not only do they help you locate children's books you know you want, they give you information on readership ages. Reverse the process and begin your search at one of these sites with a designated age range and see what titles come up. Lots of humor? Nonfiction, but not the fiction you expected? Does this help you in thinking about what you want to write?

Target the Competition & General Markets

When you're doing your audience or subject research, you might find that two or three large publishers specialize in books for a particular age or field, but the titles they list are old. That's a beginning for your competition research— looking into titles already in the marketplace similar to your idea and finding the publishers that match.

**Competitive titles.** When you are ready to pull together your submissions package, adding this competition information in a paragraph to your query or proposal, or in a separate one-page summary, will give you a definite advantage. It will show editors your professionalism, skills at research, and dedication to your work. If you use the research well, it will indicate to the editor that you know what that particular company publishes and why your book will fit its list. Doing your competition research, the questions you'll need to ask are:

- What books are in print that are similar to my idea?
- Who are the publishers, and what kinds of companies are they?
- When were they published?
- How are they different in slant, format, audience, etc., from mine?

Competition Research Form

Title	Author	Publisher	Pub. Date	Description/Differences from My Book

◆ If one or more are not different, how will I reslant my idea to make my title more distinct?

This is where you'll need to strike a balance between selecting a subject or a story that is of such significant interest to the audience you're targeting that other authors have addressed it, and the challenge of giving it a new twist. The same subjects will come up over and over again, and there's a reason—a large segment of four-year-olds are always interested in trucks and always will be, for example. But how do you write another picture book on trucks and make sure it's distinct? How do you know that your book on a kindergartener's school tribulations will attract an editor's attention?

Perhaps those kindergarteners are ready for a new book on the subject, because it's been more than five years since the last one was published by one publisher, or any publisher. To find that out, once again you might go to:

◆ bookstores, to review the selection, put your hands on the books, and peruse them
◆ *Book Markets for Children's Writers*, for an overview of companies publishing possibly competitive books
◆ online booksellers, with subject and age searches
◆ libraries for catalogues and *Subject Guide to Children's Books in Print*
◆ publisher websites and publisher catalogues

At bookstores, ask for a list of all the books on a given subject. They should be able to print one out for you from their computer system. At the library, use the computer database to do a comparable search, or look at the *Subject Guide to Children's Books in Print*.

Market types. Use *Book Markets for Children's Writers'* Category Index to generate a list of companies that publish in the category of your book and to start you thinking about the marketplace in general. You might want to use a form like that on page 13. Are the companies with competitive titles generally educational, trade, religious, special interest? Or are they all over the map? Do they have a strong backlist of older titles that they continue to support, or are titles allowed to go out of print?

The individual publisher listings in *Book Markets for Children's Writers* also give you information on how many books a company publishes each year and how many it accepts from new authors. You're another step closer to selecting the publishers to whom you'll send your submission.

Target the Publisher & Editor

It's time to look more closely at the individual listings in *Book Markets for Children's Writers* to find out what a company has published and what its editors are currently seeking. *Book Markets for Children's Writers* can be well used to create comparative lists of competitive titles, as above, and even better used to align your work with a publisher who is looking for it.

If you've followed the process here, you've focused in on an idea, determined your readership, and learned what books on that subject and readership are available. But editors' needs change. How do you know who wants what now? The listings in *Book Markets for Children's Writers* are updated annually, with an emphasis on finding exactly what the editor needs now.

Turn again to the Category Index on page 556, or leaf through the listings themselves, and write down those publishers with interests similar to your own, especially those you didn't find in your earlier research. You've done this in researching the field and competition as a whole, but now you need to focus on the publishers you will pursue for your book. Here's how the listings break down and how to use them best.

- ◆ **Publisher's Interests:** Does the publisher you have in mind produce hardbacks, paperbacks, or both? Is it an imprint of a larger company? Does it publish fiction and/or nonfiction? Does it have a specialization, such as history, regional subjects, educational? Is your book compatible with the publisher's profile? Don't stretch to make a match—make it a close one—but if you believe you can slant your book solidly toward a publisher's needs, work toward that in pulling together your proposal. If you've written fiction that just can't be reshaped, be honest, and don't consider a given publisher's needs a good target.

◆ **Freelance Potential:** How many books did the publisher produce last year? Of the books published, how many came from unpublished writers? (For an idea of your odds, compare the number of submissions the publisher received last year to the number of titles it published.) What age range does it focus on? Are there particular topics or types of books it specializes in? What genres did the company publish, in fiction or nonfiction?

◆ **Editor's Comments:** This section reveals a publisher's current needs, and the types of manuscripts it *doesn't* want to see. It may also give you insight into preferred style or other editor preferences. This information will be one of your best tools in deciding where to submit your work.

You can also keep up with current needs through many of the trade publications like *Children's Writer* newsletter (www.childrenswriter.com or 1-800-443-6078) and *Publishers Weekly* (http://publishersweekly.reviewsnews.com/), which has improved its regular coverage of children's publishing in recent years. *PW* also offers special feature issues on children's publishing every spring and fall. A *PW* subscription is expensive, but many libraries carry the publication.

Narrow your choices to 6 to 12 publishers, and if you have not yet requested their catalogues, do so, along with their writers' guidelines. Ask a final set of questions—those in the sidebar on page 18.

You're about to pull together your submissions package. First, review the writers' guidelines, if a company has them. Whether or not they do, read the *Book Markets for Children's Writers'* listing closely for specifications, and follow them exactly. Suppose you have completed a biography of Georgia O'Keeffe you'd like to propose to Lerner Publishing. It's ready to go, but it happens to be August. If you check the Lerner listing, and their guidelines, you'll see that the company only accepts submissions in November. Don't send your work anyway, assuming they'll hold it until October. They won't. Do exactly what the publisher directs.

Now you're ready to fire your arrow: Submit.

About Agents

Writers of books at some point face the question of whether or not to look for an agent. Some successful writers never work with an agent, while others much prefer to find a strong representative for their work to deal with the business side. Some publishers, a limited number and usually very large companies, will not accept unsolicited materials except through an agent. But a good manuscript or book proposal will find its home with or without an agent, if you are committed to finding the right publisher to match your work.

How to find an agent: Look at listings in *Literary Marketplace (LMP)*, or the *Writer's Digest Guide to Literary Agents*, or contact the Association of Authors' Representatives or go to their website (www.aar-online.org) for their members list. Identify agents who work with writers for children. Check in your agent guide or go online if the agent has a website for specific contact requirements. If not, send a well-written, professional cover letter describing your work and background, accompanied by an outline or synopsis and sample chapter.

What an agent does: An agent will review your work editorially before deciding to represent you, but the primary work of an agent is to contact publishers, market your material, negotiate for rights and licenses, and review financial statements. In a good working relationship, an agent will offer solid editorial advice on the direction your proposals and stories might take.

Fees: Be careful about agent fees. Increasingly, some will charge for readings and critiques, even without taking you on as a client. Compare the fees, and the commission if you do enter into a contract. A typical rate is 15 percent for domestic sales, 20 percent for foreign.

Take Close Aim

When you've narrowed your targeted publishers to a short list, review the individual publishers' catalogues closely or go to their websites (indicated in the listings) to find out about their overall list and specific titles—dates of publication, slant, format. With even greater focus now as you sight your target, ask:

◆ Is this a large house, a smaller publisher, or an independent press with 10 or fewer books published yearly?

◆ How many books are on its backlist?

◆ What audience does the publisher target?

◆ Are most books single titles, or does the publisher focus on series books?

◆ Does it aim for one or two age groups, or does it feature books for all age groups?

◆ Does the publisher use the same authors repeatedly, or are many different authors featured?

◆ Are newer authors also represented?

◆ Is there a mix of fiction and nonfiction books, or is there more of one than the other?

◆ Is there a range of subject matter? Does my book fit in their range?

◆ Does the publisher specialize in one or more types of books, such as picture books or easy-to-reads? Is my book one of these, or not?

◆ Are there books similar to yours? Too similar and too recent, so the publisher might not want duplication?

◆ Would your book fit in with others this house has published?

◆ What are the specific requirements of the writers' guidelines and how will I meet them?

Step-by-Step through Query Letters & Proposals

Many writers find query and cover letters challenging. One publisher may prefer to receive a submission consisting of a query letter and nothing else. Another wants an extended proposal packaged in a very specific format: a cover letter, outline, résumé, samples, bibliography, competition research. A query or a cover letter is always required, but how are query letters and cover letters different? How much information should they include? What tone should they take?

Query Letters

The query letter is perhaps the most important component of a book proposal package. It should capture the editor's interest and give a sense of your treatment of the topic. It should also convince an editor that you are the person to write this book. The best advice:

- Be succinct, positive, enthusiastic, and interesting.
- Briefly describe your book proposal.
- Identify the publisher's needs by indicating your familiarity with titles on their list.
- Outline your qualifications to write the book.

Review the query letter samples on pages 27 and 30. Note each of the following elements:

Opener: A direct, brief lead that:
- captures and holds the editor's interest (it could be the first paragraph of your book);
- tells what the subject is and conveys your particular angle or slant;
- reflects your writing style, but is at all times professional; you need not be overly formal, but do not take a casual tone.

Subject: A brief description of your proposed manuscript and its potential interest to the publisher.

Specifications: If applicable, include the following:
- your manuscript's word length;
- number and type of illustrations;
- a brief indication of the research and interviews to be done; if this is extensive, include it on a separate page with a reference to it in your query;
- market information and intended audience; again, if you've done more extensive competition research, attach it separately.

Reader Appeal: A brief description of why your target audience will want to read your proposed book.

Credits: If you have publishing credits, list them briefly, including magazine credits. Don't tell the editor you've read your book to your child's class, or that several teachers have encouraged you to send it in, or that you've taken a writing course. If you have particular qualifications that helped you write the book (e.g., you run obedience classes and have written a book on dog training), say so. Many publishers request résumés. If you're attaching one in your submissions package, your query should mention relevant credits, and then refer to the résumé.

Closing: Let the publisher know if this is an exclusive or simultaneous submission.

Queries are often required for nonfiction submissions, but in the past were very uncommon in fiction. Most editors preferred to see complete manuscripts or several chapters and a synopsis for novels and early reader fiction. That has changed somewhat in recent years; some editors want a query for fiction before they'll read anything more. Here are some of the distinctions in the queries and packages for nonfiction and fiction:

Nonfiction Query Package
A nonfiction package may include:

- a query or cover letter (see page 22 for which to use);
- a synopsis (see page 32);
- a detailed outline (topical or chapter) that describes each chapter's contents (see page 33);

- alternatively, a proposal that incorporates the synopsis, outline, and other information, such as the audience targeted (see page 34);
- representative chapters;
- a bibliography, consisting of the books, periodicals, and other sources you have already used to research the project, and those that you will use, including expert sources and interviews (see page 35);
- a résumé (see page 36).

Fiction Query Package

A fiction query package may also contain any or all of the following:

- one- to two-page synopsis that briefly states the book's theme and the main character's conflict, then describes the plot, major characters, and ending;
- chapter-by-chapter synopsis consisting of one to two paragraphs (maximum) per chapter, describing the major scene or plot development of each chapter. Keep the synopsis as brief as possible. You may either single space or double space a synopsis (see pages 31 and 32);
- the first three chapters (no more than 50 pages). Check the *Book Markets for Children's Writers'* listing and publisher's guidelines carefully, as some editors prefer to see only the first chapter.

Essentials

Editors need to know from the start that you write well and that you are careful in your work. Many submissions are rejected because queries are poorly written, contain grammatical errors, or show carelessness. Since form as well as content count, make sure your package:

- is free of spelling, typographical, and grammatical errors;
- is cleanly presented and readable, whether typewritten or computer-printed;
- includes an SASE—a self-addressed stamped envelope with correct postage, or International Reply Coupons for foreign publishers;
- is photocopied for your records.

Query Letter v. Cover Letter

When to use a query letter:

❑ Always when a query is the specific requirement in the publisher's writers' guidelines.

❑ When you are including no other attached information; the query should be specific, but not exceed a single page.

❑ When you are attaching some additional materials, such as a synopsis or sample chapter.

When to use a cover letter:

❑ When an editor has requested that you send a specific manuscript and it is attached. The cover letter is a polite, professional reminder to the editor.

❑ When you have had previous interactions with an editor, who will know who you are. Perhaps you've written something for the editor before, or you had a conversation at a conference when the editor clearly suggested you send your work.

❑ When your proposal package is comprehensive, and explains your book completely enough that a cover letter is all that is needed to reiterate, very briefly, the nature of the proposal.

Query Letter Checklist

Use this checklist to evaluate your query letter before you send it with the rest of your book proposal.

Basics:
- ☐ Address the letter to the current editor, or as directed in writers' guidelines or market listings (for example, Submissions Editor or Acquisitions Editor).
- ☐ Spell the editor's name correctly.
- ☐ Proofread the address, especially the numbers.

Opening:
- ☐ Create a hook—quote a passage from your manuscript, give an unusual fact or statistic, ask a question.

Body:
- ☐ Give a brief overview of what your book proposal is about, but do not duplicate the detailed information you give in the outline or synopsis.
- ☐ List your special qualifications or experience, publishing credits/organization memberships, and research sources.
- ☐ State whether you can or cannot supply artwork.

Closing:
- ☐ Provide a brief summation.
- ☐ Let this publisher know if this is an exclusive or simultaneous submission.

Last steps:
- ☐ Proofread for spelling and punctuation errors, including typos.
- ☐ Sign the letter.

Cover Letters

A cover letter accompanies a submitted manuscript and provides an overview of your fiction or nonfiction submission, but it does not go into the same level of detail as a query letter. A cover letter is a professional introduction to the materials attached. If you are attaching a large package of materials in your submission—a synopsis, outline, competition research, résumé, for example—you don't need a full-blown query, but a cover letter.

Cover letters range from a brief business format, stating, *"Enclosed is a copy of my manuscript, [Insert Title] for your review"* to something more. In a somewhat longer form, the letter may include information about your personal experience with the topic; your publication credits; if you have them, special sources for artwork; and, if relevant, the fact that someone the editor knows and respects suggested you submit the manuscript.

A cover letter is always included when a manuscript is sent at the request of the editor or when it has been reworked following the editor's suggestions. The cover letter should remind the editor that he or she asked to see this manuscript. This can be accomplished with a simple phrase along the lines of "Thank you for requesting a copy of my manuscript, [Insert Title]." If you are going to be away or if it is easier to reach you at certain times or at certain phone numbers, include that information as well. Do not refer to your work as a book; it is a manuscript until it is published.

Proposals

A proposal is a collection of information with thorough details on a book idea. Arguably, a query alone is a proposal, but here we'll consider the various other components that may go into a proposal package. Always consult—and follow to the letter—writers' guidelines to see what a publisher requires.

__Query or cover letter.__ The descriptions on pages 19–24 should help you construct your query or cover letter.

__Synopsis.__ A brief, clear description of the fiction or nonfiction project proposed, conveying the essence of the entire idea. A synopsis may be one or several paragraphs on the entire book, or it may be written in chapter-by-chapter format. Synopses should also convey a sense of your writing style, without getting wordy. See the samples on pages 31 and 32.

Outline. A formally structured listing of the topics to be covered in a manuscript or book. Outlines may consist of brief phrases, or they may be annotated with one or two-sentence descriptions of each element. See the sample on page 33.

Note that synopses are more common for fiction than outlines. Both outlines and synopses are sometimes used to describe nonfiction, but not necessarily both in the same proposal package.

Competition/market research. The importance of researching other titles in the marketplace that might be competitive to yours was discussed earlier (pages 12–15). The presentation of this information to the editor might be in synopsis form or presented as an annotated bibliography.

Bibliography. Bibliographies are important in nonfiction submissions, considerably less so with fiction, except possibly when writing in a genre such as historical fiction. A well-wrought bibliography can go a long way toward convincing an editor of the substance behind your proposal. Include primary sources, which are more and more required in children's nonfiction; book and periodical sources; Internet sources (but be particularly careful these are well-established); expert sources you've interviewed or plan to interview. For format, use a style reference such as *Chicago Manual of Style, Modern Language Association (MLA) Handbook*, or one of the major journalist references by organizations such as the *New York Times* or Associated Press. See the sample on page 35.

Résumé/publishing credits. Many publishers request a list of publishing credits or a résumé with submissions. The résumé introduces you to an editor by indicating your background and qualifications. An editor can judge from a résumé if a prospective writer has the necessary experience to research and write material for that publishing house. The résumé that you submit to a publisher is different from one you would submit when applying for a job, because it emphasizes writing experience, memberships in writing associations, and education. Include only those credentials that demonstrate experience related to the publisher's editorial requirements, not all of your work experience or every membership. In the case of educational or special interest publishers, be sure to include pertinent work experience.

No one style is preferable, but make sure your name, address, telephone number, and email address (if you have one) appear at the top of the page. Keep your résumé short and concise—it should not be more than a page long. If you have been published, those credits may be included on the one page, or listed on a separate sheet. See the sample on page 36.

Sample chapters or clips. As well-written as a query or even a synopsis might be, nothing can give an editor as clear a sense of your style, slant, and depth of the work you are proposing, or can do, than sample chapters or clips of published work. One of the obvious dilemmas of new writers is that they may not have clips, or they may be few and not suitable to a given proposal. But sample chapters, almost always the first and perhaps one or two others that are representative, help an editor make a judgment on your abilities and the project, or determine how to guide you in another direction—and toward a sale.

Sample Query Letter – Nonfiction

Street Address
City, State ZIP
Telephone Number
Email Address

Date

Carole Hall
Acquisitions, Editorial Department
John Wiley & Sons, Inc.
605 Third Avenue
New York, New York 10158

Dear Ms. Hall:

Opener/ Hook

In researching the market, I noticed that your company is a leading publisher of books for science fair projects. What makes our project unique is the authors' experience: one is an award-winning, International Science fair participant and the other, a judge with more than twenty years experience with science competition.

Credits/ Special Experience

Subject/ Reader Appeal

Ours is a how-to manual guiding a student through each step of the process, from inception of the idea through presentation of the project at the fair. While most science fair books offer specific ideas for projects, this book shows the student and parents the nitty-gritty details of how to research the topic, write a paper, the mechanics of citing references, mistakes to avoid, how to build a backboard. Each chapter concludes with winning strategies detailing what the judges are looking for. Teachers don't have time to work with an individual student in such a fashion.

Each year, three to five million junior and senior high school students participate in science fairs. One thousand from all fifty states and forty other countries progress from school to district to state and to international levels of competition. In the past fifty-nine years, millions of dollars in scholarships, grants and awards go to the participants.

Science research is a serious business, often a year-long pursuit that involves every aspect of education. These students put to work all they have learned from reading, writing, math, grammar, spelling, statistics, ethics, logic, critical thinking, computer science, graphic arts, technical skills, scientific methodology, presentation, and public speaking. If the goal of education is to teach people to use what they have learned to move toward mastering something new, science research scores one hundred percent.

Closing

Available for your consideration are the outline, author biographies and publishing credits and a brief sample of our manuscript *Sweat the Small Stuff: Strategies for Winning Science Fair Projects*. We look forward to hearing from you.

Sincerely,

Heather Tomasello

Sample Cover Letter – Nonfiction

Street Address
City, State ZIP
Telephone Number
Email Address
Date

Laura Walsh, Editor
Millbrook Press
2 Old New Milford Road
Brookfield, CT 06804

Dear Ms. Walsh,

Opener/ Subject — Please find enclosed my proposal for a book on starting seeds indoors. I've enclosed 25 pages of the text of *So You Want to Be a Dragon Farmer* and an outline of the rest of the book, plus a bibliography.

Market/ Appeal — I've focused specifically on growing snapdragons from seeds, though the principles are applicable to almost any kind of seed starting. The book is intended to fit the science curriculum. And while the text has a kind of wacky voice, the information is sound. A fourth or fifth grader might use *So You Want to Be a Dragon Farmer* to do an independent science project between mid-February and the end of school. Or the zany style might engage a young reader simply to read the book, without doing any or all of the activities.

I've gardened for years and am a committed seed starter. I've been asked to speak to garden clubs and other groups about starting seeds indoors. I've done gardening projects with kids and am currently helping a group of inner-city youths with a community garden.

Experience — Recently, I've made sales to *Guideposts for Kids, Pockets, Listen, With,* and *Flicker.* I have a Ph.D. and have taught all ages from kindergarten to college.

Submission Status/ Closing — Thank you for considering *So You Want to Be a Dragon Farmer.* This is an exclusive submission and I am willing to revise.
I look forward to hearing from you.

Very truly yours,

Sharelle Byars Moranville

SASE enclosed.

Sample Cover Letter – Fiction

Street Address
City, State ZIP
Telephone Number
Email Address
Date

Attn. Haron Houghton, Publisher
Clearlight Publishers
823 Don Diego
Santa Fe, NM 87501

Dear Mr. Houghton:

Opener/ Subject

What if you were an eleven-year-old pitcher who broke his arm on opening day? Then, to add insult to injury, you are forced to spend the summer with your estranged father, and not a baseball diamond in sight. This is not a happy scenario, until you and three new friends discover an ancient, lost world of secrets, and possibly no way home!

Specifications/ Appeal

You will follow the adventures of young Wyatt McCabe, who discovers that magic can happen somewhere besides the baseball field. You get to meet Wyatt's favorite baseball player, and discover a world that everyone thought was a myth. Then you have to convince the adults that you are not dreaming, that it really exists!

Ms Enclosed/ Synopsis

I have enclosed a copy of my manuscript, *The Secret of Oak Creek Canyon*, and a synopsis for your review. I am certain this fantasy adventure story would be a perfect fit with your catalogue of titles.

Closing

Thank you very much for your time and consideration. This is not a simultaneous submission.

Sincerely,

Cindy Thomas

Enc: SASE

Sample Query Letter – Fiction

Street Address
City, State ZIP
Telephone Number
Email Address
Date

Chronicle Books
Children's Division
85 Second Street, Sixth Floor
San Francisco, CA 94105

Dear Sir/Madam:

Opener/ Subject — Young readers are fascinated with the danger and excitement of shipwrecks. Yet there's very little material written for children on the subject of Great Lakes shipwrecks, either in fiction or nonfiction.

Synopsis — My nonfiction manuscript, *Weather-Beaten Mysteries: Great Lakes Shipwrecks*, will describe for the young reader in a lively manner many of the shipwrecks that have occurred on the five lakes since the first-known Great Lakes shipwreck, the *Griffin*, in Lake Michigan.

Included in the manuscript are maps with shipwreck positions noted and a depth chart. Pictures are available. Enclosed please find an outline and the first three chapters of my manuscript.

Also enclosed are an SASE for your convenience for a reply and an SASP for confirmation of receipt.

Experience — I have been published in *Brio* magazine, *Discoveries*, and *Wild Outdoor World*. I have also been published in an anthology of short stories, *Forget Me Knots,* from Front Porch.

Closing — This is a simultaneous submission. Thank you for considering *Weather-Beaten Mysteries: Great Lakes Shipwrecks*. Return of my submission materials is not necessary.

Sincerely,

Rita M. Tubbs
Enclosures

Sample Synopsis – Fiction

DEATH MOUNTAIN

DEATH MOUNTAIN is a fast-paced adventure survival novel for readers 10-and-up. What sets this novel apart from other adventure stories in the marketplace is that the two main characters are girls.

What begins as a day-hike in the rugged Sierra Nevada Mountains of California turns into a test of survival for Erin and her new friend Mae. The taste of freedom is soon tainted when a deadly lightning storm strikes and the girls are separated from the rest of the group.

With only each other for support, Erin and Mae are forced to face the challenges of being lost in the untamed wilderness with grit and resourcefulness. In the process, they learn to deal with unresolved personal issues and develop a life-long friendship.

The unique physical qualities of this rugged environment and its wildlife will be woven into the story. Readers will learn survival skills along with the characters:

-- Building a fire when all available wood is wet.
-- Constructing an overnight shelter from natural material.
-- Trapping fish in the style of Native Americans.
-- Using pine pitch to make torches.
-- Boiling rose hips and pine-tip tea.

This story draws on my many wilderness expeditions, including a true adventure I had while backpacking in the shadows of the highest mountain in the lower 48 states, Mt. Whitney. As in DEATH MOUNTAIN our group was caught in a deadly lightning storm on an exposed ridge. The pack horse and mule were killed and three people were airlifted off the mountain by helicopter.

Readers will sweat hour after hour as they follow Erin and Mae on their adventure.

Sample Synopsis – Nonfiction

Name   Address, Telephone, Email

Storms

Chapter One: How Storms Form

Defines a storm as a mass of rapidly moving air that redistributes energy from the sun's heat. Discusses air currents, including the Jet Stream, and their patterns of movement across the Earth. Explains that storms begin when warm, moist air meets cold, dry air and discusses the role that the sharp boundary, or front, formed at this meeting place has in the creation of storms.

Chapter Two: Rainstorms, Snowstorms, and Thunderstorms.

Provides information about about clouds and their moisture, explaining how rain, snow, and hail are produced. Describes the processes by which thunder and lightning are created. Talks about weather forecasting and storm watches and warnings. Discusses how winds influence the severity of storms, identifying the terms gale, blizzard, and cyclone.

Chapter Three: Hurricanes and Typhoons

Explains that hurricanes and typhoons are tropical cyclones. Talks about the formation of hurricanes and typhoons as well as "the eye of the storm." Discusses the effects of these storms on the environment. Gives examples of major hurricane damage and reports on scientists' attempts to study and predict the severity of hurricanes. As part of this discussion, provides information about the hurricane naming system, the Saffir-Simpson Damage-Potential Scale, hurricane watches and warnings, and hurricane safety.

Chapter Four: Tornadoes

Defines the term tornado and reports that they are the product of middle-latitude storms as opposed to tropical storms. Describes the formation of a tornado and mentions some of the most significant tornadoes in history. Discusses scientists' attempts to study and predict the severity of tornadoes, providing information about storm chasers, the Fujita Tornado Intensity Scale, tornado watches and warnings, and tornado safety.

Sample Outline – Nonfiction

SWEAT THE SMALL STUFF:
STRATEGIES FOR WINNING SCIENCE PROJECTS
Outline

INTRODUCTION

CHAPTER 1: "Why Do I Have to Learn This Stuff?"
The Benefits of Participating in Science Research and Science Fairs
Opportunities Beyond School or Local Competition

CHAPTER 2: In the Beginning
Questions to Ask Yourself to Evaluate a Topic
Pitfalls to avoid: Is My Project Possible? Is It Safe?
ISEF Categories

CHAPTER 3: There's a Method to this Madness
Basic Definitions of the Elements of a Project
Keeping an Exact Record—the Logbook
Recording the Results

CHAPTER 4: Who, What, Where, When and How
How to Write Your Research Paper
Knowing When to Stop
Putting It Together in One Page: The Abstract

CHAPTER 5: Murphy's Law of Science Research: If Anything Can Go Wrong, It Will
Establishing a Timeline
Using Proper Safety
Have a Back-up Plan

CHAPTER 6: What's Green, Glows in the Dark and is Growing on my Project?
Using Sterile Technique
Inoculation Techniques
Precautions When Working with Biological Hazards

CHAPTER 7: Data Isn't just a Star Trek Character
Statistics

CHAPTER 8: Misteaks, Mistaxe, Mistackes, Mistakes
Common Errors

Sample Proposal – Nonfiction

Name
Address
City, State, ZIP
Date

Proposal for Millbrook Press
"Invisible Invaders: New and Dangerous Infectious Diseases"

By the middle of the 20th century, it seemed like most infectious diseases were a thing of the past. However, over the past 30 years, nearly three dozen new or re-emerging infectious diseases have started to spread among humans. Each year, 1,500 people die of an infectious disease, and half of those people are children under five years old. In the United States alone, the death rate from infectious disease has doubled since 1980.

Invisible Invaders: New and Dangerous Infectious Diseases will be an addition to The Medical Library, the Millbrook/Twenty-First Century Press series on health issues. The Center for Disease Control and Prevention, and the National Institute of Allergy and Infectious Diseases have identified 35 emerging or re-emerging diseases as serious threats to human health. The book will cover the infectious diseases with the greatest real and potential impact to Americans. It will discuss why so many infectious diseases are threatening world health and where the diseases come from. The alarming appearance of new strains of organisms that are becoming ever-more resistant to antibiotics will be covered, as will the potential use of deadly microbes and bioterrorism.

One children's book about epidemics that was published in 2000 blithely announced the eradication of smallpox in the world. Yet today, the government is making contingency plans to vaccinate millions of Americans should a bioterrorist release a deadly virus. Other books fail to mention Hantavirus, West Nile Virus, or Severe Acute Respiratory Syndrome, diseases recently threatening the health and lives of Americans. Clearly, a new children's book on the subject of infectious diseases is needed.

Invisible Invaders will consist of about 25,000 words, or approximately 115 pages of text interspersed with art. It will be written for children ages 7–10 to fit into The Medical Library series format. Each section will include information about the origin and spread of the disease, its symptoms, and treatment. With knowledge comes the power to help prevent or avoid these diseases, so the text will also cover appropriate steps that young readers can follow to decrease their risk. Case studies and pertinent sidebars enhance the text.

The author will use the latest information from prestigious organizations like the CDC, World Health Organization, National Institutes of Health, the American Public Health Association, the Infectious Diseases Society of America, and the Institute of Medicine.

Sample Bibliography

SOURCES FOR <u>DANGER ON ICE: THE SHACKLETON ADVENTURE</u>

Alexander, Caroline. "Endurance." *Natural History.* vol. 108, no. 3 (April 1999): 98-100.

_____. *The Endurance: Shackleton's Legendary Antarctic Expedition.* New York: Alfred A. Knopf, 1998.

Armstrong, Jennifer. *Shipwreck at the Bottom of the World: Shackleton's Amazing Voyage.* New York: Crown Publishers, 1998.

_____. *Spirit of Endurance.* New York: Crown Publishers, 2000.

Briley, Harold. "Sail of the Century." *Geographical*, vol. 71, no. 4 (April 1999): 48-53.

Explorers and Discoverers of the World. Edited by Daniel B. Baker. Detroit: Gale Research, 1993.

"The Furthest South." *Geographical*, vol. 68 (February 1996): 30-35.

Hammel, Sara. "The Call of the Sea: It Was a Matter of Endurance." *U.S. News & World Report.* (May 31, 1999: 67)

Kimmel, Elizabeth Cody. *Ice Story: Shackleton's Lost Expedition.* New York: Clarion Books, 1999.

Lane, Anthony. "Breaking the Waves." *The New Yorker* (April 12, 1999): 96-101.

Rogers, Patrick. "Beyond Endurance." *People Weekly,* vol. 51, no. 9 (March 8, 1999): 151-153.

"A Salute to Survival." *USA Today,* vol. 129, no. 2667 (December 2000): 8-9.

Shipwrecks. Edited by David Ritchie. New York: Facts on File, 1996): 74, 117.

Shackleton, Sir Ernest. *South: A Memoir of the* Endurance *Voyage.* (New York: Carroll & Graff, 1999 reissue of 1918 edition).

Shackleton, Sir Ernest. *Shackleton: His Antarctic Writings.* (London: British Broadcasting Corp., 1983).

"Shackleton Expedition." American Museum of Natural History website. www.amnh.org/exhibitions/shackleton

Sample Résumé

Ann Purmell
Address
Telephone Number
Email

Experience

- Writer of inspirational and children's literature.
- Freelance journalist and feature writer for *Jackson Citizen Patriot* (Michigan), a Booth Communications daily. Affiliate newspapers throughout Michigan carry my articles.
- Freelance writer for *Jackson Magazine,* a monthly business publication.
- Guest lecturer for Children's Literature and Creative Writing classes at Spring Arbor College, Spring Arbor, Michigan.
- Performs school presentations for all grade levels.

Publications/Articles

Published numerous articles, including:

- "Prayers to the Dead," *In Other Words: An American Poetry Anthology* (Western Reading Services, 1998).
- "Promises Never Die," *Guideposts for Teens* (June/July 1999). Ghost-written, first-person, true story.
- "Teaching Kids the Financial Facts of Life," *Jackson Citizen Patriot* (July 20, 1999). An interview with Jayne A. Pearl, author of *Kids and Money.*
- "New Rules for Cider? Small Presses Might Be Put Out of Business," *Jackson Citizen Patriot* (December 12, 1999).
- "Jackson Public Schools Prepare for Change: Technology, Ideas Shaping Education," *Jackson Magazine* (December 1999). An interview with Dan Evans, Superintendent of Jackson Public Schools.

Education

- B.S., Nursing, Eastern Michigan University.
- Post-B.A. work, elementary education, Spring Arbor College.
- *Highlights for Children* Chautauqua Conference, summer 1999.

Sample Manuscript Pages

Title Page

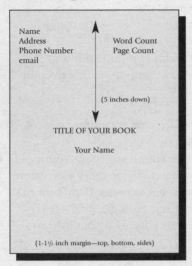

Name
Address
Phone Number
email

Word Count
Page Count

(5 inches down)

TITLE OF YOUR BOOK

Your Name

(1-1½ inch margin—top, bottom, sides)

New Chapter

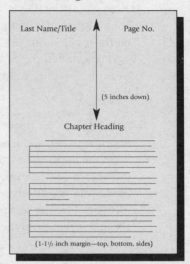

Last Name/Title   Page No.

(5 inches down)

Chapter Heading

(1-1½ inch margin—top, bottom, sides)

Following Pages

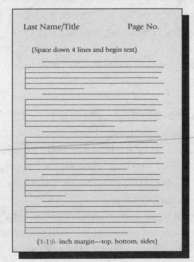

Last Name/Title   Page No.

(Space down 4 lines and begin text)

(1-1½ inch margin—top, bottom, sides)

Manuscript Preparation

P repare and mail your manuscript according to the following guidelines:

- Use high-quality 8½x11 white bond paper.
- Double-space manuscript text; leave 1- to 1½-inch margins on the top, bottom, and sides. (See page 37.)
- Send typewritten pages, letter-quality computer printouts, or clear photocopies. You may send a computer disk if the publisher requests one.

- *Title Page.* In the upper left corner, type your name, address, phone number, and email address.

  In the upper right corner, type your word count, rounded to the nearest 10 to 25 words. For anything longer than a picture book, you may also type the number of pages. (Don't count the title page.) Center and type your title (using capital letters) about 5 inches from the top of the page with your byline two lines below it.

  Start your text on the next page. (Note: if this is a picture book or board book, see page 40.)

- *Following Pages.* Type your last name and one or two key words of your title in the upper left corner, and the page number in the upper right. Begin new chapters halfway down the page.

- *Cover Letter.* Include a brief cover letter following the guidelines on page 24.

Mailing Requirements

- Assemble pages unstapled. Place cover letter on top of title page. Mail in a 9x12 or 10x13 manila envelope. Include a same-sized SASE marked "First Class." If submitting to a publisher outside the U.S., enclose an International Reply Coupon (IRC) for return postage.
- To ensure that your manuscript arrives safely, include a self-addressed, stamped postcard the editor can return upon receipt.
- Mail your submissions First Class or Priority. Do not use certified or registered mail.

Picture Book Dummy

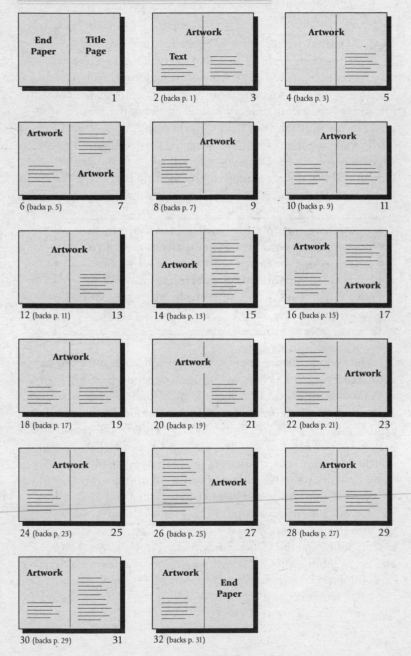

Picture Book Submissions

Most editors will accept a complete manuscript for a picture book without an initial query. Because a picture book text may contain as few as 20 words and seldom exceeds 1,500 words, it is difficult to judge if not seen in its entirety. Do not submit your own artwork unless you are a professional artist; editors prefer to use illustrators of their own choosing.

Prepare the manuscript following the guidelines for the title page on pages 37–38. Drop down four lines from the byline, indent, and begin your manuscript on the title page. Type it straight through as if it were a short story. Do not indicate page breaks.

> **Before submitting your picture book, make certain that your words lend themselves to visual representation and work well in the picture book format. Preparing a dummy or mock-up similar to the sample on page 39 can help you.**

The average picture book is 32 pages, although it may be as short as 16 pages or as long as 64 pages, depending on the age of the intended audience. To make a dummy for a 32-page book, take eight sheets of paper, fold them in half, and number them as the sample indicates; this will not include the end papers. (Each sheet makes up four pages of your book.) Lay out your text and rough sketches or a brief description of the accompanying illustrations. Move these around and adjust your concept of the artwork until you are satisfied that words and pictures fit together as they should.

Do not submit your dummy unless the editor asks for it. Simply submit your text on separate sheets of paper, typed double-spaced, following the format guidelines given on page 37. If you do choose to submit artwork as well, be sure to send copies only; editors will *rarely* take responsibility for original artwork. Be sure to include a self-addressed, stamped envelope (SASE) large enough for the return of your entire package.

Step-by-Step through the Business of Publishing

Book Contracts

Once a publisher is interested in buying your work, he or she will send a book contract for your review and signature. While book contracts vary in length and precise language from publisher to publisher, the basic provisions of these contracts are generally similar. All writers should understand publishing contract standards, know enough to acknowledge an offer as appropriate, and recognize when there may be room to negotiate. Remember, the agreement isn't complete until you sign the contract.

In Plain English
The best advice for your first contract reading is not to let the legal terminology distract you. A book contract is a complex legal document that is designed to protect you and the publisher. It defines the rights, responsibilities, and financial terms of the author, publisher, and artist (when necessary).

Because some publishers issue standard contracts and rarely change wording or payment rates for new writers, you may not need an agent or a lawyer with book-publishing experience to represent you in the negotiation of the contract. But if you choose to negotiate the contract yourself, it is advisable that you read several reference books about book contracts and have a lawyer, preferably with book-contract experience, look it over prior to signing the agreement.

In either case, you should be familiar enough with the basic premises of the contract to communicate what items you would like to change in the document. For your protection, reread the contract at every stage of negotiation.

In the following section, you'll find a primer on the basic provisions of a book contract. If a statement in your contract is not covered or remains unclear to you, ask the editor or an attorney to "translate" the clauses into plain English.

Rights and Responsibilities

A standard book contract specifies what an author and a publisher each agree to do to produce the book and place it in the marketplace. It explicitly states copyright ownership, royalty, advance, delivery date, territorial and subsidiary rights, and other related provisions.

Grant of Rights

A clause early in the contract says that on signing, the author agrees to "grant and assign" or "convey and transfer" to the publisher all or certain specified rights to a book. You thus authorize, or license, the publisher to publish your work.

Subsidiary rights are negotiated in a contract. These rights include where a book is distributed, in what language it is printed, and in what format it is published. While most publishers want world English-language rights, some publishers will consent to retaining rights only in the United States, the Philippines, Canada, and U.S. dependencies. With the United Kingdom now part of the European Community, more and more publishers want British publication rights, in English, so they can sell books to other members of the European Community.

Other subsidiary rights often included in contracts are:

Reprint Rights: These consist of publishing the work in magazines (also known as serial rights), book club editions, and hardcover or paperback versions.

Mechanical Rights: These cover audio and video cassettes, photocopying, filmstrips, and other mechanical production media.

Electronic or Computer Rights: More and more contracts include rights to cover potential use on software programs, multimedia packages, CD-ROMs, online services, etc.

Dramatic Rights: These include versions of the work for film, television, etc.

Translation Rights: These allow a work to be printed in languages other than English.

If you don't have an agent, you may want to assign a publisher broad rights since you may not have the necessary connections or experience to sell them on your own.

If possible, seek a time limit that a publisher has to use subsidiary rights. That way certain rights will revert to you if the publisher has not sold them within a specific period.

Copyright Ownership

According to the Copyright Term Extension Act of 1998, you now own all rights to work you created during or after 1978 for your lifetime plus 70 years, until you choose to sell all or part of the copyright in very specific ways. According to this law, your idea is not copyrighted; it is your unique combination of words—how you wrote something—that this law protects and considers copyrighted. A separate clause in a book contract states that you retain the copyright in your name.

Once you complete your manuscript, your work is protected. You don't need to register your work, published or unpublished, with the United States Copyright Office. In most contract agreements, a publisher is responsible for registering the published version of your work. Writers who provide a copyright notice on their submitted manuscript may be viewed as amateurs by many editors. However, registration does offer proof of ownership and a clear legal basis in case of infringement. If you decide to register your work, obtain an application form and directions on the correct way to file your copyright application. Write to the Library of Congress, Copyright Office, 101 Independence Ave. S. E., Washington, DC 20559-6000. These forms and directions are also available online in Adobe Acrobat format at: www.copyright.gov/forms. Copyright registration fees are currently $30.

If you have registered your unpublished manuscript with the Library of Congress, notify your publisher of that fact once your book is accepted for publication.

Manuscript Delivery

A book-publishing contract sets a due date by which you must complete and deliver an acceptable manuscript of the length specified in your contract. This clause allows a publisher time to request editorial changes, permits editing of the manuscript with your review and approval, establishes editorial schedules, and indicates how many author's alterations (also known as editorial changes) you may make without cost after the book has been typeset.

Warranty and Indemnification

You will be asked to ensure that the manuscript is your original work; that it contains nothing libelous, obscene, or private; and that it does not infringe on any copyright. The clause also stipulates that the author must pay the publisher's court costs and damages should it be sued over the book. This should not be an issue to the author who has exercised reasonable caution and written in good faith.

Though publishers are often reluctant to change this provision, you should still seek to limit the scope of warranty clauses. Include the phrase "to the best of the writer's knowledge" in your warranty agreement. Don't agree to pay for client's damages or attorney's fees and put a ceiling on your liability—perhaps the fee agreed upon for the assignment.

Also remember that many publishers carry their own insurance and can sometimes include writers under their house policy.

Obligation to Publish

The publisher agrees to produce and distribute the book in a timely manner, generally between one and two years. The contract should specify the time frame and indicate that if the publisher fails to publish the book within that period, the rights return to you (reversion of rights) and you keep any money already received.

Option

The option clause requires the author to offer the publisher the first chance at his or her next book. To avoid a prolonged decision-making process, try to negotiate a set period for the publisher's review of a second book, perhaps 60 or 90 days from submission of the second manuscript. Also stipulate the publisher acquire your next book on terms to be mutually agreed upon by both parties. In this way, you have room to negotiate a more favorable deal.

Payment

Calculations for the amount of money an author receives as an advance or in royalties are fairly standardized.

**Advance:** An advance is money the writer receives in a lump sum or installments when a manuscript is accepted or delivered. It is like a loan paid "against" royalties coming from anticipated profits.

Royalty: A royalty is a percentage of sales paid to the author. It is based either on a book's retail price or on net receipts (the price actually received by the publisher), and it may be fixed or arranged on a sliding scale. Standard royalty is 10% for the first 5,000 copies, 12.5% for the next 5,000 copies, and 15% thereafter. A new author may be offered only 10% or the scale may slide at a higher number of copies. Trade paperback royalties typically are 7.5% on the first 10,000 copies and 10% on all additional copies.

Depending on the extent of artwork and who supplied it to the publisher, author and artist may divide royalties or the artist may be paid a flat fee.

Accounting Statements: The publisher must provide the author with earning statements for the book. Most companies provide statements and checks semiannually, three or more months after each accounting period ends. Be sure to determine exactly when that is. For example, if the accounting periods end June 30 and December 31, you should receive statements by October 1 and April 1.

Flat Rate: Instead of paying royalties, some book packagers and smaller publishers offer a fixed amount or flat rate in return for all rights or as part of a work-for-hire agreement. This amount is paid upon completion of the book.

Before You Sign . . .

The explanations presented here include suggestions for a reasonable and (we hope) profitable approach to your book contract. Every situation presents distinct alternatives, however. Your agreements with a publisher must be undertaken in good faith on both sides and you should feel comfortable with the deal you strike. Whenever in doubt, consult an expert for advice.

You can find additional information about copyrights and publishing law in *The Copyright Handbook: How to Protect and Use Written Words* (sixth ed.) by Stephen Fishman (Nolo Press. 2000), *The Writer's Legal Guide* (second edition) by Tad Crawford (Allworth Press, 1998), and *Every Writer's Guide to Copyright and Publishing Law* by Ellen Kozak (Henry Holt, 1997).

A Note About Self, Subsidy, and Co-op Publishing Options

When you self-publish your book, you assume the cost of and responsibility for printing and distributing your book. By contrast, subsidy presses handle—for a fee—the production and, to some degree, the marketing and distribution of a writer's book. Co-op or joint-venture publishers assume responsibility for marketing and distribution of a book, while the author pays some or all of the production costs.

A newer incarnation of self-publishing is print on demand (POD), a type of printing technology that allows companies to print and bind your book in a matter of minutes. This makes it easy and cost-effective to publish books individually or in small lots, rather than investing in print runs of hundreds of books—letting you publish your work on a shoestring. POD books, however, are more expensive to produce than books done by traditional offset printing.

Another technology that's appeared as a result of the Internet boom is electronic books. Authors can publish their work without the cost of printing and binding by distributing their books in the form of computer files—Adobe PDF files are typically used. Authors can market their work individually on their own websites or utilize services such as Booklocker.com to distribute their work for a modest fee.

Based on your own needs and expectations, you may choose to try one of these approaches. If you do, exercise caution. Be sure you understand the terms of any contract, including exactly how much you will be required to pay, the marketing and distributing services the publisher is promising (if any), and the rights you are retaining. It is advisable to consult a lawyer before entering into any arrangement.

Postage Information

When you send a manuscript to a publisher, always enclose a return SASE with sufficient postage; this way, if the editor does not want to use your manuscript, it can be returned to you. To help you calculate the proper amount of postage for your SASE, here are the U.S. postal rates for first-class mailings in the U.S. and from the U.S. to Canada based on the June 2002 increase.

Ounces	8½x11 Pages (approx pgs)	U.S. 1st-Class Postage Rate	U.S. to Canada
5	21–25	$1.26	$1.60
6	26–30	1.49	1.85
7	31–35	1.72	2.10
8	36–40	1.95	2.35
9	41–45	2.18	3.10
10	46–50	2.41	3.10
11	51–55	2.64	3.10
12	56+	2.87	3.10

How to Obtain Stamps

People living in the U.S., Canada, or overseas can acquire U.S. stamps through the mail from the Stamp Fulfillment Service Center: call 800-STAMP-24 (800-782-6724) to request a catalogue or place an order. For overseas, the telephone number is 816-545-1100. You pay the cost of the stamps plus a postage and handling fee based on the value of the stamps ordered, and the stamps are shipped to you. Credit card information (MasterCard, VISA, and Discover cards only) is required for fax orders. The fax number is 816-545-1212. If you order through the catalogue, you can pay with a U.S. check or an American money order. Allow 3–4 weeks for delivery.

Frequently Asked Questions

How do I request a publisher's catalogue and writers' guidelines?

Write a brief note to the publishing company: *"Please send me a recent catalogue and writers' guidelines. If there is any charge please enclose an invoice and I will pay upon receipt."* The publisher's website, if it has one, offers a faster and less expensive alternative. Many companies put their catalogues, or at least their latest releases and their writers' guidelines on the Internet.

Do I need an agent?

There is no correct answer to this question. Some writers are very successful marketing their own work, while others feel more comfortable having an agent handle that end of the business. It's a personal decision, but if you decide to work through an agent, be an "informed consumer." Get a list of member agents from the Association of Authors' Representatives, 3rd Floor, 10 Astor Place, New York, NY 10003 (available for $7.00 and SAE with $.60 postage).

I need to include a bibliography with my book proposal. How do I set one up?

The reference section of your local library can provide several sources that will help you set up a bibliography. A style manual such as the *Chicago Manual of Style* will show you the proper format for citing all your sources, including unpublished material, interviews, and Internet material.

What do I put in a cover letter if I have no publishing credits or relevant personal experience?

In this case you may want to forego a formal cover letter and send your manuscript with a brief letter stating, *"Enclosed is my manuscript, [Insert Title], for your review."* For more information on cover letters see page 24.

I don't need my manuscript returned. How do I indicate that to an editor?

With the capability to store manuscripts electronically and print out additional copies easily, some writers keep postage costs down by enclosing a self-addressed stamped postcard (SASP) saying, *"No need to return my manuscript. Please use this postcard to advise me of the status of my manuscript. Thank you."*

Do I need to register or copyright my manuscript?

Once completed, your work is automatically protected by copyright. When your manuscript is accepted for publication, the publisher will register it for you.

Should I submit my manuscript on disk?

Do not send your manuscript on disk unless the publisher's submission guidelines note that this is an acceptable format.

When a publisher says "query with sample chapters," how do I know which chapters to send? Should they be chapters in sequence or does that matter? And how many should I send?

If the publisher does not specify which chapters it wishes to see, then it's your decision. Usually it's a good idea to send the first chapter, but if another chapter gives a flavor of your book or describes a key action in the plot, include that one. You may also want to send the final chapter of the book. For nonfiction, if one chapter is more fully representative of the material your book will cover, include that. Send two to three but if the guidelines state "sample chapter" (singular), just send one.

How long should I wait before contacting an editor after I have submitted my manuscript?

The response time given in the listings can vary, and it's a good idea to wait at least a few weeks after the allocated response time before you send a brief note to the editor asking about the status of your manuscript. If you do not get a satisfactory response or you want to send your manuscript elsewhere, send a certified letter to the editor withdrawing your work from consideration and requesting its return. You are then free to submit the work to another publishing house.

A long time ago, in 1989, I was fortunate enough to have a picture book published. If I write a query letter, should I include that information? It seems to me that it may hurt more than it helps, since I have not published anything since that.

By all means include it, though you need not mention the year it was published. Any publishing credit is worth noting, particularly if it is a picture book, because it shows you succeeded in a highly competitive field.

How do I address the editor, especially if she is female (e.g., Dear Miss, Dear Ms., Dear Mrs., Dear Editor-in-Chief, or what)?

There is no accepted preference, so the choice is really yours, but in general Ms. is used most frequently. Do use the person's last name, not his or her first. Before you decide which title to use, make sure you know if the person you are addressing is male or female.

If a publisher does not specify that "multiple submissions" are okay, does that imply they are not okay?

If a publisher has a firm policy against multiple submissions, this is usually stated in its guidelines. If not mentioned, the publisher probably does not have a hard and fast rule. If you choose to send a multiple submission, make sure to indicate that on your submission. Then it's up to the publisher to contact you if it prefers not to receive such submissions.

Publishing Terms

Advance: initial payment by publisher to author against future sales

Agent: professional who contacts editors and negotiates book contracts on author's behalf

All rights: an outright sale of your material; author has no further control over it

Anthropomorphization: attributing human form and personality to things not human, for example, animals

Backlist: list of publisher's titles that were not produced this season but are still in print

Beginning readers: children ages 4 to 7 years

Book contract: legal agreement between author and publisher

Book packager/producer: company that handles all elements of producing a book and then sells the final product to a publisher

Book proposal: see **Proposal**

Caldecott Medal: annual award that honors the illustrator of the current year's most distinguished children's book

CD-ROM: (compact-disc read-only memory) non-erasable electronic medium used for digitalized image and document storage

Clean-copy: a manuscript ready for typesetting; it is free of errors and needs no editing

Clip: sample of a writer's published work. See also **Tearsheet**

Concept book: category of picture book for children 2 to 7 years that teaches an idea (i.e., alphabet or counting) or explains a problem

Contract: see **Book contract**

Co-op publishing: author assumes some or all of the production costs and publisher handles all marketing and distribution; also referred to as "joint-venture publishing"

Copyedit: to edit with close attention to style and mechanics

Copyright: legal protection of an author's work

Cover letter: brief introductory letter sent with a manuscript

Disk submission: manuscript that is submitted on a computer disk

Distributor: company that buys and resells books from a publisher

Dummy: a sample arrangement or "mock-up" of pages to be printed, indicating the appearance of the published work

Electronic submission: manuscript transmitted to an editor from one computer to another through a modem

Email: (electronic mail) messages sent from one computer to another via a modem or computer network

End matter: material following the text of a book, such as the appendix, bibliography, index

Final draft: the last version of a polished manuscript ready for submission to an editor

First-time author: writer who has not previously been published

Flat fee: one-time payment made to an author for publication of a manuscript

Front matter: material preceding the text of a book, such as title page, acknowledgments, etc.

Galley: a proof of typeset text that is checked before it is made into final pages

Genre: category of fiction characterized by a particular style, form, or content, such as mystery or fantasy

Hard copy: the printed copy of a computer's output

Hi/lo: high-interest/low-reading level

Imprint: name under which a publishing house issues books

International Reply Coupon (IRC): coupon exchangeable in any foreign country for postage on a single-rate, surface-mailed letter

ISBN: International Standard Book Number assigned to books upon publication for purposes of identification

Letter-quality printout: computer printout that resembles typed pages

Manuscript: a typewritten, or computer-generated document (as opposed to a printed version)

Mass-market: books aimed at a wide audience and sold in supermarkets, airports, and chain bookstores

Middle-grade readers: children ages 8 to 12 years

Modem: an internal or external device used to transmit data between computers via telephone lines

Ms/Mss: manuscript/manuscripts

Newbery Medal: annual award that honors the author of that year's most distinguished children's book

Outline: summary of a book's contents, usually nonfiction, often organized under chapter headings with descriptive sentences under each to show the scope of the book

Packager: see **Book Packager**

Pen name/pseudonym: fictitious name used by an author

Picture book: a type of book that tells a story primarily or entirely through artwork and is aimed at preschool to 8-year-old children

PreK: children under 5 years of age; also known as preschool

Proofread: to read and mark errors, usually in typeset text

Proposal: detailed description of a manuscript, usually nonfiction, and its intended market

Query: letter to an editor to promote interest in a manuscript or idea

Reading fee: fee charged by anyone to read a manuscript

Reprint: another printing of a book; often a different format, such as a paperback reprint of a hardcover title

Response time: average length of time for an editor to accept or reject a submission and contact the writer with a decision

Résumé: short account of one's qualifications, including educational and professional background and publishing credits

Revision: reworking of a piece of writing

Royalty: publisher's payment to an author (usually a percentage) for each copy of the author's work sold

SAE: self-addressed envelope

SASE: self-addressed, stamped envelope

Self-publishing: author assumes complete responsibility for publishing and marketing the book, including printing, binding, advertising, and distributing the book

Simultaneous submission: manuscript submitted to more than one publisher at the same time; also known as a multiple submission

Slush pile: term used within the publishing industry to describe unsolicited manuscripts

Small press: an independent publisher that publishes a limited or specialized list

Solicited manuscript: manuscript that an editor has asked for or agreed to consider

Subsidiary rights: book contract rights other than book publishing rights, such as book club, movie rights, etc.

Subsidy publishing: author pays publisher for all or part of a book's publication, promotion, and sale

Synopsis: condensed description of a fiction manuscript

Tearsheet: page from a magazine or newspaper containing your printed story or article

Trade book: book published for retail sale in bookstores

Unsolicited manuscript: any manuscript not specifically requested by an editor; "no unsolicited manuscripts" generally means the editors will only consider queries or manuscripts submitted by agents

Vanity press: see **Subsidy publishing**

Whole language: educational approach integrating literature into class-room curricula

Work-for-hire: work specifically ordered, commissioned, and owned by a publisher for its exclusive use

Writers' guidelines: publisher's editorial objectives or specifications, which usually include word lengths, readership level, and subject matter

Young adult: children ages 12 years and older

Young reader: the general classification of books written for readers between the ages of 5 and 8

Gateway to the Markets

Write *Funny* for Kids

Humor is ageless. But humor has a special draw for the young, whether it's silly or naughty or wittily *inside*. Children's and teen books benefit from laughter, even the most serious among them, and the genre and technique of humor are welcome almost universally by editors.

Peggy Tierney, Publisher of Tanglewood Press, says the humor market "has always been there. Kids have always loved to laugh, they just didn't always get a lot of books that were genuinely funny to them." Bob Temple, Publishing Manager of Stone Arch Books, also says the market is "growing, especially among young boys. Humor is a great way to get young boys interested in reading."

Humorous fiction can have great range. "I love the fact that we are finally allowing really silly books to be published—*Captain Underpants* and *Walter the Farting Dog*—and also really sophisticated somewhat dark and ironic humor, like Lemony Snicket." says Tierney. "I think children's books used to have humor that was too lame, too *sweet*."

"Humor is almost instantaneous when someone is out of his or her normal element," explains Nancy Vorhis, Senior Editor of Eldridge Publishing, which publishes plays. She points to "the rich, snobby sorority girl stranded with backwoods mountain folks in our play, *Hollywood Hillbillies*. But humor is also natural in everyday school and home settings, especially for teens who are encountering new situations on a daily basis. Just making a teacher or principal or another student a little bit over the top, a little more emotional than normal, and you're on your way to laughs."

Stand-up & Pratfall

As wide-ranging as its appeal, humor has important subgenres, from fiction for boys and reluctant readers to popular theater to the experimental and edgy.

"We are doing books in graphic novel format," says Temple. "They are lively, cartoony books that attract kids with their funny stories and the illustration styles." Stone Arch's books target third- to fifth-graders reading at or below grade level. "The characters have to come alive in a kid's mind. Language should be smart and snappy and very colorful. Gross topics always interest young boys, too!" The new company is publishing 12 humorous books a year, and that number is expected to grow.

Reluctance of many kinds is overcome by humor, not just in reading. "From children's theater to community theater, comedies are overwhelmingly popular in our market," Vorhis says. "Someone reluctant to attend the theater is much more likely to go if the show is a comedy. Laughter is good for us emotionally and physically, too. The traditional symbol for theater consists of two drama masks, one serious and one smiling. That alone says that comedy is an equal partner with drama. We feel the need for humorous plays is growing."

"We look for depth of character and imaginative heart within a play, because no matter how funny, the work should help illuminate the human experience," Vorhis continues. "The audience should hear and enjoy the language, which should totally reflect the character and always move the plot along. Playwrights have an advantage in that an actor's expressions and physical actions also speak volumes. A pratfall introduces a comedic character before he says his first word. The story itself can range from everyday to magical—this is theater, after all!"

Tierney isn't looking for any particular kind of humorous fiction though, unlike Temple, it's thumbs down on the gross. "I can tell you what subject I'm not looking for: I've already published a fart book, and there's still real resistance to fart books in general, so I'm not really interested in publishing anything else with that particular sense of humor." She does "look for real characters, someone the kids could identify with, an original plot, writing that lives up to the plot, humor that kids like."

The Shape of a Funnybone

Humor can cross the wrong lines, and writers for children do need to take some care. "We can generalize in that we do not want anything too suggestive. In our school market, we ask writers to remember that what young actors may watch on TV or at the movies is not at all the same as what they can perform on stage in front of parents and other students," Vorhis advises.

Options for humor from picture books to middle-grade and young adult novels are wide open, however. Tanglewood Press is still a young company, and Tierney explains, "I'm new, and so far, I've only published humor picture books. I'm still looking for a great novel with humor." She wants to see originality and strong writing, and advises writers to avoid "predictability and condescending humor."

> **"The characters have to come alive in a kid's mind. Language should be smart and snappy and very colorful."**

At Eldridge, the funnybones come in plays of all shapes and sizes. "Since our market is so varied, so are our needs," says Vorhis. "We're always open to new ideas. We serve junior and senior high school drama departments, community theaters, and churches. There's just a never-ending need for comedies to entertain us and help us deal with problems in an effective yet kind way."

Vorhis describes some of Eldridge's successful works. "Recently, we published several great comedies that are distinctive. They incorporate parts of Shakespeare. In *Barbecuing Hamlet*, *Macbeth Goes Hollywood*, *The Curse of the Bard*, and others, the setting is current day, but the actors are trying to produce Shakespeare with all kinds of comedic problems. School drama departments love the fact that these comedies are not only highly entertaining for young audiences, but give a brief glimpse into great literature. The performances can be incentives to study the classics."

Eldridge publishes 25 to 30 new plays a year for school and community theater. Two-thirds are comedies. They also publish about a dozen religious plays a year; they are less likely to be comedies but usually sell well. "Currently, we need more children's theater plays," Vorhis says. "We're happy, however, to read any full-length or one-act plays for our general market and any Christmas plays for our religious market. We ask that playwrights check out our website first so that they get a better feel for what we publish. It's more efficient for all of us if they do."

Classic comedy, or classic story about the human condition: Humorous fiction has a breadth and appeal that makes it rewarding for readers and writers both.

A Life Well-Lived: Middle-Grade Biographies

A good story about a life well-lived holds appeal for readers of all ages. Whether the subject is a historical figure or a modern celebrity, whether the vehicle is theater or poetry or literature or lyric, tales of people tackling the problems and opportunities of their lives have always inspired audiences. It comes as no surprise then that the market for middle-grade biographies that capture the attention of readers is as hot as ever.

"Real life stories are popular with children and with adult publishers alike," says Catherine MacKenzie, Children's Editor for Christian Focus Publications, which publishes nine middle-grade biographies each year. "Many adults see a well-known children's biography as a *safer* purchase than the relatively unknown quantity of a fiction book. Modern day testimony books often approach their subjects imaginatively and inspiringly. History isn't really dead—history lives!"

In the educational market, "We continue to see a market for accurate, intriguing biographies as an important curriculum supplement," says Casey Cornelius, Editor in Chief of Morgan Reynolds. "We expect there will continue to be a demand for biographies that are complicated, accurate, and engage the reader."

While underlying themes still tend toward standards of moral uprightness and courage, overcoming adversity and providing leadership, the subjects of new middle-grade biographies are more often than not modern-day personalities. Chandra Howard, Senior Acquisitions Editor for Greenhaven Press believes the need for biographies on standard historical figures has reached its saturation point. "Science-oriented biographies seem to be doing well, as do a handful of contemporary celebrities. The most difficult thing to predict, however, is which biographies will sell and which won't, particularly with contemporary figures."

No matter how children's biographies have changed over the years, publishers agree the key to acceptance today is the quality of writing applied to a worthy subject.

Honest Presentations, Past & Present

"We want a well-researched, accurate presentation of each biographee, in a style that is as compelling and readable as a fine literary novel," says Nancy Lohr, Acquisitions Editor for Journey-Forth. "Our house specializes in sharing the lives of Christian statesmen of the past—men like George Mueller and David Livingston or women like Amy Carmichael and Mary Slessor. The best of these publications—such as *Fanny Crosby: Queen of Gospel Songs,* by Rebecca Davis or *Children of the Storm,* by Natash Vins—speak accurately to the target reader in compelling prose. They are honest presentations of the lives of these important figures, including not only successes and achievements, but also failures and hardships encountered along the way."

"A good biographer takes the facts compiled from research and crafts a narrative that reads like a story," says Howard, who prefers contemporary subjects. "A common pitfall among biography writers is to string together the events of a person's life without developing any underlying ties to the events."

As the market for middle-grade biographies becomes fuller, the ones that are chosen tend to be from niche groups or in particular fields of study, according to Howard. Where once well-known historical figures outsold other subjects, today readers are looking for more unique personalities. "We will be publishing more books on inventors and scientists in the next few years, and also be focusing on political leaders."

Lohr agrees that the real-life stories publishers and readers are drawn to are contemporary in subject and lesson. This fact alone helps drive the real-life story market. "The biographees of today tend to be celebrities whose contributions may not have the timeless value of the subjects of older biographies. A biography featuring the life of an athlete, for example, is likely to have a different focus and shorter shelf life than a biography featuring an inventor or American statesmen. In addition, current books seem to be less text rich, with more photos and illustrations. I would expect that trend to continue—shorter books with a higher ratio of illustration to text, and a lot more of them."

Special Interests

Some publishers do continue to look for historical biography subjects. At Morgan Reynolds, Cornelius says, "We'd like to see more curriculum-related figures proposed. We'd like submissions that offer a strong sense of theme and purpose. Writers should avoid fictionalization or oversimplifying history." The publisher is interested in a wide range of subjects, but recent series include titles on civil rights leaders and figures from European history.

> "We want a well-researched, accurate presentation of each biographee, in a style that is as compelling and as readable as a fine literary novel."

Along with subject selection, publishers are looking to expand their lists for specific age groups and niches. "I am always looking for biographical books for ages 7 to 11 and 9 to 14," says Mackenzie. "I'd like to see what some of the writers out there could do for children on the subject of the first and second world wars. Are there characters from those time periods that you could write on? Middle-grade biographies don't necessarily have to be character-based, but could be theme-based."

At JourneyForth, Lohr knows that her Christian readership is a special audience with special interests. "There is no question that our target readers make up a small niche in the children's market, but that's the beauty of publishing. A niche can be identified and its needs addressed, without the necessity of meeting every need in every market. In our case, we would like to see more stories about the men and women who carried the gospel of Christ to all parts of this world. I am not interested in biographees who are still living. I want to be able to include 'the last chapter of a life' in a biography for young readers."

Research, Research, & More Research

Greenhaven Press is one of four imprints of Thomson Gale, and publishes approximately 30 middle-grade biographies each year. Its stress on science-oriented biographies points out the growing importance of research. A good story, well-written, is not enough in this day of Internet websites, media sources, and rapid access to information. The biography written for today's middle-grader—and their book-purchasing librarian or parent—must be factually sound, accessible, and current.

"We never specifically seek out writers who market themselves as biographers because there are so many out there. Rather, when it comes to writing biographies on scientists and inventors, it is crucial that the author be able to explain complex science terminology and experiments simply," says Howard. Not only must a writer know their stuff, but they must be able to help others know it too. "We require both primary and secondary sources for our publications, as well as a secondary bibliography of age-appropriate resources that our readers can turn to for independent research."

Morgan Reynolds wants to see primary and secondary sources, interviews, and a bibliography. " Our best submissions are accurate, straightforward, do not contain fictionalization, and offer an insightful look at the subject's life and times. They weave in context and background information as necessary, without overwhelming the reader or oversimplifying history," says Cornelius.

MacKenzie indicates that good research is vital to good fiction and biography alike. "Research is a discipline all writers need," she says. "Those fiction writers who think they can get away without doing it are mistaken—it leaves a large and obvious gap in their work. I would suggest that you can't really become a good fiction writer until you can write a good true life/biographical work. That is why I think that writing true life stories and biographies is a good place to start for new writers, as they are forced to base their writing in reality. This can be a full-life manuscript or just a ghostwritten testimony for a magazine. The format is a good place to start. If you go straight into writing fiction, you can be tempted to simply base your writing in your imagination. Your writing then loses credibility."

"To write biography, you have to have a whole portfolio of skills—imagination, discipline, an eye for detail, a way with words, a love of life, an understanding of people. Much of these are only gained by experience and they aren't things that you can take a course in, unfortunately." MacKenzie goes on: "An awful lot of poor fiction arrives on my desk, yet not enough biography of any standard. This is because it's harder work to write biography. I believe that only the serious writer ever attempts it. In one sense, your story is already written and that can be difficult to deal with. You have to put in a lot of legwork before the actual writing starts."

Identify

That legwork has a big payoff, however, as more and more children's publishers look to expand their biography offerings. "We publish about four titles a year for the 9-to-14-year-old age group, but go above that number if the appropriate material is submitted," notes MacKenzie. "I would like to see more biographies, period."

Howard says the same. "We're excited about our biography on Daniel Handler—the real Lemony Snicket—written by Hayley Mitchell Haugen. We are particularly proud of our new title on J. Robert Oppenheimer in the Blackbirch Press series Giants of Science, written by Toney Allman. We hope to see more submissions like these."

"Authors and publishers must ensure that real life biography is as exciting and thrilling as real life so often is," notes MacKenzie. "If the first chapter doesn't grab me, then it's not going to grab the reader either. It should go straight into something that is adventurous or exciting or something that the reader can strongly identify with. The remaining chapters should flow seamlessly together and the book should have an underlying point—a basic ethos or theme that the reader will take away with them."

Igniting Young Adult Minds

Looking back, some of us may wonder how we survived our adolescent years. Raging hormones, peer pressure, and self-doubt often made the journey through puberty an arduous one. With statistical increases in the incidents of violence, teenage sexuality, single parent homes, and eating disorders, today's young adults face even more challenges than their parents.

Contemporary young adult fiction seeks to do more than merely entertain. It strives to address sensitive issues candidly, comfort readers who may feel isolated, and be didactic without lecturing. Today's YA audience seeks novels that go above and beyond the flawless protagonists and predictable plots of yesteryear. Anna Dorbyk, Editorial Assistant for Lobster Press, believes, "YA novels of the past were safe and conventional, but today's stories that break away from this mold are the gems."

Energized & Intense

As edgy and diverse as their readers are, says Dorbyk, "Teen novels are increasingly dealing with issues that are gritty and dark, appeal to a broader cultural and ethnic audience, and reflect the lives of today's struggling teens." Subgenres of social realism, historical adaptation, urban fantasy, free verse, and short story anthologies carve out places in publishers' lists. Megan Atwood, Acquisitions Editor for Llewellyn Worldwide, sees "the range of works being published as extraordinary at this time."

Al Forrie, Publisher at Thistledown Press, is "energized by the variety of social issues that YA writers are integrating into their fictional worlds and characters, such as those that invite gay and lesbian themes as much as they invite environmental dilemma, or adventure quest."

Publishers look for characters with a voice with which YA readers can relate. Forrie believes, "The best and worst of YA fiction seeks to address the emotional intensity of teens," and can run the gamut from lifestyle choices, violence, and death to mental disorders and spirituality. YA readers look for literary sophistication, and Thistledown "seeks out the uncompromising fidelity to language in all its forms, risk-taking with characters, and raising the bar stylistically."

Atwood is looking for books with "an edgy, gritty feel that experiment a little, play with reality, or twist something people normally take for granted."

The Workings of the Teen Mind

Not every teen novel is contemporary in setting, though its concerns must be, if not solely modern, universal. Niche publisher Beach Holme is interested in historical YA novels that "deal with important aspects that have shaped Canada's unique history and the people who settled here," says Sarah Warren, Publicity and Marketing Coordinator. She wants "strong characters who face dilemmas and make decisions on their own, and books that are written in a language that is appropriate for kids—not in an adult voice." Not wagging a parental finger in the face of the reader is essential, and Warren looks "for work that has a strong and important message, without being preachy."

YA fiction should be relevant to its target audience while relating to society as a whole. "The issues are universal and the tone is challenging and mature. I am overjoyed to read a novel that does not talk down to teens, and that, aside from the age group it is meant to target, appeals to adults," says Dorbyk.

In fact, YA fiction has a significant adult following. Perhaps parents crave a glimpse into the workings of the teenage mind or, like Forrie, they have discovered that YA fiction is full of "compelling qualities such as nonjudgmental social realism and genuine humor."

Although Llewellyn's Atwood points to the latest novel trends as "light and voyeuristic with funny, lovable protagonists on one end and gritty, novels reminiscent of the problem novel on the other," it is vital that writers resist clichés. Forrie insists, "If the settings and subjects are built upon familiar formulas, model mundane characters, or steal and modify routine YA routes, Thistledown is not interested."

Dorbyk says, "The abundance of stories about female teens that focus on shopping, gossiping, and catfights do not empower females, nor contribute anything worthwhile to the genre." Similarly, Atwood would give her kingdom to "never see a spunky, red-headed, green-eyed heroine again, and favors characters who can move off the page, stories that aren't trite, and language that is not afraid."

> **Contemporary YA fiction seeks to do more than merely entertain—it strives to address sensitive issues candidly, comfort readers who may otherwise feel isolated, and be didactic without lecturing.**

Expansive

YA's expansion as a genre doesn't seem to have an end in sight. Lobster Press, for one, has plans to increase its list in the coming year. Dorbyk is looking for submissions about "real lives and universal stories that are relevant and important to consider, and work that reflects the lives of struggling teens."

Market demand and openness to experimentation within the genre have Llewellyn planning to convert their teen line into an imprint this year, expanding their repertoire to include all types of YA books. Forrie says, "There are no subjects or settings that won't interest Thistledown if the writing is irresistible."

Young adults want to learn about life—good and bad—and writers of YA fiction have an opportunity to impart wisdom, encourage morality, and perhaps ignite a young mind.

Busy as Bees or Beavers— or Boys & Girls with Activity Books

"The sun did not shine. It was too wet to play. So we sat in the house . . . . We did nothing at all." So lament Sally and her brother in Dr. Seuss's classic *The Cat in the Hat*. The Cat in the Hat comes to their rescue with games and tricks.

Children of all ages love to be entertained with games, activities and crafts. Boredom is everyone's worst enemy.

Familiar Subjects, New Takes

Coloring books, puzzle books for car trips and rainy days, craft books of cutout paper dolls, and book kits for making everything from kites to model airplanes are mainstays of growing up. While these continue to delight new generations of children, many editors are on the lookout for fresh twists on them. "I am looking for books on topics of perennial interest to kids that get treated in a smart and unique way," says Cynthia Sherry, Associate Publisher at Chicago Review Press. "For example, a book on dinosaurs that is different than everything else that is out there or a book on weather that's really different and appealing to teachers" will get her attention.

Running Press Senior Editors Elizabeth Encarnacion and Andrea Serlin believe that the market for educationally based kits and activity books in general will continue to grow. More and more they say, parents are looking to bookstores and the books in them as alternatives to children's toys. "Nowadays when people think *activity*," says Encarnacion, "they picture hands-on, interactive, bursting-at-the-seams kits that come with everything the child needs to produce the finished product."

Publisher Jon Anderson says, "We're always looking for new takes on proven subjects, such as Egyptology and dinosaurs. Our most successful kits cover perennial subjects, but from a completely original perspective. The Deluxe Start Exploring Kits take best-selling educational coloring books and bring them to life through activities that include coloring a giant Tyrannosaurus rex poster, making a modern art mobile, playing a Matching Master-pieces card game, or decorating a 3-D dinosaur model." Running Press Kids rarely buys a complete kit from authors. They usually develop the idea in-house and find a work-for-hire author to write it. Most books currently on its list are for ages 8 to 12, but they want ideas for books appropriate for younger children.

Crossovers

Children's publishers have long known that one of the best ways to teach kids something new is to make the learning fun. "We use crafts and activities in our Bible Club curriculum," says Carol Rogers, Managing Editor of Christian Ed. Publishers. "We look for crafts that are creative and unique or have a fun twist, but that will also help teach the Bible story."

Martin Kennedy, Vice President of Didax, says the market for activity books that have a strong educational take-away is growing. "With today's classrooms focused on test-taking and achieve-ment, we need to see materials that will help teachers prepare kids for tests, so thinking skills are important. We are currently looking for cross-curricular items that can cross between such subjects as art and math, for example," says Kennedy. He cites Didax's Classroom Art texts, which inspire students to communi-cate through the visual arts and to explore their artistic interests and abilities with the use of cross-curricular activities.

As the market for activity books continues to expand, com-petition also becomes stiffer and only those ideas with a unique twist make it to finished product. "I am always looking for an author who can come up with unique, smart activities that fit with the text," says Sherry.

A Chicago Review title of which Sherry is particularly proud is *The Underground Railroad for Kids: From Slavery to Freedom.* "There are lots of books out for kids ages 9 and up dealing with the issue of slavery, but nothing that really explains it in terms that kids could understand." The text is accompanied by 21 activities that build on each other to make the topic come alive. Sherry is interested in a wide range of subjects, including art, history, science, music, and literature. While she mostly wants books for ages 9 and up, quality books for 6 to 9 are also of interest.

Activity Books for Learners of all Shapes and Sizes

Educational publishers frequently use activity books to reinforce advanced academic content for gifted students. "We wanted to find ways to bring kids new ideas for fun things to do while helping them to learn something," explains Lauri Berkenkamp, Acquisitions Editor of Nomad Press.

Nomad is launching two new series for middle-grade students. The Tools of Discovery series is "a kids' guide to history and science," explains Berkenkamp. "What is unique about our titles is that, along with telling kids' fascinating stories, each book gives them the tools to build projects themselves. In *Tools of Timekeeping*, kids learn about the science of telling time and how it has evolved. Along with learning the history of telling time, they also learn how to build their own astrolabe."

The second new Nomad series is Build it Yourself. Its titles include *Great Civil War Projects You Can Build Yourself* and *Amazing Leonardo da Vinci Projects You Can Build Yourself*. Berkenkamp is willing to consider ideas for future books. She hopes to publish between 8 and 10 titles a year should the series take off.

Jennifer Robins, Acquisitions and Development Editor of Prufrock Press, sees the market for standards-based activity books continuing to grow. "Over the past few years, we have noticed that teachers are interested in products that are standards-based, so our activity books have followed this trend. Teachers are focusing on content skills and are interested in products that provide specific content and skill support, so submissions should fit within these parameters." Prufrock features activity books for students in elementary or junior high school.

Beyond meeting the basic teacher requirements, Robins says successful activity books also look at subject matter in unique ways. "Book proposals are more likely to be accepted if they address our guidelines as well as address a topic within a subject area in a creative way." One example of a book that met these specifications is *It's Alive and Kicking: Math the Way it Ought to Be—Tough, Fun, and a Little Weird*. Geared towards students in grades three to six, the book takes the kind of yucky facts kids love (what percentage of the refrigerators in America contain moldy food?) and turns them into challenging math problems.

Direct Appeal

Another key to success, says Robins, is to "keep it simple." Activities should never take longer than 15 to 30 minutes to be completed. Proposals can be unique, but should never be too specific. Don't, for instance, suggest a book containing activities specifically for *Charlotte's Web*. It wouldn't have enough breadth.

Kennedy stresses that crafts that work the best for Didax are those that use common household materials and come with instructions that are easy to follow. Writers also need to make sure their subject matter is appropriate for the given audience. For example, Kennedy explains, writers for schools need to find topics that are, "very well considered for sensitivity issues regarding sexual content" and other concerns.

> *A key to success with activity books is to keep it simple. And, proposals can be unique, but should never too narrow.*

Rogers looks for crafts and activities that are age-targeted and don't require too much teacher preparation. Her biggest need is material for younger children. "We are using new writers for our preschool (ages four and five) and two- and three-year-old age levels. We are also looking for crafts that appeal to a combined group of children in grades one to six. The crafts and activities should be age-appropriate and should use easily obtainable supplies. We provide pattern pages for some crafts."

Rogers says that Christian Ed. is also considering launching a website devoted to Bible crafts. Though the project is "just in the hopes and dreams stage at this point, if it happens, we will be looking for additional craft writers to help fill the site." Interested writers should check guidelines for any changes in needs.

When it comes to activity books, the opportunities can be as surprising and fun as the Cat's fun-in-a-box game or Thing 1 and Thing 2. Publishers look for writers who can inspire children as much as the Cat in the Hat does with his saying, "But that is not *all* I can do. Oh, no."

Brave New Worlds: Preschoolers Learning about Self, Home, School, Community

"**A**mong preschoolers, vocabulary, letter knowledge, and phonological awareness, in addition to social and emotional factors, have a significant impact on later success in school. For example, reading scores in the tenth grade can be predicted with surprising accuracy based on a child's knowledge of the alphabet in kindergarten." (*U.S. Dept. of Health and Human Services, Feb. 3, 2003*)

Few would argue that children form their most important foundation for learning during the first five years of life. Teachers and parents seek books that expose children to the basic skills needed for reading and the more complex social skills needed for school, family, and community life. Publishers are responding to this demand with a strong showing in preschool nonfiction offerings.

Charlesbridge Trade Publishing Executive Editor Judy O'Malley says, "I believe there is a strong market for nonfiction for the youngest readers, due in part to the emphasis on early childhood education, which has led to an increasing number of children attending preschools at a very early age. Also, the range of formats and the styles of presentation for nonfiction topics for toddlers during the last decade have made nonfiction books more appealing to both adults and young children."

"We see the market growing," says Judye Groner, Editorial Director of Kar Ben, an imprint of Lerner Books. "Our niche is books for young children on Jewish themes, and with the population of children in preschools growing, we publish between 6 and 10 nonfiction books for this market each year."

Lee & Low publishes prekindergarten nonfiction in their educational imprint, BeBop Books. "We find that teachers are hungry for nonfiction for the very youngest children who are just learning to read, and they are looking for books covering topics beyond the basic concepts of colors and shapes," says Louise May, Editor in Chief. "They are also especially interested in books illustrated with photographs."

Let Me See

The visual attractiveness of books for this pre-reading audience is important. Capturing the attention of the reader and imparting information in creative ways often marks the difference between an accepted and a rejected manuscript.

"At Charlesbridge, we respond not only to topics that are appropriate for a particular age group, but to how that material is presented," explains O'Malley. "We have done several very successful young picture books that pair poetry or lyrical prose with simple, clear factual information and art that is both engaging and accurate. The topic and presentation must be accessible, but also pique the young child's desire to inquire and learn more about the world."

"We look for universal stories that present unusual nonfiction topics that young children can understand," says May. "The text must be simple, but allow for vibrant and informative illustrations to extend the text."

DNA Press focuses its attention in the preK market on various genres that reflect scientific endeavor and create a love for science discovery. "The market is very competitive," says Managing Editor Alexander Kuklin. "We publish two to three nonfiction books for preschoolers a year. Work that is unique in its approach to educating the reader, such as interactive science-oriented books, always stand out."

O'Malley "looks for originality in topic and approach that has appeal for young children, as well as a simple, lively style and clear presentation. Many writers feel rhyming text is necessary for very young books, and it can be effective if done well, but too many submissions are characterized by forced or contrived verse."

"We have a particular interest in doing picture books that introduce young children to information about people, nature, and history in a way that covers the topic as they are covered in books for slightly older children, whether as a picture book or an early reader or chapter book," says O'Malley. "In that way, a child whose imagination is captured by an idea or subject—be it bumble-bees or dinosaurs— can *grow* their understanding of that topic as he or she is ready to read and learn more."

Charlesbridge Publishing produces six to eight nonfiction books for the preschool market each year. According to O'Malley, there is ample room for writers to explore topics of a modern cultural nature as well as the educational basics. "There will always be a need for creative ways to help a toddler learn to master colors, the alphabet, shapes, etc. I think, however, we are also seeing some more sophisticated concepts, such as the ways in which people are alike and different, handled in an inviting and accessible manner for this young age group."

> *"The topic and presentation must be accessible, but also pique the young child's desire to inquire and learn more about the world."*

Community

Being part of a community—small as the family community, large as a religious denomination, and the global community—begins even in these early years. Despite the age of the preschool readership, publishers are increasingly looking for nonfiction submissions that tackle mature topics in sensitive, age-appropriate ways.

In the Jewish preschool market, Groner sees the need for nonfiction books to reach changing families. "We see an increasing number of children who are products of mixed marriages among Jews and Christians. There are issues that need to be addressed, even at the preschool level. We look, therefore, for books on Jewish holidays and life-cycle events. A good story, a good rhyme, and original take on a subject can make all the difference."

Rabbi Hara Person, Editor in Chief at URJ Press, echoes Groner's view. "We want books for this age group that reflect reality, with mothers who work and kids who may not look like their parents. We are always interested in books with liberal Jewish content, related to the holidays in particular. We want stories about real families, real lives, real kids—synagogues in which there are women rabbis, families in which everyone pitches in and prepares for holidays or cooks together, households where there aren't strict gender roles.

At the same time, the book has to be believable, says Person. "One thing we don't like is anything overly cute. No talking menorahs, no dancing dreidels. Books for this age group do not have to rhyme. Most important, they shouldn't patronize."

According to Person, *Shabbat Shalom* by Michelle Abraham is an example of good preK nonfiction. "It teaches how one family celebrates Shabbat, and provides all the basic blessings so that a family can use the book like a roadmap for creating their own authentic Shabbat experience. It stands out because the concepts are straightforward, easy-to-grasp, without being overly cute. It teaches by providing a model without lecturing or being judgmental."

SHAKTI Books for Children, published by Charlesbridge, is a program of the Global Fund of Children. "These books help young children gain an awareness of the ways in which the lives of children all over the world are similar to and different from their own," explains O'Malley. Titles in the SHAKTI series include *To Be A Kid*, by Maya Ajmera and John D. Invanko and *Be My Neighbor*, by the same authors and with a foreward by Fred Rogers (2004).

Cultural learning is central at Lee & Low Books. "Our company publishes multicultural books under our BeBob educational imprint," says May. "We are always interested in books that manage to have inherent multicultural content. We post specific guidelines about this on our website each year. Too often writers do not check these guidelines before submitting, so we receive many manuscripts that are not appropriate for us."

Bibliography as a Learning Tool

As in any nonfiction submission, evidence of sufficient research is an important part of a successful preschool nonfiction manuscript. Given the educational nature of these publications, young readers, parents and teachers alike are looking for ways to continue their *study* and a good bibliography and source list is key.

"We do like to see a list of resources the author used. When appropriate, such back matter as a glossary, an author's note, or a bibliography of related children's books can help to extend the reading and learning experience of both the child and the adult sharing the book," says O'Malley.

"Research is needed to make sure the text and illustrations are authentic and accurate," explains May. "Writers need to check whatever sources are necessary, either primary, secondary or other, to make sure they achieve this."

At DNA Press, research and source lists are vital. "We publish scientific books. A bibliography of strong science articles and sources is required in order to be published with us," notes Kuklin.

A good preK nonfiction book must incorporate all of the eye-catching style that attracts the young reader, while anchoring itself in solid research, experience, and teaching. "The simple language and bright photos or illustration that appeals to young children makes a title stand out," says Groner. "Originality is key."

Listings

How to Use the Listings

On the following pages are over 500 profiles of publishers involved in the wide range of children's publishing. Over 50 publishers are new to the directory. These publishing houses produce a variety of material from parenting guides, textbooks, and classroom resources to picture books, photo essays, middle-grade novels, and biographies.

Each year we update every listing through mailed surveys and telephone interviews. While we verify everything in the listing before we go to press, it is not uncommon for information such as contact names, addresses, and editorial needs to change suddenly. Therefore, we suggest that you always read the publisher's most recent writers' guidelines before submitting a query letter or manuscript.

If you are unable to find a particular publisher, check the Publishers' Index beginning on page 593 to see if it is cited elsewhere in the book. We do not list presses that publish over 50% of their material by requiring writers to pay all or part of the cost of publishing. While we cannot endorse or vouch for the quality of every press we list, we do try to screen out publishers of questionable quality.

To help you judge a publisher's receptivity to unsolicited submissions, we include a Freelance Potential section in each listing. This is where we identify the number of titles published in 2003 that were written by unpublished writers, authors new to the publishing house, and agented authors. We also provide the total number of query letters and unsolicited manuscripts a publisher receives each year. When possible, we list the number of books published in 2005 by category (e.g. picture books, young adult novels).

Use this information and the other information included in the listing to locate publishers that are looking for the type of material you have written or plan to write. Become familiar with the style and content of the house by studying its catalogue and a few recent titles.

Scobre Press Corporation

New Listing

Who to Contact

2255 Calle Clara
La Jolla, CA 92037

Editor: Scott Blumenthal

Publisher's Interests

High-interest, low-level sports books for middle-grade readers can be found in this publisher's catalogue. All of its material centers around character education.
Website: www.scobre.com

Website

Profile of Publisher & Readership

Freelance Potential

Published 9 titles (all juvenile) in 2005: 2 were developed from unsolicited submissions and 2 were by agented authors. Of the 9 titles, 3 were by unpublished writers and 6 were by authors who were new to the publishing house. Receives 24–60 queries yearly.

Number of Unsolicited Submissions Published & Received

Categories of Current Titles

- **Fiction:** Published 7 middle-grade books, 8–12 years. Genres include sports-related stories.
- **Nonfiction:** Published 2 middle-grade books, 8–12 years. All topics focus on sports-related issues.
- **Representative Titles:** *The Long Way Around* by Jimmie Hand (9–16 years) is a story of redemption and second chances for a high school quarterback. *Teacher's Resource Guide* (teachers) offers a step-by-step program that effectively teaches a variety of reading comprehension strategies; part of the Dream Series.

Recent Titles to Study

Submissions and Payment

How to Submit

Guidelines available. Catalogue available at website. Query. Accepts photocopies and email queries to scobre.com. SASE ($.83 postage). Responds in 1 week. Publication in 6 months. Royalty, 12%.

Editor's Comments

We offer more than simple, fluffy sports stories. We are looking for authors to create works for our "sports series." These sports books will help to create educational books that actually interest young adults. Multicultural books will continue to be a focus for our series as well. Authors should have a passion for and/or a history of creating young adult books.

Editor's Current Needs & Tips for Writers

Icon Key

☆ New Listing   🖱 E-publisher

⊗ Not currently accepting submissions

Harry N. Abrams Books for Young Readers

115 West 18th Street
New York, NY 10011

Managing Editor: Andrea Colvin

Publisher's Interests

This imprint of Harry N. Abrams, Inc., was launched in 1999. Its titles range from early picture books for infants to novels and nonfiction for young adults.

Website: www.abramsbooks.com

Freelance Potential

Published 70 titles in 2005: 1 was developed from an unsolicited submission and most were by agented authors.

- **Fiction:** Publishes early picture books, 0–4 years; easy-to-read books, 4–7 years; middle-grade books, 8–12 years; and young adult books, 12–18 years. Genres include folklore, folktales, and stories about animals, nature, and the environment.
- **Nonfiction:** Publishes easy-to-read books, 4–7 years; middle-grade books, 8–12 years; and young adult books, 12–18 years. Topics include animals and natural history. Also publishes humor.
- **Representative Titles:** *Babar the Magician* by Laurent de Brunhoff tells of a magic show that goes awry. *Chicken Bedtime Is Really Early* by Erica S. Perl is a bedtime story about farm animals who refuse to go to sleep; illustrations feature hidden clocks that help kids practice their time-telling skills.

Submissions and Payment

Guidelines available at website. Submit cover letter and complete ms for picture books; query with sample chapter for longer works and nonfiction. Accepts photocopies and computer printouts. SASE. Responds in 6 months. Publication in 1 year. Royalty, 8–15%.

Editor's Comments

We're looking for fiction and nonfiction appropriate for readers up to the age of 16, and unless it is a picture book submission, we ask that you send queries only. Note that most of the books we accept for publication are submitted by agented authors. Your chance of acceptance here is greater if you are represented by a literary agent.

Absey and Company

23011 Northcrest Drive
Spring, TX 77389

Publisher: Edward Wilson

Publisher's Interests

Award-winning titles for children and young adults can be found in the catalogue by this publisher. It offers fiction in a variety of genres, poetry, and educational nonfiction for children of all ages, as well as language arts resource materials for teachers.
Website: www.absey.com

Freelance Potential

Published 5 titles in 2005: 5 were developed from unsolicited submissions. Of the 5 titles, 2 were by unpublished writers and 2 were by authors who were new to the publishing house. Receives 10,000 queries yearly.

- **Fiction:** Published 1 story picture book, 4–10 years; 1 chapter book, 5–10 years; and 1 young adult book, 12–18 years.
- **Nonfiction:** Publishes educational titles, 0–18 years. Features biographies and books about religion and history. Also publishes educational activity books and poetry collections, as well as language arts resource titles for educators.
- **Representative Titles:** *Drowning in Secret* by Roger Leslie (YA) is the story of a picture-perfect family that keeps a lot of secrets. *Regular Lu* by Robin Nelson (4–10 years) tells the story of a mouse who discovers his own worth.

Submissions and Payment

Guidelines available. Query with résumé, outline, and sample chapters. Accepts photocopies. No simultaneous submissions. SASE. Responds in 6–9 months. Publication in 1 year. Payment policy varies.

Editor's Comments

We continue to look for high-quality material that lives up to our standards for strong, literary works in the genres of fiction, poetry, and language arts. Please query only. We work closely with our authors, and do not accept unsolicited manuscripts through the mail, email, or literary agents.

Accord Publishing

Suite 202
1732 Wazee Street
Denver, CO 80202

Editor: Ken Fleck

Publisher's Interests

Accord Publishing produces board books and picture books for infants and toddlers. For older children, it publishes science kits, books accompanied by hand or finger puppets, and drawing kits.

Website: www.accordpublishing.com

Freelance Potential

Published 20 titles in 2005: 1 was developed from an unsolicited submission and 15 were by agented authors. Of the 20 titles, 1 was by an author who was new to the publishing house. Receives 84–96 queries, 48–60 unsolicited mss each year.

- **Fiction:** Publishes concept books, toddler books, and early picture books, 0–4 years; easy-to-read books, 4–7 years; story picture books, 4–10 years; and chapter books, 5–10 years. Genres include adventure, fantasy, and humor. Also publishes novelty books, board books, and activity books.
- **Nonfiction:** Publishes "I Can't Believe It's Science!" series for children ages 7 and up. Topics include insects, rocks, and weather. Also publishes novelty books, board books, and activity books.
- **Representative Titles:** *Friends of a Feather* by Arlen Cohn is a board book about friendship that features wiggling eyeballs and rhythmic verse. *The Adventures of Max the Minnow* by William Boniface offers young readers a fish-eyed view of ocean life.

Submissions and Payment

Guidelines available at website. Query or send complete ms. SASE. Response time, publication period, and payment policy vary.

Editor's Comments

Novel, interactive books that are educational as well as entertaining are always welcome.

ACTA Publications

5557 West Howard Street
Skokie, IL 60077

Editor: Gregory Pierce

Publisher's Interests

An innovative publisher that offers Christian books, films, and audio resources, ACTA (Assisting Christians To Act) does not publish fiction. Its catalogue includes materials that help young adults and adults to enhance their faith.
Website: www.actapublications.com

Freelance Potential

Published 15 titles in 2005.

- **Nonfiction:** Publishes early picture books, 0–4 years; story picture books, 4–10 years; and young adult books, 12–18 years. Topics include history, self-help, and religion.
- **Representative Titles:** *We Were Gonna Have a Baby, But We Had an Angel Instead* by Pat Schweibert (2+ years) addresses the issues that children may face over the loss of an unborn child. *Diamond Presence* (YA) features 12 true short stories of finding God while enjoying the great American pastime of baseball.

Submissions and Payment

Catalogue available at website. Query with table of contents, sample chapter, and market analysis. Accepts photocopies and simultaneous submissions if identified. SASE. Responds in 1–3 weeks. Publication in 9–12 months. Royalty, 10%.

Editor's Comments

To be more familiar with what we publish, be sure to request a catalogue or view it at our website. Read it carefully to see if your book seems to fit. If you are certain it does, send a query letter that explains your proposal and why it would be suitable for our product line. Include a table of contents and one chapter from the book. We do not read entire manuscripts until after we have received the initial proposal and determined if it fits our current needs. First-time authors do not receive advances.

Action Publishing

P.O. Box 391
Glendale, CA 91209

Submissions Editor

Publisher's Interests
Since 1996, Action Publishing has offered products that motivate and involve readers. Its list includes fantasy and adventure books for children of all ages.
Website: www.actionpublishing.com

Freelance Potential
Published 6 titles (4 juvenile) in 2005. Of the 6 titles, 1 was by an author who was new to the publishing house. Receives 250 queries, 1,200 unsolicited mss yearly.

- **Fiction:** Publishes early picture books, 0–4 years; easy-to-read books, 4–7 years; story picture books, 4–10 years; middle-grade titles, 8–12 years; and young adult books, 12–18 years. Also publishes books in series. Genres include adventure and fantasy.
- **Nonfiction:** Publishes middle-grade titles, 8–12 years; and young adult books, 12–18 years. Topics include nature and the environment.
- **Representative Titles:** *The Legend of Snow Pookas* by Scott E. Sutton tells about the adventures of three-legged Pookas, a race of creatures who thrive in freezing temperatures. *The Family of Ree* by Scott E. Sutton introduces young readers to the colorful world of Ree, full of wizards, sea beasties, and erfs.

Submissions and Payment
Guidelines available. Accepts queries and complete mss through literary agents only. SASE. Response time and publication period vary. Royalty; advance.

Editor's Comments
An agent must submit your manuscript to us; we do not accept unsolicited material. We are currently looking for adventure and fantasy stories for young children through young adults. We are especially interested in titles that would work well in a series format, with characters or themes that continue through the series.

Adams Media Corporation

57 Littlefield Street
Avon, MA 02322

Book Proposals

Publisher's Interests

An independent publisher, Adams Media Corporation produces trade paperbacks that cover a broad range of nonfiction topics. Its goal is to provide adult and young adult readers with quality information in a highly accessible style.
Website: www.adamsmedia.com

Freelance Potential

Published 10–15 titles (1 juvenile) in 2005: all were developed from unsolicited submissions. Receives 300 queries each year.

- **Nonfiction:** Publishes young adult books, 12–18 years. Topics include animals, careers, hobbies, health, fitness, humor, social issues, relationships, and contemporary issues. Features inspirational, self-help, exam-prep, and how-to books. Also publishes books for adults on business, cooking, home improvement, parenting, personal finance, women's issues, weddings, travel, and writing.
- **Representative Titles:** *Baby Miracles* by Brad Steiger & Sherry Hansen Steiger is a collection of inspirational true stories about miraculous events involving babies. *Mean Chicks, Cliques, and Dirty Tricks* by Erika V. Shearin Karres (YA) helps girls understand what makes mean chicks tick; includes true stories of girls who fought back against teasing and bullying.

Submissions and Payment

Guidelines and catalogue available at website. Query with table of contents and brief author bio. Accepts photocopies and computer printouts. SASE. Responds only if interested. Publication period varies. Royalty.

Editor's Comments

We accept queries directly from authors, including first-time authors, as well as through literary agents. Include a description of the intended market for your book with your query and tell us why you believe it would sell.

Aladdin Paperbacks

Simon & Schuster Children's Publishing Division
4th Floor
1230 Avenue of the Americas
New York, NY 10020

Submissions Editor

Publisher's Interests
Paperback reprints of hardcover titles from Simon & Schuster imprints are the mainstay of Aladdin's list. It offers fiction and nonfiction titles for beginning readers to young adults in a variety of genres.
Website: www.simonsayskids.com

Freelance Potential
Published 150 titles in 2005: all were by agented authors.

- **Fiction:** Publishes story picture books, 4–10 years; middle-grade titles, 8–12 years; and young adult books, 12–18 years. Genres include contemporary and historical fiction, suspense, mystery, fantasy, and adventure.
- **Nonfiction:** Publishes biographies.
- **Representative Titles:** *Secret Agent* by Robyn Freedman Spizman & Mark Johnston (9–12 years) is a top-secret story about a boy who becomes his father's literary agent, unbeknownst to all concerned. *Roberto Clemente: Pride of the Pittsburgh Pirates* by Jonah Winter (4–8 years) highlights the life and times of this major league baseball player.

Submissions and Payment
Guidelines available. Accepts submissions from agented authors only. SASE. Response time, publication period, and payment policy vary.

Editor's Comments
We consider material from agented authors only. While we cannot recommend specific agents for your work, we do suggest you review *Literary Market Place*, a reference work that includes a directory of literary agents. If you have an agent who is interested in submitting your work, we are considering series titles for middle-grade and young adult readers, as well as some early-reader nonfiction titles. When working on a series, think about themes and characters that can continue throughout the books.

ALA Editions

American Library Association
50 East Huron Street
Chicago, IL 60611

Editor: Emily Moroni

Publisher's Interests
ALA Editions, the publishing division of the American Library Association, features books for library professionals, library researchers, and educators. Its list includes both reference titles and resource books.
Website: www.ala.org/editions

Freelance Potential
Published 27 titles in 2005: 3 were developed from unsolicited submissions, and 2 were reprint/licensed properties.
Receives 50 queries yearly.

- **Nonfiction:** Publishes resource materials, guides, textbooks, and reference materials for teachers and librarians. Topics include children's, young adult, and school services; acquisitions and collection development; library studies, issues, and trends; reference services; technical services and technology; digital library operations and services; and reference services and resources.
- **Representative Titles:** *Books in Bloom* by Kimberly Faurot (librarians) provides scripts and instructions for bringing stories to life. *Uncovering History: Teaching with Primary Sources* by Susan Veccia (librarians) presents practical lessons and personal stories to illustrate how American Memory resources can be used to teach history and critical thinking.

Submissions and Payment
Guidelines available at website. Query with outline/synopsis. SASE. Responds in 2–8 weeks. Publication in 7–9 months. Royalty.

Editor's Comments
Most of our projects are in book format, but nonprint and electronic publishing projects may also be accepted. Our consideration begins with your well-written proposal or brief query. Include the intended market for your book, and let us know who will read it, and why.

Alyson Books

Suite 1000
6922 Hollywood Boulevard
Los Angeles, CA 90028

Editorial Assistant: Whitney Friedlander

Publisher's Interests
A specialty publisher, Alyson Books is devoted to producing books about gay and lesbian families and lifestyles in a contemporary, thoughtful, and sensitive manner.
Website: www.alyson.com

Freelance Potential
Published 55 titles (2 juvenile) in 2005: 30 were developed from unsolicited submissions and 12 were by agented authors. Of the 55 titles, 4 were by unpublished writers and 14 were by authors who were new to the publishing house. Receives 800–900 queries yearly.

- **Fiction:** Published 2 young adult books, 12–18 years. Genres include contemporary, multicultural, and ethnic fiction. Also publishes fiction for adults.
- **Nonfiction:** Topics include gay, lesbian, and bisexual families; parenting; social issues; and self-help topics. Also publishes nonfiction titles about sexuality and parenting for adults.
- **Representative Titles:** *Pebble in the Pool* by William Taylor (YA) is a coming-of-age story about young men faced with real world problems. *Half-Life* by Aaron Krach (YA) is the story of an adolescent boy's struggle to deal with his father's untimely death. *Clay's Way* by Blair Mastbaum (YA) is a novel about an artistic boy who feels trapped in his suburban world.

Submissions and Payment
Guidelines available. Query with 1-page synopsis and available artwork. No unsolicited mss. Accepts photocopies and computer printouts. SASE. Responds in 10–12 weeks. Publication in 2 years. Royalty; advance.

Editor's Comments
We started up the young adult section of our publishing program in 2004, and we hope to see growth in this area in the coming year. We are seeking thoughtfully sensitive material about the unique challenges of being young and gay or lesbian.

Ambassador Books

91 Prescott Street
Worcester, MA 01605

Submissions Editor: Christopher Driscoll

Publisher's Interests
This Christian-focused publisher offers fiction and nonfiction books that have spiritual or inspirational elements to them. Its list includes titles for both children and adults.
Website: www.ambassadorbooks.com

Freelance Potential
Published 7 titles (3 juvenile) in 2005: 2 were developed from unsolicited submissions. Receives 2,000 queries, 500 unsolicited mss yearly.

- **Fiction:** Publishes easy-to-read books, 4–7 years; story picture books, 4–10 years; and middle-grade books, 8–12 years. Genres include adventure; mystery; suspense; and inspirational, religious, historical, and regional fiction. Also publishes sports stories.
- **Nonfiction:** Publishes easy-to-read titles, 4–7 years; story picture books, 4–7 years; and middle-grade books, 8–12 years. Topics include self-help, religion, sports, and regional subjects.
- **Representative Titles:** *Babci's Angel* by Frrich Lewandowski (4–7 years) tells an exciting tale of love and answered prayers featuring two boys, a terrible accident, and an angel. *It's Christmas Again!* by Frrich Lewandowski & Michael P. Riccards (5–8 years) is a modern parable about a time when everyone celebrates December 25th but no one remembers why.

Submissions and Payment
Guidelines available. Query. Accepts photocopies. Availability of artwork improves chance of acceptance. SASE. Responds in 4 months. Publication in 1 year. Royalty, 10%.

Editor's Comments
We're looking for imaginative and entertaining children's books with a moral. All of our material is Christian based and must be presented in a positive way. Please keep in mind that we do not accept submissions via email or fax.

Ambassador-Emerald International

427 Wade Hampton Boulevard
Greenville, SC 29609

Editor: Brenton Cook

Publisher's Interests

Pastors, professors, and lay people write the books published by Ambassador-Emerald, a company committed to promoting the Gospel of Jesus Christ and encouraging believers through its catalogue of Christian literature.
Website: www.emeraldhouse.com

Freelance Potential

Published 16–20 titles (5 juvenile) in 2005. Of the 16–20 titles, 4 were by authors who were new to the publishing house. Receives 250 queries yearly.

- **Fiction:** Publishes chapter books, 5–10 years; middle-grade novels, 8–12 years; and young adult books, 12–18 years. Genres include historical, religious, and regional fiction.
- **Nonfiction:** Publishes middle-grade books, 8–12 years; and young adult books, 12–18 years. Topics include religion, history, current events, and regional subjects. Also publishes biographies.
- **Representative Titles:** *Picnic on the Grounds* by Judy Chatham discusses the rewards of joining a church congregation and attending services regularly. *A Little Child Shall Lead Them* by Noel Davidson tells how a couple came to embrace the Christian faith after the death of their young child.

Submissions and Payment

Guidelines and catalogue available with 9x12 SASE ($1.29 postage) and at website. Query. Prefers email queries but will accept regular mail. Accepts photocopies and email to authors@emeraldhouse.com. SASE. Responds in 6 weeks. Publication in 1 year. Royalty, 5–15%; advance, $250–$1,000.

Editor's Comments

We have enjoyed long-standing relationships with our authors, but we also welcome the work of new writers. We've published quite a few first-time authors. Everything we publish is based on the truths of Christ's Gospel.

AMG Publishers

6815 Shallowford Road
Chattanooga, TN 37421

Editor: Dan Penwell

Publisher's Interests

With a broad list of biblically oriented nonfiction books, including reference titles and theology and study books for children and adults, this publisher also features fiction titles for young adults.
Website: www.amgpublishers.com

Freelance Potential

Published 35 titles (5 juvenile) in 2005: 1–2 were developed from unsolicited submissions and 12–15 were by agented authors. Of the 35 titles, 6 were by unpublished writers and 15 were by authors who were new to the publishing house. Receives 2,000 queries yearly.

- **Fiction:** Published 3 middle-grade titles, 8–12 years; and 2 young adult books, 12–18 years. Genres include contemporary fiction and fantasy.
- **Nonfiction:** Publishes Bible study materials, YA–adult. Also publishes inspirational and motivational titles, cookbooks, and books on parenting and family life.
- **Representative Titles:** *Tears of a Dragon* by Bryan Davis (YA) takes readers on an adventure while opening their eyes to themes such as faith, courage, wisdom, and redemption; part of the Dragons in Our Midst series. *Disturbing Behavior* by Lee Vukich & Steve Vandegriff (YA, parents) looks at 53 risky behaviors that can get teens into trouble and addresses how to help those who need it.

Submissions and Payment

Guidelines available at website. Query. Accepts email queries to danp@amginternational.org. Response time and publication period vary. Royalty; advance.

Editor's Comments

We seek material that encourages our readers to grow in personal devotion and faith, and that fosters skillful use of the Bible. We will also consider fantasy titles for young adults.

Amulet Books

Harry N. Abrams
5th Floor
115 West 18th Street
New York, NY 10011

Editor: Susan Van Metre

Publisher's Interests
Books for readers in the middle grades through high school make up the editorial focus of Amulet Books.
Website: www.abramsbooks.com

Freelance Potential
Published 12 titles in 2005: 9 were by agented authors. Receives 1,560 queries yearly.

- **Fiction:** Publishes middle-grade books, 8–12 years; and young adult books, 12–18 years. Genres include contemporary, historical, and science fiction; fantasy; mystery; suspense; and humor. Also publishes books in series.
- **Nonfiction:** Publishes middle-grade books, 8–12 years; and young adult books, 12–18 years. Topics include multicultural and ethnic issues, nature, the environment, and history. Also publishes books in series.
- **Representative Titles:** *The Boy Who Couldn't Die* by William Sleator (8–18 years), a spin on the classic zombie story, follows a 16-year-old boy who bargains with a psychic to gain immortality. *Dealing with Mom* by Laurence Gillot & Veronique Sibiril (YA) helps teens understand the ups and downs of their relationships with their moms and why their feelings toward mom are changing.

Submissions and Payment
Query with synopsis and first 3 chapters. SASE. Responds in 6 months. Publication period varies. Royalty; advance.

Editor's Comments
This year, we're particularly interested in receiving mysteries and contemporary stories for our middle-grade and teen readers. If you're submitting nonfiction, please include biographical information about yourself. Tell us what qualifies you to write about your subject. If other books on your topic already exist, provide the title, author, publisher, and year of publication, and explain what makes your work different.

Andersen Press Ltd.

20 Vauxhall Bridge Road
London SW1V 2SA
United Kingdom

Submissions: Elizabeth Maude

Publisher's Interests

Picture books for preschool children, middle-grade novels, and fiction for young adults appear in the catalogue of Andersen Press. Known for its high-quality, imaginative titles, this publisher does not offer nonfiction.
Website: www.andersenpress.co.uk

Freelance Potential

Published 32 titles in 2005.

- **Fiction:** Publishes story picture books, 4–10 years; chapter books, 5–10 years; middle-grade novels, 8–12 years; and young adult titles, 12–18 years. Genres include historical, contemporary, and humorous fiction; adventure; fantasy; folktales; horror; mystery; suspense; romance; animal stories; and stories about sports.
- **Representative Titles:** *Frog in Winter* by Max Velthuijs (3+ years) is a picture book about a frog who finds the warmth he seeks through the kindness of his animal friends. *Be in the Place* by Helen Hobden (12+ years) is the story of a teen who attends a music festival on her own and the family who takes her in when things go wrong.

Submissions and Payment

Guidelines available. Send complete ms for picture books. Query with synopsis and first 3 chapters for longer works. Accepts photocopies. SAE/IRC. Responds to queries in 1 week, to mss in 2 months. Publication period and payment policy vary.

Editor's Comments

We try to read all material submitted to us as quickly as possible. Therefore, we are unable to offer editorial guidance on the work we reject. Picture book manuscripts should be no longer than 1,000 words. Submissions to our juvenile fiction series, Tigers, should be 3,000 to 5,000 words. Our teen fiction runs from 15,000 to 50,000 words in length.

Annick Press

15 Patricia Avenue
Toronto, Ontario M2M 1H9
Canada

Editors

Publisher's Interests
This Canadian publisher offers award-winning fiction and nonfiction titles for middle-grade and young adult readers. It strives to produce engaging material that is stimulating.
Website: www.annickpress.com

Freelance Potential
Published 30 titles in 2005.

- **Fiction:** Publishes middle-grade books, 8–12 years; and young adult books, 12–18 years. Genres include contemporary fiction and humor.
- **Nonfiction:** Publishes middle-grade books, 8–12 years; and young adult books, 12–18 years.
- **Representative Titles:** *38 Ways to Entertain Your Babysitter* by Dette Hunter (4–9 years) is an amusing, original story with a trio of well-defined, quirky characters that sets the scene for a multitude of easy, creative home activities. *52 Days by Camel* by Lawrie Raskin with Debra Pearson (8–12 years) takes readers on a remarkable journey through the Sahara; part of the Adventure Travel Series.

Submissions and Payment
Canadian authors only. Guidelines available at website. Query with synopsis and sample chapter. Accepts email queries to annickpress@annickpress.com. SASE. Response time, publication period, and payment policy vary.

Editor's Comments
We are seeking proposals from Canadian writers for teen novels that possess a high degree of originality and capture strong and distinctive contemporary voices. Stories must involve and stimulate the reader. The use of appropriate and well-timed humor is encouraged. We are also seeking middle-grade fiction with gripping action that captures the imagination of readers and readily engages their interest. We are committed to publishing Canadian authors only.

Archimedes Press

6 Berkley Road
Glenville, NY 12302

Editor-in-Chief: Richard DiMaggio

Publisher's Interests
Since it was established in 2002, Archimedes Press has been publishing hardcover, trade paperback, and mass market paperback originals. Offering nonfiction almost exclusively, it welcomes submissions of books for children. Archimedes Press publishes three to six new titles each year.
Website: www.archimedespress.com

Freelance Potential
Published 6 titles (3 juvenile) in 2005: all were developed from unsolicited submissions and 2 were by agented authors. Of the 6 titles, 3 were by unpublished writers. Receives 1,200 queries yearly.

- **Nonfiction:** Publishes chapter books, 5–10 years; middle-grade books, 8–12 years; and young adult books, 12–18 years. Topics include current events, history, social issues, and parenting. Features self-help and how-to books, activity books, and educational titles.
- **Representative Titles:** *A Girl's Story* by Robynn Clairday is a step-by-step guide for girls who want to write their autobiographies. *Candy Around the World* by Stacy Cacciatore looks at the history and place of origin of a variety of confectionary treats.

Submissions and Payment
Guidelines available. Query or send complete ms. Prefers email queries to archimedespress@verizon.net. Accepts photocopies. SASE. No simultaneous submissions. Responds to queries in 2 months. Publication in 6 months. Royalty, 10%.

Editor's Comments
We try to avoid the limitations of the publishing industry. It's not necessary to have an agent or prior publications to submit your work to us. We're aware that there's lots of talent out there—talent that is restricted by the conventional wisdom of the publishing industry. Send us something fresh and creative.

Atheneum Books for Young Readers

1230 Avenue of the Americas
New York, NY 10020

Executive Editor: Caitlyn Dlouhy

Publisher's Interests
Children of all ages enjoy the books produced by this publisher. Its list includes picture books, chapter books, mysteries, science fiction, fantasy, and nonfiction.
Website: www.simonsayskids.com

Freelance Potential
Published 110 titles in 2005: 5 were developed from unsolicited submissions, 70 were by agented authors, and 2 were reprint/licensed properties. Receives 30,000 queries yearly.

- **Fiction:** Publishes concept books, toddler books, and early picture books, 0–4 years; story picture books, 4–10 years; chapter books, 5–10 years; middle-grade books, 8–12 years; and young adult books, 12–18 years. Genres include science fiction, historical fiction, adventure, mystery, and fantasy.
- **Nonfiction:** Publishes story picture books, 4–10 years; chapter books, 5–10 years; middle-grade books, 8–12 years; and young adult books, 12–18 years. Topics include the environment, science, nature, sports, history, and multicultural issues. Also publishes biographies.
- **Representative Titles:** *Let Me Play* by Karen Blumenthal (8+ years) tells the story of Title IX: the law that changed the future of girls in America. *The Seven Wonders of Sassafras Springs* by Betty G. Birney (8–12 years) tells a tale about a boy's journey of discovery that proves to be an adventure of a lifetime.

Submissions and Payment
Guidelines available. Query for nonfiction. Send 3 sample chapters with summary for fiction. Accepts photocopies and computer printouts. SASE. Responds in 3 months. Publication period varies. Royalty.

Editor's Comments
We produce high-quality books on a variety of subjects. We put less emphasis on particular trends, fads, and gimmicks, and more on the qualities of craftsmanship.

Augsburg Books

Suite 700
100 South 5th Street
Minneapolis, MN 55402

Submissions Editor

Publisher's Interests
Books for Christians of all denominations are available from
this publisher, which is affiliated with the Lutheran Church.
Its juvenile list features books that build sound Christian
values in children from birth through the teen years.
Website: www.augsburgbooks.com

Freelance Potential
Published several titles in 2005. Receives 1,000 queries
each year.

- **Fiction:** Publishes toddler and early picture books, 0–4 years;
  story picture books and easy-to-read books, 4–7 years; middle-
  grade fiction, 8–12 years; and young adult books, 12–18 years.
- **Nonfiction:** Publishes concept and toddler books, 0–4 years;
  story picture books, 4–7 years; middle-grade books, 8–12
  years; and young adult books, 12–18 years. Topics include
  Lutheranism, family life, spirituality, prayer, parenting, and
  Christian education.
- **Representative Titles:** *God Made Creepy Crawlies* by Sally
  Anne Conan (4–8 years) explores unique characteristics of
  a variety of animals. *Five-Minute Bible Stories* by Richard
  Johnson (4–8 years) introduces children to 20 popular Bible
  stories, including Adam and Eve, Noah's Ark, and Jonah and
  the Whale.

Submissions and Payment
Guidelines and catalogue available at website. Query with
résumé, outline, and synopsis. Accepts photocopies, com-
puter printouts, and simultaneous submissions if identified.
SASE. Responds in 1–3 months. Publication in 2–3 years.
Royalty, 5–10% of gross.

Editor's Comments
One way we determine whether a book would fit our list is if
its presentation of Christian faith would appeal to a general
audience of readers seeking answers to spiritual questions.

Avalon Books

160 Madison Avenue
New York, NY 10016

Editorial Director: Erin Cartwright-Niumata

Publisher's Interests
Wholesome adult fiction suitable for young adults and family reading is available from Avalon Books. With the exception of historical Westerns and historical romances, all of its titles feature contemporary characters and fresh plot lines.
Website: www.avalonbooks.com

Freelance Potential
Published 60 titles in 2005: 25 were developed from unsolicited submissions and 30 were by agented authors. Receives 600 queries yearly.

- **Fiction:** Publishes young adult books, 12–18 years. Genres include mystery, suspense, Western, romance, and historical fiction.
- **Representative Titles:** *Turn of Fortune* by Vicky Hunnings is a mystery set in Hilton Head, South Carolina, that features a pair of detectives struggling to solve several mysterious murders. *Found: Love* by Donna Wright depicts the romance that develops between a busy teacher and a man with a hectic job and equally full schedule.

Submissions and Payment
Guidelines and catalogue available at website. Query with 2- to 3-page synopsis and first 3 chapters. Accepts simultaneous submissions if identified. SASE. Response time and publication period vary. Flat fee.

Editor's Comments
We offer specific guidelines for each genre. Please check these guidelines, available at our website, before mailing your query package. In general, all historical fiction should be carefully researched so that it is correctly placed in time. Romances should not contain sexual situations—although kisses and embraces are acceptable—and mysteries should have tight, believable story lines in addition to the element of suspense.

A/V Concepts Corporation

30 Montauk Boulevard
Oakdale, NY 11769

Editor: Laura Solimene

Publisher's Interests

Educational software, workbooks, and study guides are the specialty of this publisher. As a division of EDCON Publishing Group, A/V Concepts offers high-interest, low-vocabulary material for students in grades two through twelve.
Website: www.edconpublishing.com

Freelance Potential

Published 5 titles (4 juvenile) in 2005. Of the 5 titles, 3 were by unpublished writers and 2 were by authors who were new to the publishing house. Receives 300 queries yearly.

- **Fiction:** Publishes middle-grade titles, 8–12 years; and young adult books, 12–18 years. Genres include the classics, science fiction, fantasy, and horror. Also publishes biographies, adapted classics, and nature and adventure stories.
- **Nonfiction:** Published 3 middle-grade titles, 8–12 years; and 1 young adult book, 12–18 years. Also publishes workbooks. Topics include reading comprehension, vocabulary development, math fundamentals, science, phonics, and writing skills.
- **Representative Titles:** *Romeo & Juliet* is a low-vocabulary, high-interest easy reader adaptation of the Shakespearean classic. *Math Mystery Theater* reinforces basic skills through CD-ROM computer exercises with humorous plots.

Submissions and Payment

Guidelines and catalogue available. Query with résumé and writing samples or clips. No unsolicited mss. All work is assigned. SASE. Responds in 3–6 weeks. Publication period varies. Flat fee.

Editor's Comments

Please note that all of our freelance work is assigned. Send us a query that demonstrates your grasp of the subject and includes why your material is suitable for our audience of educational professionals and students.

Ave Maria Press

P.O. Box 428
Notre Dame, IN 46556

Editorial Coordinator

Publisher's Interests
Educational and inspirational books for teachers, parents, and families on topics such as Scripture, prayer, meditation, and personal growth are produced by this Catholic publisher. **Website:** www.avemariapress.com

Freelance Potential
Published 40 titles in 2005: 2 were developed from unsolicited submissions, 4 were by agented authors, and 2 were reprint/licensed properties. Receives 200 queries yearly.

- **Nonfiction:** Publishes educational and religious titles for Catholic families. Topics include sacraments, prayer and spirituality, family life, Christian living, and leadership. Also publishes titles on the lives of Catholic saints.
- **Representative Titles:** *Ready for College* by Michael Pennock (YA) offers first-time college students what they need to succeed. *Child's First Catholic Dictionary* by Richard Dyches & Thomas Mustachio (grades K–3) offers clear, concise definitions and lively illustrations that inform and entertain children.

Submissions and Payment
Guidelines available at website. Query with outline, table of contents, introduction, statement of purpose, description of audience, and 1 or 2 sample chapters. Accepts photocopies and computer printouts. No simultaneous submissions. SASE. Responds in 4–6 months. Publication in 6 months. Payment rate varies.

Editor's Comments
We provide comprehensive resources for families, pastors, ministers, adolescent catechesis, and elementary catechesis. Topics related to spirituality and prayer are of interest to us, as well as material on Christian living and other works on faith and culture. When submitting a query, make sure you tell us why you are qualified to write on the topic, and who you think will read it and why.

Avisson Press

3007 Taliaferro Road
Greensboro, NC 27408

Editor: M. L. Hester

Publisher's Interests
This small publishing house features young adult biographies
and series titles of notable African American, female, and
minority personalities, both current and historical, as well as
books on specific periods in American history.

Freelance Potential
Published 8 titles in 2005: 4 were developed from unsolicited
submissions and 1 was a reprint/licensed property. Receives
300 queries yearly.

- **Fiction:** Published 1 young adult book, 12–18 years. Genres
  include contemporary and historical fiction.
- **Nonfiction:** Published 7 young adult books, 12–18 years. Topics include history, science, sports, and ethnic and multicultural issues. Also publishes biographies.
- **Representative Titles:** *I Can Do Anything* by William Schoell
  (YA) is a biography of Sammy Davis, Jr. *Mary Robinson* by Lita
  Friedman (YA) tells the story of the woman behind the fight for
  human rights.

Submissions and Payment
Query with outline, biography, and sample chapter for nonfiction. Accepts submissions for fiction from agented authors
only. Accepts photocopies, computer printouts, and simultaneous submissions if identified. SASE. Responds in 2 weeks.
Publication in 1 year. Royalty, 8–10%.

Editor's Comments
We are always interested in authors familiar with our editorial
perspective. We need titles that fit into our young adult biography series, especially biographies of minorities and women
who have accomplished great things in America. Our readers
like books about personalities they can relate to, so send us
material that focuses on contemporary social and ethnic
issues. We will consider young adult fiction titles, but only
from authors with book credits, or through an agent.

Avocus Publishing

4 White Brook Road
Gilsum, NH 03448

Editor: Craig Thorn

Publisher's Interests

This publisher values its tradition as a publishing house serving educators and offers books about independent school life, classroom teaching, academic programs, and curriculum development. Its audience also includes parents who are homeschooling their children, as well as professionals who work with gifted and special education students.
Website: www.avocus.com

Freelance Potential

Published 2 titles: 1 was developed from an unsolicited submission. Of the 2 titles, both were by unpublished writers and both were by authors who were new to the publishing house. Receives 100+ queries, 72 unsolicited mss yearly.

- **Nonfiction:** Publishes chapter picture books, 5–10 years; middle-grade books, 8–12 years; and young adult books, 12–18 years. Topics include gifted and special education.
- **Representative Titles:** *Far and Wide: Cultural Diversity in the American Boarding School* by Tim Hillman & Craig Thorn IV (teachers) offers discussions about multiculturalism at the secondary school level. *Personal Quests & Quandaries: Coming of Age in the 21st Century* by Carol W. Hotchkiss (YA) offers brief self-portraits of young adults responding to their lives and making sense of today's world.

Submissions and Payment

Guidelines and catalogue available at website. Query or send complete ms. SASE. Response time and publication period vary. Royalty; advance.

Editor's Comments

We are looking for new titles on topics related to parenting and education, homeschooling, and special needs children. In addition, hot topics such as finance, managing technology, curriculum development, and creating diverse and supportive school environments are of interest to us.

Baker Book House Company

6030 East Fulton Road
Ada, MI 49301

Submissions Editor

Publisher's Interests

In addition to books that address the needs of pastors and church leaders, Baker Book House offers books for lay Christians seeking to stimulate their thinking and titles that help parents pass their Christian faith on to their children.
Website: www.bakerbooks.com

Freelance Potential

Published 240 titles (12 juvenile) in 2005: all were by agented authors. Of the 240 titles, 1 was by an unpublished writer. Receives 100 queries yearly.

- **Fiction:** Publishes story picture books, 4–10 years. Genres include inspirational stories with Christian themes.
- **Nonfiction:** Publishes toddler books and early picture books, 0–4 years; and middle-grade books, 8–12 years. Features Bible stories and stories that show the presence of God in one's life. Also publishes parenting titles and homeschooling titles for adults.
- **Representative Titles:** *Girls!* by William Beausay & Kathryn Beausay (parents) shows how to raise caring, creative, confident daughters. *Don't Feed the Bears . . . and Other Bible Lessons for Kids* by Sheryl Bruinsma (grades 1–8) teaches discretion, virtues, and the value of living a Christian life.

Submissions and Payment

Guidelines and catalogue available at website. Accepts queries from agented authors only. No unsolicited mss. Response time varies. Publication in 1–2 years. Royalty.

Editor's Comments

We look for intelligent, engaging books that are relevant to today's Christians. For children, we seek books that show them how God is present in their everyday lives. Please note that we will only review materials sent to us through professional literary agents. Unsolicited manuscripts sent by the writer will be returned unread.

Baker's Plays

P.O. Box 699222
Quincy, MA 02269-9222

Managing Director: Deidre Shaw

Publisher's Interests
High school, university, children's, family, and regional theater groups turn to this publisher for their drama needs. Baker's offers full-length and one-act plays for all levels of actor participation and audience interest.
Website: www.bakersplays.com

Freelance Potential
Published 30 titles (15 juvenile) in 2005: 24 were developed from unsolicited submissions, 6 were by agented authors, and a few were reprint/licensed properties. Receives 1,000+ queries, 500 unsolicited mss yearly.

- **Fiction:** Publishes one-act and full-length plays, monologues, and skits for children's, high school, and family theater groups. Genres include comedy, mystery, folktales, and fairy tales. Also publishes holiday plays, the classics, and musicals.
- **Nonfiction:** Publishes textbooks and theater resource material for drama students and teachers. Topics include improvisation, teaching theater, acting techniques, theatrical history, and play writing.
- **Representative Titles:** *Adventure Faces* by Brian Way is a short play about a Carnival King who faces eviction by a large corporation; includes ideas for audience participation. *Balloon Faces* by Brian Way involves the audience in a play about the Land of Balloons on the dark side of the moon.

Submissions and Payment
Guidelines available. Query with script history, reviews, and sample pages or synopsis; or send complete ms. Accepts photocopies, computer printouts, and simultaneous submissions if identified. SASE. Responds to queries in 1 month; to mss in 3–4 months. Publication period and payment policy vary.

Editor's Comments
We prefer works that have already been staged, in order to ensure a more finished product.

Barefoot Books Ltd.

124 Walcot Street
Bath BA1 5BG
United Kingdom

Submissions Editor

Publisher's Interests
Barefoot Books is an award-winning publishing company that strives to bring art and story to today's children in a way that encourages their own creativity and honors the diversity of the world's cultures.
Website: www.barefootbooks.com

Freelance Potential
Published 40 titles in 2005: 2 were developed from unsolicited submissions and 2 were by agented authors. Of the 40 titles, 3 were by unpublished writers and 4 were by authors who were new to the publishing house. Receives 100+ unsolicited mss yearly.

- **Fiction:** Published 5 concept books, 5 toddler books, and 5 early picture books, 0–4 years; 20 easy-to-read books, 4–7 years; and 5 story picture books, 4–10 years. Genres include fairy tales, folklore, folktales, multicultural and ethnic fiction, and stories about nature and the environment.
- **Representative Titles:** *My Granny Went to Market* by Sheila Blackstone (0–7 years) follows Granny on a magic carpet ride around the world to collect souvenirs from various countries. *The Faery's Gift* by Tanya Robyn Batt (3–8 years) is the story of a poor woodcutter who faces a tricky dilemma when he saves a faery's life and is granted one wish.

Submissions and Payment
Guidelines and catalogue available at website. Send complete ms with artwork if applicable. Accepts photocopies and computer printouts. SAE/IRC. Responds only if interested. Publication period and payment policy vary.

Editor's Comments
We're selective in what we publish; we want to be sure that each of our books has enduring value as well as lots of child appeal. We welcome the opportunity to work with anyone who shares our vision.

Baycrest Books

P.O. Box 2009
Monroe, MI 48161

Acquisitions Editor

Publisher's Interests
Baycrest Books, a publisher of fiction for adults, targets young adult readers through its Orange Moon division. This division offers stories of all genres written to appeal to readers ages ten to sixteen.
Website: www.baycrestbooks.com

Freelance Potential
Published 6 titles in 2005.

- **Fiction:** Publishes young adult books, 12–16 years. Genres include adventure, fantasy, mystery, suspense, romance, science fiction, and Western fiction.
- **Representative Titles:** *The Dark Plain* by Sloan St. James (YA) is the story of a man who returns to Ireland after the death of his only son and the friendship he develops with a special woman.

Submissions and Payment
Guidelines and catalogue available at website. Query with 1-page synopsis and brief author bio. Accepts queries through website only. Accepts simultaneous submissions if identified. Responds in 1–2 months. Publication in 12–18 months. Royalty; advance.

Editor's Comments
We're looking for stories for our Orange Moon division that will captivate and perhaps educate our readers. We believe the 10- to 16-year-old age bracket is the most difficult time of life—a time of peer pressure, of finding one's way, and of searching for one's true self. We want stories that are engaging to the reader. Topics can range as far as the imagination can stretch. Fantasy books are acceptable, but plots must reflect in some way the real-life struggles that young adults face every day on the road to maturity. Your query letter should stick to the facts, but be creative in your approach. If your query and synopsis don't grab us, neither will your book.

Beach Holme Publishing

1010-409 Granville Street
Vancouver, British Columbia V6C 1T2
Canada

Publisher: Michael Carroll

Publisher's Interests

This publisher's juvenile list primarily consists of contemporary and historical novels for young adults. Only the works of Canadian authors are considered for publication.
Website: www.beachholme.bc.ca

Freelance Potential

Published 11 titles (4 juvenile) in 2005: 6 were developed from unsolicited submissions and 1 was by an agented author. Of the 11 titles, 7 were by authors who were new to the publishing house. Receives 1,000 queries yearly.

- **Fiction:** Published 1 chapter book, 5–10 years; and 3 middle-grade novels, 8–12 years. Genres include Canadian historical, contemporary, multicultural, and Native Canadian fiction.
- **Representative Titles:** *By the Skin of His Teeth* by Ann Walsh (YA) is a story of prejudice directed at a Chinese community and of a young man who is victimized for defending his Chinese friend. *Sophie's Friend in Need* by Norma Charles (YA) is a historical novel, set in British Columbia in the summer of 1950, that explores the relationship between a French Canadian girl and her camp partner, an unhappy Jewish refugee.

Submissions and Payment

Canadian authors only. Guidelines available. Query with author bio, first two chapters (30 pages maximum), market analysis, and description of intended audience. Accepts photocopies and computer printouts. SASE. Responds in 4–6 months. Publication in 1 month. Royalty; advance.

Editor's Comments

We seek novels for children between the ages of 8 and 13, especially those with a historical basis that feature Canadian settings. If your historical novel can tie in to the school curriculum, include ideas for developing teacher's guides to accompany your work.

Bebop Books

95 Madison Avenue
New York, NY 10016

Senior Editor: Jennifer Fox

Publisher's Interests

An imprint of Lee & Low Books, this multicultural publisher
provides fiction and nonfiction for beginning readers. Its
child-centered stories support literacy learning and provide
multicultural content for ages four through seven.
Website: www.bebopbooks.com

Freelance Potential

Published 8 titles in 2005: 3 were developed from unsolicited submissions. Of the 8 titles, 2 were by unpublished
writers and 3 were by authors who were new to the publishing house. Receives 1,000 unsolicited mss yearly.

- **Fiction:** Published 5 beginning reader books, 4–7 years.
  Features books in Spanish and English.
- **Nonfiction:** Published 3 beginning reader books, 4–7 year.
  Topics include multicultural and ethnic subjects.
- **Representative Titles:** *African Dance: Drumbeat in Our Feet*
  by Patricia Keeler & Júlio Leitao (Developmental Reading
  Assessment) joins an African dance troupe as they prepare for
  a show. *Leo and the Butterflies* by Jan Reynolds (Developmen-
  tal Reading Assessment) introduces a Costa Rican boy who
  explores a rainforest where butterflies live.

Submissions and Payment

Guidelines available at website or with SASE. Send complete
ms only in late summer (August) to early fall (beginning of
October). Accepts photocopies. SASE. Responds in 4 months.
Publication in 1 year. Royalty; advance.

Editor's Comments

Our policy is to review manuscripts from late summer to
early fall only. We want to see multicultural nonfiction and
stories with interesting characters (young children of color)
for beginning readers. We're also looking for stories with
simple math, science, or social studies concepts. Please do
not send us animal stories or folklore.

Behrman House

11 Edison Place
Springfield, NJ 07081

Editorial Department

Publisher's Interests

Although the primary purpose of Behrman House is to produce textbooks for use in Jewish religious schools, it also publishes books about Judaism for anyone interested in deepening their understanding of Jewish culture and practices. **Website:** www.behrmanhouse.com

Freelance Potential

Published 15–20 titles in 2005: 4–5 were developed from unsolicited submissions. Receives 50 queries, 50 unsolicited mss yearly.

- **Nonfiction:** Publishes chapter books, 5–10 years; middle-grade books, 8–12 years; and young adult books, 12–18 years. Topics include Judaism, religion, theology, prayer, holidays, the Bible, the Holocaust, history, liturgy, Hebrew, and ethics. Also publishes educational resource materials and religious instructional materials for adults.
- **Representative Titles:** *Partners with God* by Gila Gevirtz (grades 3–4) presents clear, comfortable ways to introduce Jewish concepts of God to children. *The Book of Jewish Practice* by Louis Jacobs (grades 9 and up) offers step-by-step instructions for living a Jewish life, from holiday observance and ethical business practices to reverence for life.

Submissions and Payment

Prefers query with table of contents and sample chapter. Accepts complete ms with résumé and author biography. Accepts photocopies, computer printouts, and simultaneous submissions. SASE. Responds in 2 months. Publication in 18 months. Royalty, 5–10%; advance, $1,500. Flat fee.

Editor's Comments

For the coming year, we're looking for submissions of Judaica and Hebrew materials written for children ages five through eighteen.

Benchmark Books

Marshall Cavendish
99 White Plains Road
Tarrytown, NY 10591

Editorial Director: Michelle Bisson

Publisher's Interests

Benchmark Books is known for producing outstanding educational series titles for students in kindergarten through high school. Among the subject areas it covers are American studies, the arts, human behavior, and world cultures.
Website: www.marshallcavendish.com

Freelance Potential

Published 150 titles in 2005: 10 were developed from unsolicited submissions and 10 were by agented authors. Of the 150 titles, 15 were by authors who were new to the publishing house. Receives 1,000 queries yearly.

- **Nonfiction:** Publishes easy-to-read books, 4–7 years; chapter books, 5–10 years; middle-grade books, 8–12 years; and young adult books, 12–18 years. Topics include animals, mathematics, science, social studies, history, world cultures, American studies, human behavior, the arts, and health. Also publishes activity books and biographies.
- **Representative Titles:** *Alzheimer's Disease* by Marlene Targ Brill (grades 4 and up) provides young readers with essential information about this medical condition; part of the Health Alert series. *Cholera: Curse of the Nineteenth Century* by Stephanie True Peters (grades 6 and up) combines historical narrative with first-person accounts in exploring the origins, effects, and consequences of this disease; part of the Epidemic! series.

Submissions and Payment

Query with 1–3 chapters and table of contents. Accepts photocopies and computer printouts. SASE. Responds in 6–8 weeks. Publication in 9–18 months. Flat fee.

Editor's Comments

Query us if you're experienced in writing about educational topics in a way that will engage our young readers. We're open to submissions for all curriculum areas.

Bess Press

3565 Harding Avenue
Honolulu, HI 96816

Editor: Réve Shapard

Publisher's Interests
This regional publisher specializes in educational materials
and textbooks that meet the needs of teachers working in
Hawaii and the Pacific Islands.
Website: www.besspress.com

Freelance Potential
Published 12 titles (10 juvenile) in 2005: 3 were developed
from unsolicited submissions. Of the 12 titles, 1 was by an
unpublished writer and 1 was by an author who was new to
the publishing house. Receives 10 queries, 100 unsolicited
mss yearly.

- **Fiction:** Publishes story picture books, 4–10 years; and
  coloring books. Genres include regional fiction, folklore,
  and folktales.
- **Nonfiction:** Published 9 concept books, 0–4 years;
  1 story picture book, 4–10 years; and 2 young adult books,
  12–18 years. Topics include Hawaiian and Pacific Island culture, language, natural history, literature, and biographies.
- **Representative Titles:** *Waltah Melon: Local-Kine Hero* by Carmen
  Geshell tells the story of how Waltah Melon wins the affections of
  Honey Dew. *The Magic Shark Learns to Cook* by Donivee Martin
  Laird is a humorous story about a shark who tries to learn how to
  cook.

Submissions and Payment
Writers guidelines available. Send complete ms. Accepts photocopies, computer printouts, and simultaneous submissions
if identified. SASE. Responds in 4–6 weeks. Publication in 6–12
months. Royalty; 5–10%.

Editor's Comments
We're looking for entertaining and colorful books on Hawaiian
topics only. Our target audience at this time is primarily pre-K
and early elementary readers. If you are an educator who is
familiar with curriculum guidelines, we want to hear from you.

Bethany House Publishers

11400 Hampshire Avenue South
Minneapolis, MN 55438

Submissions Editor

Publisher's Interests
An evangelical Christian publisher, Bethany House offers books for all ages, including fiction and nonfiction for children and young adults.
Website: www.bethanyhouse.com

Freelance Potential
Published 14 titles in 2005: 3 were by agented authors. Receives 50–75 queries yearly.

- **Fiction:** Published 1 story picture book, 4–10 years; and 8 middle-grade books, 8–12 years. Also publishes young adult books, 12–18 years. Genres include adventure; mystery; suspense; and inspirational, contemporary, and historical fiction.
- **Nonfiction:** Published 1 early picture book, 0–4 years; 1 middle-grade book, 8–12 years; and 3 young adult books, 12–18 years. Topics include contemporary issues, spirituality, theology, family life, and social issues. Also publishes devotionals, curriculum guides, and Christian educational resources.
- **Representative Titles:** *Mandie and the Missing Schoolmarm* by Lois Gladys Leppard imparts lessons of faith in a story about a school teacher who mysteriously disappears. *Chatting with Girls Like You* by Sandra Byrd (8–12 years) offers godly answers and advice on issues of concern to middle-grade girls.

Submissions and Payment
Guidelines available at website. Query appropriate editor by sending fax to 952-996-1304. Not currently accepting unsolicited mss. Responds in 9–12 weeks. Publication period varies. Royalty; advance.

Editor's Comments
This year, we're seeking middle-grade and young adult fiction that is a step beyond the traditional series fiction. We'd like to see savvy, contemporary characters dealing with real-life issues—characters today's readers will instantly connect with. For now, we prefer shorter series and stand-alone titles.

Beyond Words Publishing

Suite 500
20827 NW Cornell Road
Hillsboro, OR 97124-9808

Children's Editor: Summer Steele

Publisher's Interests
Books from this publisher share a common thread of inspiration. With their picture books, nonfiction, or self-help titles for young readers through young adults, Beyond Words seeks to inspire children to reach for their dreams.
Website: www.beyondword.com

Freelance Potential
Published 2 titles in 2005: 2 were developed from unsolicited submissions. Of the 2 titles, 1 was by an unpublished writer and 1 was by an author new to the publishing house. Receives 250 queries, 2,800 unsolicited mss each year.

- **Fiction:** Publishes story picture books, 4–10 years; and middle-grade books, 8–12 years. Genres include folktales and multicultural fiction.
- **Nonfiction:** Publishes story picture books, 4–10 years; middle-grade books, 8–12 years; and young adult books, 12–18 years. Also publishes middle-grade books written by young authors; and spiritual empowerment guides.
- **Representative Titles:** *Finding Fairies* by Michelle Roehm and Marianne Monson-Burton (4–10 years) shares the secrets of attracting fairies. *So You Wanna Be a Rock Star* by Stephen Anderson (8–16 years) is a how-to book that teaches young, aspiring musicians how to achieve their rock-and-roll dreams.

Submissions and Payment
Guidelines available. Send complete ms with description of market and competition. Accepts photocopies and computer printouts. SASE. Responds in 4–6 months. Publication in 1 year. Royalty, 5–10%; advance, varies.

Editor's Comments
We're looking for nature stories for ages 4–9 years, as well as books on art, self-esteem, and guide books for using your imagination, all for ages 4–14.

Blackbirch Press

Suite C
15822 Bernardo Center Drive
San Diego, CA 92127

Editorial Director: Chandra Howard

Publisher's Interests

This educational publisher produces illustrated nonfiction that correlates with elementary and middle school curricula. Its books have become known not only for their pleasing design, but for their unique editorial approaches to subjects such as natural science, social studies, and American history. **Website:** www.gale.com/blackbirch

Freelance Potential

Published 100 titles in 2005: 54 were reprint/licensed properties. Of the 100 titles, 4 were by authors who were new to the publishing house. Receives 60 queries yearly.

- **Nonfiction:** Publishes middle-grade books, 8–12 years. Topics include science, nature, the environment, ecology, biography, American history, women's history, geography, business, and multicultural subjects.
- **Representative Titles:** *A–Z Extreme Animals* by Andromeda takes a look at animals with extreme features and includes information on predators and prey, camouflage, and endangered animals. *Communities in Nature: Inland Waters* by Elizabeth Ring explores the world of freshwater plants and animals, including insects, crustaceans, frogs, turtles, fish, and birds.

Submissions and Payment

Guidelines available. Query with résumé. No unsolicited mss. Accepts photocopies and simultaneous submissions if identified. SASE. Responds in 4 months. Publication in 1 year. Flat fee.

Editor's Comments

We've been receiving too many submissions of biographies recently. Instead, we need more cutting-edge, science-based academic reference books. Our association with Thomson Gale has helped us to grow, and as we continue to do so, we will focus on the innovation, creativity, and high editorial standards we've become known for.

A & C Black

37 Soho Square
London W1D 3QZ
United Kingdom

Submissions Editor: Claire Weatherhead

Publisher's Interests

For nearly 200 years, A & C Black has been offering quality and tradition in publishing. It titles include award-winning themed activity books, curriculum books in science, math, and geography, and fiction and nonfiction series.
Website: www.acblack.com

Freelance Potential

Published 65 titles (30 juvenile) in 2005: 2 were developed from unsolicited submissions and 30 were by agented authors. Of the 65 titles, 2 were by unpublished writers and 8 were by authors who were new to the publishing house.

- **Fiction:** Published 16 chapter books, 5–10 years. Genres include historical fiction and humor.
- **Nonfiction:** Published 12 chapter books, 5–10 years; and 5 middle-grade books, 8–12 years. Topics include science, history, geography, music, art, religion, literacy, and math.
- **Representative Titles:** *A Drop in the Ocean* by Jacqui Bailey (8–12 years), follows the passage of a water droplet; part of the Science Works series. *The Gods Are Watching* by Caroline Pitcher (8–12 years) is a thriller set in ancient Egypt featuring a young boy fleeing from danger.

Submissions and Payment

Guidelines available. Send complete manuscript. Accepts photocopies and computer printouts. SAE/IRC. Responds in 2 months. Publication period and payment policy vary.

Editor's Comments

We are currently seeking authors for our children's series: Snappers emphasizes strong characterization and exciting storylines of 5,000 words for ages seven to nine; Black Cats can be any genre but should contain action-packed chapters (totaling 12,000 to14,000 words) for ages eight and up; and Flashbacks are well-researched, dramatic stories (of 12,000 to 14,000 words) set during key moments in history for ages eight and up.

Bloomsbury Children's Books

Suite 315
175 Fifth Avenue
New York, NY 10010

Submissions

Publisher's Interests

The pages of the catalogue from this publisher are filled with listings of fiction books for children of all ages. It also includes a small number of nonfiction titles.
Website: www.bloomsburyusa.com

Freelance Potential

Published 66 titles (37 juvenile) in 2005: 1 was developed from an unsolicited submission, 65 were by agented authors, and 12 were reprint/licensed properties. Of the 66 titles, 2 were by unpublished writers and 18 were by authors who were new to the publishing house. Receives 100+ queries, 1,000+ unsolicited mss yearly.

- **Fiction:** Published 2 concept books, 1 toddler book; 4 early picture books, 0–4 years; 2 easy-to-read books, 4–7 years, 8 story picture books, 4–10 years; 25 chapter and middle-grade books, 5–12 years; and 26 young adult books, 12–18 years. Genres include adventure, fantasy, multicultural and ethnic subjects, mystery, and science fiction.
- **Nonfiction:** Publishes early picture books, 0–4 years; middle-grade books, 8–12 years; and young adult books, 12–18 years. Topics include multicultural and ethnic subjects.
- **Representative Titles:** *No Bed without Ted* by Nicola Smee (3–7 years) follows a little girl and all the family pets. *Zoo* by Graham Marks (12+ years) is a shocking, fast-paced thriller about a boy trying to find the truth about his life.

Submissions and Payment

Guidelines available at website. Send complete ms for picture books; query with synopsis and first 3 chapters for longer works. Accepts photocopies, computer printouts, and simultaneous submissions if identified. SASE. Response time and publication period vary. Royalty; advance.

Editor's Comments

We're interested in fun picture books that children will love.

Blue Sky Press

Scholastic Inc.
557 Broadway
New York, NY 10012-3999

Editorial Director: Bonnie Verburg

Publisher's Interests
The titles from this imprint of Scholastic include nonfiction
for early and middle-grade readers and fiction for all age
groups, from infants to teens. Only authors who have
already achieved publication may submit queries to Blue
Sky Press.
Website: www.scholastic.com

Freelance Potential
Published 13 titles in 2005. Receives 3,000 queries yearly.

- **Fiction:** Publishes toddler books and early picture books, 0–4
  years; easy-to-read books, 4–7 years; story picture books,
  4–10 years; chapter books, 5–10 years; middle-grade books,
  8–12 years; and young adult books, 12–18 years. Genres
  include historical and multicultural fiction, folklore, fairy tales,
  fantasy, humor, and adventure.
- **Nonfiction:** Publishes story picture books, 4–8 years; and
  middle-grade books, 8–12 years. Topics include nature, the
  environment, and history.
- **Representative Titles:** *How Do Dinosaurs Say Good Night?* by
  Jane Yolen & Mark Teague (2+ years) is a story that depicts
  what young dinosaurs will do when bedtime approaches. *How
  Groundhog's Garden Grew* by Lynne Cherry (4+ years) is the
  story of a groundhog who learns how to grow a garden full of
  fruits and vegetables.

Submissions and Payment
Accepts queries from previously published authors only. Query
with synopsis and list of publishing credits. Send complete
ms for picture books. Accepts photocopies. SASE. Responds
in 6 months. Publication in 2–5 years. Royalty; advance.

Editor's Comments
We're seeking middle-grade and young adult fiction that
features strong female characters from various ethnic
backgrounds.

Boardwalk Books

Suite 200
8 Market Street
Toronto, Ontario M5E 1M6
Canada

Acquistions Editor

Publisher's Interests
This imprint of Dundurn Press publishes young adult fiction, and specializes in issue-driven fiction and historical nonfiction written by Canadian authors.
Website: www.dundurn.com

Freelance Potential
Published 60 titles (5 juvenile) in 2005: 2 were developed from unsolicited submissions and 15 were by agented authors. Of the 60 titles, 2 were by unpublished writers and 5 were by authors who were new to the publishing house. Receives 150 queries, 350 unsolicited mss yearly.

- **Fiction:** Published 4 young adult books, 12–18 years. Genres include contemporary fiction, drama, and mystery.
- **Nonfiction:** Published 1 young adult book, 12–18 years. Includes biographies.
- **Representative Titles:** *Hiding in Plain Sight* by Valerie Sherrard (YA) is a suspenseful mystery about teenage sleuth, Shelby Belgarden's, latest adventures. *Shades of Red* by kc dyer (YA) is the third and final part of the Eagle Glen Trilogy.

Submissions and Payment
Guidelines available at website. Query with cover letter, 250-word synopsis, résumé, three sample chapters, and manuscript word count; include table of contents for nonfiction. Or send complete ms. Accepts photocopies and computer printouts. SASE. Responds to nonfiction in 2–3 months, to fiction in 6–8 months. Publication period varies. Advance.

Editor's Comments
This year we are interested in issue-driven literary works for readers ages 12 through 18. Please browse our website or catalogue to make sure that your material is a good fit for our publishing program. As a Canadian publisher, please note that we rarely publish work by non-Canadian authors.

Borealis Press Ltd.

8 Mohawk Crescent
Nepean, Ontario K2H 7G6
Canada

Senior Editor: Glenn Clever

Publisher's Interests

Books by Canadian authors on subjects related to Canada distinguish this publisher's list. Its children's titles tend to be humorous with a sense of fun, although serious works that focus on the wonder and beauty of life—or, conversely, the anguishes of life—are also presented.
Website: www.borealispress.com

Freelance Potential

Published 10 titles (4 juvenile) in 2005. Receives 100 queries yearly.

- **Fiction:** Publishes story picture books, 4–10 years; and young adult books, 12–18 years. Genres include fantasy and multicultural and ethnic fiction.
- **Nonfiction:** Publishes reference titles about Canadian history. Also offers drama, poetry, and books with multicultural themes.
- **Representative Titles:** *The Aussie Six in Australia* by Paul Zann is a story about six unusual Australian animals that have been captured by a cruel circus owner; part of The Aussie Six series. *The Quest of Keppoch Mountain* by Rita Baruss is a contemporary story that involves tree spirits, spirited children, and a worldwide computer network called Kids Involved with the Wild World.

Submissions and Payment

Guidelines available. Query with outline/synopsis and sample chapter. No unsolicited mss. Accepts photocopies and disk submissions. No simultaneous submissions.SAE/IRC. Responds in 3–4 months. Publication in 1–2 years. Royalty, 10% of net.

Editor's Comments

We will review material that demonstrates mature, skillful writing on topics that seriously portray the human situation. Our goal is to publish work our readers will find meaningful.

Boyds Mills Press

815 Church Street
Honesdale, PA 18431

Manuscript Tracker: J. DeLuca

Publisher's Interests
Entertaining and informative books for children of all ages
can be found in the catalogue of this publisher. It aims to
publish high-quality stories that children will love.
Website: www.boydsmillspress.com

Freelance Potential
Published 60 titles (58 juvenile) in 2005: 25 were developed
from unsolicited submissions, 10 were by agented authors,
and 12 were reprint/licensed properties. Of the 60 titles, 10
were by unpublished writers and 15 were by new authors.
Receives 1,000 queries; 15,000 mss yearly.

* **Fiction:** Published 1 concept book, 4 toddler books, and 6
  early picture books, 0–4 years; 6 easy-to-read books, 4–7
  years; 16 story picture books, 4–10 years; 2 chapter books,
  5–10 years; 1 middle-grade book, 8–12 years; and 2 young
  adult books, 12–18 years. Genres include adventure stories
  and multicultural and ethnic fiction.
* **Nonfiction:** Published 4 early picture books, 0–4 years; 5
  easy-to-read books, 4–7 years; 10 story picture books, 4–10
  years; 2 chapter books, 5–10 years; and 1 middle-grade book,
  8–12 years. Topics include history, geography, science, and
  nature.
* **Representative Titles:** *Tap Dance Fever* by Pat Brisson (6+
  years) tells of a little girl who turns the town topsy-turvy with
  her nonstop dancing. *Cat Poems* by Dave Crawley (7–12 years)
  offers a collection of poems that pays tribute to fabulous felines.

Submissions and Payment
Guidelines available. Query with outline; or send ms. Accepts
photocopies and computer printouts. SASE. Responds in
1 month. Publication period and payment policy vary.

Editor's Comments
We're looking for fresh ideas and topics for middle-grade
fiction and picture books that are fun and imaginative.

Boynton/Cook Publishers

Heinemann
361 Hanover Street
Portsmouth, NH 03801-3912

Editorial Assistant

Publisher's Interests

Boynton/Cook provides professional resources for English teachers at the middle school, high school, and college levels. Its authors are leaders in the educational field, many of whom have won awards for their work in education. **Website:** www.boyntoncook.com

Freelance Potential

Published 75–100 titles in 2005. Receives 1,000 queries each year.

- **Nonfiction:** Publishes textbooks, grades 9 and up. Also publishes professional resource materials for educators. Topics include language arts, literature, rhetoric, communication, composition, writing, style, and drama.
- **Representative Titles:** *ESL Writers* by Shanti Bruce & Ben Rafoth (teachers) assists writing center tutors by combining practical tutoring advice with insights that foster cultural awareness of their ESL students. *Teaching English, 6–12* by Kathleen Strickland & James Strickland (teachers) is based on the philosophy that empowering students to make decisions about their learning, to set goals, and to work at their own pace results in a true learning experience.

Submissions and Payment

Guidelines and catalogue available at website. Query with project description, table of contents, sample illustrations if applicable, chapter summaries, and 3 sample chapters. Accepts photocopies, computer printouts, and simultaneous submissions if identified. SASE. Responds in 6–8 weeks. Publication in 10–12 months. Royalty.

Editor's Comments

Sample chapters are the most important part of your proposal, so be sure to select the two or three that will give us the best idea of your manuscript's content, style, and voice. If your manuscript is finished, send us the completed work.

Broadman & Holman Publishers

MNS 114
127 9th Avenue North
Nashville, TN 37234

Children's Team

Publisher's Interests
Known for its list of Bibles, textbooks, and reference titles, this publisher also offers a range of fiction and nonfiction books for children and young adults.
Website: www.broadmanandholman.com

Freelance Potential
Published 25 titles in 2005: 8 were developed from unsolicited submissions and 4 were by agented authors. Of the 25 titles, 2 were by authors who were new to the publishing house. Receives 300 unsolicited mss yearly.

- **Fiction:** Publishes story picture books, 4–10 years. Genres include historical, contemporary, and Christian fiction with biblical themes.
- **Nonfiction:** Publishes concept books and toddler books, 0–4 years; easy-to-read books, 4–7 years; story picture books, 4–10 years; middle-grade titles, 8–12 years; and young adult books, 12–18 years. Topics include religion, traditional and retold Bible stories, self-help, and contemporary social issues.
- **Representative Titles:** *Josie's Gift* by Kathy Bostrom is a heartfelt story of a young family that yearns to find happiness during the Depression. *Know God, No Fear* by Stephen Elkins takes readers on a camping adventure, and teaches them that God is always around to protect us.

Submissions and Payment
Guidelines available. Send complete ms for educational resources. Accepts agented submissions only for children's books. Accepts photocopies, computer printouts, and simultaneous submissions if identified. SASE. Responds in 3 months. Publication in 12–18 months. Royalty; advance.

Editor's Comments
We want titles that help children learn to read, and that reflect the Christian values they will grow into. Homeschooling titles are also of interest.

Brown Barn Books

119 Kettle Creek Road
Weston, CT 06883

Editor-in-Chief: Nancy Hammerslough

Publisher's Interests

Brown Barn Books publishes teen fiction only. The company is a division of Pictures of Record, Inc., a publisher of educational materials used for teaching and research by schools, universities, and museums throughout the world.
Website: www.brownbarnbooks.com

Freelance Potential

Published 4 titles in 2005. Receives 200 queries yearly.

- **Fiction:** Publishes young adult books, 12–18 years. Genres include historical and contemporary fiction, adventure, mystery, suspense, and multicultural and ethnic fiction.
- **Representative Titles:** *Idiot* by Colin Neenan (YA) is the story of a shy 16-year-old boy who makes headlines and becomes a romantic hero to millions of American girls. *Key to Aten* by Lynn Sinclair (YA) takes readers on a journey to another time and place as a 16-year-old girl tries to save a primitive world known as Aten from a future of endless warfare.

Submissions and Payment

Guidelines available at website. Query by email only to editorial@brownbarnbooks.com. Response time and publication period vary. Royalty; advance.

Editor's Comments

We accept queries by email only. Please cut and paste your query into the body of your email, instead of sending it as an attachment. We don't review unsolicited manuscripts; any manuscripts that do come in are automatically rejected unless we have specifically invited the submission after reviewing a query. Our publishing program focuses exclusively on young adult fiction—please don't submit picture books or material for middle-grade readers. Gripping stories and great characters that will appeal to readers age 12 and up are what we're looking for. Books that have been previously published in any other medium are not accepted.

The Bureau for At-Risk Youth

Suite 201
45 Executive Drive
Plainview, NY 11803

Executive Producer: Michelle Yannes

Publisher's Interests

Curriculum materials, booklets, pamphlets, multimedia products, and videos on guidance for at–risk children are the focus of this company. Its titles address current social, developmental, and cultural issues and other topics of concern.
Website: www.at-risk.com

Freelance Potential

Published 12 titles in 2005.

- **Nonfiction:** Publishes curriculum and classroom material, activity books, workbooks, and reference titles, grades K–12. Topics include special needs, anger and conflict management, sexual assault, family issues, personal health, violence prevention, substance abuse, hazing and bullying, character education, career development, self-esteem, teen sexuality, parenting, guidance, and health issues. Also publishes resource material for school guidance counselors and social work professionals.
- **Representative Titles:** *Grants for At-Risk Youth* (professionals) lists private, federal, and corporate grantmakers for funding at-risk youth programs. *Molly Mouse Learns About Stranger Safety* (grades K–3) is an activity book that helps children deal with issues important to their physical and emotional health through activities and thought-provoking questions.

Submissions and Payment

Query or send complete ms. SASE. Responds to queries in 1–3 months; to mss in 2–6 months. Publication in 6 months. Payment policy varies.

Editor's Comments

Our target audience consists of parents, educators, counselors, and other professionals who work with young people in kindergarten through grade twelve. We continue to be interested in material on drug and alcohol abuse, teen pregnancy issues, and children's health.

Buster Books

9 Lion Yard
Tremadoc Road
London, SW4 7NQ
United Kingdom

Editor: Ellen Bailey

Publisher's Interests
This English publisher, the children's book division of
Michael O'Mara Books Limited, produces nonfiction titles for
children, eight to twelve. It also features selections of board
books and novelty titles for pre-schoolers.
Website: www.mombooks.com/buster

Freelance Potential
Published 40 titles in 2005. Receives 50 queries, 200 unsolicited mss yearly.

- **Nonfiction:** Publishes early picture books, 0–4 years; easy-to-
  read books, 4–7 years; and middle-grade books, 8–12 years.
  Topics include animals and humor.
- **Representative Titles:** *Are You a Superstar?* (8–12 years) is a
  fun guide about the life of celebrities with tests and quizzes to
  determine whether readers have a future as a star. *I'm a Little
  Frog* by Tim Weare (preschoolers) is a board book containing a
  puppet frog that children can use to act out the story of a little
  frog trying to find its way home.

Submissions and Payment
Guidelines and catalogue available at website. Query with synopsis and sample text for nonfiction manuscripts. Does not
accept fiction. Accepts photocopies and computer printouts.
SAE/IRC. Responds only if interested. Publication period
varies. Flat fee.

Editor's Comments
Though we do publish fiction, we do not accept fiction submissions. We are mainly concerned with seeing nonfiction
manuscripts for children, ages eight through twelve. It is
best to review our online catalogue to get a clear idea of the
types of nonfiction that we publish. If you think your manuscript can fit in with what we offer, send us a synopsis and a
sample chapter. We do not want to see the complete work.
It is essential to include a SAE/IRC.

Butte Publications

P.O. Box 1328
Hillsboro, OR 97123-1328

Acquisitions Editor

Publisher's Interests
The field of deafness and hearing loss is supported by the resource materials that Butte Publications offers. Dictionaries; vocabulary building, reading and writing materials; myths and fables; and biographies are included in its catalogue of titles.
Website: www.buttepublications.com

Freelance Potential
Published 5 titles in 2005: all were developed from unsolicited submissions. Of the 5 titles, 1 was by an unpublished writer and 1 was by an author who was new to the publishing house. Receives 20 queries yearly.

- **Nonfiction:** Publishes resource and educational books on signing, interpreting, vocabulary, reading, writing, language skills, and lipreading. Also publishes parenting titles.
- **Representative Titles:** *Idioms* by Jocelyn & Judy Paris (teachers) introduces 24 current idiomatic expressions. *Happily Ever After: Using Storybooks in Preschool Settings* by Kate Bannister, Katy Preston, & Julie Primozich (teachers) contains storybook exercises using popular titles.

Submissions and Payment
Guidelines available. Query with table of contents, market analysis, and 2 sample chapters. Accepts computer printouts. SASE. Responds in 3–6 months. Publication in 1 year. Royalty.

Editor's Comments
We publish several new titles each year relating to deafness and hearing loss. They can be language (spoken English or sign language), skill building, professional resources, or recreational or informational in nature. We strive to bring to our audience of children, parents, professionals, and educators the best information possible. Review our catalogue to make sure your idea is unique and not a duplicate of a title we have published in the past.

Candlewick Press

2067 Massachusetts Avenue
Cambridge, MA 02140

Acquisitions: Liz Bicknell

Publisher's Interests
Books of the highest quality in text and art are published by
Candlewick Press, in operation since 1991. Its list includes
books for all ages from early picture books to young adult
fiction and nonfiction.
Website: www.candlewick.com

Freelance Potential
Published 200 titles in 2005

- **Fiction**: Publishes early picture books and toddler books,
  4–10 years; middle-grade books, 8–12 years; and young adult
  books, 12–18 years. Genres include contemporary, multicultural, historical, and science fiction; adventure; mystery;
  humor; fantasy; and stories about sports.
- **Nonfiction:** Publishes concept books and toddler books, 0–4
  years; story picture books, 4–10 years; and young adult
  books, 12–18 years. Topics include animals, history, nature,
  the environment, and geography. Also publishes biographies
  for young adults.
- **Representative Titles**: *We've All Got Bellybuttons!* by David
  Martin (3–6 years) lets little ones follow the actions of animal
  babies to discover the ways their bodies can move. *Stripes of
  the Sidestep Wolf* by Sonya Hartnett (12+ years) weaves the
  tale of two loners in a country town who find hope when one
  of them encounters a long-lost animal.

Submissions and Payment
Currently not accepting unsolicited manuscripts or queries.
Only accepts submissions from agented authors.

Editor's Comments
Due to an overwhelming amount of unsolicited submissions,
we are not accepting unsolicited manuscripts or queries at
this time. Our current policy is to only accept submissions
from agented authors or those writers that we have published in the past.

Capstone Press

151 Good Counsel Drive
Mankato, MN 56001

Editorial Director: Kay M. Olson

Publisher's Interests
Capstone Press produces nonfiction reading development tools for beginning readers, reluctant readers, and older readers who struggle with their reading ability. Each of its various imprints offers curriculum links and helps students advance through the reading development process.
Website: www.capstonepress.com

Freelance Potential
Published 400 titles in 2005. Receives numerous queries each year.

- **Nonfiction:** Published 12 concept books, 0–4 years; 163 easy-to-read books, 4–7 years; and 225 story picture books, 4–10 years. Topics include social studies, geography, health, science, animals, astronomy, math, technology, sports, arts and crafts, and the human body. Also publishes biographies.
- **Representative Titles:** *Animals in the Fall* (grades K–1) takes a look at the ways various animals prepare for the winter. *Making a First Recording* (grades 3–4) targets aspiring rock stars by taking them through the recording process.

Submissions and Payment
Guidelines available at website. Query with cover letter stating areas of interest and expertise, résumé, and 3 short writing samples. SASE. Responds in 1 month. Publication period varies. Flat fee.

Editor's Comments
We assign book topics to freelance writers on a work-for-hire, flat-rate basis. If you possess solid writing and research skills and would like to cover social studies, science, and high-interest topics for developing readers, contact us in writing (not through our website). We offer titles that are appropriate for use in preschool through high school classrooms, school and public libraries, ESL programs, Head Start, early childhood programs, and daycare centers.

Carolrhoda Books

Lerner Publishing Group
241 1st Avenue North
Minneapolis, MN 55401

Fiction Submissions Editor: Zelda Wagner

Publisher's Interests
Children of all ages have been enjoying the books published by Carolrhoda for over 35 years. An imprint of Lerner Publishing Group, its catalogue includes board books, novelty books, chapter books, and young adult novels.
Website: www.carolrhodabooks.com

Freelance Potential
Published 14 titles in 2005: 10 were developed from unsolicited submissions. Of the 14 titles, 3 were by authors who were new to the publishing house. Receives 500 queries, 2,000 unsolicited mss yearly.

- **Fiction:** Publishes story picture books, 4–10 years; and young adult books, 12–18 years. Genres include contemporary, mystery, multicultural, and historical fiction.
- **Representative Titles:** *The Girl-Son* by Anne E. Neuberger (grades 4–8) presents the true story of one girl's courage and determination to go against tradition to obtain an education. *Between the Dragon and the Eagle* by Mical Schneider (grades 4–8) takes readers on a fascinating journey back to A.D. 100, following a caravan from China to Rome.

Submissions and Payment
Guidelines available. Accepts submissions in November only. Query with outline and sample chapters; or send complete ms for shorter works. Accepts photocopies, and computer printouts. SASE. Responds in 8 months. Publication period varies. Royalty; advance.

Editor's Comments
We look for high-quality, entertaining, and informative books for young children, and are especially interested in new ideas and fresh topics. Our needs include picture books and young adult novels with multicultural and historical themes, as well as fantasy for young readers. Please note that we only accept submissions in November.

Carson-Dellosa Publishing

P.O. Box 35665
Greensboro, NC 27425-5665

Product Acquisitions: Pam Hill

Publisher's Interests
This publisher of educational resource materials features
books, activity books, and student workbooks for use in pre-K
through eighth-grade classrooms.
Website: www.carsondellosa.com

Freelance Potential
Published 100 titles in 2005: 5 were developed from unsolicited submissions, and 1 was by an agented author. Of the
100 titles, less than 5 were by unpublished writers and
5 were by authors who were new to the publishing house.
Receives 150 queries yearly.

- **Nonfiction:** Publishes supplementary educational material,
  including activity books, resource guides, classroom materials,
  and reproducibles. Topics include language arts, mathematics,
  science, arts, social studies, early childhood learning, Christian materials, and crafts.
- **Representative Titles:** *Conflict Resolution* (grades K–3) contains strategies and activities, reproducibles, and suggestions
  for parental involvement to maintain a successful, happy
  learning environment. *Bones & Hearts & Other Parts* (8+
  years) offers hands-on activities and experiments about the
  human body; part of the Real Science–Real Fun! series.

Submissions and Payment
Guidelines available. Query with outline and representative
pages. Accepts photocopies, computer printouts, and simultaneous submissions if identified. SASE. Responds in 10–12
weeks. Publication in 1–2 years. Flat fee.

Editor's Comments
We welcome book proposals from teachers and writers.
Innovative, practical, use-now materials are needed for all
levels between pre-kindergarten and grade eight, in all
curriculum areas. Fiction material and storybooks are not
considered for publication.

Cartwheel Books

Scholastic Inc.
557 Broadway
New York, NY 10012

Executive Editor

Publisher's Interests
A variety of fiction and nonfiction books for children up to the age of 10 can be found in the catalogue of this publisher. An imprint of Scholastic Inc., it only accepts material from agented or previously published authors.
Website: www.scholastic.com

Freelance Potential
Published 100 titles in 2005: 10 were developed from unsolicited submissions, many were by agented authors, and 4 were reprint/licensed properties. Receives 800–1,000 queries, 500–800 unsolicited mss yearly.

- **Fiction:** Publishes concept books, toddler books, and early picture books, 0–4 years; easy-to-read books, 4–7 years; story picture books, 4–10 years; and chapter books, 5–10 years. Genres include humor; and stories about friendship, families, animals, and holidays.
- **Nonfiction:** Publishes concept books, toddler books, and early picture books, 0–4 years; easy-to-read books, 4–7 years; and story picture books, 4–10 years. Topics include science and math.
- **Representative Titles:** *Big Bugs* by Keith Faulkner (3–5 years) is an oversized, pop-up, lift-the-flap introduction to the insect world. *Fluffy Plants a Jelly Bean* by Kate McMullan (4–8 years) follows a guinea pig as he plants a jelly bean that grows into a jelly bean stalk and leads him to the castle of a giant.

Submissions and Payment
Accepts submissions from agents and previously published authors only. Accepts photocopies and computer printouts. SASE. Responds in 3–6 months. Publication period and payment policy vary.

Editor's Comments
We're looking for interactive board books and story books that will help young children learn and have fun.

Cavendish Children's Books

99 White Plains Road
Tarrytown, NY 10591

Editorial Director: Margery Cuyler

Publisher's Interests
From picture books to chapter books to folk and fairy tales all the way up to middle-grade and young adult novels, this publisher offers a wide mix of fiction and nonfiction.
Website: www.marshallcavendish.us

Freelance Potential
Published 32 titles in 2005: 6 were by agented authors. Of the 32 titles, 8 were by authors who were new to the publishing house. Receives 1,500 queries and unsolicited mss each year.

- **Fiction:** Publishes easy-to-read books, 4–7 years; story picture books, 4–10 years; chapter books, 5–10 years; middle-grade books, 8–12 years; and young adult, 12–18 years. Genres include historical fiction, folklore, mysteries, humorous stories, and contemporary fiction.
- **Representative Titles:** *The Wacky Substitute* by Sally Derby (4–7 years) brings a hilarious day of fun to kindergarten students when the near-sighted substitute loses his eyeglasses and can't see anything clearly. *Worlds Apart* by Kathleen Karr (10+ years) is an action-packed adventure of a young colonist and his Indian friend.

Submissions and Payment
Guidelines and catalogue available. Send complete ms and short author bio. Accepts photocopies and computer printouts. SASE. Responds in 6 months. Publication period and payment policy vary.

Editor's Comments
We are especially interested in chapter books for ages six through nine. We are also looking for young adult novels that are edgy and unique and tell a great story. Many of our titles are humorous stories, so keep that in mind when submitting. To get a sense of what we publish, check out our current book list at our website.

Charlesbridge

85 Main Street
Watertown, MA 02472

Submissions Editor

Publisher's Interests
Focusing on nature, science, and multicultural topics, this publisher features a list of early readers and middle-grade chapter books.
Website: www.charlesbridge.com

Freelance Potential
Published 37 titles in 2005: 1 was developed from an unsolicited submission, 3 were by agented authors, and 4 were reprint/licensed properties. Of the 37 titles, 4 were by unpublished writers and 8 were by authors who were new to the publishing house. Receives 2,400 unsolicited mss yearly.

- **Fiction:** Publishes toddler books, early picture books, 0–4 years; and story picture books, 4–10 years. Genres include contemporary fiction, folktales, and nature stories.
- **Nonfiction:** Publishes concept books, toddler books, and early picture books, 0–4 years. Topics include animals, the alphabet, math, nature, science, multicultural and ethnic themes, and celebrations.
- **Representative Titles:** *The Bumblebee Queen* by April Pulley Sayre (3–8 years) uses lyrical text to describe the life of a typical North American bumblebee queen as she tends her colony through the seasons. *Picasso and Minou* by P. I. Maltbie (4–9 years) brings alive the people and places that surrounded Pablo in early 20th-century Paris.

Submissions and Payment
Guidelines available. Send complete ms. Accepts photocopies and computer printouts. No simultaneous submissions. SASE. Responds in 3–6 months. Publication in 2–5 years. Royalty.

Editor's Comments
We would like to see picture books and transitional "bridge books" that include lively, plot-driven stories with strong, engaging characters.

Chelsea House Publishers

Suite 201
2080 Cabot Boulevard West
Langhorne, PA 19047-1813

Editorial Assistant: Sarah Sharpless

Publisher's Interests
Award-winning curriculum-based titles for kindergarten
through college classrooms are featured on the list of this
educational publisher. The majority of its titles are published
in series format.
Website: www.chelseahouse.com

Freelance Potential
Published 243 titles (218 juvenile) in 2005: 10 were developed from unsolicited submissions, 10 were by agented
authors, and 60 were reprint/licensed properties. Of the
243 titles, 20 were by unpublished writers and 20 were by
authors who were new to the publishing house.

- **Nonfiction:** Published 97 middle-grade titles, 8–12 years; and
  121 young adult books, 12–18 years. Topics include American
  history, world history, African American studies, the classics,
  criminal justice, sports, popular culture, science, travel, drug
  education, and Christian studies. Also publishes parenting
  titles, literary criticism, and reference books for adults.
- **Representative Titles:** *Alexander the Great* (grades 6–12)
  offers a look at one of the world's most dominant figures who
  led armies to victory and ruled over a vast domain; part of the
  Ancient World Leaders series. *Birds* (grades 2–4) part of a colorful series that provides young readers with fun facts about
  their favorite birds; part of the Animal Facts series.

Submissions and Payment
Guidelines available. All books are assigned. Send résumé
with clips or writing samples. No queries or unsolicited ms.
SASE. Response time varies. Publication period varies.
Flat fee.

Editor's Comments
We like to see material that will help students write papers,
perform independent study, and delve more deeply into
their curriculum studies.

Chicago Review Press

814 North Franklin Street
Chicago, IL 60610

Associate Editor: Cynthia Sherry

Publisher's Interests
Biographies, parenting topics, and how-to titles, as well as
children's activity books appear in the listings of this mid-
sized publisher. Subjects include science and history.
Website: www.chicagoreviewpress.com

Freelance Potential
Published 40 titles (8 juvenile) in 2005: 6 were developed
from unsolicited submissions, 12 were by agented authors,
and 6 were reprint/licensed authors. Of the 40 titles, 10
were by unpublished writers and 14 were by authors who
were new to the publishing house. Receives 1,500 queries,
1,000 unsolicited mss yearly.

- **Nonfiction:** Published 8 middle-grade books, 8–12 years. Also
  publishes toddler books, 0–4 years; primary books, 6–9 years;
  and young adult titles, 12–18 years. Topics include science,
  mathematics, social issues, history, literature, and art.
- **Representative Titles:** *Bite-Sized Science* by John H. Falk &
  Kristi Rosenberg (3–8 years) offers a fun way to get young
  minds discovering the wonders of the natural world. *Civil
  Rights Movement for Kids* (4–10 years) by Mary C. Turck allows
  children to discover how students and religious leaders
  worked together to demand the protection of civil rights for
  African Americans.

Submissions and Payment
Guidelines available. Query with 1–2 sample chapters or projects; or send ms with résumé. Accepts photocopies, computer printouts, and simultaneous submissions. SASE.
Responds in 8–10 weeks. Publication in 18 months. Royalty,
7–10%; advance; $1,500–$5,000.

Editor's Comments
We're looking for books and activities that teach children
about the wonders of the world, as well as important people
who made a significant contribution to history.

Children's Book Press

2211 Mission Street
San Francisco, CA 94110

Editorial Submissions

Publisher's Interests
The goal of this publisher is to help broaden the base of children's literature by offering multicultural and bilingual stories that reflect the diversity and experiences of minority and immigrant communities in the U.S.
Website: www.childrensbookpress.org

Freelance Potential
Published 10–15 titles in 2005: 1 was developed from an unsolicited submission. Receives 1,200 unsolicited mss yearly.

- **Fiction:** Publishes story picture books, 4–10 years. Genres include multicultural, ethnic, and humorous fiction.
- **Nonfiction:** Publishes story picture books, 4–10 years. Topics include multicultural communities and cultures, social concerns, ethnic issues, diversity, immigration, heritage, family life, and relationships.
- **Representative Titles:** *Going Back Home* by Toyomi Igus (6+ years) draws on African American history to reveal the experiences of the author's sharecropping family. *Antonio's Card* by Rigoberto González (6+ years) is a sensitively crafted story of a boy's dilemma on how to express his love for his mother and her female partner.

Submissions and Payment
Guidelines available at website. Send complete ms. Accepts photocopies, computer printouts, and simultaneous submissions if identified. SASE. Responds in 8–10 weeks. Publication in 12–18 months. Royalty; advance.

Editor's Comments
We publish only picture books for elementary school children about contemporary life in the Latino/Chicano, African American, Asian American, Native American, multiracial, and other minority cultures. We like to see children in active roles and stories told from a child's point of view. Folktales are not currently part of our publishing programs.

Children's eLibrary

11th Floor
24 West 25th Street
New York, NY 10010

Submissions Editor

Publisher's Interests
This Internet publisher provides schools and libraries with high-quality e-books based on children's books from dozens of major publishers. It also makes available in electronic form many books that have gone out of print. New titles for young readers are also reviewed and accepted for original publication.
Website: www.childrenselibrary.com

Freelance Potential
Published 1,000 titles in 2005: 90 were developed from unsolicited submissions. Receives 2,000 queries yearly.

- **Fiction:** Publishes stories about nature and the environment; humor; historical, multicultural, and ethnic fiction; fantasy; fairy tales; folklore; and folktales.
- **Nonfiction:** Publishes books about nature, the environment, animals, pets, science, technology, and multicultural and ethnic subjects. Also features biographies.
- **Representative Titles:** *Ivanhound* by Nancy Holder (grades 4 and up) is a story about Wishbone, a dog who, as the brave knight Ivanhoe, hides his true identity to defeat an evil nobleman and reclaim his birthright. *Six Little Teddy Bears* by PLCMC is a multimedia story about too many bears in a bed and the sleepless night they have.

Submissions and Payment
Guidelines available at website. Query via email following instructions at website. Responds in 1–2 weeks. Publication in 1 year. Royalty.

Editor's Comments
We're dedicated to providing high-quality e-books to teachers for their students, as well as to libraries for their patrons, over the Internet. Books can be accessed from classrooms and libraries or from home—anywhere there is an Internet connection. Visit our website to learn more about our needs.

Children's Press

Scholastic Inc.
90 Sherman Turnpike
Danbury, CT 06816

Editor-in-Chief

Publisher's Interests

Nonfiction books for children of all ages are produced by this division of Scholastic. The majority of its material targets schools and libraries and is based on a variety of topics that appear as part of a series.

Website: www.scholasticlibrary.com

Freelance Potential

Published 300 titles in 2005: 50 were by agented authors. Of the 300 titles, 15 were by authors who were new to the publishing house. Receives 2,000 queries yearly.

- **Nonfiction:** Publishes concept books, 0–4 years; easy-to-read books, 4–7 years; story picture books, 4–10 years; chapter books, 5–10 years; and middle-grade books, 8–12 years. Topics include science, geography, sports, social studies, and career guidance. Also publishes biographies, Spanish titles, and hi/lo titles. All titles support elementary and middle school curricula.
- **Representative Titles:** *Abraham Lincoln* by Steven Otfinoski (grades 6–8) provides a biography of the historical figure, Abraham Lincoln. *Rookie Read-About® Science–Physical Science* (grades 1–2) features full-color photos and simple text about physical science. It strives to build early science literacy; part of the Rookie Read About® Science series.

Submissions and Payment

Query with outline/synopsis and sample chapters. No unsolicited mss. SASE. Responds in 2–6 months. Publication in 1–2 years. Flat fee.

Editor's Comments

We look for material that is fresh and interesting. We want children to learn about important topics, and have fun while doing it. We strive to produce material that will inform and entertain readers. If you have an idea for something new, or can put a twist on an old topic, send us a detailed query.

Christian Ed. Publishers

P.O. Box 26639
San Diego, CA 92196

Assistant Editor: Janet Ackelson

Publisher's Interests
For over 50 years, this religious publisher has served churches with Christ-centered Bible club materials based on the word of God. It also provides Sunday school curriculum and Christian education resources for children in pre-K through grade twelve.
Website: www.christianedwarehouse.com

Freelance Potential
Published 96 titles (48 juvenile) in 2005. Of the 96 titles, 4 were by authors who were new to the publishing house. Receives 200 queries, 90 unsolicited mss yearly.

- **Fiction:** Publishes religious fiction, pre-K–grade 12. All work is done by assignment only.
- **Nonfiction:** Publishes Christian educational titles, Bible-based curriculum, and Bible club materials, grades K–12.
- **Representative Titles:** *Five-Minute Sunday School Activities* (5–10 years) contains fun Bible lessons with reproducible crafts, games, and puzzles. *Bible Outreach Activities* (grades 1–5) includes lessons, memory verses, teaching tips, Reach Out projects, and reproducibles that teach children to share the good news of the gospel.

Submissions and Payment
Guidelines and catalogue available with 9x12 SASE (4 first-class stamps). All work by assignment only. Publication in 12–18 months. Flat fee, $.03 per word.

Editor's Comments
We are publishers of curriculum for children and youth that includes programs and student books. At this time, we are only seeking preschool materials. We also are interested in seeing Bible-teaching crafts. All of our work is done on assignment only and we seek writers who are active members of a Bible-believing church and who have hands-on experience with the children they want to write for.

Christian Focus Publications

Geanies House, Fearn by Tain
Ross-shire IV20 1TW
Scotland

Children's Editor: Catherine Mackenzie

Publisher's Interests

Children's books that are bright, fun, and full of biblical truth can be found in the catalogue of this Christian publisher. It aims to help children find out about God.

Website: www.christianfocus.com

Freelance Potential

Published 100 titles (50 juvenile) in 2005: 5 were developed from unsolicited submissions, 1 was by an agented author, and 3 were reprint/licensed properties. Of the 100 titles, 5 were by unpublished writers and 5 were by new authors. Receives 800+ queries, 500+ unsolicited mss yearly.

- **Fiction:** Publishes early picture books, 0–4 years; chapter books, 5–10 years; middle-grade books, 8–12 years; and young adult books, 12–18 years. Genres include contemporary Christian fiction.
- **Nonfiction:** Publishes toddler books, 0–4 years; easy-to-read books, 4–7 years; story picture books, 4–10 years; chapter books, 5–10 years; middle-grade books, 8–12 years; and young adult books, 12–18 years. Publishes Bible stories, biographies, devotionals, puzzle and activity books.
- **Representative Titles:** *Saved at Sea* by O. F. Walton (YA) tells the story of a young boy and a dramatic sea rescue. *A Girl of Two Worlds* by Lorna Eglin (9–12 years) tells the story of a young girl who juggles school and Christianity and Massai life.

Submissions and Payment

Guidelines available at website. Query with author information sheet, synopsis, chapter headings, and 3 sample chapters. Send ms for works shorter than 10 chapters. Accepts email to Catherine.Mackenzie@christianfocus.com. SAE/IRC. Does not return mss to authors outside the UK. Response time, publication period, and payment policy vary.

Editor's Comments

We're looking for Bible stories and fiction for all ages.

Christopher-Gordon Publishers

Suite 12
1502 Providence Highway
Norwood, MA 02062

Publisher: Susanne F. Canavan

Publisher's Interests
Since its creation in 1987, this publisher has concentrated on literacy, mathematics, science, technology, educational administration, and topics of universal interest to educators such as classroom management and teaching skills.
Website: www.christopher-gordon.com

Freelance Potential
Published 16 titles in 2005: 4 were developed from unsolicited submissions. Of the 16 titles, 4 were by unpublished writers and 4 were by authors who were new to the publishing house. Receives 150 queries, 50 unsolicited mss yearly.

- **Nonfiction:** Publishes professional enrichment materials for educators. Topics include literacy, administration, classroom management, general education, teaching skills, self-development, mathematics, science, technology, supervision, literature, education law, and cognitive thinking.
- **Representative Titles:** *Learning about Literary Genres: Reading and Writing with Young Children* by Debbie Richards and Shirl Hawes (educators) gives teachers the tools to improve writing instruction for young children. *Student Book Clubs: Improving Literature Instruction in Middle and High School* by Mark Faust et al. (educators) presents practical, ready-to-use ideas for helping students set up interesting, effective book clubs that inspire them to read.

Submissions and Payment
Guidelines and catalogue available with #10 SASE ($.57 postage) or at website. Query with table of contents, sample chapters, and market analysis; or send complete ms. Accepts photocopies. SASE. Response time varies. Publication in 18 months. Royalty; advance.

Editor's Comments
We're looking for educators to submit topics that give concrete information that teachers can use in the classroom.

Chronicle Books

Children's Division
6th Floor
85 2nd Street
San Francisco, CA 94105

Children's Division Editor

Publisher's Interests
Chronicle Books publishes an eclectic mix of traditional and innovative illustrated children's books with unusual writing styles or subjects.
Website: www.chroniclebooks.com

Freelance Potential
Published 100 titles in 2005: 2 were developed from unsolicited submissions, and 50 were by agented authors. Of the 100 titles, 2 were by unpublished writers and 2 were by new authors. Receives 240 queries, 12,000 unsolicited mss yearly.

- **Fiction:** Published 4 concept books, 6 toddler books, and 6 early picture books, 0–4 years; 4 easy-to-read books, 4–7 years; 40 story picture books, 4–10 years; 2 chapter books, 5–10 years; 4 middle-grade titles, 8–12 years; and 2 young adult books, 12–18 years. Genres include adventure, contemporary and historical fiction, science fiction, and humor.
- **Nonfiction:** Published 2 concept books, 2 toddler books, and 2 early picture books, 0–4 years; 4 easy-to-read books, 4–7 years; 10 story picture books, 4–10 years; 8 chapter books, 5–10 years; 2 middle-grade titles, 8–12 years; and 2 young adult books, 12–18 years. Topics include crafts and hobbies, geography, history, and social issues.
- **Representative Titles:** *Beyond the Great Mountains* by Ed Young (4+ years) is visual poem about the beautiful and mystical land of China. *The Oaken Throne* by Robin Jarvis (8+ years) brings readers into the dark wars between bats and squirrels.

Submissions and Payment
Guidelines available. Query or send complete ms if less than 20 pages. Accepts photocopies. SASE. Responds to queries in 3 weeks; to mss in 3 months. Publication in 2 years. Payment policy varies.

Editor's Comments
We look for titles that will give our list a distinctive flair.

Chrysalis Children's Books

The Chrysalis Building
London W10 6SP
England

Editor: Sarah Fabiny

Publisher's Interests
This British publisher offers all types of children's books, from fun titles and picture books to illustrated classics and educational books full of information and detail.
Website: www.chrysalisbooks.co.uk

Freelance Potential
Published 179 titles in 2005: 1 was developed from an unsolicited submission, 15 were by agented authors, and 4 were reprint/licensed properties. Of the 179 titles, 1 was by an unpublished writer and 3 were by authors who were new to the publishing house. Receives 200 unsolicited mss yearly.

- **Fiction:** Publishes toddler books. Genres include animal stories and humor.
- **Nonfiction:** Publishes concept books and toddler books, 0–4 years; story picture books, 4–10 years; middle-grade titles, 8–12 years; and young adult books, 12–18 years. Topics include science, geography, math, history, citizenship, special needs, sports, languages, and religion. Also publishes reference materials for students and resource materials for teachers.
- **Representative Titles:** *Mega Book of Cars* by Lynne Gibbs (7–10 years) highlights the most intriguing and amazing examples of this mode of transport. *Little Red Plane* by Ken Wilson-Max (3–6 years) is an interactive book that explain how airplanes work, and what they do best.

Submissions and Payment
Send complete ms with résumé. Accepts photocopies and Macintosh disk submissions. SAE/IRC. Responds in 2 months. Publication period varies. Flat fee.

Editor's Comments
We strongly suggest you review our line of books before you send your manuscript. We publish only pre-school, novelty books, and very young picture books, as well as older, illustrated classic story collections.

Claire Publications

Tey Brook Craft Centre
Great Tey, Colchester,
Essex, CO6 1JE
United Kingdom

Managing Director: Noel Graham

Publisher's Interests
Claire Publications seeks to provide the best in books and educational resources to support primary and secondary school teachers in the United Kingdom. Its main concentration is on mathematics and language.
Website: www.clairepublications.com

Freelance Potential
Published 20 titles in 2005: 10 were developed from unsolicited submissions. Of the 20 titles, 10 were by unpublished writers. Receives 60 queries, 25 unsolicited mss yearly.

- **Nonfiction:** Publishes activity books and educational resources. Topics include gifted education, mathematics, science and technology, social issues, special education, and multicultural subjects.
- **Representative Titles:** *The Writers Pack* (teachers) contains everything educators need to develop their students' skills in letter writing, poetry, stories, prose, and reports, as well as listening and drama skills. *Self Esteem 3* by Lou Thompson & Tim Lewson (parents and teachers) is a workbook to help adolescents who have special self-esteem needs.

Submissions and Payment
Catalogue available at website. Query with résumé and writing clips; or send complete ms. Accepts photocopies and email submissions to mail@clairepublications.com. SAE/IRC. Response time varies. Publication in 1 year. Royalty, 10%.

Editor's Comments
This year we are interested in seeing queries and manuscripts for the primary school student in all subject areas. Since our nonfiction books are for pupils in the United Kingdom, keep that in mind when writing, and make sure you are aware of our terms and of our grade correlations. We are planning to publish books for preschoolers in the near future so it is best to visit our website for updates.

Clarion Books

Houghton Mifflin Company
215 Park Avenue South
New York, NY 10003

Vice President/Associate Publisher: Dinah Stevenson

Publisher's Interests
Clarion Books publishes picture books, nonfiction, and fiction for infants and children through grade 12. This imprint of Houghton Mifflin offers a wide range of topics and styles. **Website:** www.clarionbooks.com

Freelance Potential
Published 60 titles in 2005: 30 were by agented authors, and 5 were reprint/licensed properties. Of the 60 titles, 10 were by authors who were new to the publishing house. Receives 500 queries, 2,500 unsolicited mss yearly.

- **Fiction:** Publishes picture books, 3–8 years; chapter books, 7–10 years; middle-grade novels, 8–12 years; and young adult novels, 12–18 years. Genres include adventure, folktales, fairy tales, and historical and science fiction.
- **Nonfiction:** Publishes picture books, 3–8 years; middle-grade books, 8–12 years; and young adult books, 12–18 years. Topics include nature, ecology, biography, science, history, holidays, and multicultural and ethnic issues.
- **Representative Titles:** *The Sun's Daughter* by Pat Sherman (5–9 years) is a tale based on an Iroquois legend. *Sunshine Home* by Eve Bunting (5–8 years) is the story of a grandmother's transition to a nursing home and how her family copes. *Before Hollywood* by Paul Clee (10+ years) takes readers on a historical journey through the movies.

Submissions and Payment
Guidelines available. Query or send complete ms for chapter books and novels; send complete ms for picture books. Accepts photocopies and computer printouts. SASE. Responds in 4 months. Publication in 2 years. Royalty.

Editor's Comments
We're looking for active picture books, nonfiction, and fiction for 0–12; nonfiction in the areas of social studies, science, word play, and holidays; and fiction for 8- to 12-year-old readers.

Clear Light Publishers

823 Don Diego
Sante Fe, NM 87505

Publisher: Houghton Harmon

Publisher's Interests
This publisher focuses on titles about Native American culture, religion, and history; Western Americana; Eastern philosophy and religion; U.S. and world history; and the environment. All titles are suitable for readers between the ages of four and eighteen.
Website: www.clearlightbooks.com

Freelance Potential
Published 15 titles (5 juvenile) in 2005: 12 were developed from unsolicited submissions. Receives 200 unsolicited mss each year.

- **Fiction:** Publishes story picture books, 4–10 years; and young adult books, 12–18 years. Genres include historical, regional, multicultural, and inspirational fiction.
- **Nonfiction:** Publishes middle-grade titles, 8–12 years; and young adult books, 12–18 years. Topics include animals, nature, history, religion, multicultural subjects, social issues, health, and fitness. Also publishes biographies.
- **Representative Titles:** *Tibetan Tales for Little Buddhas* by Naomi Rose (4–10 years) is a collection of three engaging stories from Tibet that offer a glimpse into Tibetan culture. *The Man Who Set the Town Dancing* by Candice Stanford is based on the true story of José Tena, the man who popularized folk dances of Mexico.

Submissions and Payment
Send complete ms. Accepts photocopies, computer printouts, and simultaneous submissions if identified. Availability of artwork improves chance of acceptance. SASE. Responds in 3 months. Publication in 1 year. Royalty.

Editor's Comments
Retold legends and folktales remain an interest to us, as well as bilingual titles for young readers. Keep in mind that we prefer material with ethnic and multicultural overtones.

Concordia Publishing House

3558 South Jefferson Avenue
St. Louis, MO 63118-3968

Editorial Assistant: Brandy Overton

Publisher's Interests
Concordia Publishing House is the publishing arm of The Lutheran Church-Missouri Synod. It provides materials for adults and children that are faithful to the scriptures and to the Lutheran Confessions.
Website: www.cph.org

Freelance Potential
Published 50 titles (32 juvenile) in 2005. Of the 50 titles, 1 was by an unpublished writer and 4 were by authors who were new to the publishing house. Receives 1,000–1,500 queries yearly.

- **Nonfiction:** Publishes early picture books, 0–4 years; easy-to-read books, 4–7 years; story picture books, 4–10 years; middle-grade titles, 8–12 years; and young adult books, 12–18 years. Topics include religious holidays, faith, Bible stories, prayer, and spirituality. Also publishes devotionals and titles for families.
- **Representative Titles:** *God, I Need to Talk to You about Bad Words* by Susan Leigh is a child-friendly way to help young readers think about behavior and pray about it. *Colors I See in Church* by Julie Stiegemeyer introduces readers to the meaning behind the symbolic colors in church.

Submissions and Payment
No unsolicited mss. All work is assigned. Query or send résumé. Response time, publication period, and payment policy vary.

Editor's Comments
Our titles range from family books that offer practical information for families and communicate the hope of the gospel for all situations, to Christian living books for teens that help readers evaluate current events and contemporary topics from a distinctly Christian viewpoint, to general books on prayer and inspiration.

Contemporary Drama Service

Meriwether Publishing Ltd.
885 Elkton Drive
Colorado Springs, CO 80907

Acquisitions: Arthur Zapel

Publisher's Interests

This publisher specializes in providing plays and books about theatrical arts to the middle-grade, junior high, and high school markets. It also offers a line of books and plays specifically for church groups.

Website: www.contemporarydrama.com

Freelance Potential

Published 40 titles (30 juvenile) in 2005. Of the 40 titles, 20 were by unpublished writers and 20 were by authors who were new to the publishing house. Receives 100–150 queries yearly.

- **Fiction:** Publishes middle-grade plays, 8–12 years; and young adult plays, 12–18 years. Publishes musicals, folktales, and fantasies. Also publishes skits, adaptations, novelty plays, parodies, and social commentaries.
- **Nonfiction:** Publishes young adult books, 12–18 years. Features books about improvisation, theater games, speech, acting techniques, and theatrical arts.
- **Representative Titles:** *Run for the Money!* by Pat Cook (8+ years) is a comical full-length play about the greedy heirs to a fortune. *Comedy Duets for Teens* by Laurie Allen (YA) offers 10 two-character comedy scenes that draw on the humor of teen issues such as grades, cliques, and crushes.

Submissions and Payment

Guidelines available. Query with outline/synopsis. Accepts photocopies, computer printouts, and simultaneous submissions if identified. SASE. Responds in 6 weeks. Publication in 6 months. Royalty. Flat fee. Special projects, negotiable.

Editor's Comments

Our focus is on material for students in the middle grades through college. With the exception of Sunday school plays for churches, we're publishing nothing for the elementary school market at this time.

Cook Communications Ministries

4050 Lee Vance View
Colorado Springs, CO 80918-7100

Editorial Assistant: Laura Riley

Publisher's Interests
In business since 1875, Cook Communications Ministries publishes Sunday school curricula, study guides, and books that help Christians gain a deeper understanding of the Bible and their faith.
Website: www.cookministries.com

Freelance Potential
Published 75 titles (30 juvenile) in 2005: 5 were developed from unsolicited submissions and 49 were by agented authors. Of the 75 titles, 1 was by an unpublished writer and 5 were by authors who were new to the publishing house. Receives 1,500 queries yearly.

- **Fiction:** Publishes concept books, toddler books, and early picture books, 0–4 years; easy-to-read books, 4–7 years; chapter books, 5–10 years; and middle-grade books, 8–12 years. Also publishes books in series, 8–12 years. Genres include inspirational and religious fiction.
- **Nonfiction:** Publishes concept books and early picture books, 0–4 years; story picture books, 4–10 years; and middle-grade books, 8–12 years. Topics include religion and social issues. Also publishes self-help titles and reference books for adults.
- **Representative Titles:** *I Know God* by Dan Foote celebrates God's revelation in all his creation and reminds kids that they can see God all around them. *Mystery in Medieval Castle* by Karla Warkentin is a story of time travelers sent back to the Middle Ages to take part in a spiritual battle.

Submissions and Payment
Guidelines available. Query with clips. Accepts photocopies and simultaneous submissions if identified. SASE. Responds in 2 weeks. Publication in 2 years. Payment policy varies.

Editor's Comments
We'll review queries for our curriculum lines at this time, but not for books. Check our website for updates to this policy.

Corwin Press

2455 Teller Road
Thousand Oaks, CA 91320

Editorial Director: Robert D. Clouse

Publisher's Interests
This publisher offers a list of substantive and practical books that contribute to the knowledge base of educators, administrators, specialists, and principals.
Website: www.corwinpress.com

Freelance Potential
Published 120 titles in 2005: 10–15 were developed from unsolicited submissions, 1–2 were by agented authors, and 3–5 were reprint/licensed properties. Of the 120 titles, 90–120 were by unpublished writers and 114 were by authors who were new to the publishing house. Receives 100+ queries yearly.

- **Nonfiction:** Publishes resource books and manuals for educators, grades K–12. Topics include administration, assessment, evaluation, professional development, curriculum development, classroom practice, special and gifted education, bilingual learning, counseling, school health, and educational technology.
- **Representative Titles:** *How to Deal with Parents Who Are Angry, Troubled, Afraid, or Just Plain Crazy* by Elaine K. McEwan provides valuable strategies for dealing with emotional or unresponsive parents. *Student Success with Thinking Maps* by David Hyerle shows how thinking maps increase student performance and teacher effectiveness.

Submissions and Payment
Guidelines available. Query with outline and prospectus, including alternative titles, rationale, prospective market, and competitive analysis. SASE. Response time varies. Publication in 7 months. Royalty.

Editor's Comments
We want reader-friendly material that offers fresh insights, conclusions, and recommendations for action. The best works draw on real-world examples and practices to illustrate key points.

Coteau Books

401-2206 Dewdney Avenue
Regina, Saskatchewan S4R 1H3
Canada

Managing Editor: Nik L. Burton

Publisher's Interests

Coteau Books is a Canadian literary press that publishes fiction, poetry, drama, and children's and young adult chapter books with Saskatchewan/Prairie content.
Website: www.coteaubooks.com

Freelance Potential

Published 18 titles (9 juvenile) in 2005: 17 were developed from unsolicited submissions, and a few were by agented authors. Receives 1,000+ queries, 500+ unsolicited mss each year.

- **Fiction:** Publishes chapter books, 5–10 years; middle-grade titles, 8–12 years; and young adult books, 12–18 years. Genres include regional, historical, and contemporary fiction; mystery, suspense, and humor.
- **Representative Titles:** *Andrei and the Snow Walker* by Larry Warwaruk (9+ years) is an intriguing story about a Ukrainian immigrant boy who learns that Canada has its own wisdom and power. *Angels in the Snow* by Wenda Young (11+ years) takes readers through the emotional life of a young woman and the landscape of Japan, with powerful imagery and unforgettable insight.

Submissions and Payment

Canadian authors only. Guidelines available with 9x12 SASE ($.90 Canadian postage). Query with summary, writing samples, and curriculum vitae; or send complete ms. Accepts photocopies and computer printouts. No simultaneous submissions. SASE. Responds in 3–6 months. Publication in 1–2 years. Royalty, 10%.

Editor's Comments

We will consider submissions by Canadian authors who demonstrate the potential for award-winning prose. Please be sure your story somehow relates to Canadian history, culture, art, or natural history.

Covenant Communications

920 East State Road
P.O. Box 416
American Fork, UT 84003-0416

Managing Editor: Shauna Humphreys

Publisher's Interests
Established in 1958, this publisher's list includes books, audio cassettes, and videos. All material supports the values of the church of Jesus Christ of the Latter-day Saints.
Website: www.covenant-lds.com

Freelance Potential
Published 70 titles in 2005: 20–30 were developed from unsolicited submissions and 10 were reprint/licensed properties. Of the 70 titles, 15–25 were by unpublished writers and new authors. Receives 700–800 mss yearly.

- **Fiction:** Publishes concept books, toddler books, early picture books, 0–4 years; chapter books, 5–10 years; middle grade books, 8–12 years; and young adult books, 12–18 years. Genres include adventure; humor; suspense; romance; science fiction; and inspirational and historical fiction.
- **Nonfiction:** Published concept books and toddler books, 0–4 years. Also publishes biographies, activity books, novelty and board books, photo essays, and reference titles. Topics include history, religion, and regional subjects.
- **Representative Titles:** *Coffin House* by Pamela Reid (8–12 years) follows the adventures of a girl who moves to New Zealand. *Beyond Perfection* by Juli Caldwell & Erin McBride (YA) is a fun read about a college girl and her family on a crash course with destiny.

Submissions and Payment
Guidelines available at website. Send complete ms with summary. Accepts photocopies, computer printouts, disk submissions, and email to shaunah@covenant.lds.com. SASE. Responds in 3 months. Publication in 6–12 months. Payment policy varies.

Editor's Comments
We seek authors who can make a positive contribution with knowledge of LDS doctrines and values.

Creative Book Publishing

36 Austin Street
St. John's, Newfoundland A1B 3T7
Canada

Sales & Marketing Coordinator: Donna Francis

Publisher's Interests
Established in 1983, Creative Book Publishing produces picture books, middle-grade literature, and young adult titles under its Tuckamore Books imprint. It only publishes the work of Canadian authors.
Website: www.nfbooks.com

Freelance Potential
Published 12 titles (4 juvenile) in 2005: all were developed from unsolicited submissions. Of the 12 titles, 3 were by unpublished writers and 3 were by authors who were new to the publishing house. Receives 240 queries, 100 unsolicited mss yearly.

- **Fiction:** Published 1 story picture book, 4–10 years; 2 middle-grade books, 8–12 years; and 1 young adult book, 12–18 years. Genres include adventure, drama, folklore, suspense, and historical fiction.
- **Nonfiction:** Publishes early story picture books, 4–10 years; middle-grade books, 8–12 years; and young adult books, 12–18 years. Topics include Canadian history and regional subjects. Also publishes biographies.
- **Representative Titles:** *Jasmine's Journey* by Cathy Brown Murphy (8–11 years) is the story of a cat who must travel to Halifax from northern Nova Scotia to reunite with her family. *At Ocean's Edge* by Susan Chalker Browne (9–11 years) depicts the dramatic events of the Cantwell family at Cape Spear lighthouse.

Submissions and Payment
Guidelines and catalogue available at website. Send complete ms with résumé, synopsis, and targeted market. Accepts photocopies. SAE/IRC. Responds in 4–6 months. Publication in 1 year. Royalty, 10%.

Editor's Comments
We only accept work from Canadian authors. Browse our website to get an idea of the children's books we publish.

Creative Bound

P.O. Box 424
151 Tansley Drive
Carp, Ontario K0A 1L0
Canada

Editor: Gail Baird

Publisher's Interests
This publisher offers a variety of nonfiction titles for adults between the ages of 25 and 50. Its list includes self-help books, and books on healing and recovery, parenting and teaching, and personal growth and life balance. It also accepts children's manuscripts for review.
Website: www.creativebound.com

Freelance Potential
Published 6 titles in 2005. Of the 6 titles, 1 was by an unpublished writer and 4 were by authors who were new to the publishing house. Receives 120 queries yearly.

- **Nonfiction:** Publishes informational and self-help books. Topics include parenting, personal growth, health, fitness, spirituality, recovery, healing, business, motivation, and teaching.
- **Representative Titles:** *In My Mind's Eye* by Mary Cook transports readers to a time when families and communities were bound together by the need to survive, and shares the remembrances of a child living on a family farm during the Depression. *Liar, Liar, Pants on Fire!* by Mary Cook shares the joys and laughter of the Haneman family during tough years.

Submissions and Payment
Guidelines available with 6x9 SAE/IRC or at website. Accepts photocopies and IBM disk submissions. SAE/IRC. Responds in 1 month. Publication in 6–12 months. Royalty.

Editor's Comments
We are looking for nonfiction works that inspire and motivate personal growth and enhanced performance. Key areas include healthy families and healthy psyches, and healthy workplaces. Please note that all submissions must be accompanied by our manuscript submission form. This form may be requested with our guidelines via mail, or downloaded from our website. Submissions not accompanied by this form will not be considered.

The Creative Company

123 South Broad Street
Mankato, MN 56001

Editor: Aaron Frisch

Publisher's Interests

The Creative Company targets the school and library markets with nonfiction series titles, as well as a limited line of trade titles. Its list includes books for children ages four to eighteen, on a variety of topics. It also publishes poetry.

Freelance Potential

Published 100 titles in 2005. Of the 100 titles, 75 were reprint/licensed properties. Receives 200 unsolicited mss each year.

- **Fiction:** Publishes story picture books, 4–10 years; and young adult books, 12–18 years. Genres include fantasy, folktales, and fairy tales.
- **Nonfiction:** Published story picture books, 4–10 years; chapter books, 5–10 years; and young adult books, 12–18 years. Topics include science, sports, music, history, zoology, architecture, geography, nature, the environment, animals, the arts, literature, humanities, world history, and explorers.
- **Representative Titles:** *I Met a Dinosaur* by Jan Wahl & Chris Sheban is a story book about a dinosaur who is discovered while visiting a gas station. *New York Yankees* by Michael E. Goodman captures the history of Yankee baseball; part of Baseball: The Great American Game series.

Submissions and Payment

Guidelines available. Send complete ms. Accepts photocopies. SASE. Responds in 10–12 weeks. Publication in 2 years. Flat fee.

Editor's Comments

Proposals for nonfiction series should include four to eight titles, and each individual title should be written for a reading audience between kindergarten and sixth grade. Our picture books tend to be written for a fairly sophisticated reading audience, and enjoyed by both juvenile and adult readers. Manuscripts may be stories, poetry, or biographical tributes.

Creative Learning Press

P.O. Box 320
Mansfield Center, CT 06250

Editor: Kris Morgan

Publisher's Interests
A publisher of educational materials, Creative Learning Press offers manuals and activity books for teachers of gifted children. A separate section of its catalogue is devoted to books that explore ways to develop critical and creative thinking skills in students by having them engage in hands-on learning activities.
Website: www.creativelearningpress.com

Freelance Potential
Published 50 titles in 2005: 5 were developed from unsolicited submissions. Receives 100 queries, 100 unsolicited mss each year.

- **Nonfiction:** Publishes textbooks, educational materials, how-to titles, teaching resources, and audio cassettes, grades K–12. Topics include science, mathematics, language arts, geography, history, research skills, business, fine arts, and leadership. Also offers materials for gifted students.
- **Representative Titles:** *Enrichment Clusters* by Joseph S. Renzulli et al. (teachers, administrators) is a guide to establishing student-driven learning programs in the school. *Opening Doors* by Nora Friedman (administrators) offers personal advice from educators who have successfully implemented the Schoolwide Enrichment Model; includes the reactions teachers and parents have had to this new program.

Submissions and Payment
Query with sample pages; or send complete ms with résumé and artwork. Accepts photocopies, computer printouts, and email to clp@creativelearningpress.com. SASE. Responds in 1 month. Publication period varies. Royalty.

Editor's Comments
We see ourselves as partners with teachers in the effort to create a better future for our children. If you share our enthusiasm and have an idea that matches our goals, contact us.

Creative Teaching Press, Inc.

15342 Graham Street
P.O. Box 2723
Huntington Beach, CA 92649

Editor

Publisher's Interests
Since 1965, this educational publisher has offered a wide variety of products for grades pre-K through grade eight, including teacher resource books and emergent readers.
Website: www.creativeteaching.com

Freelance Potential
Published 80+ titles in 2005: 4 were by unpublished writers and 20 were by authors who were new to the publishing house. Receives 300 queries, 100+ unsolicited mss yearly.

- **Fiction:** Publishes easy-to-read books, 4–7 years. Genres include ethnic and multicultural fiction, fantasy, and folktales.
- **Nonfiction:** Publishes easy-to-read books, 4–7 years. Topics include history, social issues, arts and crafts, and mathematics. Also publishes titles on special education.
- **Representative Titles:** *A Snack for Cat* by Rozanne Lanczak Williams (grades 1–2) is a emergent reader designed to build fluency through rhythm, rhyme, and repetition. *Brain Stretchers* by Linda Schwartz (grades 4–6) helps students strengthen their deductive reasoning and research skills with social studies and science-related brainteasers.

Submissions and Payment
Guidelines available. Prefers complete ms; accepts query with outline. Accepts photocopies, computer printouts, and simultaneous submissions if identified. SASE. Responds in 1–2 months. Publication period and payment policy vary.

Editor's Comments
We continue to honor our commitment to children's education by providing teaching materials that make a difference in the lives of children, teachers, and parents. We look for titles that express new ways to inspire creativity while reinforcing basic skills. This year, we need material dealing with critical thinking, test preparation, character education, self-esteem, and life skills.

Cricket Books

P.O. Box 300
Peru, IL 61354

Submissions Editor

Publisher's Interests

Offering a variety of books for children, this publisher's list includes top-notch fiction and nonfiction on a variety of subjects. It is an imprint of Cricket Magazine Group.
Website: www.cricketbooks.net

Freelance Potential

Published 6 titles in 2005: 1 was developed from an unsolicited submission, 1 was by an agented author, and 1 was a reprint/licensed property. Of the 6 titles, 2 were by unpublished writers and 1 was by an author who was new to the publishing house. Receives 600 queries and mss yearly.

- **Fiction:** Published 1 story picture book, 4–10 years; 2 chapter books, 5–10 years; 2 middle-grade books, 8–12 years; and 1 young adult book, 12–18 years. Genres include fantasy and contemporary, historical, and multicultural fiction. Also publishes poetry, bilingual and picture books, and humor.
- **Nonfiction:** Publishes chapter books, 5–10 years; and middle-grade books, 8–12 years. Topics include history, mathematics, science, technology, social issues, and sports.
- **Representative Titles:** *Perseus* by Geraldine McCaughrean (YA) explores the rich culture of Greek mythology by following Perseus on his quest to kill Medusa. *Robert Finds a Way* by Barbara Seuling (5–10 years) is a humorous drama about a boy that is having a triple-rotten day; part of the Robert series.

Submissions and Payment

Guidelines available. Only accepting submissions from agents or authors previously published by Cricket; check website for updates in submissions policy. SASE. Responds in 4–6 months. Publication in 18 months. Royalty; up to 10%; advance, $2,000+.

Editor's Comments

We continue to seek chapter books and middle-grade fiction. Please make sure you follow our submission guidelines.

Critical Thinking Company

P.O. Box 1610
Seaside, CA 93955

Director of Book Development: Cheryl Block

Publisher's Interests
This publisher is a recognized leader in teaching thinking skills to children in pre-K through grade twelve. It offers materials that develop cognitive thinking and improve standard-based learning.
Website: www.criticalthinking.com

Freelance Potential
Published 20–25 titles in 2005: Of the 20–25 titles, 2 were by unpublished writers and 5 were by authors who were new to the publishing house. Receives 25–30 unsolicited mss yearly.

- **Fiction:** Publishes concept books, 0–4 years. Features reading series that promote development of critical thinking skills.
- **Nonfiction:** Publishes concept books, and early picture books, 0–4 years; easy-to-read books, 4–7 years; and chapter books, 5–10 years. Topics include general thinking skills, grammar, spelling, vocabulary, reading comprehension, math, science and history. Also publishes activity books, 8–18 years.
- **Representative Titles:** *Reading Detective* (grades 3–4) combines short stories with multiple-choice and short-response questions to strengthen reading comprehension skills. *Punctuation Puzzler: Commas & More* (grades 3–4) uses odd, convoluted, and misleading sentences to teach students proper grammar usage.

Submissions and Payment
Guidelines available. Send complete ms. Accepts photocopies, computer printouts, and Macintosh and DOS disk submissions submissions. SASE. Responds in 6–9 months. Publication in 1–2 years. Royalty, 10%.

Editor's Comments
Our products develop young minds with fun, analytical thinking activities, not just drill and practice. We need material for all grade levels that empower students to think independently and develop better comprehension skills.

Crossway Books

Good News Publishers
1300 Crescent Street
Wheaton, IL 60187

Editorial Administrator: Jill Carter

Publisher's Interests

Christian books and Bibles are the specialty of this Evangelical publisher. Its list includes titles for adults and children that address the contemporary issues facing today's Christians.
Website: www.crossway.com

Freelance Potential

Published 79 titles (12 juvenile) in 2005: 3 were developed from unsolicited submissions, 8 were by agented authors, and 2 were reprint/licensed properties. Of the 79 titles, 1 was by an unpublished writer and 2 were by authors who were new to the publishing house. Receives 400 queries, 500 unsolicited mss yearly.

- **Fiction:** Published 2 early picture books, 0–4 years; 3 story picture books, 4–10 years; 1 middle-grade book, 8–12 years; and 2 young adult books, 12–18 years. Genres include contemporary and historical fiction, and adventure stories with Christian themes.
- **Nonfiction:** Published 2 middle-grade books. Topics include home and family life, Christian living, homeschooling, health, the Bible, and church issues. Also publishes educational resources for parents and educators.
- **Representative Titles:** *The Adventures of Nathan T. Riggins* by Stephen Bly (8–12 years) tells the adventures of a young cowboy. *The Amazing Secret* by Joni Eareckson & Steve Jensen shows how a girl learns the gift of forgiveness.

Submissions and Payment

Guidelines available. Accepts submissions from agented authors only. Responds in 6–8 weeks. Publication in 12–18 months. Payment policy varies.

Editor's Comments

If you are an agented author and seek to publish lively, inspirational books for Christian children, adults, or educators, we'd like to hear from you.

Crown Books for Young Readers

1745 Broadway
New York, NY 10019

Submissions Editor

Publisher's Interests

Children ages birth through young adult enjoy the nonfiction books offered by this publisher. A division of Random House Children's Books, its list includes titles on topics related to history, science, and social studies.
Website: www.randomhouse.com/kids

Freelance Potential

Published 30 titles in 2005: 11 were by agented authors, and 4 were reprint/licensed properties. Receives 500 queries, 1,000 unsolicited mss yearly.

- **Nonfiction:** Publishes concept books and toddler books, 0–4 years; story picture books, 4–10 years; chapter books, 5–10 years; middle-grade books, 8–12 years; and young adult books, 12–18 years. Topics include science, nature, sports, history, and social issues.
- **Representative Titles:** *My Painted House, My Friendly Chicken, and Me* by Maya Angelou (5–10 years) is an enchanting story of a girl, her village in South Africa, her mischievous brother, and her best friend—a chicken. *Little Rabbit's Loose Tooth* by Lucy Bate (4–8 years) shares the story of what happens when a rabbit girl loses her first tooth.

Submissions and Payment

Guidelines available. Accepts submissions from agented authors only. Accepts photocopies, computer printouts, and simultaneous submissions if identified. SASE. Responds in 3 months. Publication period varies. Royalty; advance.

Editor's Comments

Please note that we only publish nonfiction titles, and are only accepting submissions from agented authors. We strongly suggest you review our guidelines and the past titles we've published to get a sense of what we look for. Keep in mind that we receive hundreds of queries so competition is tough. Submissions with artwork suggestions are preferred.

CSS Publishing Company

P.O. Box 4503
517 Main Street
Lima, OH 45802-4503

Acquisitions Editor: Becky Brandt

Publisher's Interests
This publisher of Christian material serves the educational needs of pastors, worship leaders, and parish program planners. Its list incudes books and resources for both Sunday school educators and students.
Website: www.csspub.com

Freelance Potential
Published 60 titles in 2005: 30 were developed from unsolicited submissions. Of the 50 titles, 15 were by authors who were new to the publishing house. Receives 1,000 unsolicited mss yearly.

- **Nonfiction:** Publishes story picture books, 4–10 years; and young adult books, 12–18 years. Topics include religious education, prayer, worship, and family life. Also publishes resource materials, program planners, and church supplies for Christian education.
- **Representative Titles:** *Teaching the Mystery of God to Children* by Judy Gattis Smith identifies and reaffirms the spiritual experiences of young people and guides readers on a journey toward discovering the divine mystery. *When You Run out of Soap* by Mary Rose Pearson (4–7 years) adds pizzazz to Sunday school lessons with fun activities that support the teaching of Bible stories and Christian values.

Submissions and Payment
Guidelines and catalogue available at website. Send complete ms with résumé. Accepts photocopies, computer printouts, and simultaneous submissions if identified. SASE. Responds in 6 months. Publication in 6 months. Royalty. Flat fee.

Editor's Comments
We like to see ready-to-use lectionary-based materials for use with young children, children's sermons and object lessons, and resource material for working with youth.

Da Capo Press

11 Cambridge Center
Cambridge, MA 02142

Editorial Director

Publisher's Interests
An imprint of The Perseus Books Group, this publisher offers adult nonfiction titles on topics such as parenting, health, history, social issues, current events, and sports.
Website: www.dacapopress.com

Freelance Potential
Published 80 titles in 2005: 2 were developed from unsolicited submissions and 78 were by agented authors. Receives 80 unsolicited mss yearly.

- **Nonfiction:** Publishes nonfiction books for adults. Topics include parenting, biography, current events, entertainment, health, history, humor, science, nature, multicultural issues, religion, self-help, social issues, and sports.
- **Representative Titles:** *Talking to Tweens* by Elizabeth Hartley-Brewer (parents) offers practical, down-to-earth, and reassuring guidance on challenging issues for parents of children ages 8–12. *The Guy's Guide to Surviving Pregnancy, Childbirth, and the First Year of Fatherhood* by Michael Crider (parents) offers a candid, down-to-earth account of one man's transformation into fatherhood.

Submissions and Payment
Guidelines available at website. Send complete ms with author biography and credentials. Accepts photocopies. Availability of artwork improves chance of acceptance. SASE. Responds in 1–2 months. Publication in 1 year. Royalty; advance.

Editor's Comments
We're looking for books that can entertain and educate our readers at the same time. Our readers include first time parents who are looking for resources to help guide them on their parenting journey. Send us something that is unique. See our website to get an idea of the types of material we publish. Agented submissions are preferred.

Darby Creek Publishing

7858 Industrial Parkway
Plain City, OH 43064

Submissions Editor

Publisher's Interests
Titles for elementary through high school readers can be found on this small publisher's list.
Website: www.darbycreekpublishing.com

Freelance Potential
Published 12 titles in 2005: 3 were developed from unsolicited submissions, 2 were by agented authors, and 4 were reprint/licensed properties. Of the 12 titles, 1 was by an unpublished writer and 6 were by authors who were new to the publishing house. Receives 500 queries, 750 unsolicited mss yearly.

- **Fiction:** Published 1 easy-to-read book, 4–17 years; 3 chapter books, 5–10 years; 3 middle-grade books, 8–12 years; and 1 young adult book, 12–18 years. Genres include contemporary fiction, humor, romance, and sports stories.
- **Nonfiction:** Published 4 middle-grade books, 8–12 years. Topics include animals, history, and science, sports, biographies, and humor.
- **Representative Titles:** *INDY 500: The Inside Track* by Nancy Roe Pimm (9+ years) offers an inside look into the excitment of the Indy 500. *Miracle* by Gail Langer Karwoski (9+ years) is the true story of the ship *Sea Venture* and its shipwreck in the Bermuda Islands.

Submissions and Payment
Guidelines available with SASE or at website. Query with summary and 2 sample chapters; or send complete ms. Accepts photocopies and simultaneous submissions if identified. SASE. No email queries. Responds in 2–8 weeks. Publication in 12–18 months. Royalty; advance.

Editor's Comments
We're looking for material that offers a creative spin on themes for children ages eight to eighteen. Review our catalogue and guidelines and send us a query.

May Davenport, Publishers

26313 Purissima Road
Los Altos Hills, CA 94022

Publisher & Editor: May Davenport

Publisher's Interests

This small, family-owned publishing house offers books that communicate with and reach out to today's teenagers. Its list includes books that help teachers get students reading, including historical fiction, adventure, and mystery.
Website: www.maydavenportpublishers.com

Freelance Potential

Published 2 titles in 2005: all were developed from unsolicited submissions. Of the 2 titles, 2 were by unpublished writers and authors who were new to the publishing house.
Receives 1,000 queries and unsolicited mss yearly.

- **Fiction:** Published 2 young adult books, 12–18 years. Genres include historical fiction, mystery, humor, and adventure.
- **Representative Titles:** *Senioritis* by Tate Thompson (grades 8–12) tells of eight high school students who must attend an after-school program for rule infractions. *Windriders* by Blake F. Grant (grades 7–12) tells the story of a boy who learns how to fly a hang glider and teaches a 16-year-old girl who is afraid of heights to fly. In return, she teaches him karate, as they discover their family roots.

Submissions and Payment

Guidelines available. Query. SASE. Responds in 1–2 weeks. Publication in 1–2 years. Royalty, 15%. Flat fee.

Editor's Comments

We are currently seeking fine literary writing for today's teenagers (15–18 years) with both low- and high-reading levels to be used in classrooms. Writing must be purposeful enough to give students what they need to acquire the skills to write beyond the juvenile level of fantasy. At this time, we are not accepting children's color-and-read stories, juvenile novels, or young adult novels. Our website can give you the latest information and tell you what we are all about.

Jonathan David Publishers

68-22 Eliot Avenue
Middle Village, NY 11379

Editor-in-Chief: Alfred J. Kolatch

Publisher's Interests
For over 50 years, this publisher has been specializing in nonfiction Judaica for children and adults. Its list includes topics related to Jewish culture, history, and traditions.
Website: www.jdbooks.com

Freelance Potential
Published 15 titles in 2005: 9 were developed from unsolicited submissions, 2 were by agented authors, and 1 was a reprint/licensed property. Of the 15 titles, 3 were unpublished writers and 3 were by authors who were new to the publishing house. Receives 1,000 queries yearly.

- **Fiction:** Publishes easy-to-read books, 4–7 years; and story picture books, 4–10 years. Genres include folktales and stories of Jewish culture.
- **Nonfiction:** Publishes easy-to-read books, 4–7 years; and middle-grade books, 8–12 years. Topics include religion, Judaica, history, culture, and multicultural issues.
- **Representative Titles:** *My Baby Brother* by Sylvia Rouss (4–7 years) tells the story of a big sister who comes to love her new baby brother and realize what a miracle he is. *A Child's First Book of Jewish Holidays* by Alfred J. Kolatch (3–6 years) offers an engaging introduction to major Jewish holidays.

Submissions and Payment
Guidelines available. Query with résumé, table of contents, synopsis, and sample chapter. No unsolicited mss. Accepts photocopies and computer printouts. No simultaneous submissions. SASE. Responds in 1–2 months. Publication in 18 months. Royalty; advance. Flat fee.

Editor's Comments
We are interested in titles that focus on popular Judaica for juveniles and would like to see more material that covers history, heroes and heroines, culture, family life and traditions, sports, and biographies.

DAW Books

375 Hudson Street
New York, NY 10014

Associate Editor: Peter Stampfel

Publisher's Interests

Founded in 1971, this small private publisher is well-known
for discovering and publishing the hottest talents in the science fiction and fantasy fields.
Website: www.dawbooks.com

Freelance Potential

Published 48 titles (10–15 juvenile) in 2005. Of the 48 titles,
1 was by an unpublished writer and 2 were by authors who
were new to the publishing house. Receives 1,000+ unsolicited mss yearly.

- **Fiction:** Publishes science fiction, thriller, and fantasy novels
  for young adults and adults.
- **Representative Titles:** *A Flame in Hali* by Marion Zimmer
  Bradley tells how King Carolin of Hastur and his friend work
  selflessly to put an end to the destruction caused by the magical matrix Towers; part 3 of the Clingfire Trilogy. *Survival* by
  Julie E. Czerneda is a story of an Earth scientist caught up in a
  terrifying interspecies conflict; part 1 of the Species Impera-
  tive series.

Submissions and Payment

Guidelines available. Send complete ms. Accepts photocopies and computer printouts. No simultaneous submissions. SASE. Responds in 3 months. Publication in 8–12
months. Royalty, 6%; advance.

Editor's Comments

We publish first novels if they are of top-notch professional
quality. A literary agent is not necessary. We are strongly
committed to discovering and nurturing new talent, and to
keeping a personal "family" spirit at DAW. Please note that
we do not publish novellas, short stories, short story collections, poetry, nonfiction or children's books. We are strictly a
science fiction and fantasy publisher and our target audience is made up of young adult and adult readers.

Dawn Publications

12402 Bitney Springs Road
Nevada City, CA 95959

Editor: Glenn Hovemann

Publisher's Interests
Nature awareness titles for adults and children can be found in the catalogue of this publisher. Publishing mostly picture books for children, it offers books that encourage an appreciation for nature and a respectful participation in it.
Website: www.dawnpub.com

Freelance Potential
Published 6 titles in 2005: 4 were developed from unsolicited submissions and 2 were by agented authors. Of the 6 titles, 1 was by an unpublished writer and 3 were by authors who were new to the publishing house. Receives 2,000+ queries and unsolicited mss yearly.

- **Nonfiction:** Publishes easy-to-read books, 4–7 years; and story picture books, 4–10 years. Topics include the environment, conservation, ecology, family relationships, personal awareness, and multicultural and ethnic issues.
- **Representative Titles:** *Over in the Ocean* by Marianne Berkes (3–8 years) explores creatures that live in the coral reef. Children will count and clap and enjoy the colorful art in this book. *Forest Bright, Forest Night* by Jennifer Ward (3–8 years) introduces creatures of the forest to children so that they become aware of both diurnal and nocturnal animals.

Submissions and Payment
Guidelines available at website. Query or send complete ms. Accepts photocopies, computer printouts, and simultaneous submissions if identified. SASE. Responds in 2–3 months. Publication in 18–24 months. Royalty; advance.

Editor's Comments
We have very few openings for manuscripts at this time, and are not interested in material that contains animal dialogue, which presents animals in a highly anthropomorphic light. We look for simple stories that are a carrying agent for factual information about some aspect of nature.

Denlinger's Publishers

P.O. Box 1030
Edgewater, FL 32132-1030

Acquisitions Editor: Marcia Buckingham

Publisher's Interests
In 1997, Denlinger's switched from traditional publishing to electronic publishing. It now offers fiction for all ages and juvenile fiction for children eight through twelve.
Website: www.thebookden.com

Freelance Potential
Published 24 titles in 2005: all were developed from unsolicited submissions. Of the 24 titles, 5 were by unpublished writers and 6 were by authors who were new to the publishing house. Receives 1,700 unsolicited mss yearly.

- **Fiction:** Publishes chapter books, 5–10 years; and middle-grade books, 8–12 years. Genres include adventure, fantasy, folklore, and historical and inspirational fiction.
- **Representative Titles:** *Angry Angel Runaway* by Bernard L. Albertson (8–12 years) is a fast paced story about an angry, 12-year-old blind runaway who meets a truck driver. *Saltwater Summer* by Rich Eubanks (8–12 years) relates how young friends are forced to depend on each other as they fight to stay alive in the perilous sea.

Submissions and Payment
Guidelines, submission form, and catalogue available at website. Send complete ms with market analysis and biography. Accepts disk submissions, and email submissions to acquisitions@thebookden.com. SASE. Responds in 3–6 months. Publication in 6–8 months. Royalty.

Editor's Comments
We are open to most subjects but do not publish poetry, books that rely on illustrations, erotica, cookbooks, joke books or textbooks. We would like to see mysteries, adventure stories, historical fiction, self-help titles, and books on aviation, and female issues. It is best to review our online submission policy to see if electronic publishing is the right venue for you.

Dial Books for Young Readers

Penguin Group (USA) Inc.
345 Hudson Street
New York, NY 10014

Submissions Coordinator

Publisher's Interests
Books for toddlers through teens are available from this
imprint of the Penguin Group.
Website: www.penguin.com

Freelance Potential
Published 50 titles in 2005: 2 were developed from unsolicited submissions, 25 were by agented authors, and 4 were
reprint/licensed properties. Of the 50 titles, 5 were by
unpublished writers and 10 were by authors who were new
to the publishing house. Receives 2,000+ queries, 1,000+
unsolicited mss yearly.

- **Fiction:** Publishes concept books, toddler books, and early
  picture books, 0–4 years; easy-to-read books, 4–7 years; story
  picture books, 4–10 years; chapter books, 5–10 years; middle-
  grade novels, 8–12 years; and young adult books, 12–18
  years. Genres include contemporary and literary fiction.
- **Nonfiction:** Publishes concept books and early picture books,
  0–4 years; easy-to-read books, 4–7 years; story picture books,
  4–10 years; middle-grade books, 8–12 years; and young adult
  books, 12–18 years. Topics include humor, science, and
  social issues.
- **Representative Titles:** *The Amazing Thinking Machine* by
  Dennis Haseley (8–18 years) is the story of a boy who receives
  life-altering answers to his many questions. *On the Fringe* by
  Donald R. Gallo, ed. (YA) is an anthology that explores the
  teen outsider experience.

Submissions and Payment
Guidelines and catalogue available with SASE. Query with up
to 10 pages; send complete ms for picture books. SASE.
Response time, publication period, and payment policy vary.

Editor's Comments
Visit our website for up-to-date information on our submissions policy.

Didax

395 Main Street
Rowley, MA 01969

Vice President: Martin Kennedy

Publisher's Interests
Didax specializes in producing innovative hands-on, print, and software tools created *by* teachers *for* teachers at the preschool through high school levels.
Website: www.didax.com

Freelance Potential
Published 25 titles in 2005: 2 were developed from unsolicited submissions and 21 were by agented authors. Receives 120 queries, 24 unsolicited mss yearly.

- **Nonfiction:** Publishes reproducible activity books and teacher resources, pre-K–grade 12. Topics include basic math, fractions, geometry, algebra, probability, problem-solving, the alphabet, pre-reading, phonics, word study, spelling, vocabulary, writing, reading comprehension, and social studies.
- **Representative Titles:** *Classroom Art* by Amelia Ruscoe (grades K–3) focuses on the development of drawing, painting, and printmaking skills to inspire students to communicate through visual art. *Bullying* (grades 3–4) teaches students the skills they need to identify bullying, cope with it, and prevent bullying from starting.

Submissions and Payment
Guidelines available. Query with résumé and outline; or send complete ms. Accepts photocopies, computer printouts, disk submissions (Microsoft Word), email submissions to development@didaxinc.com, and simultaneous submissions if identified. SASE. Responds to queries in 2 weeks, to mss in 1 month. Publication in 1 year. Royalty; advance.

Editor's Comments
We're committed to helping teachers succeed in communicating concepts of math, language arts, and social studies to their students. We look for products developed by experienced educators that offer original approaches to teaching concepts or skills.

Different Books

3900 Glenwood Avenue
Golden Valley, MN 55422

Editor: Roger Hammer

Publisher's Interests

A small press, Different Books has a tightly focused publishing program that features books about persons with disabilities. Its titles target children from preschool through sixth grade, and all feature a disabled child as the main character.

Freelance Potential

Published 4 titles in 2005: all were developed from unsolicited submissions. Of the 4 titles, 3 were by authors who were new to the publishing house. Receives 100 queries, 500 unsolicited mss yearly.

- **Fiction:** Published 1 story picture book, 4–10 years; 1 chapter book, 5–10 years; and 2 middle-grade books, 8–12 years. Genres include fantasy, fairy tales, adventure, and multicultural and ethnic fiction.
- **Representative Titles:** *Wayne's Trail* is a story about overcoming obstacles that shows what happens when a group of friends decide to take a wheelchair-bound boy to the top of their favorite hill to watch the sunset; part of the Mona and Friends in the Land of Ican series. *Simon the Daredevil Centipede* features a centipede who buys 50 pairs of roller skates and, with great determination, becomes such a good skater that he lands his dream job.

Submissions and Payment

Guidelines available. Query or send complete ms. Accepts photocopies and computer printouts. No simultaneous submissions. SASE. Responds to queries in 1 week, to mss in 2 months. Publication in 1 year. Royalty. Flat fee for each new printing.

Editor's Comments

For the coming year, we're interested in receiving submissions that reflect our publishing goal—to portray children with disabilities who face adversity and overcome it. We seek stories that are sensitive to all American cultures.

Discovery Enterprises

25 Leslie Road
Auburndale, MA 02466

General Manager: Lisa Gianelly

Publisher's Interests

Featuring material based on primary- and secondary-source documents, this publisher offers fiction and nonfiction titles for students in kindergarten through grade twelve.
Website: www.ushistorydocs.com; www.historycompass.com

Freelance Potential

Published 10 titles in 2005: 2 were developed from unsolicited submissions. Of the 10 titles, 1 was by an unpublished writer and 3 were by authors who were new to the publishing house. Receives 50–60 queries yearly.

- **Fiction:** Publishes plays, grades 4–12. Also publishes middle-grade titles, 8–12 years; and young adult books, 12–18 years. Genres include historical fiction.
- **Nonfiction:** Publishes easy-to-read books, 4–7 years; chapter books, 5–10 years; middle-grade titles, 8–12 years; and young adult books, 12–18 years. Topics include American history. Also publishes biographies.
- **Representative Titles:** *Seaman's Adventures with Lewis and Clark* by Duncan Brown (grades 1–4) is a story based on actual accounts of the Lewis and Clark expedition, and focuses on Seaman, the dog who accompanied the group. *Message for a Spy* by Dorothy A. Heibel (grades 4–8) is a story of the American Revolution and a brave boy who helps both his father and the Patriots.

Submissions and Payment

Guidelines available. Query with résumé, outline, and nonfiction clips. No unsolicited mss. Accepts photocopies and simultaneous submissions if identified. SASE. Responds in 3 months. Publication in 2–8 months. Royalty.

Editor's Comments

Our titles include primary source materials that relate to American history. Our goal is to make students aware of the exciting history of the United States.

DiskUs Publishing

P.O. Box 43
Albany, IN 47320

Submissions Editor: Holly Janey

Publisher's Interests

A pioneer in the development of the e-publishing business, this publisher offers a variety of quality children's fiction and nonfiction. Its material may be ordered or downloaded from its website.

Website: www.diskuspublishing.com

Freelance Potential

Published 90 titles (25 juvenile) in 2005: 45 were developed from unsolicited submissions. Receives 15,000 queries each year.

- **Fiction:** Publishes concept books and toddler books, 0–4 years; easy-to-read books, 4–7 years; middle-grade books, 8–12 years; and young adult books, 8–12 years. Genres include science fiction, fantasy, horror, mystery, Western, action, adventure, and mainstream fiction.
- **Nonfiction:** Publishes concept and toddler books, 0–4 years. Also publishes puzzle books, religious titles, and adult self-help books.
- **Representative Titles:** *The Candi Striped Reindeer* by Cia Leah tells the story of a reindeer that looked different from all the other reindeer and wanted to fit in. *Thanksgiving with Grandpa* by Cia Leah is the story of a girl who tries to save a turkey on her Grandpa's farm from becoming the Thanksgiving dinner.

Submissions and Payment

Guidelines available at website. Query with résumé, word count, synopsis, and first 3 chapters. Accepts email queries to editors@diskuspublishing.com (put "DiskUs" in the subject line). SASE. Responds in 3–6 months. Publication in 5 months. Royalty.

Editor's Comments

We're looking for informative and entertaining books for children. Stories with twists and turns are popular with us.

DNA Press

P.O. Box 572
Eagleville, PA 19408

Acquisitions Editor

Publisher's Interests

DNA Press specializes in books about science in any form
and for any audience. In addition to academic monographs
and thrillers for adults, it also publishes middle-grade and
young adult titles, all of which are related to the advance-
ment and spreading of scientific knowledge.
Website: www.dnapress.com

Freelance Potential

Published 10 titles (5 juvenile) in 2005: 8 were developed
from unsolicited submissions. Receives 500 queries yearly.

- **Fiction:** Publishes middle-grade books, 8–12 years; and
  young adult books, 12–18 years. Genres include science
  and technology.
- **Nonfiction:** Publishes middle-grade books, 8–12 years; and
  young adult books, 12–18 years. Topics include contemporary
  and science fiction.
- **Representative Titles:** *Feebie Brainiac and the Lysis Virus* by
  David A. Sutcher (YA) is a novel that incorporates issues such
  as euthanasia, human cloning, and genetic manipulation into
  the plot to provoke thought in the reader. *The Prometheus
  Project* by Douglas E. Richards (9–12 years) is a science fiction
  adventure novel that is intended to stimulate interest in science and technology.

Submissions and Payment

Guidelines and catalogue available at website. Query with
synopsis; or send complete ms. SASE. Responds to queries
in 6 weeks. Publication period varies. Royalty.

Editor's Comments

We're always looking for exciting book proposals. If you can
share your thoughts and experience related to science with
our audience, then we're your publisher. Your query should
tell us why your work should be published, who your intended
audience is, and which books it would be competing with.

Dorchester Publishing

200 Madison Avenue
New York, NY 10016

Editor: Kate Seaver

Publisher's Interests

Striving to bring top-notch fiction to its large reading audience, this independent publisher, mostly known for its romance novels, also produces horror, thrillers, Westerns, and young adult titles.
Website: www.dorchesterpub.com

Freelance Potential

Published 225 titles (12 juvenile) in 2005: 12 were developed from unsolicited submissions and 112 were by agented authors. Of the 225 titles, 18 were by unpublished writers and 27 were by authors who were new to the publishing house. Receives 3,000 unsolicited mss yearly.

- **Fiction:** Publishes young adult books, 12–18 years. Genres include contemporary fiction.
- **Representative Titles:** *Custer, Terry and Me* by G. G. Boyer tells the story of how the only eyewitness to the most famous Cavalry and Indian battle in frontier history fights to survive to preserve the truth. *Terror Stalks the Border* by Bradford Scott tells the story of two of the most celebrated rangers in fiction and how they bring down a vicious criminal organization terrorizing the Texas border.

Submissions and Payment

Guidelines available. Query with first three chapters. Accepts photocopies. SASE. Responds in 6–8 months. Publication in 9–12 months. Royalty; advance.

Editor's Comments

We are only considering contempory fiction and present-day paranormals for our young adult line. While our stories do include romance, plots should be centered upon the pressing issues teens face in life. As our primary audience is children ages 12 to 16, there should be no sex scenes. Manuscripts should be approximately 45,000 words. Send us an idea for something filled with adventure that our readers will love.

Dorling Kindersley

375 Hudson Street
New York, NY 10014

Submissions: Beth Sutinis

Publisher's Interests
Lively, interactive picture books are the speciality of this
international publisher. Its list incudes top-notch material,
including nonfiction for children, interactive software, CD-
ROMs, and fiction and nonfiction for adults.
Website: www.dk.com

Freelance Potential
Published 250 titles in 2005: 3 were by agented authors and
50 were reprint/licensed properties. Receives 1,000 queries
each year.

- **Nonfiction:** Publishes concept books and toddler books, 0–4
  years; easy-to-read books, 4–7 years; middle-grade titles, 8–12
  years; and young adult books, 12–18 years.
- **Representative Titles:** *Fishy Tales* (3–5 years) takes a journey
  through a coral reef watching small fish swim and jellyfish
  float; part of the DK Readers series. *Human Body* by Dr. Sue
  Davidson (8+ years) explores the human body using a completely unique system of show-and-tell that combines cutting-
  edge computerized photomontage and acetate technology.
  Survival by Barbara Taylor (8+ years) takes a fresh look at
  familiar subjects such as history and science.

Submissions and Payment
Guidelines available. Accepts queries through agents only.
No unsolicited mss. SASE. Responds in 6 months. Publica-
tion in 2 years. Royalty, 10%; advance, varies.

Editor's Comments
We're look for engaging children's books that make reading
fun. While our main focus is on picture books, we are also
looking for novelty books and some nonfiction with visuals
on a variety of topics. Please note that we only accept
queries through agents, and that most of our writers are published. In order to get a sense of the types of material we
are looking for, please review our catalogue.

Dover Publications

31 East 2nd Street
Mineola, NY 11501-3582

President: Paul Negri

Publisher's Interests

Dover Publications is a well-known publisher of fiction reprints for children, as well as educational titles, biographies, and activity books.
Website: www.doverpublications.com

Freelance Potential

Published 160 titles in 2005. Receives 125 queries, 400 unsolicited mss yearly.

- **Fiction:** Publishes reprints of children's classics and storybooks. Genres include folktales, fantasy, and fairy tales. Also publishes stories about animals.
- **Nonfiction:** Publishes educational titles, anthologies, and biographies. Topics include American history, Native Americans, ancient history, needlework, fashion, languages, architecture, archaeology, literature, hobbies, adventure, and fine art. Also publishes coloring and activity books.
- **Representative Titles:** *The Railway Children* by E. Nesbit (9–12 years) is a classic reprint of the charming story of three children who must change their comfortable lifestyle and move to a cottage by the railroad. *Uncle Wiggily* by Howard R. Garis (8–11 years) includes eleven delightful stories of the adventures of an old gentleman rabbit.

Submissions and Payment

Catalogue available at website. Query or send complete ms. Accepts photocopies and computer printouts. SASE. Response time and publication period vary. Flat fee.

Editor's Comments

The only fiction we publish is reprints of classic children's literature. However, we are looking for original, historically accurate submissions that are suitable for children and young adults. Craft and activity books with an unusual way to make something are of interest. New and established writers are encouraged to send us their work.

Down East Books

P.O. Box 679
Camden, ME 04843

Managing Editor: Michael Steere

Publisher's Interests

Focusing on Maine and New England themes, this small publisher offers fiction and nonfiction books for children. 5% self-, subsidy-, co-venture, or co-op published material.
Website: www.downeastbooks.com

Freelance Potential

Published 30 titles (5 juvenile) in 2005: 5 were developed from unsolicited submissions and 1 was a reprint/licensed property. Of the 30 titles, 3 were by unpublished writers and 6 were by authors who were new to the publishing house. Receives 1,000 queries, 300 unsolicited mss yearly.

- **Fiction:** Published 1 concept book, 0–4 years; 5 easy-to-read books, 4–7 years; and 1 middle-grade book, 8–12 years. Genres include contemporary fiction, adventure, mystery, and humor.
- **Nonfiction:** Publishes books about New England and Maine.
- **Representative Titles:** *Lobsterman* by Dahlov Ipcar (4+ years) tells the story of a day in the life of a lobsterman's son, working alongside his father. *The Gazebo* by Ethel Pochocki (8+ years) is a richly illustrated story that features a little girl who grows up to build the gazebo of her dreams on the coast of Maine.

Submissions and Payment

Guidelines available. Query with clips or writing samples; or send complete ms. Accepts photocopies, computer printouts, and simultaneous submissions. No email. SASE. Responds in 2–8 weeks. Publication in 1 year. Royalty, 9–12%; advance, $300–$600.

Editor's Comments

We're looking for true-to-life adventure stories or nature or animal stories, as well as children's titles that include elements of universally applicable character building as part of the story. All stories must take place in Maine or New England.

Dramatic Publishing

311 Washington Street
Woodstock, IL 60098

Acquisitions Editor: Linda Habjan

Publisher's Interests
Since 1885, this publisher has been providing new plays and musicals for theater groups in high schools, community groups, professional companies, and children's programs. **Website:** www.dramaticpublishing.com

Freelance Potential
Published 60 titles (30 juvenile) in 2005. Of the 60 titles, 25 were by authors who were new to the publishing house. Receives 250 queries, 600 unsolicited mss yearly.

- **Fiction:** Publishes full-length and one-act plays, monologues and anthologies. Genres include drama, humor, fairy tales, musicals, and holiday plays.
- **Nonfiction:** Publishes books and resource materials. Topics include teaching theater arts, stagecraft, stage dialects, production techniques, playwriting, and audition and competition presentations.
- **Representative Titles:** *The Imaginators* by Dwayne Hartford is a play about three children and the power of their imagination. *Live Drawing; A Portrait of the Mona Lisa* by Jules Tasca is a dramatic play about the famous Mona Lisa and her painter, Leonardo DaVinci.

Submissions and Payment
Guidelines available. Send complete ms with résumé, synopsis, production history, reviews, cast list, and set and technical requirements; include audiocassette for musicals. Accepts photocopies and computer printouts. SASE. Responds in 10–12 weeks. Publication in 18 months. Royalty.

Editor's Comments
We still need plays and musicals for an audience of children and young adults. Plays that feature large casts, such as in a school production, are welcome, as well as those with limited casting, such as in small community theater groups.

Dutton Children's Books

Penguin Young Readers Group
14th Floor
345 Hudson Street
New York, NY 10014

Queries Editor

Publisher's Interests

For more than 150 years, Dutton has been publishing fiction and nonfiction, beginning readers, middle-grade books and young adult novels. Their mission is to create high-quality books that show a commitment to excellence.
Website: www.penguin.com/youngreaders

Freelance Potential

Published 100 titles in 2005: 75 were by agented authors. Of the 100 titles, 10 were by unpublished writers and 25 were by authors who were new to the publishing house.

- **Fiction:** Published 3 concept books, 0–4 years; 2 toddler books, 0–4 years; 10 early picture books, 0–4 years; 2 easy-to-read books, 4–7 years; 30 story picture books, 4–10 years; 5 chapter books, 5–10 years; 19 middle-grade books, 8–12 years; and 15 young adult books, 12–18 years. Genres include adventure, mystery, fantasy, and humor.
- **Nonfiction:** Published 2 concept books, 0–4 years; 1 toddler book, 0–4 years; 5 early picture books, 0–4 years; and 6 story picture books, 4–10 years. Topics include history and nature.
- **Representative Titles:** *If I Built a Car* by Chris Van Dusen (3–7 years) is the story of a boy who designs his perfect car of the future. *Dread Locks* by Neal Shusterman (12+ years) is a tale of a modern-day girl with magical powers; part of the Dark Fusion series.

Submissions and Payment

Guidelines available. Query with brief synopsis and publishing credits. No unsolicited mss. SASE. Responds in 2–3 months. Publication in 1+ years. Royalty; advance.

Editor's Comments

Remember that we only accept queries. Keep them to one-page and include any relevant background that you think we might find helpful. If you have a special reason for sending it to Dutton, let us know that also.

Eakin Press

Sunbelt Media, Inc.
P.O. Box 90159
Austin, TX 78709-0159

Publisher: Virginia Messer

Publisher's Interests
The books available from this regional publisher focus on the American Southwest. Its children's division offers books for beginning readers, picture books, and fiction and nonfiction for middle-grade children and teens.
Website: www.eakinpress.com

Freelance Potential
Published 200–300 titles (100–150 juvenile) in 2005. Receives 2,500 queries yearly.

- **Fiction:** Publishes picture books, 4–10 years; easy-to-read books, 4–7 years; chapter books, 5–10 years; and middle-grade books, 8–12 years. Genres include historical and multicultural fiction, folklore, and stories about animals.
- **Nonfiction:** Publishes easy-to-read books, 4–7 years; story picture books, 4–10 years; chapter books, 5–10 years; and middle-grade books, 8–12 years. Features biographies and books about regional subjects and history.
- **Representative Titles:** *Mystery at Saddlecreek* by Marcia Allen Bennett is a suspense story featuring young sleuths trying to discover who is committing acts of vandalism in the Hill Country of Texas. *The Borrowed Grave* by Jacqueline Stem is an adventure story set at a summer camp in historic Fort Davis, Texas.

Submissions and Payment
Guidelines available. Query with résumé, sample chapter, and clips or writing samples. Accepts photocopies, computer printouts, and simultaneous submissions if identified. SASE. Responds in 6 months. Publication in 1–2 years. Royalty.

Editor's Comments
If your manuscript is intended for a mainstream audience or focuses on a region other than the Southwest, you should look for a different publisher. Books that include elements such as a glossary, maps, or teacher's guide will appeal to the school market.

E & E Publishing

Suite 227
1001 Bridgeway
Sausalito, CA 94965

Submissions Editor: Eve Bine-Stock

Publisher's Interests

Picture books and story books that appeal to children of all ages, and nonfiction for adults can be found in the catalogue of this publisher. It produces high-quality paperback books as well as e-books.

Website: www.eandegroup.com/publishing

Freelance Potential

Published 5 titles in 2005. Of the 5 titles, 3 were by authors who were new to the publishing house.

- **Fiction:** Publishes early picture books and concept books, 0–4 years; easy-to-read books, 4–7 years; and story picture books, 4–10 years. Genres include adventure, fantasy, and humor.
- **Nonfiction:** Publishes early picture and concept books, 0–4 years; easy-to-read books, 4–7 years; and story picture books, 4–10 years. Topics include animals and poetry.
- **Representative Titles:** *Charlotte's Garden* by Charlotte Corry Partin (0+ years) is a book of poetry of the seasons exquisitely illustrated with pressed flower art. *The Beetle and the Berry* by Anne Applefield (8+ years) follows a tiny beetle as he tries to move the large, juicy berry he finds.

Submissions and Payment

Send complete ms for picture books; query for longer works. Prefers email to eandegroup@eandegroup.com. Accepts photocopies and computer printouts. SASE. Responds in 1 week. Publication period and payment policy vary.

Editor's Comments

We're looking for well-written concept books. Our stories are enjoyed by children and adults of all ages. Our e-books combine early learning with modern technology and are a fun way to read great stories and use the computer at the same time. Send us something that will delight children and intrigue adults. Please note that we do not accept young adult books, or holiday material.

Educational Ministries

165 Plaza Drive
Prescott, AZ 86303-5549

Submissions Editor: Linda Davidson

Publisher's Interests
Practical, innovative, and creative resources for Christian
educators in mainline Protestant churches are the mainstay
of this publisher. Its list includes supplementary resources,
manuals, and curriculum guides for church educators and
worship leaders.
Website: www.educationalministries.com

Freelance Potential
Published 2–3 titles (1 juvenile) in 2005: 1 was developed
from an unsolicited submission. Receives 190 unsolicited
mss yearly.

- **Fiction:** Publishes toddler books, 0–4 years. Genres include
  Christian and educational fiction. Also publishes adult fiction.
- **Nonfiction:** Publishes educational resource materials for use
  by Protestant denominations. Topics include Lent, vacation
  Bible school programs, children's and youth ministry, worship,
  and crafts.
- **Representative Titles:** *Being Human: Learning Thru Feelings*
  by Elaine M. Ward (educators) helps teachers understand how
  children learn through emotions such as contrition, forgiveness, joy, trust, and love. *Creative Arts & Crafts* by Anne
  Gilbert (8–12 years) supplements New Testament stories with
  projects that accompany stories from John the Baptist through
  the early church.

Submissions and Payment
Guidelines available. Send complete ms. Accepts photocopies, computer printouts, and simultaneous submissions if
identified. SASE. Responds in 6–8 weeks. Publication in 1–4
months. Flat fee.

Editor's Comments
Our theology leans to the liberal side; we would not be clas-
sified as conservative or fundamental. Our resources seek to
ask questions, not give pat answers.

Educators Publishing Service

P.O. Box 9031
Cambridge, MA 02139-9031

Vice President, Publishing: Charlie Heinle

Publisher's Interests
This publisher is committed to producing high-quality, research-based teaching materials that provide literary solutions for every child. It offers a variety of language arts and reading resources for classroom use.
Website: www.epsbooks.com

Freelance Potential
Published 100 titles (40 juvenile) in 2005: 3 were developed from unsolicited submissions. Of the 100 titles, 5 were by unpublished writers and 5 were by authors who were new to the publishing house. Receives 250 queries yearly.

- **Fiction:** Publishes easy-to-read books, 4–7 years; chapter books, 5–10 years.
- **Nonfiction:** Publishes reading, writing, vocabulary, grammar, and comprehension workbooks, grades K–8. Also publishes educational materials for students with learning disabilities.
- **Representative Titles:** *Thinking about Mac and Tab 2* (grades K–1) contains early comprehension exercises designed for beginning readers. *Explode the Code* by Nancy M. Hall & Rena Price (grades K–4) provides a sequential, systematic approach to phonics in which students blend sounds to build vocabulary and read words, phrases, sentences, and stories.

Submissions and Payment
Query with résumé, outline, sample chapter, and table of contents. Accepts photocopies, computer printouts, and simultaneous submissions if identified. SASE. Responds in 2–3 months. Publication in 1 year. Royalty.

Editor's Comments
We accept queries from educators writing for the school market, authoring materials (primarily K–8) in the reading and language arts area. We strive to meet the needs of all students, and are looking for material for the general classroom, as well as for students with learning disabilities.

Edupress

P.O. Box 800
W5527 Highway 106
Fort Atkinson, WI 53538

Director: Nancy Craine

Publisher's Interests

This publisher provides teachers with quality resource materials that feature innovative activities. To help ensure student success, the award-winning books and products from Edupress are created by educators and designed by talented artists whose goal is to make learning fun. Edupress has been in business since 1979.
Website: www.edupressinc.com

Freelance Potential

Published 30 titles in 2005: 3 were developed from unsolicited submissions. Receives 30 queries yearly.

- **Nonfiction:** Publishes books and resource materials for educators, pre-K–grade 8. Topics include social studies, science, curriculum coordination, language arts, early learning, math, holidays, arts and crafts, and classroom decor.
- **Representative Titles:** *Landforms Activity Book* (grades 2–6) shows how to use everyday materials to create landforms in the classroom and introduces kids to the scientific method of inquiry. *Plants Activity Book* (grades 2–6) includes step-by-step directions for creating projects that teach plant facts and that help kids learn to relate scientific concepts to their everyday world.

Submissions and Payment

Guidelines available. Query with outline and sample pages. Accepts photocopies and computer printouts. SASE. Responds in 4–5 months. Publication in 1 year. Flat fee.

Editor's Comments

We take great pride in the development of our products. Our goal is to make learning an enjoyable experience for kids in preschool through eighth grade. If you're an educator with a creative idea for a book or resource that supports the curriculum, send us your query. We welcome products designed for all levels of learning abilities.

Eerdmans Books for Young Readers

255 Jefferson Avenue SE
Grand Rapids, MI 49503

Editor-in-Chief: Judy Zylstra

Publisher's Interests
The picture books, middle-grade, and young adult titles by
Eerdmans Books for Young Readers are designed to nurture
faith in God and to help young readers explore the joys—as
well as the challenges—of life in God's world.
Website: www.eerdmans.com/youngreaders

Freelance Potential
Published 12–16 titles in 2005: 5 were developed from
unsolicited submissions, 10 were by agented authors, and 2
were reprint/licensed properties. Of the 15 titles, 2 were by
unpublished writers and 7 were by authors who were new to
the publishing house. Receives 1,000 queries, 6,000 unsolicited mss yearly.

- **Fiction:** Published 2 early picture books, 0–4 years; 4 easy-to-
  read books, 4–7 years; 6 story picture books, 4–10 years; 2
  middle-grade books 8–12 years; and young adult books,
  12–18 years. Genres include multicultural and religious fiction.
  Also publishes retellings of classic tales.
- **Nonfiction:** Publishes early picture books, 0–4 years; and middle-grade books, 8–12 years. Also publishes biographies.
- **Representative Titles:** *Circles of Hope* by Karen Lynn
  Williams (4 and up) tells the story of a young boy who plants a
  tree for his new baby sister. *The Beautiful World that God
  Made* by Rhonda Gowler Greene (3–8) answers the question of
  how the world began.

Submissions and Payment
Guidelines available. Send complete ms for picture books.
Query with 3–4 sample chapters for longer works. Accepts
photocopies and computer printouts. SASE. Responds in 3–4
months. Publication period varies. Royalty.

Editor's Comments
We are looking to publish titles that are not overly religious
for the general school market.

Egmont Books Ltd.

239 Kensington High Street
London W8 6SA
United Kingdom

Submissions: Jo Spooner

Publisher's Interests

A publisher of books for children, Egmont offers a range of titles from board books for toddlers to novels and nonfiction on subjects of interest to teens.
Website: www.egmont.co.uk

Freelance Potential

Published 70 titles in 2005: most were by agented authors.

- **Fiction:** Publishes concept books, toddler books, and early picture books, 0–4 years; easy-to-read books, 4–7 years; story picture books, 4–10 years; chapter books, 5–10 years; middle-grade books, 8–12 years; and young adult novels, 12–18 years. Genres include adventure; drama; fairy tales; fantasy; mystery; horror; humor; multicultural, inspirational, and historical fiction; and stories about nature and the environment. Also publishes activity, novelty, and board books.
- **Nonfiction:** Publishes concept books, toddler books, and early picture books, 0–4 years; easy-to-read books, 4–7 years; story picture books, 4–10 years; chapter books, 5–10 years; middle-grade books, 8–12 years; and young adult books, 12–18 years. Topics include history and humor. Also publishes activity, novelty, and board books.
- **Representative Titles:** *Mr. Wolf's Nursery Time* by Colin Hawkins (1–10 years) follows Mr. Wolf through the day as he meets a medley of nursery rhyme characters. *The Flowing Queen* by Kai Meyer (8–10 years) is a fantasy set in Venice, a city besieged by the armies of a revived Egyptian Pharaoh.

Submissions and Payment

Guidelines available. Query with outline/synopsis and 2 sample chapters. Accepts photocopies. SAE/IRC. Response time and payment policy vary.

Editor's Comments

Writers are encouraged to submit novelty books that feature innovative formats. We want to entice children to explore the written word by offering them books they'll enjoy.

Eldridge Publishing

P.O. Box 14367
Tallahasse, FL 32317

Editor: Susan Shore

Publisher's Interests

Established nearly one hundred years ago, Eldridge Publishing offers theatrical material, including plays, skits, and musicals, for junior high and high school students.
Website: www.histage.com; www.95church.com

Freelance Potential

Published 35 titles in 2005: most were developed from unsolicited submissions, 3 were by agented authors, and 3 were reprint/licensed properties. Of the 35 titles, most were by unpublished writers and 7 were by authors who were new to the publishing house. Receives 50–60 queries, 500 unsolicited mss yearly.

- **Fiction:** Publishes full-length plays, skits, and musicals; grades 6–12. Genres include contemporary and classical drama, humor, folktales, melodrama, Westerns, and Bible stories. Also publishes plays about holidays and adult drama for community theater.
- **Representative Titles:** *The Million-Heirs* by Delmar Burkitt (YA) is a play about three unusual requests made of his children by their millionarie father. *Hercules* by Craig Sodaro (YA) is a humorous, modern version of the Greek classic.

Submissions and Payment

Send complete ms stating play length and age ranges for actors and audience. Include cassette and sample score with musical submissions. Accepts photocopies, computer printout, and simultaneous submissions if identified. SASE. Responds in 2 months. Publication in 6–12 months. Royalty, varies. Flat fee for religious plays.

Editor's Comments

Please send plays and theatrical works that have been previously performed. We focus on material that requires the actors be junior high age and up. We are always looking for religious holiday plays.

Encore Performance Publishing

Suite 250
2181 West California Avenue
Salt Lake City, UT 84104

President: Michael Perry

Publisher's Interests
The plays that appear in this publisher's catalogue focus on the family and are written to uplift, edify, and entertain. The plays, many of which highlight moral issues, are aimed at audiences of all ages. School and church groups and community and professional theaters turn to Encore Performance Publishing in search of appropriate material.
Website: www.encoreplay.com

Freelance Potential
Published 10–20 titles (11–16 juvenile) in 2005: 2 were by agented authors. Receives 100+ queries yearly.

- **Fiction:** Publishes easy-to-read books, 4–7 years; middle-grade books, 8–12 years; and young adult books, 12–18 years. Features dramas with multicultural, religious, and ethnic themes, as well as educational, bilingual, and humorous plays.
- **Nonfiction:** Publishes books about theater arts for all ages. Topics include acting, auditions, improvisation, stage management, set design, lighting, and makeup.
- **Representative Titles:** *The Old Curiosity Shop* by Gawen Robinson & Stephen Robertson is a musical composed in the tradition of *Phantom of the Opera*. *Notre Dame* by Gawen Robinson & Stephen Robertson is a musical based on the Victor Hugo novel about two babies swapped at birth in 15th-century Paris.

Submissions and Payment
Guidelines available. Query with résumé, synopsis, and production history. Accepts photocopies and computer printouts. SASE. Responds in 2 weeks. Publication in 2 months. Royalty, 50% performance, 10% book.

Editor's Comments
One of our priorities is to choose plays that show how the consequences of our actions affect not only our own lives, but the lives of those around us.

Enslow Publishers, Inc.

Box 398
40 Industrial Road
Berkeley Heights, NJ 07922-0398

Vice President: Brian Enslow

Publisher's Interests

Quality nonfiction books for students and young adults that support the school curriculum comprise Enslow's list. Multicultural titles, biographies, history, health, and science are featured topics.
Website: www.enslow.com

Freelance Potential

Published 175 titles (50 juvenile) in 2005: 25 were developed from unsolicited submissions. Of the 175 titles, 25 were by unpublished writers and 60 were by authors who were new to the publishing house. Receives 1,000 queries each year.

- **Nonfiction:** Published 50 easy-to-read books, 4–7 years; 100 middle-grade books, 8–12 years; and 25 young adult books, 12–18 years. Topics include the environment, science, multicultural and ethnic subjects, history, and social issues.
- **Representative Titles:** *Exploring Ancient Rome* by Elaine Landau (grades 3–4) takes readers on a whirlwind tour of ancient Rome from the aqueducts to the Colosseum. *A Student's Guide to William Shakespeare* by Walt Mittelstaet (grades 8+) examines the life and major works of this literary genius.

Submissions and Payment

Guidelines available. Query with outline, table of contents, sample chapter, and market analysis. Accepts photocopies and computer printouts. SASE. Responds in 1–6 months. Publication in 1 year. Royalty; advance. Flat fee.

Editor's Comments

Submit biographies of influential people both historical and contemporary. We want to see the lives and works of scientists and inventors. We're also looking for American history topics; literary criticism; and multicultural themes. Writers need to submit text that is simple, clear, and interesting.

Evan-Moor Educational Publishers

18 Lower Ragsdale Drive
Monterey, CA 93940

Senior Editor: Marilyn Evans

Publisher's Interests
The focus of this publisher is helping children learn. Its supplemental educational materials, that meet core curriculum standards, has been serving the needs of teachers and of students in pre-kindergarten through grade six for over twenty-five years.
Website: www.evan-moor.com

Freelance Potential
Published 65 titles in 2005. Of the 65 titles, 5 were by authors who were new to the publishing house. Receives 350 queries, 250 unsolicited mss yearly.

- **Nonfiction:** Publishes classroom and homeschooling resources, teaching materials, and activity books, pre-K–grade 6. Topics include social studies, mathematics, science, technology, reading, writing, language arts, early learning, arts and crafts, and thematic units.
- **Representative Titles:** *Read & Understand Poetry* (teachers) is a series of four books, each containing 25 poems, two activity sheets, and a teacher lesson plan. *U.S. Facts & Fun* (grades 1–6) presents factual stories and fun activities to broaden students' knowledge of the United States.

Submissions and Payment
Guidelines available at website. Query with outline, sample pages, and résumé; or send complete ms. Accepts photocopies, computer printouts, and simultaneous submissions if identified. SASE. Responds in 3 months. Publication in 1–2 years. Flat fee.

Editor's Comments
Materials for learning the English language in classroom settings are what we are most interested in. We are also open to submissions of educational activities in all subjects for students in pre-kindergarten. We do not publish fiction, music materials, or books in languages other than English.

Facts On File

17th Floor
132 West 31st Street
New York, NY 10001

Editorial Director: Laurie Likoff
Senior Editor, Young Adult: Nicole Bowen

Publisher's Interests

This reference publisher is known for its strength in American history. It offers curriculum-based books for children ages nine and up. Subjects include math, science, social studies, history, language, and literature. It markets its titles to schools, libraries, and educational bookstores.
Website: www.factsonfile.com

Freelance Potential

Published 300 titles in 2005: 50 were by agented authors. Of the 300 titles, 5 were by authors who were new to the publishing house. Receives 150 queries yearly.

- **Nonfiction:** Publishes chapter books, 5–10 years; middle-grade books, 8–12 years; and young adult books, 12–18 years. Topics include history, social issues, current affairs, politics, multicultural subjects, mathematics, science, and the environment.
- **Representative Titles:** *The Thirteen Colonies Set* (grades 3–6) investigates the formation of the founding colonies of the United States. *The History of Mathematics Set* (grades 6+) focuses on different areas of math by thoroughly examining the processes, notable events, and key individuals who played a role in developing the particular mathematical area.

Submissions and Payment

Query with outline, sample chapter, description of audience, competitive titles, and marketing ideas. Accepts photocopies, computer printouts, and simultaneous submissions if identified. SASE. Responds in 2 months. Publication in 1 year. Royalty; advance.

Editor's Comments

We're looking for comprehensive, authoritative, and easy-to-use reference books. You may submit a proposal that fits with an existing series, or is an original work. Writers must be experts or have extensive research experience to draw upon.

Fairview Press

2450 Riverside Avenue
Minneapolis, MN 55454

Submissions: Lane Stiles or Stephanie Billecke

Publisher's Interests
This publishing house is a division of Fairview Health Services, a regional health care provider affiliated with the University of Minnesota. It produces books that deal with the physical, emotional, and spiritual health of children, adults, and seniors.
Website: www.fairview.org

Freelance Potential
Published 4 titles (2 juvenile) in 2005: 1 was developed from an unsolicited submission. Receives 240–360 queries each year.

- **Nonfiction:** Publishes middle-grade books, 8–12 years; and young adult books, 12–18 years. Topics include grief and bereavement, aging and seniors, caregiving, health, medicine, and patient education.
- **Representative Titles:** *Beyond the Rainbow* by Marge Eaton Heegaard is a workbook for children who are in the advanced stages of serious illnesses. *Help Me Say Goodbye* by Janis Silverman addresses the fears kids may have when someone close to them dies and includes activities for helping them through the stages of grief.

Submissions and Payment
Guidelines and catalogue available at website. Query with outline, sample chapter, and marketing plan. Accepts photocopies and computer printouts. SASE. Response time and publication period vary. Contracts for payment are negotiated on a case-by-case basis.

Editor's Comments
We do not publish fiction, and although our audiences include children, teens, and adults, we are not acquiring children's picture books at this time. We will consider proposals for any of the topics listed above and on other topics of broad interest to families.

Faith Kidz

4050 Lee Vance View
Colorado Springs, CO 80918

Editorial Assistant

Publisher's Interests

This division of Cook Communications Ministries produces books, toys, and games designed to give Christian parents age-appropriate tools to excel as spiritual mentors to their children. Its titles range from board books for babies to stories and nonfiction for young readers up to the age of 12.
Website: www.cookministries.com/faithkidz

Freelance Potential

Published 120 titles (31 juvenile) in 2005. Of the 120 titles, 5 were by authors who were new to the publishing house. Receives 1,000+ queries yearly.

- **Fiction:** Publishes concept books and toddler books, 0–4 years; easy-to-read books, 4–7 years; chapter books, 5–10 years; and middle-grade books, 8–12 years. Genres include religious and inspirational fiction.
- **Nonfiction:** Publishes easy-to-read books, 4–7 years; chapter books, 5–10 years; and middle-grade books, 8–12 years. Topics include Christianity, the Bible, and life skills.
- **Representative Titles:** *Humble Bee* by Matt Whitlock teaches kids about the virtue of humility. *That's Not All I Found in the City* by Sue Buchanan & Lynn Hodges is a story that tells how a young girl learned many things about New York City, the Easter Parade, and the real meaning of Easter.

Submissions and Payment

Query with writing credits and market analysis of comparative products. Accepts photocopies and computer printouts. SASE. Response time and publication period vary. All books are written on a work-for-hire basis.

Editor's Comments

Our writers' guidelines change with our changing needs, and we're advising all prospective authors to visit our website for up-to-date contact information and submission procedures. We're reviewing only curriculum proposals at this time.

Falcon Publishing

246 Goose Lane
P.O. Box 480
Guilford, CT 06437

Acquisitions Editor

Publisher's Interests
This small publisher is an imprint of Globe Pequot Press, a regional publisher specializing in New England history, biography, and travel. Falcon Publishing features a list of titles for children and adults on regional outdoor recreation and local history.
Website: www.globepequot.com

Freelance Potential
Published 300 titles (15 juvenile) in 2005: 3 were developed from unsolicited submissions, and 30 were by agented authors. Receives 1,000 queries yearly.

- **Nonfiction:** Publishes chapter books, 5–10 years; middle-grade titles, 8–12 years; and young adult books, 12–18 years. Topics include regional subjects, natural history, nature, the environment, and history.
- **Representative Titles:** *A House for Wanda Wood Duck* by Patricia Barnes-Svarney (4–8 years) is a charming tale of discovery that includes an important lesson in conservation; includes instruction for building a wooden nest box. *Liberty's Children* by Scotti McAuliff Cohn compiles behind-the-scenes stories of American children who displayed courage, devotion, and wisdom during the American colonies' fight for freedom.

Submissions and Payment
Guidelines available. Query with synopsis, table of contents, and sample chapter. Accepts photocopies and computer printouts. SASE. Responds in 3 months. Publication in 1 year. Royalty.

Editor's Comments
The core of our offerings continues to include outdoor recreation titles, including hiking, biking, paddling, and wildlife viewing. Titles for children should introduce them to to idea of natural history and conservation with out preaching. Be sure to review our guidelines before querying.

Farrar, Straus & Giroux

19 Union Square West
New York, NY 10003

Children's Editorial Department

Publisher's Interests

Focusing on children ages three to thirteen, this publisher offers fantasy, humor, and contemporary fiction titles, as well as some nonfiction.

Website: www.fsgkidsbooks.com

Freelance Potential

Published 80 titles in 2005: 5 were developed from unsolicited submissions, 35 were by agented authors, and 5 were reprint/licensed properties. Of the 80 titles, 5 were by unpublished writers. Receives 1,000 queries, 6,000 unsolicited mss yearly.

- **Fiction:** Publishes easy-to-read books, 4–7 years; story picture books, 3–10 years; chapter books, 6–10 years; middle-grade novels, 8–12 years; and young adult books, 12–18 years. Genres include fantasy, humor, and contemporary fiction.
- **Nonfiction:** Publishes story picture books, 4–10 years; middle-grade books, 8–12 years; and young adult books, 12–18 years. Topics include history, science, and nature.
- **Representative Titles:** *Boy2Girl* by Terence Blacker (YA) is the story of an American boy in London who takes on the challenge of going to school posing as a girl. *Five Creatures* by Emily Jenkins (3–6 years) is a picture book that depicts scenes in a happy household of three humans and two cats.

Submissions and Payment

Guidelines available. Query for mss longer than 20 pages; or send complete ms for shorter works. Accepts photocopies, computer printouts, and simultaneous submissions if identified. SASE. Responds in 2–3 months. Publication in 18–36 months. Royalty, 3–10% of list price.

Editor's Comments

We are seeking humorous children's stories. The length of a story should be based on the age of the intended audience; our house has no fixed lengths.

Frederick Fell Publishers, Inc.

Suite 305
2131 Hollywood Boulevard
Hollywood, FL 33020

Publisher: Donald L. Lessne

Publisher's Interests
With over 60 years in publishing, Frederick Fell Publishers produces a list of books on health and how-to subjects, parenting and child care, and inspirational and religious fiction for young adults.
Website: www.fellpub.com

Freelance Potential
Published 24 titles in 2005: 22 were developed from unsolicited submissions and 2 were by agented authors. Of the 24 titles, 8 were by unpublished writers and 2 were by authors who were new to the publishing house. Receives 4,000 queries, 3,900 unsolicited mss yearly.

- **Fiction:** Publishes young adult books, 12–18 years. Genres include inspirational and religious fiction.
- **Nonfiction:** Publishes young adult books, 12–18 years. Topics include spirituality and health. Features how-to and self-help titles. Also publishes biographies and books about parenting, as well as child care, business, science, and entertainment for adults.
- **Representative Titles:** *The Tiniest Acorn: A Story to Grow By* by Marsha T. Danzig (YA) is the story of a tiny acorn who comes to realize that all things are possible, no matter what your size. *Help Your Child Excel in Math* by Margaret Berge & Philip Gibbons (parents) presents games and puzzles to make learning math more enjoyable.

Submissions and Payment
Guidelines available. Query with résumé, table of contents, and marketing plan. Accepts photocopies and simultaneous submissions if identified. SASE. Responds in 1 month. Publication in 9–12 months. Royalty.

Editor's Comments
Submissions on spiritual themes for young adults are always welcome. If you have a unique concept, we'd like to see it.

Ferguson Publishing

17th Floor
132 West 31st Street
New York, NY 10001

Editorial Director: Laurie Likoff

Publisher's Interests
For over 60 years, this imprint of Facts on File has been a source for career education resources for students in middle-school through college. Materials on financial aid and occupational outlooks are also included in their catalogue.
Website: www.fergpubco.com/www.factsonfile.com

Freelance Potential
Published 50–60 titles in 2005: 1 was developed from an unsolicited submission and 25 were by agented authors. Of the 50–60 titles, 1 was by an unpublished writer and 5 were by authors who were new to the publishing house. Receives 25–30 queries, 10 unsolicited mss yearly.

- **Nonfiction:** Published 20–30 middle-grade books, 8–12 years; and 20–30 young adult books, 12–18 years. Topics include college planning, career awareness, and job training. Also publishes development titles and general reference books.
- **Representative Titles:** *What Can I Do Now?* (grades 6–12) helps students take a proactive approach to career exploration and preparation. *College Majors and Careers* (grades 9+) provides updated information that is crucial to making decisions about academic and career opportunities.

Submissions and Payment
Guidelines available at website. Query with table of contents; or send complete ms with proposal. Accepts photocopies, computer printouts, email submissions to editorial@factsonfile.com, and simultaneous submissions if identified. SASE. Responds in 3–6 months. Publication period varies. Work-for-hire and some royalty assignments.

Editor's Comments
We are looking for material on career skills and career exploration for grades 6–12. We expect our authors to have a college degree, professional degree, or doctorate in their area of expertise or be familiar with the subject on which they write.

Finney Company

3943 Meadowbrook Road
Minneapolis, MN 55426

President: Alan E. Krysan

Publisher's Interests
This publisher specializes in material for career development, and focuses on books, monographs, videos, and educational resources to meet the needs of today's career education and development programs.
Website: www.finney-hobar.com

Freelance Potential
Published 4 titles in 2005: 3 were developed from unsolicited
submissions, 1 was a reprint/licensed property. Of the 4
titles, 1 was by an unpublished writer and 3 were by authors
who were new to the publishing house. Receives 100
queries, 80 unsolicited mss yearly.

- **Nonfiction:** Published 1 middle-grade title, 8–12 years; and 3
  young adult books, 12–18 years. Also publishes resource
  materials for guidance counselors, coloring books for young
  children, and career-oriented posters. Topics include occupational guidance, careers, technical education, counseling, port-
  folios, skills development, applying for employment, résumé
  writing, and interpersonal skills.
- **Representative Titles:** *The Global Citizen* guides readers
  through the ins and outs of living and working in a foreign
  country. *Planning My Career* (young adult) stresses the importance of career development and school-to-work transitions.

Submissions and Payment
Guidelines available at website. Query or send complete ms.
SASE. Response time varies. Publication period varies. Royalty,
10% of net.

Editor's Comments
We believe career development is a lifelong process that
should start in elementary school and continue throughout
life. We would like to see manuscripts for books and monographs that address contemporary career choices.

Flashlight Press

3709 13th Avenue
Brooklyn, NY 11218

Editor: Shari Dash Greenspan

Publisher's Interests
This publisher of picture story books targets readers ages four to ten years old. The books it produces explore and illuminate the touching and humorous moments of family situations and social interactions.
Website: www.flashlightpress.com

Freelance Potential
Published 2 titles in 2005: both were developed from unsolicited submissions. Receives 1,200 queries yearly.

- **Fiction:** Publishes easy-to-read books, 4–7 years; and story picture books, 4–10 years. Features contemporary fiction with universal themes.
- **Nonfiction:** Publishes easy-to-read books, 4–7 years; and story picture books, 4–10 years. Topics include family and social issues.
- **Representative Titles:** *Alley Oops* by Janice Levy (5–9 years) relates the painful and embarrassing aftermath of bullying from the perspective of the bully. *Carla's Sandwich* by Debbie Herman (4–8 years) is the story of a girl who is shunned by her classmates for bringing "weird" sandwiches to school, but her strong sense of individuality eventually wins them over.

Submissions and Payment
Guidelines available at website. Query or send complete ms. Accepts email (queries only) to editor@flashlightpress.com. SASE. Responds to queries in 1–2 weeks, to mss in 3–4 months. Publication period and payment policy vary.

Editor's Comments
Submissions of illustrated picture books are welcome. Stories should deal with family life or with social problems such as intolerance, playground bullies, and aggressive behavior. We seek books that help kids take a look at their own actions and reactions, and books that teach them the values of acceptance, tolerance, and the importance of individuality.

Floris Books

15 Harrison Gardens
Edinburgh
EH11 1SH
Scotland, UK

Editor: Gail Winskill

Publisher's Interests

Floris Books is a specialty publisher focusing on Scottish topics
and subject matter. Its young fiction imprint is Kelpies, whose
audience is comprised of 7- to 12-year-old readers.
Website: www.florisbooks.co.uk

Freelance Potential

Published 12 titles (11 juvenile) in 2005: 1 was developed
from an unsolicited submission and 9 were by agented
authors. Of the 12 titles, 1 was by an unpublished writer and
1 was by an author who was new to the publishing house.
Receives 150 unsolicited mss yearly.

- **Fiction:** Published 4 story picture books, 4–10 years;
  6 middle-grade books, 8–12 years; and 2 young adult books,
  12–18 years. Genres include contemporary, multicultural, and
  regional fiction; drama; and fantasy.
- **Representative Titles:** *In the Land of Elves* by Daniela
  Drescher (5–8 years) is the story about a clan of elves who
  play through the seasons. *Goldie at the Farm* by Martha Sand-
  wall-Bergstrom (5–8 years) tells the tale of Goldie, a young girl
  working on a farm as a maid. *Making Flower Children* by
  Sybille Adolphi is a craft book with simple instructions on how
  to make flower figures.

Submissions and Payment

Guidelines available. Query or send complete ms. Agented
submissions improve chance of acceptance Does not accept
nonfiction. Accepts photocopies. SAE/IRC. Responds to
queries in 1 week; to mss in 3 months. Publication in 18
months. Royalty.

Editor's Comments

We are focusing on contemporary situations and characters
with which today's children can relate. Although we focus on
Scottish subject matter, we are interested in material that
will be appreciated by a wide audience.

Focus on the Family Book Development

8765 Explorer Drive
Colorado Springs, CO 80920

Editorial Assistant

Publisher's Interests
Focus on the Family is a nonprofit organization dedicated to the preservation of the home. All of its titles reflect Christian values and deal specifically with family issues.
Website: www.family.org

Freelance Potential
Published 40 titles (6 juvenile) in 2005: 36 were by agented authors.

- **Fiction:** Published 2 young adult books, 12–18 years. Fiction that deals with family issues and promotes traditional family values, for the time period of 1900 to present day only.
- **Nonfiction:** Published 4 young adult books, 12–18 years. Topics include family advice topics, including marriage and parenting, teen issues, encouragement for women, and topics for seniors.
- **Representative Titles:** *The DNA of Parent-Teen Relationships* by Gary Smalley & Greg Smalley, Ph.D. helps parents of teens forge a strong, lasting, and loving bond with their young adults. *Blue Genes* by Paul Meier, M.D. helps adults break free of the chemical imbalances that affect their moods, lives, and loved ones.

Submissions and Payment
Guidelines available. Query only through recognized agent. SASE. Response time varies. Publication in 1 year. Payment policy varies.

Editor's Comments
We have a narrow focus and do not publish outside of our mission. Our guidelines are very specific as to what we can publish and how to submit work. All our products have an evangelical Christian slant. Please note that we no longer accept unsolicited manuscripts or queries. Please submit through a recognized agent or an editorial service such as The Writer's Edge, www.WritersEdgeService.com.

Forest House Publishing Company

P.O. Box 13350
Chandler, AZ 85248

President: Dianne Spahr

Publisher's Interests
Focusing on school and library markets, this publisher offers educational fiction and nonfiction books, as well as bilingual and Spanish titles.
Website: www.forest-house.com

Freelance Potential
Published 12 titles (6 juvenile) in 2005. Receives 100 queries yearly.

- **Fiction:** Publishes concept books, toddler books, and early picture books, 0–4 years; easy-to-read books, 4–7 years; story picture books, 4–10 years; chapter books, 5–10 years; and middle-grade titles, 8–12 years. Genres include contemporary and multicultural fiction, fairy tales, and adventure stories.
- **Nonfiction:** Publishes easy-to-read books, 4–7 years; and chapter books, 5–10 years. Topics include nature, animals, arts and crafts, special education, sigh language, history, the environment, and ethnic and multicultural issues.
- **Representative Titles:** *The Seventh Door* by Norman Leach (grades K–3) teaches a valuable lesson thanks to seven sisters and seven rocks. *The Amazing Adventures of Abiola* by Jeffrey & Debra Dean (grades 4–6) highlights some of the contributions African Americans have made to the world.

Submissions and Payment
Query with résumé. No unsolicited mss. Accepts photocopies, computer printouts, and faxes to 480-802-1957. Availabilty of artwork improves chance of acceptance. SASE. Responds in 6 months. Publication in 1 year. Royalty; advance. Flat fee.

Editor's Comments
We do not accept unsolicited manuscripts; if we are interested in your query, we will let you know. We are seeking educational material for all reading levels from kindergarden through grade six. Books on crafts are also needed.

Formac Publishing Company, Ltd.

5502 Atlantic Street
Halifax, Nova Scotia B3H 1G4
Canada

Senior Editor: Elizabeth Eve

Publisher's Interests
Featuring the culture, people, and places of Canada, the fiction and nonfiction books by this publisher are read by children and young adults.
Website: www.formac.ca

Freelance Potential
Published 20 titles (10 juvenile) in 2005: 4 reprint/licensed properties. Of the 20 titles, 1 was by an unpublished writer and 1 was by an author who was new to the publishing house. Receives 80 queries yearly.

- **Fiction:** Publishes easy-to-read books, 4–7 years; chapter books, 5–10 years; and middle-grade titles, 8–12 years. Genres include mystery, suspense, fantasy, adventure, humor, historical fiction, and sports stories.
- **Nonfiction:** Published middle-grade titles, 8–12 years. Topics include regional, multicultural, and ethnic subjects; sports; nature; and the environment.
- **Representative Titles:** *At Risk* by Jacqueline Guest (YA) is an edgy and suspenseful novel that explores contemporary topics that affect teens in today's society. *Dear Old Dumpling* by Gilles Gauthier is the story about the mixed feelings of loss and hope experienced by children of single-parent families, and about the love between a boy and his dog.

Submissions and Payment
Guidelines available at website. Query with résumé, outline, and sample chapters. No unsolicited mss. Accepts photocopies, computer printouts, and simultaneous submissions if identified. SAE/IRC. Responds in 1–12 months. Publication in 1–2 years. Royalty.

Editor's Comments
This year, we continue to need historical fiction books for middle-grade and young adults. All material should relate to Canadian history and culture.

Forward Movement Publications

2nd Floor
300 West Fourth Street
Cincinnati, OH 45202

Submissions Editor: Edward S. Gleason

Publisher's Interests
Publishing fiction and nonfiction for middle-grade and young
adult readers, this religious publisher, an official agency of
the Episcopal church, specializes in books and pamphlets
related to the life of the church.
Website: www.forwardmovement.org

Freelance Potential
Published 10 titles in 2005: 1 was developed from an unsolicited submission and 2 were reprint/licensed properties. Of
the 10 titles, 5 were by unpublished writers and 5 were by
authors new to the publishing house. Receives 500 queries
each year.

- **Fiction:** Publishes middle-grade books, 8–12 years; and young
  adult books, 12–18 years. Features contemporary fiction with
  Christian themes.
- **Nonfiction:** Publishes middle-grade books, 8–12 years; and
  young adult books, 12–18 years. Topics include meditation,
  spirituality, church history, and contemporary issues such as
  drug abuse and AIDS.
- **Representative Titles:** *Anglican Learning Centres—All Saints* by
  Patricia Bays (teachers) shows how to set up a Sunday school
  learning center for children ages 6–12. *Can't Talk to Your Parents?* by Ashley Rooney (YA) explores the challenges faced by
  young people and the relevance of their Christian faith.

Submissions and Payment
Guidelines, catalogue, and sample pamphlet available
($1.65 postage; no SASE). Query with sample chapters.
Accepts photocopies and computer printouts. SASE.
Responds in 1 month. Publication period varies. Flat fee.

Editor's Comments
There is a special need for 4–8 page pamphlets that Sunday
school teachers can use in the classroom. Read our catalogue
to find out what topics we have already covered.

Frances Foster Books

Farrar, Straus & Giroux
19 Union Square West
New York, NY 10003

Children's Editorial Department

Publisher's Interests

Since 1996, this imprint of Farrar, Straus & Giroux offers a select list of quality fiction and some nonfiction titles for children to young adults.
Website: www.fsgkidsbooks.com

Freelance Potential

Published 20 titles in 2005: 2 were developed from unsolicited submissions and 10 were by agented authors. Of the 20 titles, 5 were by authors who were new to the publishing house. Receives 75–100 queries, 200 unsolicited mss yearly.

- **Fiction:** Published 3 early picture books, 0–4 years; 10 story picture books, 4–10 years; 2 chapter books, 5–10 years; 10 middle-grade books, 8–12 years; and 10 young adult books, 12–18 years. Genres include contemporary, historical, and ethnic fiction; fantasy, adventure, and drama.
- **Nonfiction:** Published 2 story picture books, 4–10 years; and 2 young adult books, 12–18 years. Genre is history.
- **Representative Titles:** *Peach Heaven* by Yangsook Choi (4–8 years) is the tale of a Korean girl who dreams of a peach orchard where she can play and eat as much of the fruit as she wishes. *Magic By the Book* by Nina Bernstein (10+ years) details what happens to two sisters who choose a book with magical powers that takes them away to adventures.

Submissions and Payment

Guidelines available. Query with 3 sample chapters and synopsis for novels. Send complete ms for picture books. Accepts photocopies, computer printouts, and simultaneous submissions if identified. SASE. Responds in 3+ months. Publication in 2+ years. Royalty; advance.

Editor's Comments

We want to see strong young adult literature with well-defined characters, believable plots, and good writing.

Free Spirit Publishing

Suite 200
217 5th Avenue North
Minneapolis, MN 55401–1299

Acquisitions Editor: Douglas J. Fehlen

Publisher's Interests

High-quality nonfiction books in the areas of self-help for
children and teens, enrichment activities for teachers and
youth workers, and successful parenting and teaching strategies, are the main focus of this publisher.
Website: www.freespirit.com

Freelance Potential

Published 24 titles (15 juvenile) in 2005: 12 were developed
from unsolicited submissions and 2 were by agented
authors. Receives 2,500 queries yearly.

- **Nonfiction:** Published 1 toddler book, 0–4 years; 6 easy-to-
  read books, 4–7 years; 8 middle-grade books, 8–12 years;
  and 4 young adult books, 12–18 years. Topics include family
  and social issues, stress management, character building, relationships, creativity, self awareness, and self-esteem. Also publishes titles on learning disorders, psychology, and gifted and
  talented education.
- **Representative Titles:** *Too Stressed to Think?* by Annie Fox,
  M.Ed., and Ruth Kirschner (12+ years) is a teen guide to staying
  sane when life makes you crazy. *How to Help Your Child with
  Homework* by Jeanne Shay Schumm, Ph.D. (parents) guides
  parents in encouraging good study habits and ending the
  homework wars.

Submissions and Payment

Guidelines available. Query with résumé, outline, and 2 sample
chapters. Accepts photocopies and computer printouts.
Responds in 1–4 months. Publication in 1–3 years. Royalty;
advance.

Editor's Comments

We are looking for strong proposals in the following areas:
learning differences, bullying, conflict resolution, manners,
gender issues, health, social skills, and character education.
We do not publish fiction, picture books, or biographies.

Samuel French, Inc.

45 West 25th Street
New York, NY 10010

Editor: Lawrence Harbison

Publisher's Interests
Serving the theatrical community since 1830, Samuel French offers a variety of plays from Broadway hits and intimate revues to productions suitable for children and teens. It also publishes resource materials and books for theater educators and students.
Website: www.samuelfrench.com

Freelance Potential
Published 60–70 titles in 2005: 20 were developed from unsolicited submissions, 40+ were by agented authors. Receives 1,000 unsolicited mss yearly.

- **Fiction:** Publishes full-length and one-act plays, monologues, readings, and anthologies for theater groups of all ages. Genres include musicals, operettas, religious and holiday plays, and Shakespearean drama.
- **Nonfiction:** Publishes books and resource materials for theater teachers and directors. Topics include acting methods, directing, stage design, lighting, theater management, auditions, comedy, improvisations, and film production.
- **Representative Titles:** *The Fisherman and His Wife* by Ruth Newton is an adaptation of the beloved Grimm tale about a magic fish with the power to grant wishes. *Jack and the Giant* by Ruth Newton is a comic version of the classic fairy tale with audience participation.

Submissions and Payment
Guidelines available. Query or send complete ms. Accepts photocopies. SASE. Responds to queries in 1 week; to mss in 2–3 months. Publication in 1 year. Payment policy varies.

Editor's Comments
We continue to need original plays for production groups of varying abilities. Monologues and audition material that express the concerns of today's youth are of interest. We are not considering adaptations of fables or fairy tales at this time.

Front Street

862 Haywood Road
Asheville, NC 28806

Editor: Joy Neaves

Publisher's Interests

This independent publisher specializes in books for children
and young adults. Its mission is to expose young readers to
the best literature available from various countries, cultures,
and languages.
Website: www.frontstreetbooks.com

Freelance Potential

Published 24 titles in 2005. Receives 1,000 queries, 3,000
unsolicited mss yearly.

- **Fiction:** Published 2 story picture books, 4–10 years; 10 middle-
  grade books, 8–12 years; and 8 young adult books, 12–18
  years. Genres include humor; adventure; fantasy; and multicultural, historical, contemporary, and science fiction.
- **Nonfiction:** Publishes young adult books, 12–18 years. Also
  publishes novelty books, educational titles, and poetry.
- **Representative Titles:** *The Lace Dowry* by Andrea Cheng
  (10+ years) is a story of an overbearing mother and a determined teen. *Kalpana's Dream* by Judith Clarke (10+ years)
  tells of a high school English class who must write an essay
  describing who they are.

Submissions and Payment

Guidelines available at website. No longer accepting unsolicited picture book mss. Query with sample chapter for nonfiction. Send complete ms for fiction under 100 pages, or
2 sample chapters for longer works. Accepts photocopies
and computer printouts, but discourages simultaneous submissions. SASE. Responds in 3 months. Publication in 12–18
months. Royalty; advance.

Editor's Comments

Our middle-grade chapter books address the settings and
activities of school-age children while our YA fiction deals
with children in crisis or at risk, and offers hope. We believe
in new voices; half our authors are previously unpublished.

Fulcrum Publishing

Suite 300
16100 Table Mountain Parkway
Golden, CO 80403-1672

Submissions Editor: T.J. Baker

Publisher's Interests

Fulcrum Publishing offers an eclectic mix of titles for teachers, librarians, parents, and children in elementary and middle school. Its program focuses on educational titles that offer insight into various cultures.
Website: www.fulcrum-books.com

Freelance Potential

Published 30 titles (3 juvenile) in 2005: 2 were by agented authors. Receives 250 queries, 1,500 unsolicited mss yearly.

- **Nonfiction:** Publishes story picture books, 4–10 years; chapter books, 5–10 years; middle-grade books, 8–12 years. Topics include Native American culture, outdoor activities, history, the American West, natural history, and the environment. Also publishes educational activity books for educators and parents.
- **Representative Titles:** *Native American Games and Stories* by James Bruchac & Joseph Bruchac (8+ years) is full of educational games based on the Native American concept that you can learn while you play. *Ignacio's Chair* by Gloria Evangelista (6–12 years) takes readers on a journey through the ages. *Cucumber Soup* (4–8 years) by Vickie Leigh Krudwig teaches children about different types of insects.

Submissions and Payment

Guidelines available. Query or send sample chapter with résumé and competition analysis. Accepts photocopies, computer printouts, and simultaneous submissions if identified. SASE. Responds to queries in 1 month. Publication in 18–24 months. Royalty; advance.

Editor's Comments

In the coming year, we are interested in publishing well-researched nonfiction in the areas of the environment and multicultural issues. Please review our catalogue for an overview of the types of material we publish.

Laura Geringer Books

HarperCollins Children's Books
1350 Avenue of the Americas
New York, NY 10019

Editor: Laura Geringer

Publisher's Interests
Laura Geringer Books publishes picture books, I-Can-Read books, chapter books, and young adult novels. Its list includes exceptionally written titles that involve the reader and appeal to a child's imagination.
Website: www.harperchildrens.com

Freelance Potential
Published 12 titles (all juvenile) in 2005: all were by agented authors. Receives 500 queries yearly.

- **Fiction:** Published 2 easy-to-read books, 4–7 years; 6 story picture books, 4–10 years; 1 middle-grade title, 8–12 years; and 3 young adult books (12–18 years). Also publishes young adult novels, 12–18 years. Genres include contemporary, mystery, multicultural, and historical fiction; adventure; folklore; fantasy; humor; drama; and nature stories.
- **Representative Titles:** *Algernon Graeves Is Scary Enough* by Peter Bollinger (4–8 years) is a holiday tale about the scariest Halloween costume ever. *Saint Francis and the Wolf* by Richard Egielski (all ages) is a classic tale of love, friendship, and living together in harmony.

Submissions and Payment
Guidelines available. Query. Prefers submissions from agented authors. No unsolicited ms. Accepts photocopies. SASE. Responds in 2–10 weeks. Publication period varies; payment policy varies.

Editor's Comments
Because of the tremendous amount of manuscripts we receive, we are no longer accepting unsolicited manuscripts. We do, however, accept query letters and proposals. We look for ideas that are fresh, imaginative, and keep kids turning the pages. Excellent writing that involves the reader in a story that has appeal for children is essential.

Gibbs Smith, Publisher

1877 East Gentile Street
Layton, UT 84040

Submissions Editors: Madge Baird & Suzanne Taylor

Publisher's Interests

This small company is known for its collection of original titles for children, including titles that enrich and inspire readers of all ages.
Website: www.gibbs-smith.com

Freelance Potential

Published 80 titles (12 juvenile) in 2005: 3 were developed from unsolicited submissions, 4 were by agented authors, and 2 were reprint/licensed properties. Of the 80 titles, 5 were by unpublished writers and 30 were by authors who were new to the publishing house. Receives 800 queries, 2,500 unsolicited mss yearly.

- **Fiction:** Published 4 story picture books, 4–10 years. Also publishes easy-to-read books, 4–7 years. Genres include adventure, Westerns, humor, fantasy, and folktales. Also publishes animal, nature, and environmental stories.
- **Nonfiction:** Publishes activity books, 4–10 years. Topics include the outdoors, nature, crafts, and holidays.
- **Representative Titles:** *The Big Book of Boy Stuff* by Bart King (9–13 years) has all the important information boys need to know, including what to do if a bean gets stuck in your nose. *Children's Songbag* by Paul DuBois Jacobs & Jennifer Swender is a collection of 50 fun and easy songs, plus sheet music, fun facts, games, and activities.

Submissions and Payment

Guidelines available. Send complete ms for picture books. Query with outline and writing samples for nonfiction. Accepts photocopies, computer printouts, and simultaneous submissions if identified. SASE. Responds in 10–12 weeks. Publication in 1–2 years. Royalty; advance.

Editor's Comments

Activity books for children ages four to ten remain on our wish list, as well as Western stories.

Gifted Education Press

P.O. Box 1586
10201 Yuma Court
Manassas, VA 20108

Editor: Maurice D. Fisher

Publisher's Interests
Books to stimulate gifted students can be found in the catalogue of this educational publisher. In addition, it publishes a quarterly newsletter. Its target audience includes teachers, administrators, librarians, parents, and homeschoolers. Topics include philosophy and logic, social studies and the humanities, science, math, technology, and language arts.
Website: www.giftedpress.com

Freelance Potential
Published 5 titles in 2005: all were developed from unsolicited submissions. Of the 5 titles, 5 were by authors who were new to the publishing house. Receives 50 queries yearly.

- **Nonfiction:** Publishes middle-grade books, 8–12 years. Also publishes educational resources for teachers and parents working with gifted students, and school administrators running gifted-education programs.
- **Representative Titles:** *Humanities Education for the 21st Century: Essays and Reviews* by Michael E. Walters (grades 4–12) includes essays on great writers and thinkers in literature, history, architecture, and politics, as well as discussions of ideas and concepts. *Bright Child: An Educational Guide for Parents and Teachers of Young Gifted Students* by Lynn H. Fox & Andrea I. Prejean (grades K–6) emphasizes characteristics of development and examples for teaching.

Submissions and Payment
Submit 1-page query only. No unsolicited mss. SASE. Responds in 3 months. Publication in 3 months. Royalty, 10%.

Editor's Comments
We're looking for books for ages 10+ on science and physics, and the humanities. We look for material on topics we haven't already covered, and authors must be experts on their subject. See our website for details.

The Globe Pequot Press

825 Great Northern Boulevard
Helena, MT 59601

Executive Editor: Erin H. Turner

Publisher's Interests

Travel guides, and regional history and natural history titles
are the specialty of this publishing company. Its list includes
books for children, young adults, and adults.
Website: www.globepequot.com

Freelance Potential

Published 300 titles (15–20 juvenile) in 2005: 45 were
developed from unsolicited submissions, 15 were by agented
authors, and 15 were reprint/licensed properties. Of the
300 titles, 75 were by unpublished writers and 45 were by
authors who were new to the publishing house. Receives
1,000–1,200 queries yearly.

- **Nonfiction:** Publishes story picture books, 4–10 years; middle-
  grade titles, 8–12 years; and young adult books, 12–18 years.
  Topics include animals, pets, history, nature, the environment,
  travel, conservation, and regional subjects, Also publishes
  biographies.
- **Representative Titles:** *A Tale of Two Cities* by Tony Massarotti
  & John Harper tells about the ongoing rivalry between the
  Boston Red Sox and the New York Yankees. *Decade of the
  Wolf* by Douglas W. Smith & Gary Ferguson recounts a project
  to release 31 gray wolves into Yellowstone National Park.

Submissions and Payment

Guidelines available at website. Query with clips. Accepts
photocopies and disk submissions. SASE. Responds in 3
months. Publication in 18 months. Royalty, 8–12%; advance,
$500–$1,500.

Editor's Comments

Check the guidelines at our website to see if your book idea
is right for our list. Be sure to include a definition of your
book's projected target audience and market, and an analysis
of competing titles. Tell us who the book is for, and why it is
better than what is already on the bookshelves.

Goodheart-Willcox

18604 West Creek Drive
Tinley Park, IL 60477-6243

Editor, Family & Consumer Sciences: Teresa Dec

Publisher's Interests
Since its inception in 1921, Goodheart-Willcox has provided training guides, textbooks, and career education titles for technical and trade training programs, schools, and industries. All of its books offer a variety of features designed to make learning easier.
Website: www.g-w.com

Freelance Potential
Published 50 titles in 2005. Receives 100+ queries yearly.

- **Nonfiction:** Publishes textbooks and how-to titles. Topics include life management, personal development, family living, child care, child development, parenting, consumer education, food and nutrition, housing and interiors, fashion and clothing, career education, and professional development. Also features instructor's guides, resource guides, and software.
- **Representative Titles:** *Working with Young Children* introduces students to the fast-growing field of child care services by applying child development principles to child care settings; helps students develop skills for guiding children effectively while keeping them healthy and safe. *Changes & Choices* helps students develop the relationship skills they need as they face the transition to adulthood.

Submissions and Payment
Guidelines available. Query with résumé, outline, sample chapter, and list of illustrations. SASE. Responds in 2 months. Publication in 2 years. Royalty.

Editor's Comments
Our goal is to provide resources that serve as excellent learning tools. The books and supplements we produce are known for providing the latest information about the theories, techniques, tools, and operations of our focus areas. All are designed to train everyone from students through practicing professionals.

Graphia

Houghton Mifflin Co.
222 Berkeley Street
Boston, MA 02116

Senior Editor: Eden Edwards

Publisher's Interests
A 2004 imprint of Houghton Mifflin, Graphia offers quality
paperbacks for today's teens. Its fiction, nonfiction, poetry,
and graphic novels feature believable characters, recogniz-
able situations, and dilemmas.
Website: www.graphiabooks.com

Freelance Potential
Published 10–12 titles in 2005: 5 were by unpublished writers
and 7 were by authors who were new to the publishing
house. Receives 200–250 queries, 200 unsolicited manuscripts each year.

- **Fiction:** Published 7–8 young adult books, 12–18 years. Gen-
  res include contemporary, historical, and science fiction; mystery; suspense; and humor.
- **Nonfiction:** Published 3–5 young adult books, 12–18 years.
  Topics include history, multicultural, and informational issues.
- **Representative Titles:** *Comfort* by Carolee Dean (12+ years)
  is a gritty story of poetry slams, country music, and small town
  Texas conflicts that mix tragedy and hope. *Dunk* by David
  Lubar (12+ years) weaves a story of a boy who spends a summer
  sitting inside a dunk tank, goading people into taking a shot
  and sending him spilling into the water.

Submissions and Payment
Guidelines available. Query with synopsis and sample chapters for nonfiction. Send complete ms for fiction. Responds
only if interested. Publication period varies. Royalty;
advance.

Editor's Comments
Send us nonfiction and sophisticated, engaging fiction for
teens. Due to the volume of submissions, we are unable to
return manuscripts, so do not enclose an SASE. If we are
interested, we will notify you in 12 weeks.

Graphic Arts Center Publishing Co.

P.O. Box 10306
Portland, OR 97296-0306

Editorial Assistant: Jean Bond-Slaughter

Publisher's Interests
Books for children of all ages that celebrate the people and wildlife in Alaska, the Northwest, Canada, and the Western United States are produced by this regional publisher.
Website: www.gacpc.com

Freelance Potential
Published 20 titles in 2005: 10 were developed from unsolicited submissions, 3 were by agented authors, and 5 were reprint/licensed properties. Of the 20 titles, 5 were by unpublished writers and 10 were by new authors. Receives 250 queries, 100 unsolicited mss yearly.

- **Fiction:** Publishes early picture books, 0–4 years; story picture books, 4–10 years; chapter books, 5–10 years; and young adult books, 12–18 years. Genres include historical fiction; folklore; suspense; and stories about animals, nature, and the environment.
- **Nonfiction:** Publishes early picture books, 0–4 years; story picture books, 4–10 years; middle-grade books, 8–12 years; and young adult books, 12–18 years. Topics include animals, natural history, and humor. Also publishes biographies.
- **Representative Titles:** *The Animal in Me* by Laurie Tye (2–6 years) is a richly illustrated book that entices children to imagine what kind of animal they resemble. *Winter Is* by Ann Dixon (3–6 years) is about the excitement of a child awaiting the joys of winter.

Submissions and Payment
Guidelines available. Query with clips for fiction; send ms for children's books. Accepts photocopies, disk submissions, and simultaneous submissions if identified. SASE. Responds in 2–4 months. Publication in 2 years. Payment policy varies.

Editor's Comments
We seek children's fiction and nonfiction books with themes related to Alaska, the Northwest, or Western United States.

Greene Bark Press

P.O. Box 1108
Bridgeport, CT 06601-1108

Associate Publisher: Tara Maroney

Publisher's Interests
This book publisher focuses on colorful picture books for children age three to nine. It also offers interactive CD-ROMs, games, and videos, as well as teacher resource guides.
Website: www.greenebarkpress.com

Freelance Potential
Published 1 title in 2005: it was developed from an unsolicited submission. Receives 1,200 unsolicited mss yearly.

- **Fiction:** Publishes story picture books, 3–9 years. Genres include fantasy, mystery, the environment, and ethnic and multicultural themes. Also offers teachers' guide videos, math board games, card games, classroom accessories, and CD-ROMs.
- **Representative Titles:** *Words Are Not for Hurting* by Elizabeth Verdick (2–6 years) teaches little readers big ideas about taking responsibility about what they say, and how they say it. *Hey! There's a Goblin under My Throne!* by Rhett Ransom Pennell (3–9 years) follows brave King Edwin on his quest to protect his kingdom from many strange mythological creatures from around the world.

Submissions and Payment
Guidelines available. Send complete ms with illustrations and story board. Prefers one story per submission. Accepts photocopies and simultaneous submissions if identified. SASE. Responds in 2–6 months. Publication in 12–18 months. Royalty, 10–15%.

Editor's Comments
We specialize in picture books for young readers that make learning fun. We rarely publish juvenile novels, and we do not even consider adult titles, other than teaching guides that accompany our books. Your manuscript must have a unique story line, with lots of color and imagery to involve the reader.

Greenhaven Press

Suite C
15822 Bernardo Center Drive
San Diego, CA 92127

Senior Acquisitions Editor: Chandra Howard

Publisher's Interests
An imprint of Thomas Gale, this educational publisher offers nonfiction books for high school students. It strives to offer a wide spectrum of points of view on every topic covered including American and world history, social issues, literary criticism, and biographies.
Website: www.galegroup.com/greenhaven

Freelance Potential
Published 180 titles in 2005. Of the 180 titles, 18 were by unpublished writers and 18 were by authors who were new to the publishing house. Receives 300 queries yearly.

- **Nonfiction:** Publishes young adult books, 12–18 years. Features anthologies and books in series about history, contemporary social issues, world authors, and literary criticism. Also features biographies of famous history makers.
- **Representative Titles:** *Great Disasters: Volcanoes* (YA) offers a fascinating look at volcanos and the natural phenomena that causes them; part of the Great Disasters series. *Current Controversies: Hate Crimes* (YA) presents a balanced presentation for highly controversial views on hate crimes; part of the Current Controversies series.

Submissions and Payment
Guidelines available. Query acquisitions editor for guidelines. All work done on a work-for-hire basis. Response time varies. Publication in 1 year. Flat fee, varies.

Editor's Comments
We're looking for quality nonfiction educational books for the high school market. Please note that our writers are hired on a work-for-hire basis only and must have the appropriate credentials and experience to write for us. See our guidelines for details. University professors and graduate students are encouraged to send a query. Our current needs include ideas for social issues.

Groundwood Books

Suite 500
720 Bathhurst Street
Toronto, Ontario M5S 2R4
Canada

Acquisitions Editor

Publisher's Interests
This publisher is dedicated to producing high-quality children's books that are read and loved by children of all ages. It strives to publish character-driven literary fiction.
Website: www.groundwoodbooks.com

Freelance Potential
Published 25 titles in 2005: Of the 25 titles, 5 were by authors who were new to the publishing house.

- **Fiction:** Publishes concept books, 0–4 years; story picture books, 4–10 years; chapter books, 5–10 years; middle-grade books, 8–12 years; and young adult books, 12–18 years. Genres include contemporary, and multicultural fiction.
- **Representative Titles:** *Salmon Creek* by Annette LeBox (4–8 years) tells the story of one coho, from her birth in a remote creek to her final hours when she spawns and then dies. *Breaking Trail* by Joanne Bell (9–12 years) tells how a young girl and her dog-sled team embark on a grueling race.

Submissions and Payment
Guidelines and catalogue available at website. Query with synopsis and sample chapters. Accepts photocopies and computer printouts. No simultaneous submissions. SAE/IRC. Responds in 4–6 months. Publication period varies. Royalty; advance.

Editor's Comments
Due to the enormous number of submissions we receive, we regret we can no longer accept unsolicited manuscripts for picture books. However, we are always looking for new authors of novel-length fiction for children in all age areas. We do not publish high-interest/low-vocabulary fiction or stories with anthropomorphic animals or elves/fairies as the main characters. We encourage you to familiarize yourself with the kinds of books we publish in order to judge your work's compatibility.

Gryphon House

P.O. Box 207
Beltsville, MD 20704-0207

Editor-in-Chief: Kathy Charner

Publisher's Interests

Nonfiction books and creative activities that enrich the lives of young children can be found in the catalogue of this educational publisher. Topics include science, math, language development, and teaching strategies. It also includes material on bilingual education.

Website: www.gryphonhouse.com

Freelance Potential

Published 12 titles in 2005: 2 were developed from unsolicited submissions and 1was by an agented author. Of the 12 titles, 1 was by an unpublished writer and 6 were by authors who were new to the publishing house. Receives 150 queries yearly.

- **Nonfiction:** Publishes titles for parents and teachers working with children under the age of eight. Topics include art, math, science, language development, teaching strategies, conflict resolution, program development, and bilingual education.
- **Representative Titles:** *The Learning Power of Laughter* by Jackie Silberg (3–6 years) offers fun activities that use the power of laughter to encourage children to be creative while learning. *My Big World of Wonder* by Sherri Griffin (educators) allows teachers to heighten young children's awareness of nature and natural resources.

Submissions and Payment

Guidelines available. Query with table of contents, introductory material, and 20–30 pages of activities. Accepts photocopies, and computer printouts. SASE. Responds in 3–4 months. Publication in 1–2 years. Payment policy varies.

Editor's Comments

Make sure your ideas are developmentally appropriate for children up to the age of eight. We look for material that is creative and offers a participatory experience. We are not interested in books of paper and pencil activities.

Gulliver Books

Harcourt Trade Publishers
15 East 26th Street
New York, NY 10010

Editorial Director: Elizabeth Van Doren
Editor: Tamson Weston

Publisher's Interests
This publisher is interested in topics that address universal childhood experiences such as school, anxieties, sibling relationships, and common childhood fascinations, such as pirates and dinosaurs.
Website: www.harcourtbooks.com

Freelance Potential
Published 18 titles in 2005.

- **Fiction:** Publishes concept books, toddler books, and early picture books, 0–4 years; story picture books, 4–10 years; chapter books, 5–10 years; middle-grade books, 8–12 years; and young adult books, 12–18 years. Genres include adventure; and historical and contemporary fiction. Also publishes animal stories and poetry.
- **Nonfiction:** Publishes story picture books, 4–10 years. Topics include history, sports, nature, science, and the environment.
- **Representative Titles:** *Please Bury Me in the Library* by J. Patrick Lewis (6–9 years) is a collection of original poems inspired by Edward Lear, X. J. Kennedy, and Lewis Carroll about books and reading that range from sweet to silly to funny. *Each Little Bird that Sings* by Deborah Wiles (8–12 years) is a Southern coming-of-age novel about a spunky 10-year-old who learns about life, loss, and triumph.

Submissions and Payment
Accepts submissions only from agented and previously published authors or members of the Society of Children's Book Writers and Illustrators (SCBWI). SASE. Responds in 6–8 weeks. Publication in 2–4 years. Royalty; advance.

Editor's Comments
Due to the overwhelming volume of submissions we receive, we are only reviewing material from agented authors, members of SCBWI, and authors who have previously published with us.

Hachai Publishing

156 Chester Avenue
Brooklyn, NY 11218

Editor: Devorah L. Rosenfeld

Publisher's Interests
Hachai Publishing is dedicated to producing books that convey the joy of Jewish traditions and a love of Judaism to young children.
Website: www.hachai.com

Freelance Potential
Published 5 titles in 2005: 3 were developed from unsolicited submissions. Of the 5 titles, 4 were by authors who were new to the publishing house. Receives 500 unsolicited mss each year.

- **Fiction:** Published 1 toddler book and 3 early picture books, 0–4 years; and 1 chapter book, 5–10 years. Genres include religious and historical fiction, folktales, and adventure.
- **Nonfiction:** Publishes concept books, 0–4 years; and story picture books, 4–10 years. Topics include Jewish holidays, mitzvos, and middos. Also publishes biographies of Jewish figures and personalities.
- **Representative Titles:** *Is It Shabbos Yet?* by Ellen Emmerman (2–5 years) is an illustrated book that helps children understand Shabbos preparations. *Nine Spoons* by Marci Stillerman (5–8 years) is a moving Chanukah story of devotion and sacrifice set in a Nazi concentration camp.

Submissions and Payment
Guidelines available. Query with outline and sample chapter; or send complete ms. Accepts photocopies, computer printouts, and simultaneous submissions if identified. SASE. Responds in 2–6 weeks, Publication in 12–18 months. Flat fee.

Editor's Comments
We look for books that show good character traits like sharing, kindness, and forgiveness. Our stories are excellent tools for imparting a love of Hashem. We currently need biographies of spiritually great men and women in Jewish history, and historical fiction for readers ages seven to ten.

Hampton-Brown Books

26385 Carmel Rancho Boulevard
Carmel, CA 93923

Special Projects Coordinator

Publisher's Interests
This educational publisher is known for meeting the needs of linguistically and culturally diverse student populations. Its list includes books for young children, middle-grade readers, and English-as-a-Second-Language materials.
Website: www.hampton-brown.com

Freelance Potential
Published 220 titles (165 juvenile) in 2005: 110 were by agented authors and 110 were reprint/licensed properties. Of the 220 titles, most were by authors who were new to the publishing house. Receives 132 queries yearly.

- **Fiction:** Publishes early picture books, 0–4 years; easy-to-read books, 4–7 years; story picture books, 4–10 years; chapter books, 5–10 years; and middle-grade books, 8–12 years. Genres include fairy tales, folklore, drama, and contemporary and multicultural fiction.
- **Nonfiction:** Publishes early picture books, 0–4 years; easy-to-read books, 4–7 years; story picture books, 4–10 years; chapter books, 5–10 years; and middle-grade books, 8–12 years. Also publishes textbook anthologies on phonics, ESL, early literacy, dual-language programs, content-area reading, and home-schooling.
- **Representative Titles:** *Language Songs Big Book and Song CD* offers engaging songs and chants for building background, language, and vocabulary. *Vocabulary Builders Kit* offers ten free-standing scenes with manipulatives, teachers' guide, and song CD for interactive vocabulary development.

Submissions and Payment
Query. No unsolicited mss. SASE. Responds in 3–6 months. Publication period varies. Flat fee.

Editor's Comments
We strive to produce material that improves education for all students. We look for educational materials that motivate.

Harbour Publishing

P.O. Box 219
Madeira Park, British Columbia V0N 2H0
Canada

Editor: Shyla Seller

Publisher's Interests

This publisher's catalogue includes fiction that focuses on topics concerning the west coast of British Columbia. Previously published titles included history, science, nature, and folklore books for children, as well as fiction, travel, and cookbooks for adults.
Website: www.harbourpublishing.com

Freelance Potential

Published 20 titles (1 juvenile) in 2005: 3 were developed from unsolicited submissions. Of the 20 titles, 1 was by an unpublished writer and 1 was by an author who was new to the publishing house. Receives 10–20 queries, 100+ unsolicited mss yearly.

- **Fiction:** Publishes young adult books, 12–18 years. Genres include contemporary, historical, multicultural, and regional fiction; adventure; folklore; folktales; and nature stories relating to the Pacific West coast.
- **Nonfiction:** Publishes titles for adults. Topics include multicultural and ethnic issues, current events, history, social issues, geography, the environment, and biographies.
- **Representative Titles:** *Runaway at Sea* by Mary Razzell (YA) is the story of a young heroine dealing with family issues, budding sexuality, and adulthood. *Alsek's ABC Adventure* by Chris Caldwell (3–5 years) follows a hungry grizzly bear on his journeys through the Yukon wilderness in search for food.

Submissions and Payment

Guidelines available with 9x12 SASE. Query or send complete ms. Accepts photocopies. SASE. Responds in 6 months. Publication in 2 years. Royalty.

Editor's Comments

We publish both fiction and nonfiction titles, and YA books are of particular interest to us. Keep in mind that competition is tough, so send us your top-notch material.

Harcourt Children's Books

Harcourt Trade Publishers
15 East 26th Street
New York, NY 10010

Submissions Editor

Publisher's Interests

Children of all ages enjoy the high quality books produced by this popular publisher. Its list includes fiction, picture books, board books, and novelty books. It will only accept submissions from agented authors.
Website: www.harcourtbooks.com

Freelance Potential

Published 175 titles in 2005: all were by agented authors.

- **Fiction:** Publishes concept books, toddler books, and early picture books, 0–4 years; easy-to-read books, 4–7 years; story picture books, 4–10 years; chapter books, 5–10 years; middle-grade novels, 8–12 years; and young adult books, 12–18 years. Genres include mystery; fantasy; suspense; and contemporary, historical, and multicultural fiction. Also publishes poetry and stories about sports, nature, and the environment.
- **Representative Titles:** *What Do You Love?* by Jonathan London (0–3 years) joins a mother and her little one as they spend the day doing all of their favorite things together. *The Napping House* by Audrey Wood (3–7 years) is a bedtime favorite that features a cozy bed, a snoring granny, a dreaming child, a dozing dog, and an unexpected visitor who wakes up the house on a rainy afternoon of napping.

Submissions and Payment

Accepts submissions from agented authors only. No simultaneous submissions. Responds to agents in 1 month. Publication in 2 years. Royalty; advance.

Editor's Comments

Our focus is mainly picture books, but we also publish middle-grade and young adult fiction. Please do not send any unsolicited manuscripts or queries. We only accept work through literary agents. If you do not have an agent, you may want to check *The Literary Market Place*, which provides a listing of agents and publishers and appears annually.

Harcourt Religion Publishers

6277 Sea Harbor Drive
Orlando, FL 32887

Managing Editor: Sabrina Magnuson

Publisher's Interests
This publisher provides the Catholic educational market with practical catechetical resources that assist students and teachers in the process of faith formation and reflect the teachings of the Catholic church.
Website: www.harcourtreligion.com

Freelance Potential
Published 30 titles in 2005: 2 were by unpublished writers and 4 were by authors who were new to the publishing house. Receives 30–35 queries yearly.

- **Nonfiction:** Publishes easy-to-read books, 4–7 years; chapter books, 5–10 years; middle-grade titles, 8–12 years; and young adult books, 12–18 years. Also publishes Catholic high school textbooks. Topics include faith, catechism, education, Christian lifestyles, parish life, contemporary issues, prayer, worship, and family life.
- **Representative Titles:** *The Catholic Family in a Changing World* by Rev. Robert Hater (families) uses personal and biblical stories to offer pastoral insight, spiritual wisdom, and guidance to Catholic families of today. *Nurturing the Spiritual Growth of Your Adolescent* by Mike Carotta (parents) encourages adults to reinforce Christian life skills and to mentor young teens in the same skills.

Submissions and Payment
Guidelines available. Query with outline, résumé, and 3 sample chapters. No unsolicited mss. Accepts photocopies, computer printouts, and simultaneous submissions if identified. SASE. Responds in 3–6 months. Publication in 1 year. Royalty; Flat fee.

Editor's Comments
We are continuing to revise and expand our major publishing programs to provide a more integrated approach to the spiritual needs of the whole parish.

HarperCollins Children's Books

1350 Avenue of the Americas
New York, NY 10019

Executive Editor: Ruth Katcher

Publisher's Interests

This division of HarperCollins has long been known for its tradition of publishing quality books for children. From early reader series through young adult novels, it offers fiction only. The editors will review queries only from authors experienced enough to have acquired literary agents.
Website: www.harperchildrens.com

Freelance Potential

Published 6–8 titles in 2005: all were by agented authors. Of the 6–8 titles, 3–4 were by authors who were new to the publishing house. Receives 1,080 queries yearly.

- **Fiction:** Publishes easy-to-read books, 4–7 years; chapter books, 5–10 years; middle-grade novels, 8–12 years; and young adult books, 12–18 years. Genres include adventure; drama; fantasy; folklore; folktales; horror; humor; mystery; suspense; Westerns; and contemporary, historical, multicultural, and science fiction. Also publishes stories about sports.
- **Representative Titles:** *Beetle McGrady Eats Bugs!* by Megan McDonald is the story of a girl who dreams of doing something adventurous, so she decides to eat an ant. *Russell the Sheep* by Rob Scotton tells the story of a sheep who is out of step with the rest of his flock.

Submissions and Payment

Catalogue available at website. Accepts queries from agented authors only. Query with résumé and clips. SASE. Responds in 1 month. Publication in 18 months. Royalty, varies; advance, varies.

Editor's Comments

We found that the number of submissions we were receiving far exceeded our limited resources for reviewing them. Because of this, and because of our extremely high standards, we decided to review material submitted through literary agents only. We are continuing to adhere to this policy.

Hayes School Publishing Company

321 Pennwood Avenue
Pittsburgh, PA 15221

President: Clair Hayes

Publisher's Interests

This publisher produces supplementary teaching aids for teachers in kindergarten through senior high school. Resources include bulletin board materials, classroom posters, charts, educational games, reproducibles, and workbooks.

Website: www.hayespub.com

Freelance Potential

Published 30 titles in 2005: 2–3 were developed from unsolicited submissions. Of the 30 titles, 1 was by an author who was new to the publishing house. Receives 200–300 queries each year.

- **Nonfiction:** Publishes educational resource materials, grades K–12. Topics include language arts, multicultural studies, math, computer literacy, foreign language, social studies, science, health, creative thinking, handwriting, geography, health, and standardized testing.
- **Representative Titles:** *Mythology of Ancient Greece & Rome* (grade 6 and up) introduces students to the world of mythology, its symbols and its vocabulary. *Reading About Famous Explorers* (grades 3–6) includes classroom lessons and activities on well-known international explorers.

Submissions and Payment

Guidelines available. Query with résumé, outline, table of contents, and sample pages. Accepts photocopies, computer printouts, and simultaneous submissions if identified. SASE. Responds in 2–3 weeks. Publication period varies. Flat fee.

Editor's Comments

We are constantly looking for new material in all academic subject areas. We are especially interested in material for music, foreign language, and early childhood programs. Information on standardized testing is always of interest to our teaching audience.

Hazelden Foundation

P.O. Box 176
Center City, MN 55012-0176

Manuscript Coordinator

Publisher's Interests
Founded as a treatment center for persons with alcohol or drug dependencies, Hazelden developed into a publisher of books for professionals in the treatment and criminal justice fields, educators and prevention specialists, and individuals seeking recovery for themselves or a loved one.
Website: www.hazeldenbookplace.org

Freelance Potential
Published 100 titles in 2005: 60 were developed from unsolicited submissions and 5 were by agented authors. Receives 300 queries yearly.

- **Nonfiction:** Publishes middle-grade books, 8–12 years; and young adult books, 12–18 years. Topics include alcohol and substance abuse, health, fitness, and social issues.
- **Representative Titles:** *Understanding Borderline Personality Disorder Program* by Juergen E. Korbanka & Randy M. Huntington consists of pamphlets and workbooks that explore ways to cope with common behaviors associated with borderline personality disorder. *A Guide for the Family of the Alcoholic* by Joseph L. Kellermann assists family members in defending themselves against the weapons of control often used by alcoholics.

Submissions and Payment
Guidelines available. For catalogue, call 1-800-328-0098. Query with outline/synopsis, 3 sample chapters, and clips or writing samples. Accepts photocopies. SASE. Responds in 3 months. Publication in 12–18 months. Royalty. Flat fee.

Editor's Comments
For young readers, we're interested in reviewing research-based curricula materials for use with students in kindergarten through grade 12. We look for curricula with real-life content that will engage our readers, help prevent risky behaviors, and build resilient character in them.

Health Press NA Inc.

P.O. Box 37470
Albuquerque, NM 87176

Editor: Kathleen Frazier

Publisher's Interests
Easy-to-understand books about health and medical issues for children and their families are the mainstay of this publisher. Written by health professionals, its titles focus on providing explanations, reassurances, and answers to the questions patients ask.
Website: www.healthpress.com

Freelance Potential
Published 4 titles (2 juvenile) in 2005: all were developed from unsolicited submissions. Receives 500 queries yearly.

- **Fiction:** Publishes concept books, 0–4 years; easy-to-read books, 4–7 years; middle-grade books, 8–12 years; and young adult books, 12–18 years. Genres include humor, adventure, and contemporary fiction.
- **Nonfiction:** Publishes concept books, 0–4 years; easy-to-read books, 4–7 years; middle-grade titles, 8–12 years; and young adult books, 12–18 years. Topics include health, disabilities, medical conditions, nutrition, grief, psychology, parenting, and tolerance.
- **Representative Titles:** *The Girl with No Hair* by Elizabeth Murphy-Melas discusses the condition of alopecia areata, and how one girl learns to cope with the disease that causes hair loss. *Dad's Falling Apart* by Jennifer Crown Smith explains how multiple sclerosis affects people and their families.

Submissions and Payment
Guidelines available at website. Query with brief synopsis, résumé, and 3 sample chapters. SASE. Response time varies. Publication period varies. Royalty.

Editor's Comments
We want to see material that gives children and their peers accessible information about health conditions and promotes tolerance and understanding.

Heinemann

361 Hanover Street
Portsmouth, NH 03801-3912

Acquisitions Editor

Publisher's Interests

Heinemann publishes educational resources by professionals for professionals, and provides educational services for teachers in kindergarten through college.
Website: www.heinemann.com

Freelance Potential

Published 75–100 titles in 2005. Receives 1,000+ queries each year.

- **Nonfiction:** Publishes educational resource and multimedia material for teachers and school administrators. Topics include math, science, social studies, art education, reading, writing, ESL, bilingual education, special and gifted education, early childhood development, school reform, curriculum development, and the creative arts. Also publishes professional development and assessment materials.
- **Representative Titles:** *Powerful Units on Childhood, Money, and Government* by Janet Alleman & Jere Brophy (grades K–3) presents instructional units on cultural universals for the primary grades. *And Justice for Some* by Wendy Lement & Bethany Dunakin (grades 9–12) presents four original plays that document instances of injustice perpetrated in cases from key epochs of U.S. history.

Submissions and Payment

Guidelines available. Query with résumé, proposal, outline, table of contents, and chapter summaries. Accepts photocopies, computer printouts, and email submissions to proposals@heinemann.com. SASE. Responds in 6–8 weeks. Publication in 10–12 months. Payment policy varies.

Editor's Comments

We strive to give voice to those who share our respect for the professionalism and compassion of teachers, and those who support them, to help children become literate, empathetic, and knowledgeable citizens.

Helm Publishing

3923 Seward Avenue
Rockford, IL 61108

Editor: Dianne Helm

Publisher's Interests

Fiction and nonfiction for readers ages 13 and up are featured on this publisher's list. Many of its titles target parents and educators. 20% subsidy-published material.
Website: www.publishersdrive.com

Freelance Potential

Published 15 titles in 2005: 13 were developed from unsolicited submissions and 2 were by agented authors. Receives 3,000 queries yearly.

- **Fiction:** Publishes young adult books, 12–18 years. Genres include historical fiction, fantasy, mystery, suspense, romance, and science fiction. Also publishes titles for adults.
- **Nonfiction:** Publishes young adult books, 12–18 years. Topics include entertainment and history. Also publishes books for adults on topics such as business, parenting, and women's contemporary issues.
- **Representative Titles:** *Becky's Rebel* by Sherry Derr-Wille is a novel set during the Civil War about a Confederate soldier who falls in love with a woman from the North. *My Mother's Black Child* by N. Johnson Beck is the story of a woman's fight to gain the love of a mother who rejected her from birth because of the color of her skin. *Summer's Child* by Sherry Derr-Wille is the story of a family that moves from Norway to Minnesota and the conflict that arises between them and their American-born child.

Submissions and Payment

Guidelines and catalogue available at website. Query. Accepts photocopies and computer printouts. SASE. Response time and publication period vary. Royalty.

Editor's Comments

Our books cover a broad range of subjects and styles. For young adults, we will consider queries for our new series, Bubblegum Babes. Visit our website for more information.

Hendrick-Long Publishing Company

Suite D
10635 Tower Oaks
Houston, TX 77070

Vice President: Vilma Long

Publisher's Interests
This independent Texas-based publisher specializes in non-fiction and historical fiction about Texas and the Southwest for children in kindergarten through high school.
Website: www.hendricklongpublishing.com

Freelance Potential
Published 2 titles in 2005: both were developed from unsolicited submissions. Receives 200+ queries yearly.

- **Fiction:** Published 1 middle-grade book, 8–12 years. Also publishes story picture books, 4–10 years; and young adult books, 12–18 years. Genres include historical fiction, regional fiction, and folklore.
- **Nonfiction:** Published 1 middle-grade book, 8–12 years. Also publishes young adult books, 12–18 years. Topics include animals, biography, nature, history, and geography related to Texas and the Southwest.
- **Representative Titles:** *The Ghost at the Old Stone Fort* by Martha Tannery Jones (9+ years) weaves facts about 18th-century Nacogdoches into a story that takes place during the Depression of the 1930s. *The Armadillo from Amarillo* by Lynne Cherry (8+ years) follows an armadillo on a journey from San Antonio north through the canyons and prairies of Texas.

Submissions and Payment
Guidelines available. Query with résumé, outline/synopsis, table of contents, and 1–2 sample chapters. Accepts photocopies, computer printouts, and simultaneous submissions if identified. SASE. Responds in 4–6 months. Publication in 18 months. Royalty; advance.

Editor's Comments
All material submitted to us should relate to our primary focus and should be suitable for young readers. For the coming year, we're particularly interested in reviewing submissions of cookbooks that feature the foods of Texas.

Heuer Publishing LLC

Suite 200
211 1st Avenue SE
Cedar Rapids, IA 52401

Editor: Geri Albrecht
Publisher: Steven S. Michalicek

Publisher's Interests

Schools and community theaters turn to this publisher for its one-act plays, full-length plays, and musical monodramas/monologues. It also publishes theater-related texts.
Website: www.hitplays.com

Freelance Potential

Published 35 titles (5–10 juvenile) in 2005: 17 were developed from unsolicited submissions, 3 were by agented authors, and 3 were by reprint/licensed properties. Of the 35 titles, 2 were by unpublished writers and 5 were by authors who were new to the publishing house. Receives 400 queries, 300 unsolicited mss yearly.

- **Fiction:** Publishes middle-grade books, 8–12 years; and young adult books, 12–18 years. Genres include comedy, musicals, drama, suspense, mystery, and satire.
- **Nonfiction:** Publishes young adult books, 12–18 years. Topics include theater arts, stage production, auditions, sound effects, and theater resources for young adults.
- **Representative Titles:** *Teenage Nightmare* by Laura Toffenetti is a one-act satire that brings the trials and tribulations of teen life to stage. *Sure As You're Born* by Donald Payton is a comedy about a boy named Wilbur who wins a writing contest by submitting his sister's story under his own name. His father wishes Wilbur was a girl, and dreams his wish is granted.

Submissions and Payment

Guidelines available. Query or send complete ms with synopsis, cast list, running time, and set requirements. Accepts submissions online through website. SASE. Responds in 2 months. Publication period varies. Royalty. Flat fee.

Editor's Comments

Keep in mind that subject matter and language must be appropriate for students and younger audiences. Most of the actors performing in our plays are new to the stage.

Holiday House

425 Madison Avenue
New York, NY 10017

Editorial Department

Publisher's Interests

Books for young people from picture books through middle-grade readers to young adult fiction and nonfiction have been a hallmark of this publisher. It does not publish board books, activity books, or paperback originals.
Website: www.holidayhouse.com

Freelance Potential

Published 50 titles in 2005: 15 were by agented authors and 5 were reprint/licensed properties. Of the 50 titles, 2 were by unpublished writers. Receives 8,000 queries yearly.

- **Fiction:** Published 30 story picture books, 4–10 years; 5 chapter books, 5–10 years; 5 middle-grade books, 8–12 years; and 10 young adult books, 12–18 years. Genres include humor, mystery, fantasy, and historical and multicultural fiction.
- **Nonfiction:** Publishes early picture books, 0–4 years; easy-to-read books, 4–7 years; and middle-grade books, 8–12 years. Topics include history, social issues, and science. Also publishes biographies.
- **Representative Titles:** *Dr. Clock-sicle* by Martha Weston (5–8 years) follows Dr. Clock on an adventure as he takes his time machine to look for saber-toothed cats. *Poe Park* by Agnes Martinez (8–12 years) relates how a young teen who is entering high school must deal with a terrible event in his life.

Submissions and Payment

Guidelines available. Query only for picture books as well as novels. Accepts photocopies. SASE. Responds in 2 months. Publication period varies. Royalty; advance.

Editor's Comments

Since we are a small publisher, we only accept queries. Describe your book idea to us and, if we find your idea suited to our needs, we will notify you by mail. Read through our catalogue to get a better idea of the types of books we are looking for.

Holloway House Publishing Group

8060 Melrose Avenue
Los Angeles, CA 90046

Submissions Editor: Neal Colgrass

Publisher's Interests

Holloway House is known as the world's largest publisher of paperbacks about the African American experience. Most of its titles are for adult readers, but its series of biographies, entitled Black Americans, spotlights personalities of interest to adults as well as to young adults.
Website: www.hollowayhousebooks.com

Freelance Potential

Published 8 titles in 2005. Receives 500+ queries, 100 unsolicited mss yearly.

- **Fiction:** Publishes young adult books, 12–18 years. Genres include crime, Westerns, mystery, and historical and contemporary fiction.
- **Nonfiction:** Publishes young adult books, 12–18 years. Topics include contemporary and social issues. Also publishes biographies.
- **Representative Titles:** *Jackie Robinson* by Richard Scott traces the life of the Brooklyn Dodger from childhood to baseball legend. *Wilma Rudolph* by Tom Biracree tells the story of the young woman who overcame a harrowing childhood to become an Olympic gold medalist in 1960 and a role model for young athletes.

Submissions and Payment

Guidelines available. Query with résumé; or send complete ms. Accepts photocopies, computer printouts, and disk submissions. SASE. Responds to queries in 3 weeks, to mss in 3 months. Publication period and payment policy vary.

Editor's Comments

We assign most of our books, but we will look at queries or submissions for our Black American series. Meticulous research is a hallmark of this series. We also look for a direct, entertaining writing style that presents facts in a way that will fascinate readers of all ages.

Henry Holt Books for Young Readers

175 Fifth Avenue
New York, NY 10010

Submissions Editor

Publisher's Interests
Literature for children of all ages fills the catalogue from this division of Henry Holt and Company. Its offerings include concept books for very young children, titles for beginning readers, and books on subjects of interest to teens. This company publishes fiction, nonfiction, and poetry.
Website: www.henryholtchildrensbooks.com

Freelance Potential
Published 65 titles in 2005. Receives 2,000 unsolicited mss each year.

- **Fiction:** Publishes concept books and early picture books, 0–4 years; easy-to-read books, 4–7 years; story picture books, 4–10 years; chapter books, 5–10 years; middle-grade books, 8–12 years; and young adult books, 12–18 years. Genres include historical, multicultural, and ethnic fiction; adventure and nature stories; drama; and fantasy. Also publishes poetry.
- **Nonfiction:** Publishes story picture books, 4–10 years; chapter books, 5–10 years; and middle-grade books, 8–12 years. Topics include history, multicultural and ethnic issues, nature, and the environment.
- **Representative Titles:** *My First Chinese New Year* by Karen Katz follows a young girl as she is introduced to the festivities surrounding the Chinese New Year. *Brave Little Raccoon* by Erica Wolf is a story based on the themes of separation, being brave, and growing up.

Submissions and Payment
Guidelines and catalogue available with 9x12 SASE ($.80). Send complete ms. Accepts photocopies. No simultaneous submissions. SASE. Responds in 3–4 months. Publication period and payment policy vary.

Editor's Comments
If you're thinking of submitting your work to us, remember that we do not publish board, novelty, or activity books.

Honor Books

Cook Communications Ministries
4050 Lee Vance View
Colorado Springs, CO 80918

Product/Brand Manager

Publisher's Interests
This Christian publisher specializes in spiritual books that
inspire, encourage, and motivate young, middle-grade, and
teen readers to experience God's grace.
Website: www.honorbooks.com

Freelance Potential
Published 30 titles (5 juvenile) in 2005. Receives 120 unsolicited mss yearly.

- **Nonfiction:** Publishes concept books, toddler books, and early
  picture books, 0–4 years; easy-to-read books, 4–7 years; story
  picture books, 4–10 years; middle-grade titles, 8–12 years;
  young adult titles, 12–18 years. Also publishes activity, novelty,
  and board books; titles in series; and devotionals. Topics
  include Christian living, faith, and prayer.
- **Representative Titles:** *Daily Grace for Teens* (YA) is a compi-
  lation of reflections by well-known authors that illustrate God's
  amazing grace and goodness. *God's Little Devotional Book for
  Students* combines powerful Bible verses, thought-provoking
  quotes, and entertaining stories for a daily devotional guide.

Submissions and Payment
Guidelines available. Send complete ms with interior sample
spreads. Accepts simultaneous submissions if identified.
Availability of artwork improves chance of acceptance. SASE.
Responds in 3 months. Publication in 1–2 years. Royalty;
advance. Flat fee.

Editor's Comments
Although we are in the process of assessing our editorial
needs, we will consider material that stresses the importance
of God in our lives. Current interests are nonfiction devotionals, Bible stories, and board books for young readers. All fiction material must have religious or spiritual themes; we do
not consider fantasy.

Horizon Publishers

191 North 650 East
Bountiful, UT 84010-3628

Submissions Editor: Dwayne Crowther

Publisher's Interests

Targeting readers who are members of the Church of Jesus Christ of Latter-day Saints, as well as the general Christian marketplace, this publisher features titles on raising and teaching children, family life, and Bible study.
Website: www.horizonpublishersbooks.com

Freelance Potential

Published 30 titles (3–5 juvenile) in 2005: 180 were developed from unsolicited submissions. Of the 30 titles, 24 were by authors who were new to the publishing house. Receives 200 queries and unsolicited mss yearly.

- **Nonfiction:** Publishes activity and educational books for children. Topics include the Mormon faith, spirituality, and social issues. Also publishes books about parenting, family life, crafts, outdoor life, and scouting.
- **Representative Titles:** *Dating & Courting Done Right* by Jennifer Blewster Richardson (YA–adult) discusses topics such as personal preparedness, honesty, avoiding abuse, divorce, moral cleanliness, and having fun. *Planting Seeds of Faith* by Alison Palmer (teachers and parents) offers lesson plans with corresponding scripture lessons, songs, learning activities, and treats.

Submissions and Payment

Guidelines available. Query or send complete ms. Accepts photocopies and computer printouts. SASE. Responds to queries in 1–3 months; to mss in 4–5 months. Publication period varies. Royalty, 8%; advance, $100–$500. Flat fee.

Editor's Comments

Although our material is directed toward LDS readers, we are not affiliated with the Church. We are looking for titles that focus on scriptural studies, Christian doctrine, defense of the faith, and prophecy and the last days. We will also consider wholesome, inspirational fiction.

Houghton Mifflin Children's Books

222 Berkeley Street
Boston, MA 02116

Editorial Assistant: Erica Zappy

Publisher's Interests
The list for this popular publisher of children includes fiction and nonfiction titles designed to educate, inform, and entertain young readers.
Website: www.houghtonmifflinbooks.com

Freelance Potential
Published 60 titles (35 juvenile) in 2005: 2 were developed from unsolicited submissions, 51 were by agented authors, and 2 were reprint/licensed properties. Receives 500 queries, 5,000 unsolicited mss yearly.

- **Fiction:** Published 3 toddler books, 0–4 years; 1 easy-to-read book, 4–7 years; 15 story picture books, 4–10 years; 5 middle-grade titles, 8–12 years; and 5 young adult books, 12–18 years. Genres include historical and multicultural fiction, adventure, and humor.
- **Nonfiction:** Published 5 middle-grade titles, 8–12 years; and 1 young adult book, 12–18 years. Topics include history, science, nature, and natural history. Also publishes biographies.
- **Representative Titles:** *Carmine: A Little More Red* by Melissa Sweet (4–8 years) is a fresh, yet faithful, retelling of Little Red Riding Hood. *The Silent Witness* by Robin Friedman (4–8 years) is a picture book about a young girl and her doll, told in the larger story of the Civil War.

Submissions and Payment
Guidelines available with SASE, at website, or by calling 617-351-5959. Send complete ms for fiction. Query with synopsis and sample chapters for nonfiction. Accepts photocopies and computer printouts. SASE. Responds in 3 months if interested. Publication period varies. Royalty; advance.

Editor's Comments
High-quality, unforgettable picture and storybooks are our specialty. Competition for our attention is fierce, so send us your best work. We'll let you know if we're interested.

Humanics

Suites 200–203
12 South Dixie Highway
Lake Worth, FL 33460

Acquisitions Editor: W. Arthur Bligh

Publisher's Interests
With an emphasis on early childhood education, Humanics produces quality teacher-resource guides and activity books for classroom and parent use.
Website: www.humanicspub.com

Freelance Potential
Published 12 titles in 2005: 12 were developed from unsolicited submissions. Of the 12 titles, 2 were by unpublished writers and 1 was by an author who was new to the publishing house. Receives 150 queries and 125 unsolicited mss each year.

- **Nonfiction:** Publishes teacher-resource books. Topics include science and math; art; crafts. Also publishes parenting books.
- **Representative Titles:** *The Infant and Toddler Handbook* by Gary B. Wilson covers every aspect of a child's development from birth to two years. *Homespun Curriculum: A Developmentally Appropriate Activities Guide* by Denise Theobald contains complete lesson plans adapted to the skill levels of infants to toddlers to school-age children.

Submissions and Payment
Guidelines available at website. Send complete manuscript with resume, synopsis, and marketing plan. A one-time, non-refundable submission fee of $50 is required with all submissions. Accepts photocopies, computer printouts, and disk submissions (Microsoft Word or WordPerfect). SASE. Response time, publication period, and payment policy vary.

Editor's Comments
Qualified writers with a sound knowledge of the education field are who we look for. We also publish activity books for children up to the age of nine, so we want submissions that are creative and fun and well presented. We take time to review each submission, so expect the process to be quite a lengthy one.

Hunter House Publishers

P.O. Box 2914
Alameda, CA 94501-0914

Acquisitions Editor: Jeanne Brondino

Publisher's Interests
Health and family books that appeal to the reading public
and health-care and mental health professionals are featured
on this Hunter House's list.
Website: www.hunterhouse.com

Freelance Potential
Published 18 titles in 2005: 6 were developed from unsolicited
submissions. Of the 18 titles, 1 was by an unpublished
writer and 7 were by authors who were new to the publishing
house. Receives 1,000 queries yearly.

- **Nonfiction:** Publishes resource titles for educators, parents,
  and social workers. Topics include relationships, sexuality,
  health, fitness, violence prevention, and trauma. Also publishes
  activity books.
- **Representative Titles:** *Kids' Food for Fitness* by Anita Bean,
  B.Sc., helps parents to ensure that their child's diet supports
  their physical needs and helps them get the most out of life.
  101 Improv Games for Children and Adults by Bob Bedore
  explains the basics of improv, and how to teach it to children.

Submissions and Payment
Guidelines available. Query with résumé, overview, chapter
by chapter outline, competitive analysis, and marketing
ideas. Accepts computer printouts, and simultaneous submissions if identified. SASE. Responds in 3–4 months. Publication in 1–3 years. Royalty.

Editor's Comments
We only publish nonfiction and do not publish children's
books. We want to see books that focus on health, including
symptoms, medical theories, and treatments. Personal
growth is a current topic of interest and we are also seeking
additions to our Growth & Recovery Workbooks series that
helps children who have experienced trauma and abuse.

John Hunt Publishing

The Bothy Deershot Lodge
Park Lane Ropley
Hantz SO24 OBE
United Kingdom

Editor: John Hunt

Publisher's Interests
Since 1988 John Hunt Publishing has offered a variety of
fiction and nonfiction titles dealing with religious and
spiritual themes. Its children's list includes Bible stories,
religious holidays, faith, family, lifeskills, and books on
prayer and meditation. 5% self-, subsidy-, co-venture, or
co-op published.
Website: www.o-books.net

Freelance Potential
Published 50 titles (5 juvenile) in 2005: 5 were developed
from unsolicited submissions and 10 were by agented
authors. Of the 50 titles, 10 were by unpublished writers.
Receives thousands of queries, and hundreds of unsolicited
mss yearly.

- **Fiction:** Publishes easy-to-read books, 4–7 years; story picture
  books, 4–10 years; chapter books, 5–10 years; middle-grade
  books, 8–12 years; and young adult books, 12–18 years.
  Genres include religious and spiritual fiction.
- **Representative Titles:** *Fairy Lullabies* by Alan & Linda Parry
  (3–7 years) is the story of a magical land of fairies and elves.
  Patrick and the Cat that Saw Beyond by Zoe d'Ay (8–12 years)
  is a mythical story about life and death. *Relax Kids: Aladdin's
  Magic Carpet* (3+ years) introduces children to relaxation and
  meditation through nursery rhymes.

Submissions and Payment
Query with clips. Accepts photocopies. SASE. Responds in
1 week. Publication in 18 months. Royalty. Flat fee.

Editor's Comments
This year we are interested in books for all ages that deal
with spirituality and all religions. Material that teaches young
readers how to cope effectively with difficult life challenges
such as death, stress, and questions about spirituality are
also of interest.

Illumination Arts

P.O. Box 1865
Bellevue, WA 98009

Editorial Director: Ruth Thompson

Publisher's Interests
For over 16 years, this publisher's book collection inspires love, respect, forgiveness, inner peace and self-awareness. Geared towards children ages two through ten, it specializes in books with inspirational and spiritual themes.
Website: www.illumin.com

Freelance Potential
Published 4–5 titles in 2005: all were developed from unsolicited submissions. Of the 4–5 titles, 3 were by unpublished writers and 3 were by authors who were new to the publishing house. Receives 2,000–3,000 mss yearly.

- **Fiction:** Published 4–5 story picture books, 4–10 years.
- **Representative Titles:** *Your Father Forever* by Travis Griffith reveals the promises a devoted father makes to nurture, guide, protect and respect his children. *Little Yellow Pear Tomatoes* by Demian Elainé Yumei examines the universal circle of life through the innocent eyes of a young girl, who sees all the energy and collaboration it takes to grow her pear tomatoes.

Submissions and Payment
Guidelines available. Send complete ms, résumé, and market analysis. Accepts photocopies, computer printouts, and simultaneous submissions if identified. SASE. Responds in 1 month. Publication period and payment policy vary.

Editor's Comments
At this time, we are seeking fiction and nonfiction stories that are 500–2,000 words in length. Writers are requested to submit inspirational, spiritual, and uplifting manuscripts that are in keeping with the wholesome values of our publishing company. Stories that border on the adventurous are also welcome. Keep in mind that our age range for readers is two through ten years of age. We do not accept chapter, or full-length books.

Impact Publishers

P.O. Box 6016
Atascadero, CA 93423

Acquisitions Editor: Freeman Porter

Publisher's Interests

Publishing only popular psychology and self-help books, Impact Publishers offers nonfiction titles focused on personal growth, relationships, emotional issues, families, communities, and health.

Website: www.impactpublishers.com

Freelance Potential

Published 5 titles (1 juvenile) in 2005: 1 was developed from an unsolicited submission, 2 were by agented authors, and 1 was a reprint/licensed property. Of the 5 titles, 1 was by an unpublished writer. Receives 500–750 queries each year.

- **Nonfiction:** Publishes middle-grade books, 8–12 years; and young adult books, 12–18 years. Topics include social issues; marriage, mental health; self-esteem; creativity; relationships; social and emotional growth; parenting; popular psychology; and multicultural and ethnic issues.
- **Representative Titles:** *Jigsaw Puzzle Family* by Cynthia MacGregor helps children fit together the pieces of their new family. *Calming the Family Storm: Anger Management for Moms, Dad, and All the Kids* by Gary D. McKay, Ph.D, and Steven A. Mayhell, Ph.D, is a practical manual of helpful skills for handling anger that every family experiences.

Submissions and Payment

Guidelines available. Query with résumé and sample chapters. Accepts photocopies, computer printouts, and simultaneous submissions if identified. SASE. Responds in 1–3 months. Publication in 1 year. Royalty; advance.

Editor's Comments

Our books are written in "everyday language" by professionals with advanced degrees. We are always open to qualified new authors, but please remember to keep your audience in mind and present material in a clear, simple, and comprehensive manner.

Imperial International

30 Montauk Boulevard
Oakdale, NY 11769

Editor-in-Chief: Laura Solimene

Publisher's Interests
As a division of EDCON Publishing Group, Imperial International offers supplemental instructional materials for students and teachers in elementary school through high school.
Website: www.edconpublishing.com

Freelance Potential
Published 5 titles in 2005. Of the 5 titles, all were by unpublished writers who were new to the publishing house.
Receives 60 unsolicited mss yearly.

- **Fiction:** Publishes easy-to-read books, 4–7 years; chapter books, 5–10 years; and middle-grade titles, 8–12 years. Genres include science fiction, adventure, multicultural and ethnic fiction, and fairy tales. Also publishes hi/lo fiction, 6–18 years; and activity books, 6–12 years.
- **Nonfiction:** Publishes chapter books, 5–10 years; and young adult books, 12–18 years. Topics include reading comprehension, mathematics, science, and technology. Also publishes educational materials for homeschooling.
- **Representative Titles:** *Sharpening Writing Skills* (grades 3–7) hones students' ability to write clear, concise and technically accurate short stories using music and special effects to enhance mental imagery. *Sports Math* (grades 7–12) introduces math concepts and principles through the excitement of popular sports.

Submissions and Payment
Guidelines available with 9x12 SASE ($1.35 postage). Send complete ms. Accepts photocopies and simultaneous submissions if identified. Submissions are not returned. Responds in 1–2 weeks. Publication in 6 months. Flat fee, $300–$1,000.

Editor's Comments
Our forte is high-interest/low-readability books and materials for reluctant readers of all levels.

Incentive Publications

3835 Cleghorn Avenue
Nashville, TN 37215

Editor: Blake Parker

Publisher's Interests

Established in 1969, this company publishes supplemental educational books and materials to meet the needs of students and educators at all grade levels. It offers workbooks, resource titles, videos, and creative materials for home and classroom use.

Website: www.incentivepublications.com

Freelance Potential

Published 30–32 titles in 2005: 3 were developed from unsolicited submissions. Of the 30–32 titles, 1 was by a new author. Receives 300 queries yearly.

- **Nonfiction:** Publishes early picture books, 0–4 years; chapter books, 5–10 years; middle-grade titles, 8–12 years; and young adult books, 12–18 years. Topics include literacy, social awareness, science, arts and crafts, math, reading, and early learning.
- **Representative Titles:** *Art for Young Children* by Donna Hussain is a resource book filled with stimulating art activities designed for the abilities and attention spans of preschool children. *Newbery & Caldecott Books in the Classroom* by Claudette Comfort offers units of instruction for classroom use on each winner of the Newbery & Caldecott award since 1922.

Submissions and Payment

Guidelines available. Query with table of contents, outline/synopsis, and 1–3 sample chapters. Accepts photocopies and simultaneous submissions if identified. SASE. Responds in 4–6 weeks. Publication period varies. Royalty. Flat fee.

Editor's Comments

Our needs change as the needs of our audience change. At this time, we will consider queries for assessment materials, such as kindergarten readiness books and middle-grade study resources.

International Reading Association

P.O. Box 8139
800 Barksdale Road
Newark, DE 19714-8139

Submissions: Becky Zell

Publisher's Interests

This nonprofit professional organization seeks to promote literacy and improve reading instruction for children of all ages, as well as for adults. To achieve this goal, it publishes numerous books, booklets, and pamphlets written by educators experienced in the reading field.
Website: www.reading.org

Freelance Potential

Published 30 titles in 2005. Receives 100 queries yearly.

- **Nonfiction:** Publishes educational titles, research reports, and monographs. Topics include literacy programs, reading research and practice, language comprehension at all levels, and professional development.
- **Representative Titles:** *Using Children's Literature in Preschool* by Lesley Mandel Morrow & Linda B. Gambrell (teachers) explores ways to use children's literature to help preschoolers understand concepts about books, learn within the content areas, and develop reading comprehension. *Teaching Vocabulary* by Gail E. Tompkins & Cathy Blanchfield (teachers) provides strategies and creative ideas for teaching vocabulary to elementary, middle school, and high school students.

Submissions and Payment

Guidelines available. Request a Publication Proposal Form before sending ms. Accepts photocopies. No simultaneous submissions. SASE. Response time, publication period, and payment policy vary.

Editor's Comments

If you are an experienced reading teacher, we're interested in your contribution to the literacy field. Your proposal will be reviewed by committee members who are experts on your topic. If your proposal is deemed promising, we will invite you to develop a complete manuscript.

JayJo Books

Guidance Channel Company
Suite 201
45 Executive Drive
Plainview, NY 11803-0760

Editor-in-Chief: Michelle Yannis

Publisher's Interests
Established in 1992 to provide quality children's health education, this publisher offers simple, non-technical, and colorful picture books to teach readers about chronic illnesses and disabilities.
Website: www.jayjo.com

Freelance Potential
Published several titles in 2005. Receives 250 queries each year.

- **Fiction:** Publishes story picture books, 5–12 years. Features books on children's health issues and learning disabilities, including asthma, ADHD, diabetes, food allergies, cystic fibrosis, arthritis, Tourette Syndrome, autism, dyslexia, speech and hearing disorders, cancer, depression, cerebral palsy, cystic fibrosis, and Down Syndrome.
- **Representative Titles:** *Sportsercise!* (grades 1–5) is a delightful story about exercise-induced asthma and how kids learn to cope with it. *Taking ADD to School* (grades 1–5) educates classmates of children with Attention Deficit Disorder about this syndrome, and how it affects their friends who have it.

Submissions and Payment
Guidelines available with #10 SASE ($.37 postage). Query. Accepts photocopies. SASE. Responds in 3 months. Publication in 2 years. Flat fee.

Editor's Comments
Our books promote understanding and acceptance of children with special physical and educational needs and conditions. We continue to need titles that deal with health and guidance issues for students in kindergarten through grade eight, especially contemporary issues such as substance abuse and smoking. Although our books are written for children, they are also used by parents, teachers, caregivers, and physicians.

Jewish Lights

P.O. Box 237
Sunset Farm Offices
Route 4
Woodstock, VT 05091

Submissions Editor

Publisher's Interests
Drawing on the Jewish wisdom and tradition to deal with
issues such as the quest for self and the meaning of life,
Jewish Lights publishes inspirational books for people of all religious beliefs. Its children's titles explore faith and spirituality
in age-appropriate forms.
Website: www.jewishlights.com

Freelance Potential
Published 60 titles (4 juvenile) in 2005: 10 were developed
from unsolicited submissions and 1 was by an agented
author. Of the 60 titles, 9 were by unpublished writers and
12 were by authors who were new to the publishing house.
Receives 1,000+ queries, 700 unsolicited mss yearly.

- **Nonfiction:** Publishes toddler books, 0–4 years; easy-to-read
  books, 4–7 years; story picture books, 4–10 years; and young
  adult books, 12–18 years. Topics include religious and inspirational subjects and self-help.
- **Representative Titles:** *The JGirl's Guide* by Penina Adelman
  et al. (YA) provides Jewish writings, traditions, and advice to
  help young Jewish women as they come of age. *Adam & Eve's
  First Sunset: God's New Day* by Sandy Eisenberg Sasso (4+
  years) offers a lesson in faith and hope when coping with situations that are beyond one's control.

Submissions and Payment
Guidelines available. Query with résumé, table of contents,
sample chapter, and marketing plan. Send complete ms for
picture books. Accepts photocopies, computer printouts,
and simultaneous submissions if identified. SASE. Responds
in 4 months. Publication in 1 year. Payment policy varies.

Editor's Comments
While people of Jewish heritage are our primary audience,
our books speak to Christians as well. They broaden their
understanding of Judaism and the roots of their own faith.

JIST Publishing

8902 Otis Avenue
Indianapolis, IN 46216-1033

Acquisitions Editor

Publisher's Interests

JIST Publishing's books on job search and careers are used in schools, colleges, government agencies, and workforce-development programs. Other life issues covered in its titles, include anger and stress management, suicide, self-esteem, personal finances, and mentoring. JIST's focus is on helping readers improve their lives.
Website: www.jist.com

Freelance Potential

Published 40–50 titles (16 juvenile) in 2005. Of the 40–50 titles, 5 were by unpublished writers and 5 were by authors who were new to the publishing house. Receives 250 queries yearly.

- **Fiction:** Published 1 easy-to-read book, 4–7 years; and 5 middle-grade books, 8–12 years. Genres include contemporary fiction about social issues.
- **Nonfiction:** Published 5 middle-grade books, 8–12 years; and 5 young adult books, 12–18 years. Topics include job search, career exploration, occupational information, life skills, character education, domestic violence, and elder and child abuse.
- **Representative Titles:** *The World of Work and You* by Michael Farr (YA) helps students plan their futures with job charts, worksheets, and activities. *Creating Your High School Résumé* by Kathryn Kraemer Troutman (YA) shows students how to prepare a résumé that gets results.

Submissions and Payment

Guidelines available at website. Query with résumé, outline/synopsis, and audience/market analysis. Accepts photocopies and computer printouts. SASE. Responds in 3–4 months. Publication in 1–2 years. Royalty, 8–10%.

Editor's Comments

Your work stands a better chance of being accepted if you follow our book proposal guidelines, available at our website.

Journey Forth

1700 Wade Hampton Boulevard
Greenville, SC 29614-0060

Acquisitions Editor: Nancy Lohr

Publisher's Interests

Well-written books for readers of varying abilities and interests are produced by this Christian publisher. Its list includes fiction, nonfiction, and biographies for children and teens.
Website: www.bjup.com

Freelance Potential

Published 10 titles in 2005: 1 was developed from an unsolicited submission, 1 was by an agented author, and 2 were reprint/licensed properties. Of the 10 titles, 2 were by unpublished writers and 3 were by authors who were new to the publishing house. Receives 70 queries, 500 mss yearly.

- **Fiction:** Published 3 easy-to-read books, 4–7 years; 2 chapter books, 5–10 years; 3 middle-grade books, 8–12 years; and 2 young adult books, 12–18 years. Genres include Christian living, mystery, historical and contemporary fiction, fantasy, animal adventure, and fictional biographies.
- **Nonfiction:** Publishes middle-grade books, 8–12 years; and young adult books, 12–18 years. Features Christian biographies.
- **Representative Titles:** *The Secret of the Golden Cowrie* by Gloria Repp (YA) tells the story of a girl and her aunt who share a secret that leads them on a mystery. *A King for Brass Cobweb* by Dawn L. Watkins (3–5 years) tells of a chipmunk that leaves home to seek a king who is wise, brave, and true.

Submissions and Payment

Guidelines available. Query with 5 sample chapters; or send complete ms. Accepts photocopies, computer printouts, and simultaneous submissions if identified. No email. SASE. Responds in 3 months. Publication in 18–24 months. Royalty, negotiable.

Editor's Comments

We are dedicated to excellence in children's literature, and seek high-quality Christian fiction and nonfiction. Send us something realistic and true to Christian tenants.

The Judaica Press

123 Ditmas Avenue
Brooklyn, NY 11218

Editor: Norman Shapiro

Publisher's Interests

The juvenile books from Judaica Press are intended for
children who already possess some knowledge of Judaism.
These books are written to entertain young readers, as well
as instruct them about Jewish life and customs.
Website: www.judaicapress.com

Freelance Potential

Published 12 titles (7–8 juvenile) in 2005: 5 were developed
from unsolicited submissions and 1–2 were reprint/licensed
properties. Receives 100 queries, 90 unsolicited mss yearly.

- **Fiction:** Publishes early picture books, 0–4 years; easy-to-read
  books, 4–7 years; story picture books, 4–10 years; and young
  adult books, 12–18 years. Genres include religious mystery
  and suspense; and religious fiction.
- **Nonfiction:** Publishes story picture books, 4–10 years. Topics
  include Jewish traditions, self-help issues, Bible stories, crafts,
  and hobbies.
- **Representative Titles:** *Count with Mendel* by Naftali Cisner
  (1–3 years) is a board book that helps toddlers learn to count
  while teaching them about the Jewish holidays. *The Most
  Beautiful Picture in the World* by Menucha Fuchs (2–5 years) is
  a story that teaches about cooperation.

Submissions and Payment

Query with outline; or send complete ms. Accepts photocopies and computer printouts. Availability of artwork
improves chance of acceptance. SASE. Responds in 3
months. Publication in 1–2 years. Royalty.

Editor's Comments

We're open to submissions on any topic related to traditional
Jewish life. Authors who feel confident they can convey
concepts of Judaism to children in an entertaining way are
invited to submit. Accompanying artwork in the form of
color prints or drawings is especially welcome.

Just Us Books

3rd Floor
356 Glenwood Avenue
East Orange, NJ 07017

Submissions Manager

Publisher's Interests
Specializing in African American books for young people, this publisher offers realistic, contemporary fiction and biographies with cultural authenticity.
Website: www.justusbooks.com

Freelance Potential
Published 10 titles (all juvenile) in 2005: 2 were developed from unsolicited submissions, 1 was by an agented author, and 5 were reprint/licensed properties. Of the 10 titles, 2 were by unpublished writers and 2 were by authors who were new to the publishing house. Receives 1,000+ queries each year.

- **Fiction:** Published 2 concept books, 0–4 years; 2 easy-to-read books, 4–7 years; 2 story picture books, 4–10 years; 3 middle-grade books, 8–12 years; and 1 young adult book, 12–18 years. Genres include contemporary, multicultural, and historical fiction; adventure; and mystery.
- **Nonfiction:** Publishes middle-grade books, 8–12 years. Topics include history and culture. Also publishes biographies.
- **Representative Titles:** *Ma Dears' Old Green House* by Denise Lewis Patrick (3–7 years) recalls childhood memories of visiting a warm, safe, comforting place. *Eddie's Ordeal* by Kelly Starling Lyons (9–12 years) tells about a family secret that changes a boy's life forever; part of the NEATE series.

Submissions and Payment
Guidelines available. Query with outline/synopsis and biography. SASE. Responds in 3–4 months. Publication period varies. Royalty.

Editor's Comments
We encourage queries from new writers. We seek fiction and nonfiction for ages thirteen to sixteen. Plots must be compelling, and introduce conflict and resolution by realistic characters. A tie-in to African American history or culture is necessary.

Kaeden Books

P.O. Box 16190
Rocky River, OH 44116

Editor: Craig Urmston

Publisher's Interests

Kaeden Books is an educational publisher that offers materials for emergent and early readers. Its leveled readers are aimed at students between the ages of five and ten.
Website: www.kaeden.com

Freelance Potential

Published 16–20 titles (all juvenile) in 2005: 12 were developed from unsolicited submissions. Receives 10,000 queries and unsolicited mss yearly.

- **Fiction:** Published 2 easy-to-read books, 4–7 years; and 6 story picture books, 4–10 years. Genres include contemporary fiction.
- **Nonfiction:** Published 8 story picture books. Topics include nature, biography, science, and social studies.
- **Representative Titles:** *We Like Puddles* (4–10 years) takes a fun look at weather and springtime through the eyes of children and some ducks. *What Am I?* (4–10 years) uses clever clues and riddles to help students predict the name of animals and write a book of their own. *We Need Trees* (4–7 years) uses a colorful story to show how we need trees, and the products they offer us.

Submissions and Payment

Guidelines available at website. Send complete ms; no originals. Accepts photocopies and computer printouts. SASE. Responds only if interested. Response time and publication period vary. Royalty. Flat fee.

Editor's Comments

This year we plan to focus on nonfiction for children ages five through ten. Subjects we are looking for include social studies, science, plants, animals, and communities. We seek material that is in line with current curriculum guidelines, so please familiarize yourself before submitting.

Kar-Ben Publishing

Suite 2
11430 Strand Drive
Rockville, MD 20852

Submissions Editor: Madeline Wikler

Publisher's Interests
A division of Lerner Publishing Group, Kar-Ben is a specialty publisher that offers titles on Jewish themes for children and families.
Website: www.karben.com

Freelance Potential
Published 12 titles (all juvenile) in 2005: 3 were developed from unsolicited submissions and 1 was by an agented author, and 1 was a reprint/licensed property. Receives 300–400 queries, 350 unsolicited mss yearly.

- **Fiction:** Published 2 concept books, 0–4 years; 2 toddler books, 0–4 years; 2 early picture books, 0–4 years; 2 story picture books, 4–10 years; and 2 chapter books, 5–10 years. Features folktales; and Bible, holiday, and lifecycle stories.
- **Nonfiction:** Published 2 story picture books, 4–10 years. Topics include animals, natural history, and humor. Includes activity and board books.
- **Representative Titles:** *It's Hanukkah Time!* by Latifa Berry Kroph (2–6 years) introduces children to the holiday of Hanukkah. *The Mouse in the Matzah Factory* by Francine Medoff (3–8 years) is the story of a mouse who journeys from a wheat field to a city matzah factory.

Submissions and Payment
Guidelines available. Send complete ms. Accepts photocopies, computer printouts, and simultaneous submissions if identified. SASE. Responds in 3–5 weeks. Publication period varies. Royalty; 5–8%; advance, $500–$2,000.

Editor's Comments
We are interested in stories that reflect the ethnic and cultural diversity of today's Jewish and interfaith families. We are looking for concise stories about characters with whom today's readers can relate. Please do not send artwork with submissions.

Key Curriculum Press

1150 65th Street
Emeryville, CA 94608

President and Editorial Director: Steve Rasmussen

Publisher's Interests

For innovative math textbooks, software, and supplemental materials that educators can use in secondary and middle school classrooms, this publisher provides an extensive catalogue of helpful titles.
Website: www.keypress.com

Freelance Potential

Published 70 titles in 2005. Receives 150 queries yearly.

- **Nonfiction:** Publishes textbooks, software, and supplemental materials for grades 6–12.
- **Representative Titles:** *Discovering Geometry: An Investigative Approach* by Michael Serra (grades 8–10) involves students in active participation in their own learning of geometric relationships using a wide variety of tools. *Sensor Sensibility* by Jack Randall (grades 9–12) reveals the fascinating connections between mathematics and science to broaden students' understanding of algebra.

Submissions and Payment

Guidelines available on website. Query with résumé, prospectus, a detailed table of contents, and 1–3 sample chapters. Accepts photocopies, computer printouts, disk submissions, and simultaneous submissions if identified. SASE. Responds in 2 months. Publication period varies. Royalty, 6–10%.

Editor's Comments

We are interested in seeing math materials for grades six through twelve. For all materials, the reading level should be appropriate to the skill level of the students and the nature of the materials. Everything that we publish must conform to the standards of the National Council of Teachers of Mathematics (NCTM). Be sure and browse our catalogue to get an idea of what types of educational materials we publish on mathematics.

Kids Can Press

29 Birch Avenue
Toronto, Ontario M4V 1E2
Canada

Acquisitions Editor

Publisher's Interests

Producing books for children from birth to age 14, Kids Can Press offers picture books, young adult novels, and nonfiction on topics of interest to teens. It publishes the work of Canadian authors only.
Website: www.kidscanpress.com

Freelance Potential

Published 60 titles (11 juvenile) in 2005: 12 were by agented authors. Receives 3,600–4,800 unsolicited mss yearly.

- **Fiction:** Publishes early picture books, 0–4 years; easy-to read books, 4–7 years; story picture books, 4–10 years; middle-grade books, 8–12 years; and young adult books, 12–18 years. Genres include fantasy, folklore, folktales, mystery, and suspense.
- **Nonfiction:** Publishes early picture books, 0–4 years; easy-to read books, 4–7 years; story picture books, 4–10 years; and young adult books, 12–14 years. Topics include animals, pets, crafts, hobbies, nature, and the environment.
- **Representative Titles:** *The Turning* by Gillian Chan (YA) is a novel about a teen who encounters mysterious people and events when he moves to England to live with his father. *Walking with the Dead* by L. M. Falcone (9–12 years) is a novel that revolves around a perfectly preserved ancient Greek corpse that wakes from the dead and the boy who tries to help him.

Submissions and Payment

Canadian authors only. Guidelines and catalogue available at website. Send complete ms. Accepts photocopies and computer printouts. SASE. Response time and publication period vary. Royalty; advance.

Editor's Comments

Our award-winning books have earned us a reputation for excellence. We seek books that entertain, inform, and delight the most important audience in the world—young readers.

Alfred A. Knopf Books for Young Readers

1745 Broadway
New York, NY 10019

Submissions Editor

Publisher's Interests

Picture books, board books, and novels for children from birth through young adult fill the list of this publisher. An imprint of Random House Children's Books, its produces top-notch fiction from award-winning authors.
Website: www.randomhouse.com/kids

Freelance Potential

Published 50 titles in 2005: all by agented authors. Receives 4,000 unsolicited mss yearly.

- **Fiction:** Publishes picture books, 0–8 years; chapter books, 5–10 years; middle-grade novels, 8–12 years; and young adult books, 12–18 years. Genres include historical, contemporary, and multicultural fiction.
- **Representative Titles:** *Kate, the Cat and the Moon* by David Almond (4–8 years) is a dreamy tale of a girl that changes into a cat and roams her familiar neighborhood for one glorious night. *Winter Friends* by Mary Quattlebaum (2–5 years) is a lively story in poems that celebrates the good times to be had by all in winter. *Flush* by Carl Hiaasen (10+ years) is a story that follows a boy's plans to uncover a crooked casino boat owner who is polluting the harbor.

Submissions and Payment

Guidelines available at website. Accepts agented submissions only. Accepts photocopies, computer printouts, and simultaneous submissions if identified. SASE. Responds in 3 months. Publication in 1–2 years. Royalty; advance.

Editor's Comments

We look for quality literature for children of all ages. Due to the volume of materials we receive, we now only accept unsolicited manuscripts if they are submitted to one of our two contests. Check our website for rules and guidelines. All other types of manuscripts must be submitted through an agent or by the request of an editor.

Wendy Lamb Books

1745 Broadway
New York, NY 10019

Editor: Wendy Lamb

Publisher's Interests
Targeting young adult and middle-grade readers, this imprint of Random House publishes both fiction and nonfiction. Its list covers topics such as history, adventure, mystery, humor, and multicultural themes.
Website: www.randomhouse.com

Freelance Potential
Published 12 titles (12 juvenile) in 2005: 1 was developed from an unsolicited submission and 11 were by agented authors. Of the 12 titles, 3 were by unpublished writers and 3 were by authors who were new to the publishing house. Receives 1,000 unsolicited queries yearly.

- **Fiction:** Published 5 middle-grade books, 8–12 years; and 7 young adult books, 12–18 years. Genres include adventure, humor, multicultural, and mystery.
- **Nonfiction:** Publishes middle-grade books, 8–12 years; and young adult books, 12–18 years. Topics include history, and multicultural themes.
- **Representative Titles:** *My Big Sister Is So Bossy* by Mary Hershey (8–12 years) tells the story of a girl who has big plans to win a science prize, find a best friend, and get back at her older sister. *The Crimes and Punishments of Miss Payne* by Barry Jonsberg (12+ years) is a unique story about two friends who set out to prove their horrible teacher is crooked.

Submissions and Payment
Guidelines available. Query with age group and publishing credits, along with 3 sample chapters. Accepts photocopies, computer printouts, and disk submissions (Microsoft Word). SASE. Responds in 6 weeks. Publication period and payment policy vary.

Editor's Comments
After submitting your query, please do not phone, email, or fax to inquire about your submission. Queries and questions about submissions should be made in writing.

Lark Books

67 Broadway
Asheville, NC 28801

Editorial Director: Joe Rhatigan

Publisher's Interests

Activity and craft books for middle-grade, young adult, and adult readers are the specialty of this publisher. From ceramics to beaded bags, from creative writing to science activities, this publisher covers a wide variety of topics.
Website: www.larkbooks.com

Freelance Potential

Published 60 titles (20 juvenile) in 2005: 10 were developed from unsolicited submissions and 5 were reprint/licensed properties. Receives 25 queries yearly.

- **Nonfiction:** Publishes middle-grade books, 8–12 years; and young adult books, 12–18 years. Topics include art instruction, creative writing, general activities, and crafts. Also publishes reference books.
- **Representative Titles:** *Out-of-this-World Astronomy* by Joe Rhatigan, Rain Newcomb, & Greg Doppmann (8–12 years) offers fabulous images, projects, and fascinating scientific information on astronomy. *Gross Me Out!* by Ralph Retcher & Betty Poo (8–12 years) offers wonderfully repulsive projects kids will love including exploring the slimy side of the human body, and meeting critters that live under the skin.

Submissions and Payment

Guidelines available at website. Prefers query with résumé, table of contents, introduction, 2–3 sample projects, and a description of artwork and illustrations. SASE. Response time varies. Publication period and payment policy vary.

Editor's Comments

We are currently de-emphasizing craft books and are interested in more activity books that emphasize science and reference. Material must pique the readers curiosity, and be both educational and entertaining. First-time and published writers are welcome to submit a query. If we are interested, we will ask you to submit a complete proposal.

Leadership Publishers Inc.

P.O. Box 8358
Des Moines, IA 50201-8358

Editor/Owner: Dr. Louis Roets

Publisher's Interests

Enrichment programs for gifted students in kindergarten through grade twelve, as well as reference books and curriculums for teachers, educational professionals, and parents can be found in the catalog of this publisher. It covers topics such as leadership skills, staff development, serving gifted and talented students, instructional strategies, and understanding success and failure.

Website: www.leadershippublishers.com

Freelance Potential

Published 2 titles in 2005. Receives 10 queries yearly.

- **Nonfiction:** Publishes acceleration and enrichment programs, grades K–12. Also publishes resource and reference materials for school administrators, teachers, counselors, and parents.
- **Representative Titles:** *Gifted and Standard Education: Issues of Mutual Concern* by Lois F. Roets (teachers) uses question and response on many issues related to gifted and standard curriculum for teachers of K–12. *Effective Student Councils for Elementary—A Resource Book for Teachers and Administrators* by Pamela Zielske (teachers) offers a ready-to-use guide for effective Student Councils.

Submissions and Payment

Send for guidelines and catalog before submitting (SASE with 2 first-class stamps). Then query with table of contents, outline, and 2 sample chapters. Accepts photocopies and computer printouts. SASE. Responds in 2 months. Publication in 6–12 months. Royalty, 10%; flat fee.

Editor's Comments

We are only looking for updates of titles that are selling. Our readers turn to us for the latest educational materials for gifted and high ability students. Check our website for the type of books that we publish. Currently, we are only soliciting titles and do not accept unsolicited manuscripts.

Learning Horizons

1 American Road
Cleveland, OH 44144

Editorial Manager: Colleen Tsironis

Publisher's Interests

Striving to make learning fun and exciting, this educational publisher offers a variety of resources for teachers and parents of children up to grade six. Its list includes workbooks, activity books, and game cards, as well as stationery, stickers, and other educational materials.
Website: www.learninghorizons.com

Freelance Potential

Published 34 titles (all juvenile) in 2005: all were assigned and most titles are from reprint/licensed properties. Of the 34 titles, 1 was by an unpublished writer and 4 were by authors who were new to the publishing house. Receives 600 queries yearly.

- **Nonfiction:** Published 4 story picture books, 4–10 years; and 30 workbooks. Features educational and informational titles and novelty and board books. Topics include math, language, science, social studies, holidays, nature, and the environment.
- **Representative Titles:** *Beginning Reading* (3–12 years) is a workbook that offers a variety of educational activities that promote reading; part of the Learn on the Go series. *Seals!* (4–9 years) offers awesome life-like illustrations and engaging text about where seals live, how they look, and how they change as they grow; part of the Know-It-Alls series.

Submissions and Payment

Query. SASE. Responds in 3–4 months. Publication in 18 months. Payment policy varies.

Editor's Comments

We're looking for workbooks and other novelty books on subjects such as language skills, reading, writing, math for preschool through third grade. Many of our products are developed by professional educators who know best the skills children need to succeed and how to present and teach those skills. We target both teachers and parents.

Learning Resources

380 North Fairway Drive
Vernon Hills, IL 60061

Editorial Director

Publisher's Interests
Learning Resources provides teachers in kindergarten through grade six classrooms with supplemental materials for teaching math, science, language arts, and geography.
Website: www.learningresources.com

Freelance Potential
Published 50 titles in 2005. Of the 50 titles, 3 were by unpublished writers and 5 were by authors who were new to the publishing house. Receives 25 queries yearly.

- **Nonfiction:** Publishes educational materials, manipulatives, workbooks, and activity books, pre-K–grade 6. Topics include reading, ESL, ELL, early childhood learning, math, measurement, Spanish, science, geography, and nutrition. Also publishes teacher resources.
- **Representative Titles:** *Improving Student Reading Comprehension* (grades 1–6) uses engaging stories and related activities to help students master basic reading skills. *Terrifying Tornadoes!* (grades 3–8) is a cross-curriculum title that combines science and math facts with reading and research skills; part of the Weather Wise series.

Submissions and Payment
Catalogue available with 9x12 SASE ($3 postage). Query with résumé and writing samples. Accepts photocopies, computer printouts, and disk submissions. SASE. Responds in 6–12 weeks. Publication in 1–2 years. Flat fee.

Editor's Comments
Most of our authors have a strong background in education and in the areas we cover with our materials. We continue to need activity books with corresponding manipulatives and reproducibles, especially for ESL, ELL, and Spanish programs. Remember that we specialize in kindergarten through grade six materials, so make sure your submission is age appropriate.

Lee & Low Books

95 Madison Avenue
New York, NY 10016

Submissions Editor

Publisher's Interests
Lee & Low Books strives to meet the needs of children of color by publishing fictional stories and informational books that promote the understanding of people across cultural and racial lines.
Website: www.leeandlow.com

Freelance Potential
Published 20 titles in 2005: 2 were developed from unsolicited submissions and 6 were by agented authors. Of the 20 titles, 4 were by unpublished writers and 6 were by authors who were new to the publishing house. Receives 2,000 unsolicited mss yearly.

- **Fiction:** Publishes story picture books, 4–10 years; middle-grade books, 8–12 years. Genres include historical, realistic, contemporary, multicultural, and ethnic fiction.
- **Nonfiction:** Publishes picture books, 4–10 years; middle-grade books, 8–12 years; and young adult books, 12–18 years. Topics include people and multicultural issues.
- **Representative Titles:** *Brothers in Hope* by Mary Williams (7+ years) follows a courageous Sudanese boy who walks thousands of miles to a refugee camp after he is orphaned by civil war. *Destiny's Gift* by Natasha Anastasia Tarpley (6–10 years) is the heartwarming story about a girl's love of reading.

Submissions and Payment
Guidelines and catalogue available at website or with 9x12 SASE ($1.75 postage). Send complete ms. Accepts photocopies, computer printouts, and simultaneous submissions. SASE. Responds in 2–4 months. Publication in 1–2 years. Royalty; advance.

Editor's Comments
This year we are seeking multicultural fiction and nonfiction for ages six through twelve, as well as picture books and middle-grade projects.

Legacy Press

P.O. Box 261129
San Diego, CA 92196

Editorial Director: Christy Scannell

Publisher's Interests
Legacy Press focuses on evangelical nonfiction books for children ages two to twelve that promote Christian values, as well as devotionals and activity books. It also offers a limited line of contemporary Christian fiction series titles.
Website: www.rainbowpublishers.com

Freelance Potential
Published 16 titles (4 juvenile) in 2005: 8 were developed from unsolicited submissions. Receives 500 queries yearly.

- **Fiction:** Publishes series books, 2–12 years. Genres include contemporary religious and Christian fiction.
- **Nonfiction:** Publishes evangelical-based titles, 2–12 years. Topics include the Bible, religion, holidays, crafts, and hobbies. Also publishes activity books and devotionals.
- **Representative Titles:** *Instant Bible Lessons for Toddlers* (1–3 years) gets little ones excited about Bible learning through puzzles, games, crafts, and snacks. *Teaching Children to Pray* (grades 1–2) helps children learn four types of prayer using cut, color, and paste activities.

Submissions and Payment
Guidelines and catalogue available with 9x12 SASE (2 first-class stamps). Query with table of contents and first 3 chapters. Accepts photocopies. SASE. Responds in 3 months. Publication in 6–36 months. Royalty, 8%+; advance, $500+.

Editor's Comments
We are actively seeking reproducible classroom resource books that use crafts, games, puzzles and other activities to creatively teach the Bible to children. We prefer creative writers who have accepted Jesus and are dedicated to serving him, are active participants in a Bible-believing church, and relate well to the needs of the evangelical Christian market. Be sure to tell us how your book differs from others currently on the market.

Lerner Publishing Group

241 First Avenue North
Minneapolis, MN 55401

Submissions Editor: Jennifer Zimian

Publisher's Interests

Nonfiction children's titles for the school library market
are the specialty of this publisher. Educational books cover
topics of interest to readers age four to eighteen.
Website: www.lernerbooks.com

Freelance Potential

Published 250 titles in 2005: 5 were developed from unsolicited submissions, 50 were by agented authors, and 12
were reprint/licensed properties. Of the 250 titles, 5 were by
authors who were new to the publishing house. Receives
500 queries, 2,000 unsolicited mss yearly.

- **Nonfiction:** Publishes easy-to-read books, 4–7 years; chapter
  books, 5–10 years; middle-grade titles, 8–12 years; and young
  adult books, 12–18 years. Topics include natural and physical
  science, current events, ancient and modern history, world
  cultures, and sports. Also publishes biographies.
- **Representative Titles:** *The Art of Making Comic Books* by
  Michael Pellowski (grades 4–9) introduces readers to the many
  different aspects of producing a comic book. *My Pet Cats* by
  LeeAnne Engler (grades 2–6) follows a girl as she discovers
  that it's twice the adventure to keep up with her playful pets.

Submissions and Payment

Guidelines and catalogue available with 9x12 SASE ($3.50
postage). Query with outline and sample chapter; or send
complete ms with résumé. Accepts submissions in November only. Accepts photocopies, computer printouts, and
simultaneous submissions if identified. SASE. Responds in
6–8 months. Publication period and payment policy vary.

Editor's Comments

We continue to consider manuscripts for contemporary and
historical biographies, especially those that would appeal to
boys. We are not interested in religious topics, workbooks,
or activity books.

Arthur A. Levine Books

Scholastic Inc.
557 Broadway
New York, NY 10012

Editorial Director: Arthur A. Levine

Publisher's Interests

Literary fiction and nonfiction for children and young adults are found on this publisher's list. Its titles feature strong writing and authentic emotion, and its editors welcome submissions from new authors.

Website: www.arthuralevinebooks.com

Freelance Potential

Published 15 titles in 2005: 2 were developed from unsolicited submissions, 11 were by agented authors, and 5 were reprint/licensed properties. Receives 2,000 queries yearly.

- **Fiction:** Published 7 story picture books, 4–10 years; 1 middle-grade novel, 8–10 years; and 6 young adult books, 12–18 years. Genres include multicultural fiction. Also publishes poetry.
- **Nonfiction:** Published 1 concept book, 0–4 years. Also publishes picture books, 4–10 years; middle-grade books, 8–12 years; and young adult books, 12–18 years; and biographies.
- **Representative Titles:** *The Legend of the Wandering King* by Laura Gallego García (10+ years) is a historical fantasy based on the true story of a prince in pre-Islamic Arabia. *Birdwing* by Rafe Martin (YA) is a mythic story of a boy torn between his human nature and the swan he used to be.

Submissions and Payment

Guidelines available. Query. Accepts complete ms from agented and previously published authors only. Accepts photocopies. SASE. Responds to queries in 4 weeks; to mss in 6–8 months. Publication in 18–24 months. Payment policy varies.

Editor's Comments

Strive to write a query letter that reveals the character of your writing and gives us an overall feel for the work. A good query reads like jacket or catalogue copy—don't think of a query letter as a dull form to fill out. One page is sufficient.

Libraries Unlimited

88 Post Road
Westport, CT 06881

Acquisitions Editor: Barbara Ittner

Publisher's Interests
This educational publisher provides books and reference guides for educators, librarians, and media specialists.
Website: www.lu.com

Freelance Potential
Published 100 titles (40 juvenile) in 2005: 7 were developed from unsolicited submissions and 8 were by agented authors. Of the 100 titles, 5 were by unpublished writers and 30 were by authors who were new to the publishing house. Receives 400 queries, 7 unsolicited mss yearly.

- **Fiction:** Publishes toddler books, 0–4 years; story picture books, 4–10 years; and chapter books, 5–10 years. Genres include historical fiction; folklore; suspense; and stories about animals, nature, and the environment.
- **Nonfiction:** Publishes curriculum titles. Features bilingual books, grades K–6; and activity books, grades K–12. Also features biographies, professional reference titles, gifted education titles, and regional books. Topics include science, mathematics, social studies, whole language, and literature.
- **Representative Titles:** *Storytelling for Young Adults* by Gail de Vos (YA) is an annotated bibliography of stories from around the world. *Talk about Books!* by Elizabeth Knowles & Martha Smith (8–12 years) features a book list and discussion topics for book clubs.

Submissions and Payment
Guidelines available. Query with sample chapters, table of contents, and résumé; or send complete ms. Accepts photocopies, computer printouts, and simultaneous submissions. SASE. Responds in 2–3 months. Publication in 10–12 months. Royalty.

Editor's Comments
We are looking for material for educators that is written by educators who have used the ideas in their library or classroom. Please review our catalogue prior to submission.

Lillenas Publishing Company

2923 Troost Avenue
Kansas City, MO 64109

Drama Editor: Kimberly R. Messer

Publisher's Interests
For over 20 years, this publisher has been providing Christian schools and churches with quality creative resources for drama ministry. Its catalogue includes sketch collections, full-length and one-act plays, musicals, puppet scripts, worship resources, and how-to books.
Website: www.lillenasdrama.com

Freelance Potential
Published 15 titles in 2005. Receives 300–400 unsolicited mss yearly.

- **Fiction:** Publishes full-length and one-act plays, monologues, sketches, skits, recitations, puppet plays, and dramatic exercises, 6–18 years. Also publishes dramatic material on Christmas, Thanksgiving, Mother's Day, and other holiday themes.
- **Nonfiction:** Publishes theater resource materials. Topics include stage design, scenery, production techniques, and drama ministry.
- **Representative Titles:** *Just for the Play of It* by Debbie Salter Goodwin approaches drama as a fun experience involving movement, storytelling, imagination, and learning. *Over the Airwaves* by Martha Bolton offers a collection of sketches and monologues for children and young teens.

Submissions and Payment
Writers' guidelines available. Send complete ms with cast list, scene description, and prop list. Accepts computer printouts. SASE. Responds in 2–3 months. Publication period varies. Flat fee.

Editor's Comments
We're looking for adult, youth, and children's drama with a spiritual viewpoint, as well as current events and church calendars. We look for material that will create an impact on the audience. Before submitting, we recommend you acquaint yourself with our publications and style.

Linnet Books

The Shoe String Press
2 Linsley Street
New Haven, CT 06473

President: Diantha C. Thorpe

Publisher's Interests

Specializing in nonfiction for children in grades six through twelve, this publisher offers titles that include biographies, reference books, history, memoirs, folktales, and multicultural children's materials. It targets the school and library markets.
Website: www.shoestringpress.com

Freelance Potential

Published 8 titles in 2005: Receives 500 queries yearly.

- **Nonfiction:** Publishes interdisciplinary books, memoirs, biographies, reference books, literacy companions, and multicultural children's publishing materials. Topics include social studies, natural history, folktales, storytelling, art, archaeology, and anthropology.
- **Representative Titles:** *Daisy Bates* by Amy Polakow (grades 12+) portrays the life of this proud civil rights activist who was instrumental in breaking down the racial barriers of the South. *Theodore Roosevelt* by Matt Donnelly (grades 7+) offers an engaging and informative biography of this prominent figure in American history.

Submissions and Payment

Query with 2 sample chapters. Accepts photocopies, computer printouts, and simultaneous submissions if identified. SASE. Responds in 4 months. Publication in 1 year. Royalty; advance.

Editor's Comments

We strive to provide nonfiction books that ignite the imagination and enrich the knowledge of readers from varying ages and backgounds. We like books that are interdisciplinary, multicultural or multiethnic, and that are solid works of research, scholarship, and understanding. Folktales and first-person narratives continue to be of interest to us, as well as books about significant historical or cultural influences.

Linworth Publishing

Suite L
480 East Wilson Bridge Road
Worthington, OH 43085

Acquisitions Editor: Donna King

Publisher's Interests

Professional resources for school librarians and media specialists are available from Linworth Publishing. Its books address the real-world challenges of librarians, enhance their professional development, and contribute to the enrichment of their students.
Website: www.linworth.com

Freelance Potential

Published 20 titles in 2005: 10 were developed from unsolicited submissions. Receives 120 queries yearly.

- **Nonfiction:** Publishes books about school libraries, school media centers, literature, and technology for librarians, media specialists, and teachers, grades K–12. Also offers professional development titles.
- **Representative Titles:** *Essentials of Elementary School Library Management* by Laurie Thelen is a handbook of activities and project ideas for daily practice that also includes time-management tips and sample spreadsheets to master grant-writing strategies. *Learning Right from Wrong in the Digital Age* by Doug Johnson helps media specialists understand today's information technology ethics, from downloading explicit pictures to guessing passwords to respect for privacy, property, and the law.

Submissions and Payment

Guidelines and catalogue available at website. Query or send 2 hard copies of complete ms with IBM disk. Accepts email queries to linworth@linworthpublishing.com. SASE. Responds in 1 week. Publication in 6 months. Royalty.

Editor's Comments

Our authors are school librarians and media specialists themselves, leaders in the profession with ideas that are backed up by years of experience. Our books help our readers keep up with the latest developments in their field.

Lion Publishing

Mayfield House
256 Banbury Road
Oxford OX2 7DH
England

Editorial Secretary: Catherine Giddings

Publisher's Interests

Books that reflect Christian values and inspire a Christian world view are the specialty of this British publisher. Its list includes fiction, nonfiction, and biographies for children.
Website: www.lionhudson.com

Freelance Potential

Published 150 titles (83 juvenile) in 2005: 3 were developed from unsolicited submissions, and 30 were by agented authors. Of the 150 titles, 2 were by authors who were new to the publishing house. Receives 1,000 unsolicited mss each year.

- **Fiction:** Publishes concept books, toddler books, and early picture books, 0–4 years; easy-to-read books, 4–7 years; story picture books, 4–10 years; chapter books, 5–10 years; middle-grade titles, 8–12 years; and young adult books, 12–18 years. Genres include fairy tales, inspirational fiction, and adventure.
- **Nonfiction:** Publishes early picture books, 0–4 years; easy-to-read books, 4–7 years; story picture books, 4–10 years; and middle-grade titles, 8–12 years. Topics include current events, history, humor, nature, the environment, religion, social issues, health, and fitness. Also publishes biographies.
- **Representative Titles:** *Chilling Out* by Meg Harper is a charming story about a little girl who wants to live a simple life. *Jonah and the Whale* is an illustrated version of the well-known Bible story.

Submissions and Payment

Guidelines available. Query with résumé. Accepts photocopies. SASE. Responds in 1 week. Publication period and payment policy vary.

Editor's Comments

We receive hundreds of manuscripts every year, and publish very few of them. Most of our material is commissioned by our editors, rather than submitted on spec.

Little, Brown and Company Books for Young Readers

1271 Avenue of the Americas
New York, NY 10020

Editor-in-Chief: Megan Tingley

Publisher's Interests
The books that appear in this publisher's catalogue are written by agented authors and include picture books, middle-grade and young adult titles, and some books for toddlers.
Website: www.lb-kids.com or www.lb-teens.com

Freelance Potential
Published 12 titles in 2005: all were by agented authors. Of the 12 titles, 1 was by an author who was new to the publishing house. Receives 600+ queries yearly.

- **Fiction:** Publishes toddler books, 0–4 years; story picture books, 4–10 years; middle-grade books, 5–10 years; and young adult books, 12–18 years. Genres include contemporary and multicultural fiction. Also publishes stories about holidays and music.
- **Nonfiction:** Publishes toddler books, 0–4 years; story picture books, 4–10 years; middle-grade books, 8–12 years; and young adult books, 12–18 years. Topics include multicultural and ethnic issues, crafts, and hobbies.
- **Representative Titles:** *Mummies, Pyramids, and Pharaohs* by Gail Gibbons (4–8 years) introduces young readers to ancient Egypt. *Never, Ever Shout in a Zoo* by Karma Wilson (3–6 years) depicts the chain of chaotic events that take place when a young girl innocently shouts at the zoo.

Submissions and Payment
Accepts submissions sent by literary agents or those sent at the request of the editors only. No unsolicited mss or queries. Accepts photocopies. SASE. Responds in 2 months. Publication period varies. Royalty; advance.

Editor's Comments
We're currently reviewing agented submissions on topics that include humor, music, multicultural issues, and the supernatural. Right now, our editorial focus is on books for middle-grade and young adult readers rather than on picture books.

Little Simon

Simon & Schuster Children's Publishing Division
1230 Avenue of the Americas
New York, NY 10020

Editorial Department

Publisher's Interests

Young children enjoy the variety of novelty books produced by this publisher. Its list includes pop-up books, board books, lift-the-flap books, interactive books, and touch-and-feel books. An imprint of Simon & Schuster Children's Publishing, it offers mainly fiction.
Website: www.simonsayskids.com

Freelance Potential

Published 65 titles in 2005: 20 were by agented authors and 15 were reprint/licensed properties. Receives 200 queries each year.

- **Fiction:** Publishes concept, toddler, and board books, 0–4 years; and pop-up books, 4–8 years. Topics cover animals, holidays, trucks and automobiles, and the weather.
- **Representative Titles:** *Mommy, I Love You* by Quentin Greban (4–8 years) follows an artistic ladybug who has lost her way and meets various animals while trying to find her mommy. *Ocean Babies* by Deborah Lee Rose (4–8 years) provides lyrical text and colorful illustrations that capture new ocean life.

Submissions and Payment

Query only. No unsolicited mss. Accepts agented submissions only. SASE. Responds in 6 months. Publication in 2 years. Royalty; advance. Flat fee.

Editor's Comments

We look for unique novelty books that children and parents will love. Our products make reading fun and excite and motivate children to read. We have strict guideline procedures and accept queries and agented submissions only. Unsolicited material will be returned unread. If you have an idea for something other than the standard type of picture, chapter, or young adult book, send us a query. If we feel it matches our needs, we will contact you.

Little Tiger Press

1 The Coda Centre
189 Munster Road
London SW6 6AW
United Kingdom

Editor: Laura Workman

Publisher's Interests
Little Tiger Press specializes in children's books. Its titles blend age-appropriate humor, drama, and imagination with education and inspiration.
Website: www.littletigerpress.com

Freelance Potential
Published 40–50 titles in 2005: 2–3 were developed from unsolicited submissions, 10 were by agented authors, and 3 were reprint/licensed properties. Of the 40–50 titles, 6 were by unpublished writers and 6 were by authors who were new to the publishing house. Receives 200 queries each year.

- **Fiction:** Publishes toddler books and early picture books, 0–4 years; story picture books, 3–7 years; and easy-to-read books, 4–7 years. Genres include classic and contemporary fiction, animal stories, novelty books, and board books.
- **Nonfiction:** Publishes early picture books, 0–4 years; and story picture books, 3–7 years. Also publishes novelty and board books. Topics include animals, pets, nature, the environment, and holidays.
- **Representative Titles:** *Lazy Ozzie* by Michael Coleman & Gwyneth Williamson (3–6 years) involves a lazy owl, a clever plan, and all the animals on the farm. *I've Seen Santa* by David Bedford & Tim Warnes (3–7 years) tells of a little bear who is determined to stay awake on Christmas Eve.

Submissions and Payment
Guidelines available at website. Send complete ms. Accepts photocopies and computer printouts. SAE/IRC. Responds in 2 months. Publication period varies. Payment policy varies.

Editor's Comments
We're looking for cozy, comical, and crazy stories that fit every mood of our young readers.

Llewellyn Publications

P.O. Box 64383
St. Paul, MN 55164-0383

Acquisitions Editor: Megan C. Atwood

Publisher's Interests

Llewellyn offers fiction and nonfiction for middle-grade through young adult readers. Mystery, suspense, witchcraft, spells, magic, metaphysics, self-help, fantasy, science fiction, and astrology make up a large portion of its list.
Website: www.llewellyn.com

Freelance Potential

Published 21 titles in 2005: 5 were developed from unsolicited submissions and 16 were by agented authors. Receives 300 queries, 200 unsolicited mss yearly.

- **Fiction:** Publishes middle-grade books, 8–12 years; and young adult books, 12–18 years. Genres include mystery, fantasy, science fiction, suspense, and shamanism.
- **Nonfiction:** Publishes young adult books, 12–18 years. Topics include astrology, wicca, and magic.
- **Representative Titles:** *Red Is for Remembrance* by Laurie Faria Stolarz (YA) is the fourth addition to a series of best-selling teen thrillers. *The Ghost of Shady Lane* by Dotti Enderle (8–12 years) is an apparition known as the Grey Lady that turns up at a historical landmark; part of the Fortune Tellers Club series.

Submissions and Payment

Guidelines available with #10 SASE ($.74 postage) or at website. Catalogue available at website. Send complete ms with a formatted disk (Microsoft Word), author questionnaire, author data and book information form. Accepts photocopies. SASE. Responds in 2–6 months. Publication in 1–2 years. Royalty, 10%.

Editor's Comments

We want to see cutting-edge, well-written young adult books for ages 12–18. Topics can range from fantasy/sci fi to realism. Know your competition—read current bestsellers and magazines for teens, and talk to librarians.

Lobster Press

Suites C & D
1620 Sherbrooke Street West
Montreal, Quebec H3H 1C9
Canada

Publishing Assistant: Stephanie Normandin

Publisher's Interests
High-quality fiction and nonfiction for children up to teens, including picture books, easy-to-read chapter books, and contemporary young adult works, are on this publisher's list.
Website: www.lobsterpress.com

Freelance Potential
Published 12 titles in 2005: 1 was developed from an unsolicited submissions and 2 were by agented authors. Of the 12 titles, 3 were by unpublished writers, and 2 were by authors who were new to the publishing house. Receives 100 queries, 1000 unsolicited mss yearly.

- **Fiction:** Publishes story picture books, 4–10 years; middle-grade books, 8–12 years; and young adult books, 12–18 years. Also publishes chapter books, 5–10 years. Genres include contemporary fiction, humorous stories, and fantasy.
- **Nonfiction:** Publishes early picture books, 0–4 years; story picture books, 4–10 years; middle-grade books, 8–12 years; and young adult books, 12–18 years. Topics include science, health, sports, and family travel guides.
- **Representative Titles:** *Fighting the Current* by Heather Waldorf (YA) is a story of family dysfunction, challenged by having a relative with a disability. *The Baseball Card* by Jack Siematycki & Avi Slodovnick (2–7 years) details a little boy's first trip to the ballpark and a tale of a baseball legend.

Submissions and Payment
Guidelines available at website. Send complete manuscript or three chapters with resume and synopsis. Accepts photocopies and simultaneous submissions. SAE/IRC. Responds in 6–8 months. Publication in 12–18 months. Royalty; advance.

Editor's Comments
We're looking for YA fiction and nonfiction, especially high interest stories for reluctant readers. There's also a need for Christmas picture books for ages two through seven.

James Lorimer & Company

35 Britain Street
Toronto, Ontario M5A 1R7
Canada

Children's Book Editor: Hadley Dyer

Publisher's Interests
Canadian life is depicted in the books produced by James Lorimer & Company. It offers fiction and nonfiction ranging from easy-to-read books to young adult titles, all written by Canadian authors.
Website: www.lorimer.ca

Freelance Potential
Published 20 titles (10 juvenile) in 2005: 2 were developed from unsolicited submissions and 2 were reprint/licensed properties. Of the 20 titles, 2 were by unpublished writers. Receives 96 queries yearly.

- **Fiction:** Publishes easy-to-read books, 4–7 years; chapter books, 5–10 years; middle-grade books, 8–12 years; and young adult books, 12–18 years. Genres include mystery, suspense, fantasy, adventure, humor, and historical fiction.
- **Nonfiction:** Publishes easy-to-read books, 4–7 years; and middle-grade books, 8–12 years. Topics include multicultural subjects, nature, sports, and contemporary social concerns.
- **Representative Titles:** *Arthur's Problem Puppy* by Ginette Anfousse is the story of a young boy who learns the meaning of responsibility when he gets a puppy who resists being trained. *Carrie's Camping Adventure* by Lesley Choyce demonstrates that going beyond everyday experience can make a young person stronger and more resourceful.

Submissions and Payment
Canadian authors only. Guidelines available. Query with outline/synopsis and 2 sample chapters. SASE. Responds in 4–6 months. Publication period varies. Royalty; advance.

Editor's Comments
The literary value of a work, rather than any lesson or moral it seeks to convey, is our first concern when considering a proposal. We look for realistic, contemporary stories that feature Canadian backdrops.

LTDBooks

Suite 301, Unit 1
200 North Service Road West
Oakville, Ontario L6M 2Y1
Canada

Submissions Editors: Dee Lloyd & Nara Petchsy

Publisher's Interests

An electronic book publisher, LTDBooks produces books of
all fictional genres for adults and young adults. Horror and
paranormal works are primary areas of interest.
Website: www.ltdbooks.com

Freelance Potential

Published 30 titles in 2005: 5 were developed from unsolicited submissions. Of the 30 titles, 10 were by unpublished
writers and 5 were by authors who were new to the publishing house. Receives 200 queries yearly.

- **Fiction:** Publishes young adult books, 12–18 years. Genres
  include suspense, horror, mystery, and stories about the paranormal. Also publishes books for adults.
- **Representative Titles:** *Seven Words for Sand* by Allan Serafino
  (YA) is an adventure story about a teenager and his father who
  are deserted by their guides while crossing the Sahara Desert.
  The Right Hand of Velachaz by Rie Sheridan (YA) is a fantasy
  that centers around a wizard and a 12-year-old boy who discovers he has the gift of magic.

Submissions and Payment

Guidelines and sample contracts available at website. Query
with synopsis. Accepts email queries to editor@ltdbooks.com.
Response time and publication period vary. Royalty, 30%.

Editor's Comments

Authors who seek to be published in electronic format are
invited to submit. We accept only about 10 works each year,
however, so selection will be limited. At this time, we're
especially interested in acquiring more horror, mystery, and
paranormal books (paranormal romances in particular). Visit
our website and follow our specific submission guidelines if
you'd like us to consider your work. Note that we accept
only emailed submissions, and those that do not strictly
adhere to our guidelines will automatically be rejected.

Lucent Books

Suite C
15822 Bernardo Center Drive
San Diego, CA 92127

Senior Acquisitions Editor: Chandra Howard

Publisher's Interests
Since its inception in 1987, Lucent Books has developed a
number of series and titles covering topics in history, biography, current issues, geography, health, science, and sports.
An imprint of Thompson Gale since 2000, it continues to
publish quality nonfiction for middle-grade through high
school students.
Website: www.gale.com/lucent

Freelance Potential
Published 200 titles in 2005: 5 were developed from unsolicited submissions and 2 were by agented authors. Of the
200 titles, 15 were by unpublished writers and 20 were by
authors who were new to the publishing house. Receives
100 queries, 25 unsolicited mss yearly.

- **Nonfiction:** Publishes middle-grade books, 8–12 years; and
  young adult books, 12–18 years. Topics include political, cultural, and social history; science; geo-politics; and current
  events.
- **Representative Titles:** *Filmmakers* offers students insight
  into the lives and personalities of important filmmakers such
  as Steven Spielberg; part of the History Makers biography
  series. *Dyslexia* offers young readers and researchers an
  understanding of what this condition is, and the latest treatment updates; part of the Diseases and Disorders series.

Submissions and Payment
Guidelines available. All books written on a work-for-hire
basis, by assignment only. Query with résumé and list of
published work. Response time varies. Publication in 1 year.
Flat fee, $2,500 for first book; $3,000 for subsequent books.

Editor's Comments
We are interested in topics on scientific breakthroughs; hot
spots around the world; and controversial issues. Our books
are assigned on a work-for-hire basis.

Luna Rising

2900 North Fort Valley Road
Flagstaff, AZ 86001

Editor: Theresa Howell

Publisher's Interests
Bilingual English and Spanish picture books are the specialty
of this publisher. Its list also includes educational books,
biographies, and activity books, as well as fiction.
Website: www.lunarisingbooks.com

Freelance Potential
Published 2 titles in 2005: 1 was developed from an unsolicited submission and 1 was by an agented author. Receives
240 queries yearly.

- **Fiction:** Publishes story picture books, 4–10 years; and middle-grade books, 12–18 years. Genres include adventure, suspense, and bilingual stories.
- **Nonfiction:** Publishes story picture books, 4–10 years. Also publishes activity books, biographies, bilingual, and educational
  books.
- **Representative Titles:** *Baby Gecko's Colors* by Nancy Twinem
  (1–5 years) follows baby gecko as she visits the red rocks,
  gazes at the blue sky, and smells the yellow flowers. It offers a
  wonderful introduction to the world of color. *Danger in the
  Desert* by T. S. Fields (8–12 years) tells how two boys are car-
  jacked and left in the brutally hot desert with no food or
  water, and must survive using only what they have in their
  station wagon.

Submissions and Payment
Guidelines available. Query. SASE. Responds in 3 months.
Publication period and payment policy vary.

Editor's Comments
We are especially interested in material written by Latino
authors. Please note that manuscripts do not have to be
translated into Spanish. We continue to seek contemporary
fiction with a focus on Latino themes, well-written stories
with Latino role models, and bilingual picture books for children
4–8 years old. Send us an idea for something new.

Magination Press

750 First Street NE
Washington, DC 20002

Managing Editor: Darcie Johnston

Publisher's Interests
Books to help children deal with a wide variety of concerns and challenges are what this publisher produces. Well-crafted books for children up to 13 years are featured on its list.
Website: www.maginationpress.com

Freelance Potential
Published 10–12 titles in 2005: 8 were developed from unsolicited submissions. Of the 10–12 titles, 10 were by unpublished writers and 10 were by authors who were new to the publishing house. Receives 25+ queries, 700+ unsolicited mss yearly.

- **Fiction:** Published 4 early picture books, 0–4 years; 4 story picture books, 4–10 years; and 4 middle-grade books, 8–12 years. Stories address psychological concerns and medical issues, family relationships, fears, and learning difficulties.
- **Nonfiction:** Topics include grief, divorce, learning disabilities, and family issues.
- **Representative Titles:** *Blue Cheese Breath and Stinky Feet* by Catherine DePino, Ed.D (6–12 years) is the story of how one boy gets help in dealing with a school bully. *Learning to Slow Down and Pay Attention* by Kathleen Nadeau, Ph.D, and Ellen Nixon, Ph.D (6–11 years) is the updated edition of a book that deals with ADHD, from a child's point of view.

Submissions and Payment
Guidelines and catalogue available with 10x13 SASE (2 first-class stamps). Send complete ms. Accepts photocopies and computer printouts. SASE. Responds in 2–6 months. Publication in 24–36 months. Royalty.

Editor's Comments
Submissions must have a strong self-help component grounded in psychological theory and research. We look for realistic, positive characters. All manuscripts are reviewed by psychologists and other professionals for accuracy.

Maple Tree Press Inc.

Suite 200
51 Front Street East
Toronto, Ontario M5E 1B3
Canada

Associate Editor: Victoria Hill

Publisher's Interests

Maple Tree Press offers nonfiction books about science and nature, as well as craft books, for children age three to twelve. It almost exclusively publishes Canadian authors.
Website: www.mapletreepress.com

Freelance Potential

Published 13 titles in 2005. Of the 13 titles, 1 was by an author who was new to the publishing house. Receives 50+ queries, 1,000 unsolicited mss yearly.

- **Fiction:** Publishes story picture books, 4–10 years. Genres include contemporary fiction.
- **Nonfiction:** Publishes middle-grade titles, 8–12 years. Topics include science, history, sports, nature, and crafts. Also publishes biographies.
- **Representative Titles:** *Daniel's Dinosaurs* by Charles Helm (7–10 years) is the true story of a boy who unearths dinosaur footprints almost in his own backyard. *Mummies* by Sylvia Funston (8–12 years) combines gory details and fascinating facts to introduce young readers to some mummies from around the world.

Submissions and Payment

Send complete ms for fiction. Query with outline, sample chapter, and slips or writing samples for nonfiction. Accepts photocopies, computer printouts, and simultaneous submissions if identified. SAE/IRC. Responds in 3–6 months. Publication in 2 years. Royalty.

Editor's Comments

We want innovative nonfiction and fact-based fiction books that respect children's intelligence and curiosity above all. Dealing with subjects that have enduring appeal, our titles have a special style that captivates children, their parents, their teachers, and librarians alike. Our list is full at this time, and we will consider only the best manuscripts.

Master Books

P.O. Box 726
Green Forest, AR 72638

Acquisitions Editor: Roger Howerton

Publisher's Interests
The goal of Master Books is to advance the biblical truths of creation. It publishes scholarly works, books for children, as well as homeschooling resources.
Website: www.masterbooks.net

Freelance Potential
Published 16 titles (4 juvenile) in 2005. Of the 16 titles, 1 was by an unpublished writer and 3 were by authors who were new to the publishing house. Receives 300 queries, 250 unsolicited mss yearly.

- **Nonfiction:** Published 2 story picture books, 4–10 years; 2 middle-grade books, 8–12 years. Topics include science, technology, and animals. Also publishes homeschooling materials with Christian themes.
- **Representative Titles:** *Dragons of the Deep* by Carl Wieland looks at now-extinct giants and monsters of the oceans and includes charts, diagrams, and interesting facts. *'A' Is for Adam* by Ken & Mally Ham and Dan Lietha (3–5 years) teaches about creation and the gospel using the alphabet.

Submissions and Payment
Writers' guidelines and catalogue available with 9x12 SASE (5 first-class stamps). Query with table of contents, synopsis, and sample chapter. Accepts photocopies and computer printouts. SASE. Responds in 3–4 months. Publication in 1 year. Royalty.

Editor's Comments
We only publish nonfiction books that are unique, well written, and portray a positive Christian message for the reader. Find unique ways to present creation and a Gospel message that will appeal to a large audience. We expect our authors to be able to plainly express themselves in their writing. You must also be able to sell us on the project by explaining how it is marketable.

Maval Publishing

567 Harrison Street
Denver, CO 80206

Editor: George Luder

Publisher's Interests
Colorful and educational children's books in English and
Spanish are produced by this publisher. Its catalogue
includes fiction and nonfiction for children of all ages.
Website: www.maval.com

Freelance Potential
Published 10 titles in 2005: all were developed from unsolicited submissions, 1 was by an agented author, and 1 was
a reprint/licensed property. Of the 10 titles, 8 were by
unpublished writers and 8 were by authors who were new to
the publishing house. Receives 2,000 unsolicited mss yearly.

- **Fiction:** Publishes toddler books, 0–4 years; easy-to-read
  books, 4–7 years; story picture books, 4–10 years; middle-
  grade books, 8–12 years; and young adult books, 12–18
  years. Genres include historical, religious, multicultural, and
  ethnic fiction; adventure; folklore; fantasy; mystery; humor;
  Westerns; and suspense.
- **Nonfiction:** Publishes easy-to-read titles, 4–7 years; story picture books, 4–10 years; middle-grade books, 8–12 years; and
  young adult books, 12–18 years. Topics include animals and
  multicultural and ethnic subjects. Also publishes humor and
  biographies.
- **Representative Titles:** *Anything But a Shot* by Sean McKeown
  (2–8 years) teaches a child that getting a shot is nothing to be
  scared of. *Mommy Gave Me* by Mary L. Hernandez tells a story
  about the things moms do for their little ones as they grow.

Submissions and Payment
Guidelines available with 9x5 SASE ($.80 postage). Send ms
with artwork (color prints or transparencies). Accepts simultaneous submissions. SASE. Responds in 4–6 months. Publication in 18 months. Royalty.

Editor's Comments
We're looking for educational and entertaining books.

Mayhaven Publishing

P.O. Box 557
803 Buckthorn Circle
Mahomet, IL 61853

Editor: Doris Wenzel

Publisher's Interests

Offering fiction and nonfiction for children through young adults, this publisher features such genres as humor, adventure, history, and coming-of-age stories. 20% subsidy, or co-op published.

Website: www.mayhavenpublishing.com

Freelance Potential

Published 10 titles (5 juvenile) in 2005: 7 were developed from unsolicited submissions and 1 was by an agented author. Of the 10 titles, 5 were by unpublished writers and 5 were by authors who were new to the publishing house. Receives 2,000+ queries, yearly.

- **Fiction:** Publishes easy-to-read books, 4–7 years; story picture books, 4–10 years; middle-grade books, 8–12 years; and young adult books, 12–18 years. Genres include adventure, humor, coming-of-age stories, and historical fiction.
- **Nonfiction:** Publishes chapter books, 5–10 years. Topics include nature, travel, cooking, history, and the West.
- **Representative Titles:** *You Will Come Back* by Terri DeMitchell (8–12 years) is a mystery centered around strange coins that two friends discover along the rocky New England coast. *Valley of the Flames* by Herman White (YA) centers around a boy searching for his lost dog before a wild fire races out of control.

Submissions and Payment

Guidelines available. Query with 3 sample chapters. Accepts photocopies and computer printouts. SASE. Responds in 9–12 months. Publication in 12–18 months. Royalty; advance, varies.

Editor's Comments

We welcome new talent with a fresh voice. In addition to our publishing program, we also feature an annual fiction contest with a first prize of publication of the work.

Margaret K. McElderry Books

Simon & Schuster Children's Publishing Division
1230 Avenue of the Americas
New York, NY 10024

Associate Publisher: Emma Dryden

Publisher's Interests
This well-known imprint of Simon & Schuster publishes
hardcover books for preschool through young adult readers
on a wide array of topics.
Website: www.simonsayskids.com

Freelance Potential
Published 31 titles in 2005: 8 were by agented authors and
7 were foreign reprint/licensed properties. Of the 30 titles, 2
were by unpublished writers and 6 were by authors who
were new to the publishing house. Receives 2,500 queries
each year.

- **Fiction:** Published 12 story picture books, 4–10 years;
  13 middle-grade books, 5–10 years; and 4 young adult books,
  12–18 years. Genres include historical fiction, folklore, fantasy,
  humor, and poetry.
- **Nonfiction:** Published 2 story picture books, 4–10 years.
  Topics include animals, natural history, and humor.
- **Representative Titles:** *Golden & Grey* by Louise Arnold
  (8–12 years) is a humorous novel about a boy and a ghost
  who decides to be the boy's "invisible friend." *Black Storm
  Comin'* by Diane Lee Wilson (8–12 years) is a historical fiction
  adventure novel. *Daddy Hugs 1 2 3* by Karen Katz (0–4 years)
  is a brightly illustrated book about Daddy and baby.

Submissions and Payment
Guidelines available. Query with résumé, outline/synopsis,
and first three chapters for novels. No unsolicited mss.
SASE. Responds in 1–2 months. Publication in 2–4 years.
Royalty; advance.

Editor's Comments
While we do not publish textbooks, coloring and activity
books, science fiction, or religious publications, our list of
topics is nearly limitless. Please note that we are not currently
accepting unsolicited manuscripts.

Meadowbrook Press

5451 Smetana Drive
Minnetonka, MN 55343

General Submissions Editor

Publisher's Interests
For over 30 years, this Midwest publisher has been specializing in pregnancy, baby care, child care, and party planning books. It also publishes children's activities books, as well as children's poetry anthologies.
Website: www.meadowbrookpress.com

Freelance Potential
Published 11 titles (2 juvenile) in 2005: 1 was developed from an unsolicited submission and 1 was by an agented author. Receives 100 queries yearly.

- **Nonfiction:** Publishes concept books, 0–4 years; and middle-grade books, 8–12 years. Features activity, joke, and game books for children, as well as books on child care, parenting, and family activities for adults.
- **Representative Titles:** *The Wiggle and Giggle Busy Book* by Trish Kuffner (2–5 years) offers creative, lively games and activities that keep little ones busy and active. *When the Teacher Isn't Looking* by Kenn Nesbitt (5–10 years) pokes fun at silly school topics with wacky poems.

Submissions and Payment
Guidelines available. Query. No unsolicited mss. Accepts photocopies, computer printouts, and simultaneous submissions if identified. SASE. Responds in 4 months. Publication in 2 years. Royalty; advance.

Editor's Comments
We are interested in material on pregnancy, breastfeeding, child care (birth–elementary school), children's activities (birth–elementary school), and children's poetry. Send us a well-written query for your ideas. Remember, neatness counts—typos and sloppiness will have a negative impact. Also, we are currently looking for funny poems for inclusion on our Giggle Poetry website and for possible inclusion in our future poetry anthologies. See guidelines for details.

Medallion Press

27825 North Forest Garden Road
Wauconda, IL 60084

Acquisitions Editor: Wendy Burbank

Publisher's Interests
Medallion Press publishes mainstream young adult and adult fiction in a variety of genres, including contemporary and historical romance, science fiction, fantasy, and suspense. It does not publish nonfiction or poetry.
Website: www.medallionpress.com

Freelance Potential
Published 45+ titles (2 juvenile) in 2005: 22+ were developed from unsolicited submissions and 5 were by agented authors. Of the 45+ titles, 36 were by unpublished writers, and 43 were by authors who were new to the publishing house. Receives 500+ queries yearly.

- **Fiction:** Publishes young adult books, 12–18 years. Genres include adventure; historical, contemporary and multicultural fiction; fantasy; suspense; horror; humor; science fiction; and romance.
- **Representative Titles:** *The Secret of Shabaz* by Jennifer Macaire (YA) is a fantasy adventure about a servant girl and her war horse who share many adventures while seeking to save the world from destruction. *Ellie and the Elven King* by Helen A. Rosburg concerns magical realms, a fairy kingdom, and a romance between a king and a beautiful maiden.

Submissions and Payment
Guidelines available at website. Query with outline and 3 sample chapters. Accepts photocopies, computer printouts, and simultaneous submissions if identified. SASE. Responds in 3–6 months. Publication in 2 years. Royalty; advance.

Editor's Comments
We are looking for serious fiction in the genres of mystery, suspense, science fiction, dark horror, and thrillers. Keep in mind the age of the reader you are writing for, 13–18, and gear your story, characters, and dialogue accordingly. Word count should be between 55,000 and 80,000 words.

Meriwether Publishing Ltd.

885 Elkton Drive
Colorado Springs, CO 80907

Associate Editor: Arthur Zapel

Publisher's Interests
Catering to the needs of middle-grade through college
theater groups, this publisher offers plays, monologues, contest material, and theater resource titles.
Website: www.meriwetherpublishing.com

Freelance Potential
Published 60 titles in 2005: 60 were developed from unsolicited submissions. Of the 25 titles, 15 were by unpublished
writers and 30 were by authors who were new to the publishing house. Receives 1,500 queries, 900 unsolicited mss
each year.

- **Fiction:** Publishes middle-grade titles, 8–12 years. Features
  one-act and full-length dramas, musicals, comedies, folktales,
  and social commentaries, dialogues, and monologues.
- **Nonfiction:** Publishes theater reference books and how-to
  titles, 12–25 years. Topics include theater arts, stagecraft,
  costume, directing, improvisation, and makeup.
- **Representative Titles:** *Sketch-O-Frenia* by Josh Dessler &
  Lawrence Phillis is a collection of short and witty comedy
  sketches suitable for stage, television, or film. *Introduction
  to Stage Lighting* by Charles I. Swift includes the fundamentals
  of theatrical stage lighting, including light and shadow, balance, focus, and mood.

Submissions and Payment
Guidelines available. Prefers query with outline/synopsis and
sample chapter. Will accept complete ms. Accepts photo-
copies and simultaneous submissions if identified. SASE.
Responds in 4–6 weeks. Publication in 6 months. Royalty.
Flat fee.

Editor's Comments
We need one-act comedy farces and two-act full length plays.
Submissions should include cast and prop lists, information
on costumes, and set specifications.

Messianic Jewish Publishers

6204 Park Heights Avenue
Baltimore, MD 21215

Managing Editor: Janet Chaiet

Publisher's Interests
This religious publisher of nonfiction gears its books to Jewish evangelism, the Jewish roots of Christianity, or Messianic Judaism, always keeping in mind an awareness of Jewish culture and thought.
Website: www.messianicjewish.net

Freelance Potential
Published 3 titles in 2005.

- **Nonfiction:** Publishes concept books, 0–4 years; toddler books, 0–4 years; story picture books, 4–10 years; and middle-grade books, 8–12 years. Topics include religious and inspirational subjects.
- **Representative Titles:** *My First Hanukkah Board Book (0–4 years)* features photos and explanations of Hanukkah customs such as lighting the menorah and eating latkes. *Celebrations of the Bible: A Messianic Children's Curriculum* (teachers) uses easy-to-follow lesson plans, crafts, Bible study worksheets, games, reproducible handouts, and other activities to highlight 8 Jewish holidays.

Submissions and Payment
Query first for guidelines. Send book proposal, outline, 3 sample chapters, résumé, market analysis, and 3 references. Accepts photocopies and computer printouts. SASE. Responds in 6–8 months. Publication period and payment policy vary.

Editor's Comments
We are particularly interested in themes that deal with Messianic Judaism and the Jewish roots of the Christian faith. Book proposals should not be faxed or emailed. Be sure to include a brief description of each chapter in your nonfiction manuscript and tell us why your story is unique to our Jewish market. For the three references, they may be a rabbi, pastor, supervisor, editor, or business associate.

Milet Publishing

6 North End Parade
London W14 0SJ
United Kingdom

Director: Patricia Billings

Publisher's Interests

This British publisher features bilingual books, English-only titles, picture dictionaries, translated fiction, and fiction books for young readers.
Website: www.milet.com

Freelance Potential

Published 57 titles (56 juvenile) in 2005: 1 was by an agented author. Receives 360 queries, 100+ unsolicited mss each year.

- **Fiction:** Publishes toddler books and early picture books, 0–4 years; easy-to-read books, 4–7 years; and middle-grade titles, 8–12 years. Genres include contemporary, multicultural, and ethnic fiction, and adventure.
- **Nonfiction:** Publishes picture dictionaries, language books, and flashcards for children and young adults. Also publishes Turkish reference books.
- **Representative Titles:** *Alphabet Poem* by Michael Rosen and Hervé Tullet is an imaginative and hilarious look at the letters we love. *Welcome to Lizard Lounge* by Laura Hambleton tells the story of a lizard who discovers his uniqueness.

Submissions and Payment

Guidelines and catalogue available at website. Send complete ms for picture books; query with synopsis and sample text for all others. Accepts photocopies. SASE. Responds in 2 months. Publication in 12–18 months. Payment policy varies.

Editor's Comments

We continue to look for children's books that are innovative, non-traditional, international, and multicultural. We focus on one-of-a-kind books—stories that are set in diverse locations with unusual or original themes, or with new takes on popular themes. This year we are seeking picture books for children 0–7 years and young fiction for readers 8–12 years.

Milkweed Editions

Suite 300
1011 Washington Avenue South
Minneapolis, MN 55415

First Reader: Elisabeth Fitz

Publisher's Interests
Founded in 1979, this publisher offers fiction titles for young readers ages 8 through 13. It also publishes adult fiction, literary nonfiction, and poetry for adults.
Website: www.milkweed.org

Freelance Potential
Published 16 titles (5 juvenile) in 2005: 1 was developed from an unsolicited submission, and 1 was by a reprint/licensed property. Of the 16 titles, 1 was by an unpublished writer and 6 were by authors who were new to the publishing house. Receives 3,000 queries, 4,000 unsolicited mss each year.

- **Fiction:** Publishes middle-grade titles, 8–12 years. Genres include historical, multicultural and ethnic fiction; and stories about nature.
- **Representative Titles:** *Perfect* by Natalie Friend (9–13 years) is the story of Isabella Lee's attempt to come to terms with the death of her father. She takes a wrong turn toward bulimia, but finds unexpected help from the most popular girl in her class. *Parents Wanted* by George Harrar (8–13 years) tells the story of a boy with a troubled past that faces new challenges as he is placed with adoptive parents.

Submissions and Payment
Guidelines available. Query with outline and sample chapter(s) or send complete ms. Accepts photocopies and simultaneous submissions if identified. SASE. Responds in 1 month; to mss in 1–6 months. Publication in 2 years. Royalty, 6% of list price; advance, varies.

Editor's Comments
We are happy to accept manuscripts from authors of all backgrounds (previously published or not). In return, we ask that you take the time to familiarize yourself with our list in order to determine if we are a good fit for your manuscript.

The Millbrook Press

2 Old New Milford Road
Brookfield, CT 06804

Editorial Director: Jean Reynolds

Publisher's Interests
Now a division of Lerner Publishing Group, this publisher specializes in curriculum-oriented nonfiction books for students in grades five through twelve on topics from the arts and social studies to science and sports. It has recently resumed its publishing program.
Website: www.millbrookpress.com

Freelance Potential
Resumed publishing in 2005.

- **Nonfiction:** Publishes concept books and toddler books, 0–4 years; middle-grade titles, 8–12 years; and young adult books, 12–18 years. Topics include the arts, sports, social studies, history, math, science, nature, the environment, and crafts. Also publishes biographies.
- **Representative Titles:** *All New Holiday Crafts for Kids* (grades K–3) features craft ideas for all ages that bring holidays to life. *Cooking through Time* (grades 4–8) takes readers on a time-traveling adventure, with a look at food preparation from certain time periods. It includes recipes and an appendix. *Dilly's Adventure* (grades 2–4) takes readers on an adventure with a young girl as she details her first summer camp experience through diary entries.

Submissions and Payment
Guidelines available at website. Query with résumé, outline, and sample chapter. SASE. Responds in 6–8 weeks. Publication in 12–18 months. Royalty; advance. Flat fee.

Editor's Comments
Nonfiction for middle grades is our specialty, and we are currently interested in titles about American history, math, science, and social studies with ties to the school curriculum. We are also interested in contemporary issues for young adults. We will consider queries from both agented authors and non-agented writers.

Mirrorstone Books

P.O. Box 707
Renton, WA 98057-0707

Senior Editor: Nina Hess

Publisher's Interests
This imprint of Wizards of the Coast publishes fantasy and horror books for teens, middle-grade adventure, and fantasy titles on a work-for-hire basis.
Website: www.mirrorstonebooks.com

Freelance Potential
Published 20 titles in 2005: 2 were developed from unsolicited submissions and 9 were by agented authors. Of the 20 titles, 3 were by unpublished writers and 6 were by authors who were new to the publishing house. Receives 100+ queries, 100+ unsolicited mss yearly.

- **Fiction:** Published 20 middle-grade books, 8–12 years. Genres include adventure; science fiction; and medieval, mystical, heroic, and epic fantasy.
- **Representative Titles:** *The Dragon Well* by Dan Willis (10+ years) pits a group of young friends against the bandit king terrorizing their village home. *Eye of Fortune* by Denise Graham (8+ years) follows the adventures of the young knights of the silver dragon as they head back to the Dungeons of Doom in search of buried treasure; part of the Knights of the Silver Dragon series.

Submissions and Payment
Guidelines available. Query with approximately 10-page writing sample (sample chapter preferred). Accepts photocopies and simultaneous submissions if identified. SASE. Responds in 4 months. Publication in 1 year. Payment policy varies.

Editor's Comments
If you plan on submitting your work to us, be familiar with the novels we currently publish. Go to our website to get an idea of our book series. The books in each of our series are written on a work-for-hire basis. We are interested in fantasy and horror stories for ages 12 to 16 and middle-grade adventures for ages 8 to 12.

Mitchell Lane Publisher

P.O. Box 196
Hockessin, DE 19707

President: Barbara Mitchell

Publisher's Interests
Mitchell Lane Publishers specializes in authorized biographies for children between the ages of eight and fourteen.
Its titles spotlight the lives of contemporary and historical
business people, politicians, actors, scientists, media personalities, musicians, and sports players.
Website: www.mitchellane.com

Freelance Potential
Published 80 titles in 2005: Of the 80 titles, 10 were by
authors who were new to the publishing house. Receives
20 queries yearly.

- **Nonfiction:** Publishes chapter books, 5–10 years; middle-
  grade titles, 8–12 years; and young adult books, 12–18 years.
  Topics include contemporary multicultural personalities,
  sports figures, entertainers, inventors, scientists, and past and
  present political leaders.
- **Representative Titles:** *Bow Wow: Hip-Hop Superstar* (grades
  4–8) highlights the life and music of this contemporary young
  hip-hop artist. *Condoleezza Rice* (grades 4–8) is a biography of
  one of America's foremost female political leaders, following
  her career from Stanford University Provost to United States
  Secretary of State.

Submissions and Payment
All work is assigned. Query with writing samples and
résumé. Flat fee.

Editor's Comments
All of our publications fit into a series format. We are looking
for titles that can be used in our Series of Soccer Players for
young readers; and Series of Natural Disasters for older grades.
This year, we are introducing a new series, Monumental Mile-
stones, that covers current events of modern times, such as
the Tsunami in Indonesia. Following your query, we will contact you if we are interested in your work.

Mondo Publishing

980 Avenue of the Americas
New York, NY 10018

Senior Editor: Susan DerKazarian

Publisher's Interests
Children up to the age of ten enjoy the books and sing-along music tapes produced by this publisher. Its list includes folktales, fantasy, and adventure stories, as well as books on science, history, crafts, music, and hobbies.
Website: www.mondopub.com

Freelance Potential
Published 12 titles in 2005: 6 were developed from unsolicited submissions, 3 were by agented authors, and 1 was a print/licensed property. Of the 12 titles, 1 was by an unpublished writer and 9 were by authors who were new to the publishing house. Receives 400 unsolicited mss yearly.

- **Fiction:** Publishes easy-to-read books, 4–7 years; story picture books, 4–10 years; chapter books, 5–10 years; and middle-grade books, 8–12 years. Genres include fantasy, mystery, folktales, adventure, humor, stories about sports, and contemporary and historical fiction.
- **Nonfiction:** Publishes early picture books, 0–4 years; story picture books, 4–10 years; and young adult books, 12–18 years. Topics include science, nature, animals, the environment, language arts, history, music, crafts, and hobbies.
- **Representative Titles:** *A House for Hickory* by Kelly Mazzone (4–7 years) tells the story of Hickory the mouse and his search for a new house. *Atu's Story* by Sandra Clayton (4–7 years) is a folktale about the son of a village chief and a visitor that tells stories of faraway places that the villagers want to go and see.

Submissions and Payment
Send complete ms. SASE. Response time varies. Publication in 1–3 years. Royalty, varies.

Editor's Comments
Please be advised that our list for 2006 is full. However, if you send us something unique that inspires children to read, we may consider it for a future publication.

Moody Publishers

Moody Bible Institute
820 North LaSalle Boulevard
Chicago, IL 60610-3284

Acquisitions Coordinator

Publisher's Interests

This publisher strives to educate and edify Christians and to
evangelize the non-Christians by ethically publishing conservative, evangelical Christian literature for all ages.
Website: www.moodypublishers.org

Freelance Potential

Published 60 titles (20 juvenile) in 2005: 8 were by agented
authors. Of the 80 titles, 1 was by an unpublished writer and
10 were by authors who were new to the publishing house.
Receives 1,000+ queries and unsolicited mss yearly.

- **Fiction:** Publishes middle-grade books, 8–12 years; and
  young adult books, 12–18 years. Genres include adventure,
  Western, fantasy, mystery, suspense, and contemporary and
  historical fiction. Also publishes biblical fiction.
- **Nonfiction:** Publishes toddler books, 0–4 years; easy-to-read
  books, 4–7 years; story picture books, 4–10 years; and young
  adult books, 12–18 years. Topics include religion, social
  issues, and sports.
- **Representative Titles:** *The Five Love Languages of Children*
  by Rose Campbell & Gary Chapman (parents) helps couples
  develop stronger, more fulfilling relationships by teaching
  them to speak each others love language. *The New Bible in Pictures for Little Eyes* by Kenneth N. Taylor (3–6 years) is an
  interactive way to share the truths of the Bible with children.

Submissions and Payment

Guidelines available. Query with résumé, outline/synopsis,
and 3 sample chapters, or send ms for fiction. Accepts nonfiction proposals through agents or manuscript services only.
SASE. Responds in 2–3 months. Publication in 12–18
months. Payment policy varies.

Editor's Comments

We're looking for authors that can get out the message of
God to children through their well-written stories.

Moose Enterprise

684 Walls Side Road
Sault Ste. Marie, Ontario P6A 5K6
Canada

Editor: Richard Mousseau

Publisher's Interests
This Canadian publisher features the work of experienced
and first-time authors. Its list includes titles on history,
biographies, and adventure for readers age eight to adult.
It also publishes book collections in all genres for children
and adults.

Freelance Potential
Published 6 titles (3 juvenile) in 2005: 6 were developed
from unsolicited submissions. Of the 6 titles, 1 was by an
unpublished writer and 5 were by authors who were new to
the publishing house. Receives 96 queries yearly.

- **Fiction:** Published 1 middle-grade novel, 8–12 years; and
  2 young adult books, 12–18 years. Genres include adventure,
  drama, fantasy, historical fiction, humor, horror, mystery, suspense, science fiction, and Westerns.
- **Nonfiction:** Publishes titles for ages 10–adult. Topics include
  local, Canadian, and military history; and humor. Also publishes
  biographies.
- **Representative Titles:** *A Long Exciting Trip to Peace* by Hap
  Harnden (all ages) is a factual account of the author's life,
  including his service in the Royal Air Force during the Second
  World War. *Gentle Thoughts* (YA) is a collection of short stories
  with a hint of mystery, magic, and humor.

Submissions and Payment
Guidelines available. Query. SAE/IRC. Responds in 1 month.
Publication in 1 year. Royalty, 10–30%.

Editor's Comments
We welcome the work of authors who have the courage to
submit their work in hopes of acceptance. Be willing to
accept the guidance, comments, and opinions of our
editors. No two people write or edit exactly the same. We
do not compare ourselves to other publishers or share their
views or editorial procedures.

Morgan Reynolds Publishing

Suite 223
620 South Elm Street
Greensboro, NC 27406

Editor: Casey Cornelius

Publisher's Interests

Morgan Reynolds publishes curriculum-based nonfiction books for juvenile and young adult readers. Its list includes lively biographies of contemporary and historical figures, and exciting looks at critical events in world history.
Website: www.morganreynolds.com

Freelance Potential

Published 30 titles in 2005: 10 were developed from unsolicited submissions. Of the 30 titles, 1 was by an unpublished writer and 5 were by authors who were new to the publishing house. Receives 400–500 queries, 300 unsolicited mss yearly.

- **Nonfiction:** Published 2 middle-grade titles, 8–12 years; and 28 young adult books, 12–18 years. Topics include history, music, science, business, feminism, and world events. Also features biographies on notable Americans, music makers, business leaders, and sports figures.
- **Representative Titles:** *Ulysses S. Grant: Defender of the Union* by Earle Rice Jr. (grades 6–12) is a biography of one of America's great leaders, from his education at West Point to his election as President of the United States. *Uh Huh!* by John Duggleby (grades 6–12) follows the life of the Emmy-award winning blind musician Ray Charles.

Submissions and Payment

Guidelines available. Query with outline and sample chapter; or send complete ms. Accepts photocopies, computer printouts, and simultaneous submissions if identified. SASE. Responds to queries in 1 month; to mss in 1–3 months. Publication in 12–18 months. Royalty; advance.

Editor's Comments

This year we are looking for titles about civil rights, science, literature, social studies, and history for ages 10 and up. Historical events should be treated with attention to detail and context.

Mott Media

112 East Ellen Street
Fenton, MI 48430

Curriculum Consultant: Lori Coeman

Publisher's Interests

Material for homeschooled students and teachers are the specialty of this small publishing house. Its list includes non-fiction books for all levels of study, including stand-alone and series titles on math, history, and religion, as well as biographies of contemporary and historical personalities.
Website: www.homeschoolingbooks.com

Freelance Potential

Published several titles in 2005: 2 were assigned. Receives 48 queries yearly.

- **Nonfiction:** Publishes middle-grade titles, 8–12 years; and young adult books, 12–18 years. Topics include animals, history, humor, language arts, grammar, spelling, phonics, and religion. Also publishes biographies.
- **Representative Titles:** *Backyard Scientist: Magical Super Crystals* (4–12 years) includes exciting non-toxic and environmentally safe experiments to entertain and stimulate young minds. *Four Trojan Horses of Humanism* (15 years) studies the philosophy of humanism, and how it affects the mind and soul of Christians.

Submissions and Payment

Guidelines available. Query with outline and sample chapter; or send complete ms. Accepts photocopies, computer print-outs, and simultaneous submissions if identified. SASE. Responds in 1–2 months. Publication in 6 months. Royalty; advance. Flat fee.

Editor's Comments

We continue to expand our publishing program for middle-grade and young adult students. As our list of titles grows, we will need books for homeschool study in all areas of the curriculum. A particular need at this time is books with a Christian worldview. We do not publish fiction, storybooks, or activity books.

Mountain Press Publishing Company

P.O. Box 2399
Missoula, MT 59806-2399

Submissions Editor

Publisher's Interests

Mountain Press publishes nonfiction trade books for children and adults. Its list includes titles on western U.S. history, earth science, and natural history. This publisher is well-known for its state-by-state series on Roadside Geology, Roadside History, and Geology Underfoot.
Website: www.mountain-press.com

Freelance Potential

Published 15 titles in 2005: 1 was by an agented author. Receives 25 queries yearly.

- **Nonfiction:** Publishes story picture books, 4–10 years; chapter books, 5–10 years; middle-grade titles, 8–12 years; and young adult books, 12–18 years. Topics include history, nature, the environment, science, technology, natural history, geology, and regional history.
- **Representative Titles:** *Nature's Yucky* by Lee Ann Landstrom and Karen I. Shragg (grades K–5) uses kids' natural fascination with the stinky, the gross, and the icky to help them learn about wild animals. *Look-See with Uncle Bill* by Will James (10+ years) joins two boys and their uncle on an adventurous Western round-up full of mishaps, close calls, and excitement; part of the Tumbleweed series.

Submissions and Payment

Guidelines available at website. Query with outline and sample chapter. Accepts photocopies and computer printouts. SASE. Responds in 3 months. Publication in 2 years. Royalty.

Editor's Comments

Other than reprints of the works of Will James, we do not publish fiction, including historical fiction. We do not publish memoirs or personal stories. Children's books must be factual, without anthropomorphizing or storytelling. We encourage you to review our website to help determine if your book is appropriate for our publishing goals.

National Association for the Education of Young People

1509 16th Street NW
Washington, DC 20036-1426

Publications Editor: Carol Copple

Publisher's Interests
NAEYC is a nonprofit organization that provides professional growth services to adults working with children. In addition to other services, it publishes books and resource materials for teachers and parents.
Website: www.naeyc.org

Freelance Potential
Published 5 titles in 2005: 3 were developed from unsolicited submissions, and 1 was a reprint/licensed property. Of the 5 titles, 3 were by authors who were new to the publishing house. Receives 50 queries yearly.

- **Nonfiction:** Publishes educational materials for teachers, caregivers, and parents. Topics include professional development, early childhood education, family relationships, health, nutrition, assessment, language and literacy, diversity, play, school programs, social and emotional development, stress, and violence prevention.
- **Representative Titles:** *Children as Illustrators* by Susan C. Thompson (educators) shows how art and literacy experiences can be integrated into the classroom through interpreting and creating pictorial representations. *Writing in Preschool* by Judith A. Schickedanz & René M. Casbergue (educators) examines writing programs in preschool, from letter strings to real words to detailed messages.

Submissions and Payment
Guidelines available. Query with outline and 3 sample chapters. Accepts photocopies and computer printouts. No simultaneous submissions. SASE. Responds in 1 month. Publication period varies. No payment.

Editor's Comments
We want titles that make creative and insightful recommendations for practice, or present basic principles pulled from expert practice, theory, and research.

National Council of Teachers of English

1111 West Kenyon Road
Urbana, IL 61801-1096

Director of Book Publications: Zarina Hock

Publisher's Interests
Resource books for educators of English and language arts for kindergarten through college-level students are featured on this publisher's list. The list of books closely matches what teachers need in the classroom.
Website: www.ncte.org

Freelance Potential
Published 15 titles in 2005. Receives 175 queries, 80 unsolicited mss yearly.

- **Nonfiction:** Publishes books for English and language arts teachers on writing, reading, grammar, literature, diversity, society, poetry, censorship, media studies, technology, research, and teaching ideas.
- **Representative Titles:** *New Visions for Linking Literature and Mathematics* by David & Phyllis Whitin (teachers, K–6) features math-related literature and how to use it effectively in the classroom. *Accent on Meter* by Joseph Powell and Mark Halperin (teachers) offers practical ways of teaching students about the close connection between the meaning, rhythm, and meter of poetry.

Submissions and Payment
Guidelines available. Query with cover letter, formal proposal, chapter summaries, and table of contents. SASE. Responds in 1–2 weeks. Publication in 18 months. Royalty, varies.

Editor's Comments
Do not send proposals for anthologies or single-authored works of creative writing, personal journals, student writing, or articles more suited in length to journals. Each potential book is carefully evaluated by experts in the field, and all our publications are subject to the strategic oversight of the National Council of Teachers of English Editorial Board. Carefully read over our submission guidelines.

National Geographic Society

Children's Books
1145 17th Street NW
Washington, DC 20036-4688

Editorial Coordinator: Priyanka Lamichhane

Publisher's Interests

The children's list of National Geographic includes biographies, history, geography, science, nature, and reference books. It publishes quality nonfiction for ages four through young adult.
Website: www.nationalgeographic.com/books

Freelance Potential

Published 60 titles in 2005: 5 were developed from unsolicited submissions and 5 were by agented authors. Of the 60 titles, 1 was by an unpublished writer and 12 were by authors who were new to the publishing house. Receives 200 queries yearly.

- **Nonfiction:** Publishes story picture books, 4–10 years; middle-grade books, 8–12 years; and young adult books, 12–18 years. Topics include life, earth, and general science; American and world cultures and history; animals; multicultural stories; and geography. Also publishes biographies.
- **Representative Titles:** *Ghandi: The Young Protester Who Founded a Nation* by Philip Wilkinson (8–12 years) is a tribute to the influential political and social leader who practiced non-violent resistance. *Remember World War II: Kids Who Survived Tell Their Stories* by Dorinda Makanaonalani Nicholson (10+ years) commemorates war life through the eyes of children.

Submissions and Payment

Query with outline and sample chapter. No unsolicited mss. SASE. Responds in 3–4 months. Publication period varies. Flat fee.

Editor's Comments

We do not accept unsolicited manuscripts. To better gage what types of books we publish, check out our list of titles. We place a strong emphasis on biographies and history and feature several nonfiction series, including Voices from Colonial America and History Biographies.

Naturegraph

P.O. Box 1047
3543 Indian Creek Road
Happy Camp, CA 96039

Managing Editor: Barbara Brown

Publisher's Interests

Known for its books on Native American legends, culture, and spirituality, Naturegraph also publishes field guides and other books about outdoor activities and the natural world.
Website: www.naturegraph.com

Freelance Potential

Published 2 titles in 2005: both were developed from unsolicited submissions. Receives 400 queries yearly.

- **Fiction:** Publishes middle-grade novels, 8–12 years; and young adult books, 12–18 years. Genres include mythology, folktales, and Native American folklore.
- **Nonfiction:** Published 2 young adult books, 12–18 years. Topics include Native Americans, western U.S. wildlife, the environment, crafts, hiking, backpacking, and natural history. Also publishes field guides for all ages
- **Representative Titles:** *Warriors of the Rainbow* by William Willoya is the story of a great-grandmother who instills the Indian spirit in her great-grandson. *Turtle Going Nowhere in the Plenty of Time* by Davis Many Voices features legends from the Southwest.

Submissions and Payment

Guidelines available at website. Query with outline and 1–2 sample chapters. Accepts photocopies and computer printouts. SASE. Response time and publication period vary. Royalty.

Editor's Comments

Most of our titles are for adults but young adults enjoy them, too. If you can write knowledgeably about topics such as edible plants, backpacking, or the wildlife and marine life of the American West, send us your query. We're always interested in Native American legends, as well as their history, wisdom, arts and crafts, spirituality, and visions. Craft books that feature the use of natural materials would also fit our list.

Neal-Schuman Publishers

Suite 2004
100 William Street
New York, NY 10038

Director of Publishing: Charles Harmon

Publisher's Interests

Neal-Schuman specializes in providing books that advance the knowledge of information specialists including school, college, university, and public librarians.
Website: www.neal-schuman.com

Freelance Potential

Published 36–40 titles in 2005. Receives 300 queries, 300 unsolicited mss yearly.

- **Nonfiction:** Publishes resource materials for school media specialists and public librarians. Topics include curriculum support, the Internet, technology, literary skills, reading programs, collection development, reference needs, the first amendment, staff development, management, and communications.
- **Representative Titles:** *Public Relations for School Library Media Programs* by Helen F. Flowers (librarians) offers strategies for developing and executing a successful public relations plan. *Developing Academic Library Staff for Future Success* by Margaret Oldroyd, ed. (librarians) highlights how roles of university and college librarians are changing and evaluates the implications of these changes for skill needs and development routes.

Submissions and Payment

Guidelines available. Prefers query with résumé, outline, table of contents, and sample chapter. Will accept complete ms. Accepts photocopies and computer printouts. SASE. Responds to queries in 2 weeks, to mss in 1–2 months. Publication in 10–12 months. Royalty.

Editor's Comments

In addition to providing a description of your subject and explaining why your book will fill a void in the field, we'd also like you to include a preface addressed to your potential readers detailing who the book is for and how it can be used.

New Age Dimensions

P.O. Box 772097
Coral Springs, FL 33077

Editor: Melissa Alvarez

Publisher's Interests

In addition to books for adults, New Age Dimensions publishes picture books, books for middle-grade readers, and
young adult titles. Its list features trade paperbacks, e-books,
and books on CD.
Website: www.newagedimensionspublishing.com

Freelance Potential

Published 50+ titles (6 juvenile) in 2005: 45 were developed
from unsolicited submissions and 2 were by agented
authors. Receives 7,200 queries yearly.

- **Fiction:** Publishes early picture books, 0–4 years; middle-grade
  books, 8–12 years; and young adult books, 12–18 years. Genres include inspirational, contemporary, and science fiction;
  romance; fantasy; adventure; and mystery.
- **Nonfiction:** Publishes early picture books, 0–4 years; middle-
  grade books, 8–12 years; and young adult books, 12–18
  years. Publishes books on all nonfiction topics. Also offers
  how-to and self-help titles for parents and educators.
- **Representative Titles:** *Echoes of a Distant Storm* by Wendy
  Simpson (YA) is a fantasy about an evil being who seeks to
  enslave the world. *Piney's Summer* by Dorothy Baughman (9–
  12 years) follows a young boy on his summer escapades.

Submissions and Payment

Guidelines available at website. Query with synopsis and
first 3 chapters. Accepts email queries to melissaalvarez@
newagedimensionspublishing.com. No simultaneous submissions. Responds in 1–2 months. Publication period varies.
Royalty, 40%.

Editor's Comments

We're looking for quality nonfiction at this time, as well as
inspirational fiction, science fiction, and fantasy. We have
enough romances. Be sure to follow the submissions guidelines posted at our website—we're very strict about them.

New Harbinger Publications

5674 Shattuck Avenue
Oakland, CA 94609

Acquisitions Editor: Tesilya Hanauer

Publisher's Interests
Launched in 1973, New Harbinger Publications specializes in books that deliver effective, reliable information on a range of mental health, medical, and personal growth topics. The general public, as well as mental health professionals, seek out the self-help and psychology books produced by this press.
Website: www.newharbinger.com

Freelance Potential
Published 40 titles in 2005: 10 were developed from unsolicited submissions and 10 were by agented authors. Of the 40 titles, 10 were by unpublished writers and 30 were by authors who were new to the publishing house. Receives 600 queries yearly.

- **Nonfiction:** Publishes self-help, psychology, and health books for lay persons and professionals. Topics include parenting, divorce, pregnancy, self-esteem, addictions, stress, depression, eating disorders, grief, and sexuality.
- **Representative Titles:** *The Emotional House* by Kathryn L. Robyn & Dawn Ritchie teaches readers to use psychological and design principles to transform their homes into nurturing and supportive living spaces. *Do the Right Thing* by Thomas G. Plante describes a system for making ethical choices in daily life, a practice that contributes to good mental health.

Submissions and Payment
Guidelines available. Query. Accepts photocopies and email queries to acquisitions@newharbinger.com. SASE. Responds in 2–4 weeks. Publication in 1 year. Royalty, 10%.

Editor's Comments
We look for research-based, clinically sound books written by professionals with degrees in their areas of expertise. While our books tackle familiar subjects, we also strive to provide information on newer diagnoses—fibromyalgia, for example.

New Hope Publishers

P.O. Box 12065
Birmingham, AL 35201-2065

Manuscript Submissions

Publisher's Interests
The goal of this Christian publisher is to help families seek biblical answers to daily concerns and life's heartbreaks. Its list includes titles for children and adults.
Website: www.newhopepubl.com

Freelance Potential
Published 24 titles in 2005: 2 were developed from unsolicited submissions, 4 were by agented authors, and 2 were reprint/licensed properties. Of the 24 titles, 4 were by unpublished writers and 12 were by authors who were new to the publishing house. Receives 40–50 queries, 300 unsolicited mss yearly.

- **Fiction:** Publishes story picture books, 4–10 years; chapter books, 5–10 years; middle-grade titles, 8–12 years; and young adult books, 12–18 years. Genres include inspirational fiction.
- **Nonfiction:** Publishes inspirational and spiritual books for women and families. Topics include spiritual growth, women's issues, parenting, prayer, relationships, Christian living, and Bible studies.
- **Representative Titles:** *Robyn Flies Home* by Renée Kent (8–12 years) is the story of a physically challenged girl who turns out to be stronger inside than she seems. *The Joyful Shepard* by Cyncie Smith (4–10 years) portrays the joy and compassion of the Parable of the Lost Sheep.

Submissions and Payment
Guidelines available. Prefers proposal and sample chapter; query with outline or complete ms. Accepts photocopies, computer printouts, and email to new_hope@wmu.org. SASE. Response time and publication period vary. Royalty. Flat fee.

Editor's Comments
We are looking for titles that equip readers with the tools and skills they need to grow in Christ and share His vision.

New Leaf Press

P.O. Box 726
Green Forest, AR 72638

Acquisitions Editor: Roger Howerton

Publisher's Interests
For more than 30 years, this Christian publisher has featured children's titles that explain the Christian doctrine and help build positive character traits.
Website: www.newleafpress.net

Freelance Potential
Published 19 titles (9 juvenile) in 2005: 4 were by unpublished writers and 10 were by authors who were new to the publishing house. Receives 300 queries, 250 unsolicited mss yearly.

- **Fiction:** Published 4 easy-to-read books, 4–7 years; Genres include adventure, inspirational, and stories about character building. Titles include an activity section and audio CD.
- **Nonfiction:** Published 4 easy-to-read books, 4–7 years; and 1 young adult book, 12–18 years. Topics include current events, history, social issues, Christian growth and Bible doctrine.
- **Representative Titles:** *Big Thoughts for Little Thinkers* is a *four-book* series by Joey Allen (4–8 years) that presents the Christian doctrines of the Trinity, the gospel, Scripture, and missions for young children. *Character Billders* by Tony Salerno (6–12 years) is a four-book activity set that follows the adventures of Little Bill and his friends as they learn the value and benefits of good character.

Submissions and Payment
Guidelines and catalogue available with 9x12 SASE (5 first-class stamps). Query with cover letter, table of contents, synopsis, and sample chapter. Accepts photocopies and simultaneous submissions if identified. SASE. Responds in 3 months. Publication in 12–18 months. Royalty, 10% of net.

Editor's Comments
We are looking for books that promote Christian growth and development in children and teens. We like biblically-based submissions with a positive message for the reader. Our books surpass the standard for excellence in the Christian market.

Newmarket Press

15th Floor
18 East 48th Street
New York, NY 10017

Editor: Shannon Berning

Publisher's Interests

For more than 20 years, this company has published a list of nonfiction titles, as well as a limited list of fiction for young adults and adults.
Website: www.newmarketpress.com

Freelance Potential

Published 45 titles in 2005: most were by agented authors. Receives 1,200 queries yearly.

- **Fiction:** Publishes contemporary fiction for young adults.
- **Nonfiction:** Publishes parenting and self-help books. Topics include childcare, health, fitness, nutrition, sports, business, history, and multicultural and ethnic issues. Also publishes biographies.
- **Representative Titles:** *Kazan: Father of Baree* by James Oliver Curwood (YA) follows the story of Kazan, part wolf and part dog, as he struggles to find his place in the world of men. *My Body, My Self for Boys* by Area & Lynda Madaras (YA) is a fact-filled journal/activity book to help young adults learn about the physical and mental changes that take place in their bodies during puberty.

Submissions and Payment

Query with outline, table of contents, marketing information, clips, sample chapter, and author biography. Accepts photocopies. SASE. Responds in 3–6 months. Publication in 1 year. Royalty; advance.

Editor's Comments

We are one of the few independent trade publishing houses. We publish approximately 15 to 20 books each year, primarily in the areas of parenting, health, and self-help. Although we do not have a specific set of guidelines for submissions, we suggest you consider the following areas before you submit your manuscript to us: audience, market, and competition.

New Society Publishers

P.O. Box 189
Gabriola Island, British Columbia V0R 1X0
Canada

Publisher: Christopher Plant

Publisher's Interests
To promote its vision of a just society and ecological sustainability, this publisher offers inspirational, motivational, and pro-active nonfiction. Its commitment is to fundamental social change through nonviolent, skill-driven action.
Website: www.newsociety.com

Freelance Potential
Published 24 titles in 2005: 8 were developed from unsolicited submissions, 2 were by agented authors, and 1 was a reprint/licensed property. Receives 300 queries yearly.

- **Nonfiction:** Publishes college guides and career resources for young adults. Also publishes titles on education systems, family issues, parenting, child development, sustainability, business practices, leadership, feminism, diversity, and community issues for adults.
- **Representative Titles:** *The Natural Child: Parenting from the Heart* by Jan Hunt (parents) promotes a return to attachment parenting. *Connecting Kids: Exploring Diversity Together* by Linda Hill (parents, educators) helps children explore differences, build acceptance, and embrace an inclusive culture that reduces prejudice and discrimination.

Submissions and Payment
Guidelines available. Query with proposal, table of contents, and sample chapter. SAE/IRC. Responds in 2–3 months. Publication in 1 year. Payment policy varies.

Editor's Comments
Please review our detailed guidelines, available at our website. They list the key ingredients to a proposal, and we cannot guarantee a serious consideration of your proposal if it does not address all the questions listed. Topics that interest us include nonviolent strategies that can be applied to local, national, and international affairs; cultural diversity; and building a sense of community with humankind and nature.

New World Library

14 Pamaron Way
Novato, CA 94949

Submissions Editor

Publisher's Interests

Spiritual and practical books for children and adults are the specialty of this publisher. It strives to provide inspirational materials that focus on improving personal growth, overall health, and the quality of life.
Website: www.newworldlibrary.com

Freelance Potential

Published 40 titles in 2005: 2 were developed from unsolicited submissions and 20 were by agented authors. Of the 40 titles, 5 were by unpublished writers and 10 were by authors who were new to the publishing house. Receives 1,000 queries yearly.

- **Fiction:** Publishes story picture books, 4–10 years. Genres include inspirational and religious fiction, and retellings of classic tales.
- **Representative Titles:** *The Lovables in the Kingdom of Self-Esteem* by Diane Loomans (YA) is a charming book filled with characters that children can relate to while learning the qualities of positive self-image. *Secret of the Peaceful Warrior* by Dan Millman (3–5 years) is the story of a boy that learns the meaning of courage and friendship when he is confronted by, and befriends, the school bully.

Submissions and Payment

Guidelines available at website. Query with 2 or 3 sample chapters, outline or table of contents, market assessment, and biographical information. SASE. Responds in 3 months. Publication period and policy vary.

Editor's Comments

We're looking for story ideas that focus on helping children deal with issues they may face in their everyday lives such as bullying, building self-esteem, dealing with death, and other obstacles. Our works appeal to a large, general audience. Send us a query for something motivational.

Nightwood Editions

RR #2
3692 Beach Avenue
Roberts Creek, British Columbia V0N 2W2
Canada

Editor: Silas White

Publisher's Interests
Native legends for children are available from this regional publisher, which offers mostly adult titles on topics related to the West Coast of Canada. Poetry, art books, cookbooks, how-to books, and anthologies make up the bulk of its list. Nightwood Editions produces several books per year, at least one of which is likely to be a book for young readers.
Website: www.nightwoodeditions.com

Freelance Potential
Published 7 titles in 2005: 4 were by unpublished writers and 2 were by authors who were new to the publishing house.

- **Fiction:** Publishes Native British Columbian folklore and folk-tales for children. Also publishes anthologies for adults.
- **Nonfiction:** Publishes titles for young adults and adults. Topics include history and natural history. Also publishes cookbooks, guide books, how-to titles, and art books.
- **Representative Titles:** *Bonk on the Head* by John-James Ford (YA) is a coming-of-age novel about a young man's grueling journey through military indoctrination and the strange family life that drove him to it. *Bear Stories* by Hubert Evans recounts four true stories of encounters people had with bears.

Submissions and Payment
Guidelines available. Catalogue available with 9x12 SAE/IRC. Query with 1-paragraph summary of content, outline, and writing sample. Accepts photocopies and email queries to info@nightwoodeditions.com. SAE/IRC. Responds in 3–6 months. Publication period varies. Royalty; advance.

Editor's Comments
We do not review unsolicited manuscripts. We do solicit submissions once or twice a year, so if your work is not familiar to us, feel free to email a bio, a synopsis of your manuscript, and a 15-page sample of your work. When we're soliciting manuscripts, we'll contact you if we want to see more.

Nimbus Publishing Ltd.

P.O. Box 9166
Halifax, Nova Scotia B3K 5M8
Canada

Managing Editor: Sandra McIntyre

Publisher's Interests
For 30 years, Nimbus Publishing has been bringing the works of Atlantic Canadian authors to Atlantic Canadian readers. It offers a limited number of books for children, all of which reflect the Atlantic experience.
Website: www.nimbus.ns.ca

Freelance Potential
Published 30–35 titles (5 juvenile) in 2005: 3 were developed from unsolicited submissions. Of the 30–35 titles, 25 were by unpublished writers and 20 were by authors who were new to the publishing house. Receives 200–300 queries and unsolicited mss yearly.

- **Fiction:** Publishes story picture books, 4–10 years; and middle-grade books, 8–12 years. Genres include folklore and historical, multicultural, and regional fiction.
- **Nonfiction:** Publishes titles for young adults and adults. Topics include geography, social and cultural history, natural history, sports, plant and animal lore, and the environment. Also publishes regional cookbooks, guidebooks, personal travel books, and photographic books.
- **Representative Titles:** *Lena and the Whale* is the story of a girl with a sixth sense who comes to the rescue of a baby humpback that swims too close to shore. *Smallest Rabbit* by Joyce Barkhouse tells of a rabbit's first winter.

Submissions and Payment
Guidelines available. Query with outline and sample chapter; or send complete ms. Accepts photocopies, computer printouts, and simultaneous submissions if identified. SASE. Response time varies. Publication in 1–2 years. Royalty; advance. Flat fee.

Editor's Comments
We no longer review unsolicited manuscripts for children's books; please send queries only.

NL Associates

P.O. Box 1199
Highstown, NJ 08520

President: Nathan Levy

Publisher's Interests
The books from NL Associates are designed to stimulate the critical and creative thinking skills of children in the elementary grades through high school. It offers brain-game activity books and books about mathematics, language arts, writing, public speaking, and time management. Resources for teachers of gifted students are also included in its catalogue, along with child development titles.
Website: www.storieswithholes.com

Freelance Potential
Published 5 titles in 2005. Receives 10 queries, 10 mss yearly.

- **Nonfiction:** Publishes educational materials and activity books designed to help critical thinking skills, grades 1–12. Features books on special education and titles for parents and educators.
- **Representative Titles:** *Teaching Young Gifted Children in the Regular Classroom* by Smutny, Walker & Meckstroth (teachers) helps primary-grade teachers identify their gifted students and explains how they can nurture and challenge these children in the classroom. *Thinking and Writing Activities for the Brain* by Nathan Levy & Amy Burke blends quotations and proverbs with critical thinking and writing skills to help children enhance their cognitive and affective abilities.

Submissions and Payment
Query or send complete ms. SASE. Response time, publication period, and payment policy vary.

Editor's Comments
All the educational materials we produce stress the development of critical thinking skills. Our resources must be fun to use as well. Visit our website for a sampling of our titles and to see if your idea will fit in with our publishing program and our goal: to provide "books for people who stretch their minds and free their spirits."

North Country Books

311 Turner Street
Utica, NY 13501

Publisher: Sheila Orlin

Publisher's Interests
This regional company publishes and distributes books about New York State exclusively. Topics range from history and folklore to field guides and cookbooks. All of its fiction for children has a New York setting or focus.
Website: www.NorthCountryBooks.com

Freelance Potential
Published 6 titles (1 juvenile) in 2005. Receives 75 queries each year.

- **Fiction:** Publishes story picture books, 4–10 years. Features folklore about New York State.
- **Nonfiction:** Publishes easy-to-read books, 4–7 years; and middle-grade books, 8–12 years. Also publishes biographies; field and trail guides; cookbooks; and books about history, art, photography, and nature for adults—all related to New York State.
- **Representative Titles:** *Excuse Me, Sir . . . Your Socks Are on Fire* by Larry Weill describes the experiences of a Wilderness Park Ranger during his three years of service in the Adirondack Mountains. *Dead End* by Liza Frenette is an adventure story involving a group of middle school kids on an overnight hike in the Adirondacks.

Submissions and Payment
Guidelines and catalogue available with 9x12 SASE ($2 postage). Query or send complete ms. Accepts photocopies. SASE. Responds to queries in 1–2 months, to mss in 6–12 months. Publication in 2–5 years. Royalty.

Editor's Comments
Our books appeal to a general audience seeking information about New York State, particularly the Capital district, central New York, the Finger Lakes region, and the Hudson River Valley. Most of what we accept is nonfiction, although fiction for children is welcome as long as it features a New York setting.

NorthWord Books for Young Readers

11571 K-Tel Drive
Minnetonka, MN 55343

Submissions Editor

Publisher's Interests

NorthWord strives to instill a love of the natural world through the board books, picture books, and nonfiction it offers for children up to the age of 12.
Website: www.tnkidsbooks.com

Freelance Potential

Published 17 titles in 2005: 3 were developed from unsolicited submissions and 2 were by agented authors. Of the 17 titles, 2 were by unpublished writers and 5 were by authors who were new to the publishing house. Receives 500 queries, 400 unsolicited mss yearly.

- **Fiction:** Published 2 concept books, 0–4 years; and 2 story picture books, 4–10 years. Publishes stories about animals, nature, and the environment.
- **Nonfiction:** Published 2 concept books, 2 toddler books, and 4 early picture books, 0–4 years; 1 easy-to-read book, 4–7 years; 2 story picture books, 4–10 years; and 2 middle-grade books, 8–12 years. Topics include animals, natural history, nature, the environment, and wildlife. Also publishes biographies of naturalists.
- **Representative Titles:** *The Sunset Switch* by Kathleen Kudlinski (5–8 years) illustrates the balance of nocturnal and diurnal animals and how they take turns. *Zebras* by Jill Anderson (2–5 years) portrays a day in the life of this animal; part of the Wild Ones series.

Submissions and Payment

Guidelines available. Query with writing sample for nonfiction. Send complete ms for picture books. Accepts photocopies. SASE. Responds in 1–3 months. Publication in 2 years. Payment policy varies.

Editor's Comments

We'd like to receive biographies of naturalists and books about nature, outdoor activities, and environmental issues.

Novalis

Saint Paul University
223 Main Street
Ottawa, Ontario K1S 1C4
Canada

Commissioning Editor: Kevin Burns

Publisher's Interests
Novalis publishes books to help children and adults explore their religious heritage, to live their faith, and to create a more spiritual world.
Website: www.novalis.ca

Freelance Potential
Published 60 titles (7 juvenile) in 2005: 7 were developed from unsolicited submissions, 2 were by agented authors, and 10 were reprint/licensed properties. Of the 60 titles, 5 were by unpublished writers and 5 were by new authors. Receives 150+ queries each year.

- **Fiction:** Published 2 early picture books, 0–4 years; 2 easy-to-read books, 4–7 years; and 1 story picture book, 4–10 years. Genres include religious and spiritual fiction.
- **Nonfiction:** Published 2 middle-grade titles, 8–12 years. Also publishes early picture books, 0–4 years; story picture books, 4–10 years; and young adult novels, 12–18 years. Topics include religion, spirituality, theology, and history. Also publishes biographies for adults.
- **Representative Titles:** *What You Will See Inside a Catholic Church* by Rev. Michael Keane introduces children to traditional houses of worship, liturgical celebrations, and rituals of the Catholic faith. *Growing Up with God* by Nancy Cocks uses stories to explore childrens' faith and spiritual life.

Submissions and Payment
Guidelines available. Query with clips and 2 sample chapters. Accepts photocopies and email queries to kburns@ustpaul.ca. No simultaneous submissions. SAE/IRC. Responds in 8 weeks. Publication in 12–18 months. Royalty; advance.

Editor's Comments
Every book is unique, and each writer follows a unique journey from idea to print. We look for material that follows the Scriptures and traditional theology.

The Oliver Press

5707 West 36th Street
Minneapolis, MN 55416-2510

Publisher: Mark Lerner

Publisher's Interests
For more than a decade, The Oliver Press has published nonfiction that provides the facts and views that responsible citizenship requires. Its history, biography, and science books are for children ages five through eighteen.
Website: www.oliverpress.com

Freelance Potential
Published 12 titles in 2005. Of the 12 titles, 3 were by authors who were new to the publishing house. Receives 50 queries yearly.

- **Nonfiction:** Publishes chapter books, 5–10 years; middle-grade books, 8–12 years; and young adult books, 12–18 years. Topics include current events, archaeology, astronomy, aviation, business, communications, law, government, the environment, medicine, meteorology, space, history, forensics, and genetics.
- **Representative Titles:** *Obesity: Causes and Consequences* by Joanne Mattern (grade 5+) includes the latest information, explains the health risks, and discusses the causes of this epidemic; part of the Behind the News series. *Voyageurs, Lumberjacks, and Farmers: Pioneers of the Midwest* by Kieran Doherty (grade 7+) offers candid portraits of the individuals who shaped Midwest history.

Submissions and Payment
Guidelines available. Query with résumé, outline, and writing sample. Accepts photocopies, computer printouts, and simultaneous submissions if identified. SASE. Response time varies. Publication in 1–2 years. Flat fee, $1,000.

Editor's Comments
We want to see topics that provide historical perspective, depth, and context to the subjects that are being covered in elementary and high school classrooms today.

OnStage Publishing

214 East Moulton Street NE
Decatur, AL 35601

Senior Editor: Diane Hamilton

Publisher's Interests
The focus of this publisher is on middle-grade chapter books
and titles for young adults. Plans for a line of picture books
are currently in the works.
Website: www.onstagebooks.com

Freelance Potential
Published 5–10 titles in 2005: most were developed from
unsolicited submissions. Of the 5–10 titles, 3 were by
unpublished writers and 2 were by authors who were new to
the publishing house. Receives 500 queries, 3,500 mss yearly.

- **Fiction:** Published 3 middle-grade books, 8–12 years; and
  2 young adult novels, 12–18 years. Genres include adventure;
  drama; fantasy; horror; mystery; suspense; contemporary,
  historical, humorous, and science fiction; sports stories; and
  stories about nature and the environment.
- **Nonfiction:** Publishes story picture books, 4–10 years; chapter
  books, 5–10 years; middle-grade books, 8–12 years; and young
  adult titles, 12–18 years. Topics include animals, history, nature,
  the environment, and sports. Also publishes biographies.
- **Representative Titles:** *The Legacy of Bletchley Park* by Annie
  Laura Smith (YA) is the story of an English girl's struggles with
  her German heritage during WWII. *The Secret of Crybaby Hollow* by Darren Butler (8–12 years) follows a sixth-grade sleuth
  as she solves a series of mysteries.

Submissions and Payment
Guidelines available with 9x12 SASE (3 first-class stamps).
Send ms for picture books. Query with sample chapters for
longer fiction and nonfiction. Accepts simultaneous submissions if identified. SASE. Responds in 2–4 months. Publication in 1–2 years. Royalty, varies; advance, varies.

Editor's Comments
We will look at any picture book manuscript to see if it will
fit in with our future plans. Please query first for nonfiction.

Orca Book Publishers

P.O. Box 468
Custer, WA 98240-0468

Editor: Bob Tyrrell

Publisher's Interests

Picture books, chapter books, juvenile and young adult fiction, and graphic novels relating to Canadian history and culture are the specialty of this regional publisher. All of its titles are written by Canadian authors.
Website: www.orcabook.com

Freelance Potential

Published 50–60 titles in 2005: 25–30 were developed from unsolicited submissions, and 15 were by agented authors. Of the 50–60 titles, 7–8 were by unpublished writers and 7–8 were by authors who were new to the publishing house. Receives 2,000 queries, 500 unsolicited mss yearly.

- **Fiction:** Publishes easy-to-read books, 4–7 years; story picture books, 4–10 years; chapter books, 5–10 years; middle-grade titles, 8–12 years; and young adult books, 12–18 years. Genres include regional historical and contemporary fiction.
- **Representative Titles:** *Summer on the Run* by Nancy Belgue is the story of a down-and-out boy who decides that risky rum-running will help his family. *The Bachelors* by Don Trembath follows the escapades of three boys and their grumpy grandfather as they try to make it through a whole week together.

Submissions and Payment

Canadian authors only. Guidelines available at website. Query with 2–3 sample chapters for novels; send complete ms for picture books. Accepts photocopies and computer printouts. SASE. Responds in 8–12 weeks. Publication in 18–24 months. Royalty, 10% split; advance.

Editor's Comments

We are currently seeking manuscripts in the following categories: picture books with engaging plots and strong writing; contemporary stories of fantasy with a universal theme and a sympathetic child protagonist; and high-interest teen novels that reflect the universal struggles that young people face.

Orchard Books

Scholastic, Inc.
557 Broadway
New York, NY 10012-3999

Editorial Assistant: Bethany Bezdecheck
Fiction Editor: Lisa Sandell

Publisher's Interests
A wide range of fiction and nonfiction titles, from charming picture books to adventurous young adult books, are offered by this imprint of Scholastic, Inc. 10% self-, subsidy-, co-venture, or co-op published material.
Website: www.scholastic.com

Freelance Potential
Published 20 titles in 2005: 15–20 were by agented authors ann 6 were reprint/licensed properties. Receives 1,000+ queries yearly.

- **Fiction:** Publishes concept books, toddler books, and early picture books, 0–4 years; story picture books, 4–10 years; chapter books, 5–10 years; middle-grade books, 8–12 years; and young adult books, 12–18 years. Genres include historical, contemporary, and multicultural fiction; fairy tales; folktales; fantasy; humor; and stories about animals; nature; and sports.
- **Nonfiction:** Publishes story picture books, 4–10 years. Topics include history, nature, the environment, and social issues.
- **Representative Titles:** *The Wheels on the Race Car* by Alexander Zane (4–8 years) is a fun, read-aloud picture book with rhyming text and amusing illustrations. *Montmorency on the Rocks* by Eleanor Updale (9–12 years) a compelling historical thriller, brimming with intrigue, humor, and suspense.

Submissions and Payment
Guidelines available. Query only. Send fiction queries to Lisa Sandell, Editor, and queries for picture books to Bethany Bezdecheck, Editorial Assistant. No unsolicited mss. SASE. Responds in 3 months. Royalties; advance.

Editor's Comments
We look for entertaining and educational books that children will enjoy reading. Our list includes titles from award-winning authors, as well as first time authors.

O'Reilly Media, Inc.

1005 Gravenstein Hwy North
Sebastopol, CA 95472

Editorial Assistant: Michele Filshie

Publisher's Interests

A wide variety of books that focus on topics related to computers can be found on the pages of this publisher's catalogue. It targets young adults and adults and includes programming topics, data technology, hardware, system administration, email administration, games and game programming, digital media, security, and networking.
Website: www.oreilly.com/oreilly/author/intro.html

Freelance Potential

Published 150 titles in 2005: 60 were developed from unsolicited submissions. Of the 60 titles, all were by unpublished writers who were new to the publishing house.

- **Nonfiction:** Publishes young adult books, 12–18 years. Topics include computers, science, and technology.
- **Representative Titles:** *Jakarta Struts Cookbook* by Bill Siggelkow (YA) is a timely reference that is high on practicality and low on theory, providing solutions to a wide range of problems. *Revolution in the Valley* by Andy Hertzfeld traces the development of the Macintosh computer and offers a vivid, firsthand account of its introduction and beyond. *Internet Annoyances* by Preston Gralla (YA) is a guide that addresses and presents solutions for glitches to make using the Internet as stress-free as possible.

Submissions and Payment

Guidelines and catalogue available at website. Send query with proposal. SASE. Response time varies. Publication in 12 months. Royalty, 10%; advance. Flat fee.

Editor's Comments

This year we are looking for books on computers, technology, math, and science. All the material we publish is computer-related. Before submitting a manuscript, you must send a query and proposal. See our website for further information on submitting, and our publishing philosophy.

Our Sunday Visitor

200 Knoll Plaza
Huntington, IN 46750

Acquisitions Editor

Publisher's Interests

Established in 1912, Our Sunday Visitor is the largest non-profit Catholic publishing company in the U.S. Its publishing division produces books, pamphlets, and booklets on topics of interest to Catholic lay people, such as prayer, church history, the saints, and family life. Its juvenile list features titles for infants through young adults.
Website: www.osv.com

Freelance Potential

Published 55 titles (6 juvenile) in 2005. Receives 1,300 queries yearly.

- **Nonfiction:** Publishes concept books, 0–4 years; story picture books, 4–10 years; chapter books, 5–10 years; middle-grade books, 8–12 years; and young adult books, 12–18 years. Topics include family issues, parish life, church heritage, and the lives of the saints.
- **Representative Titles:** *We Have a Pope! Benedict XVI* by Matthew E. Bunson is a biography of the Holy Father, the former Cardinal Joseph Ratzinger of Germany. *Teach Me about the Life of Jesus* by Joan Ensor Plum & Paul S. Plum (3–7 years) includes activities and discussion ideas that introduce young children to the life of Jesus as depicted in Scripture.

Submissions and Payment

Guidelines available. Query with résumé and sample chapter. Accepts photocopies, computer printouts, and simultaneous submissions if identified. SASE. Responds in 2–3 months. Publication in 1+ years. Royalty; advance. Flat fee.

Editor's Comments

We don't publish fiction or poetry, but we do look for books that explain the essentials of the faith, reference books that provide trustworthy information to Catholics, books that cultivate a sense of prayer and devotion, books that serve the needs of priests, and books about marriage and family life.

The Overmountain Press

P.O. Box 1261
Johnson City, TN 37605

Managing Editor: Daniel Lewis

Publisher's Interests
Focusing on the Southern Appalachian area, this publisher offers children's books, cookbooks, guidebooks, ghost lore, mysteries, regional nonfiction, and folklore.
Website: www.overmountainpress.com

Freelance Potential
Published 25 titles (7 juvenile) in 2005: 3 were developed from unsolicited submissions, 3 were by agented authors, and 1 was a reprint/licensed property. Receives 500 queries each year.

- **Fiction:** Publishes early picture books, 0–4 years; middle-grade books, 8–12 years; and young adult books, 12–18 years. Genres include folklore, folktales, mystery, and regional fiction.
- **Nonfiction:** Publishes story picture books, 4–10 years; and chapter books, 5–10 years. Topics include Southern Appalachia.
- **Representative Titles:** *Ten Friends* by Gayla Dowdy Seale introduces young children to the Ten Commandments through the use of colorful illustrations and simple, rhyming language. *Bloody Mary* by Patrick Bone summons spooky memories of magic and fantasy, where good overcomes evil, and violence takes a back seat to imagination and humor.

Submissions and Payment
Guidelines available at website or with 6x9 SASE ($.85 postage). Query with résumé and sample chapters; send complete ms for the History Series for Young Readers. Accepts photocopies and computer printouts. SASE. Responds in 2–3 months. Publication in 1 year. Royalty, 15%.

Editor's Comments
We're always looking for new titles. If you think your book fits our list, review our guidelines and submit accordingly. Remember, all books must have a strong regional flavor.

Richard C. Owen Publishers

P.O. Box 585
Katonah, NY 10536

Director of Children's Books: Janice Boland

Publisher's Interests

Richard C. Owen Publishers supports the belief that students will become enthusiastic, independent, life-long learners—as well as accomplished readers and writers—with the proper support. All of its materials, which are aimed at children in preschool through age 10, strive to provide that support.
Website: www.rcowen.com

Freelance Potential

Published 15 titles in 2005: 2 were developed from unsolicited submissions. Receives 1,000 queries, 1,000 unsolicited mss yearly.

- **Fiction:** Publishes easy-to-read books, 4–7 years; story picture books, 4–10 years; and chapter books, 5–10 years. Genres include mystery; humor; folktales; contemporary fiction; stories about animals and nature; and books about social, ethnic, and multicultural issues.
- **Nonfiction:** Publishes easy-to-read books, 4–7 years; story picture books, 4–10 years; and chapter books, 5–10 years. Topics include current events, geography, music, science, nature, and the environment. Also publishes professional development titles and parenting books.
- **Representative Titles:** *The Artist* by Lois Podoshen introduces children to primary and secondary colors and the color wheel. *Andi's Wool* by Rhonda Cox is a nonfiction account of a pet sheep's annual shearing.

Submissions and Payment

Guidelines available. Send complete ms. Accepts photocopies, computer printouts, and simultaneous submissions if identified. SASE. Responds in 3–6 months. Publication period and payment policy vary.

Editor's Comments

We're looking for high-interest stories that will appeal to five-, six-, and seven-year-old children.

Pacific Educational Press

6365 Biological Sciences Road
Faculty of Education, University of British Columbia
Vancouver, British Columbia V6T 1Z4
Canada

Director: Catherine Edwards

Publisher's Interests
In addition to providing textbooks for teacher education programs and professional resources for practicing teachers, this publishing house also produces books on education topics and contemporary issues for students at all grade levels.
Website: www.pep.educ.ubc.ca

Freelance Potential
Published 5 titles (1 juvenile) in 2005: 1 was developed from an unsolicited submission. Of the 5 titles, 1 was by an author new to the publishing house. Receives 50 queries yearly.

- **Fiction:** Publishes chapter books, 5–10 years; and middle-grade books, 8–12 years. Genres include historical and multi-cultural fiction.
- **Nonfiction:** Publishes middle-grade books, 8–12 years; and young adult books, 12–18 years. Also publishes books for teachers, grades K–12. Topics include mathematics, science, social studies, multicultural education, critical thinking, fine arts, and administration.
- **Representative Titles:** *Trapped by Coal* by Constance Horne (8–12 years) is the story of a coal-mining family determined to escape from a cruel working life. *In the Street of the Temple Cloth Printers* by Dorothy Field (9–12 years) provides a look at the traditional way of life of the craftspeople who live in India.

Submissions and Payment
Guidelines available. Query with résumé, outline, and 2 sample chapters. Accepts photocopies, computer printouts, and simultaneous submissions if identified. SAE/IRC. Responds in 2–6 months. Publication in 10–18 months. Royalty.

Editor's Comments
This year, we're looking for resources for art teachers, as well as critical thinking math and science resources for teachers and students at all levels.

Pacific Press Publishing Association

1350 North Kings Road
Nampa, ID 83687

Acquisitions Editor: Tim Lale

Publisher's Interests

Pacific Press publishes Christian books with a Seventh-day Adventist perspective. Its juvenile list targets kids between the ages of four and fourteen and includes picture books that illustrate a distinctive Adventist belief, Bible story sets, and truth-based stories with Christian themes.
Website: www.pacificpress.com

Freelance Potential

Published 40 titles (10 juvenile) in 2005: 5 were developed from unsolicited submissions. Receives 200+ queries yearly.

- **Fiction:** Publishes easy-to-read books, 4–7 years; chapter books, 5–10 years; and middle-grade books, 8–12 years. Genres include adventure, mystery, and suspense—all with Christian themes.
- **Nonfiction:** Publishes easy-to-read books, 4–7 years; chapter books, 5–10 years; and middle-grade books, 8–12 years. Topics include children, animals, and Seventh-day Adventist beliefs. Also publishes Bible stories.
- **Representative Titles:** *Flying High* by Katy Pistole is the story of a young girl struggling with anger and forgiveness issues. *What's Wrong with Rusty?* by Heather Grovet portrays a 12-year-old athlete who learns he has juvenile diabetes.

Submissions and Payment

Guidelines available at website or with SASE. Query. Accepts photocopies, computer printouts, disk submissions, and email submissions to booksubmissions@pacificpress.com. SASE. Responds in 3 months. Publication in 6–12 months. Royalty, 6–12%; advance, to $1,500.

Editor's Comments

We're looking for books that teach children and teens how to pray; books that explore the life of Jesus; and material that teaches young people about eternal life and their futures with God. We also need Christian historical fiction for all ages.

P & R Publishing Company

P.O. Box 817
Phillipsburg, NJ 08865

Director of Publications: Al Fisher

Publisher's Interests
P & R Publishing is dedicated to producing books that promote biblical understanding and godly living as summarized in The Westminister Confession of Faith and Catechisms.
Website: www.prpbook.com

Freelance Potential
Published 40 titles in 2005: 1 was by an agented author. Receives 360 queries yearly.

- **Fiction:** Publishes middle-grade books, 8–12 years; and young adult books, 12–18 years. Genres include inspirational and religious fiction, and fantasy.
- **Nonfiction:** Publishes middle-grade titles, 8–12 years; and young adult books, 12–18 years. Topics include Christian living, counseling, theology, apologetics, study aids, Christian issues and ethics, resources for youth, and women's issues.
- **Representative Titles:** *Beyond the Summerland* by L. B. Grahm is an original adventure/fantasy story based on the book of Isaiah; part of the Binding of the Blade series. *Ultimate Issues* by R. C. Sproul (YA) helps young adults work through tough personal issues such as the relative value of human and animal life, a standard of rightness, and being acceptable to God.

Submissions and Payment
Guidelines available at website. Query with outline, 2 sample chapters, and proposal. Accepts photocopies, computer printouts, and simultaneous submissions if identified. SASE. Responds in 2 months. Publication period varies. Royalty.

Editor's Comments
Our titles range from academic works that advance biblical and theological scholarship to popular books designed to help readers grow in Christian thought and service. Your manuscript should include clear, engaging, insightful applications of Reformed theology to life.

Parenting Press, Inc.

P.O. Box 75267
Seattle, WA 98175-0267

Publisher: Carolyn Threadgill

Publisher's Interests
Practical advice on building life skills is offered by this publisher. Its list includes titles that help toddlers, tweens, teens, and their parents and teachers cope with social and behavioral issues.
Website: www.parentingpress.com

Freelance Potential
Published 4 titles (1 juvenile) in 2005: 1 was developed from an unsolicited submission. Of the 4 titles, 3 were by authors who were new to the publishing house. Receives 300–500 queries yearly.

- **Fiction:** Publishes toddler books, 0–4 years; story picture books, 4–10 years; and middle-grade books, 8–12 years. Topics include stories that understand feelings and build self-esteem.
- **Nonfiction:** Publishes concept books, 0–4 years; and easy-to-read books, 4–7 years. Also publishes adult titles. Topics include loss and grief, child guidance, children's safety, emotions, problem solving, and social studies.
- **Representative Titles:** *Dealing with Disappointment* by Elizabeth Crary (2–12 years) provides self-calming techniques and problem-solving tools that help kids learn to handle obstacles and frustrations throughout life. *The Way I Feel* by Janan Cain (2–8 years) explains various emotions with the help of two zany characters who soar, sniffle, and shriek their way through feelings like joy, boredom, and anger.

Submissions and Payment
Guidelines available. Query with outline and clips or writing samples. Accepts photocopies, computer printouts, and simultaneous submissions if identified. SASE. Responds in 2 months. Publication in 18–24 months. Royalty, 4–8% of net.

Editor's Comments
This year, we are looking for titles that deal with anger, teen concerns, and contemporary children's issues.

Parkway Publishers

P.O. Box 3678
Boone, NC 28607

President: Rao Aluri

Publisher's Interests

Parkway Publisher's catalogue includes nonfiction and fiction books. Topics focus on the history, nature, and culture of western North Carolina. It also features folklore, legends, and mysteries for children and young adults.

Website: www.parkwaypublishers.com

Freelance Potential

Published 20 titles (5 juvenile) in 2005: all were developed from unsolicited submissions. Of the 20 titles, 15 were by unpublished writers and 15 were by authors who were new to the publishing house. Receives 25 unsolicited mss yearly.

- **Fiction:** Publishes story picture books, 4–10 years; chapter books, 5–10 years; and young adult books, 12–18 years. Genres include historical fiction, folktales and legends, science, mysteries, and animal adventures.
- **Nonfiction:** Publishes story picture books, 4–10 years; middle-grade books, 8–12 years; and young adult books, 12–18 years. Topics include history, culture, and nature of western North Carolina.
- **Representative Titles:** *Zebordee's Caper* by Ann Goode Cooper (4–10 years) tells the adventures of an ant who escapes from an ant farm and explores a kitchen. *The Gold Bug of Farrow Point* by Jack R. Pyle (YA) is a mystery that follows the adventures of a brother and sister who decode a message while on vacation that leads them into dangerous situations.

Submissions and Payment

Guidelines available. Send complete ms. Accepts photocopies, computer printouts, and IBM disk submissions. SASE. Responds in 2–6 weeks. Publication in 6–12 months. Royalty, 10%.

Editor's Comments

We are interested in books about the history of North Carolina, as well as stories about local legends and folktales.

Pauline Books & Media

50 St. Paul's Avenue
Jamaica Plain, MA 02130-3491

Children's Editor: Sister Patricia Edward, F.S.P.

Publisher's Interests
Seeking to provide wholesome and entertaining reading that
can help children develop Christian values, this publisher
offers prayerbooks, nonfiction books on the lives of the
saints, coloring books, Bible stories, Christmas and Easter
stories, and seasonal activities.
Website: www.pauline.org

Freelance Potential
Published 45 titles (20 juvenile) in 2005: 5 were developed
from unsolicited submissions. Of the 45 titles, 4 were by
unpublished writers and 12 were by authors who were new
to the publishing house. Receives 360–480 queries yearly.

- **Nonfiction:** Publishes early picture books, 0–4 years; easy-to-
  read books, 4–7 years; story picture books, and middle-grade
  books, 8–12 years. Also publishes prayer books. Topics
  include religious holidays, the lives of saints, and the sacraments. Features coloring books and activity books.
- **Representative Titles:** *Squishy, Squishy* by Chérie B. Stihler
  (3–6 years) is a whimsical, radiantly illustrated book of
  rhyming text that gives thanks to God. *Little Book of Saints* by
  Kathleen M. Muldoon (7–9 years) tells the stories of ten
  beloved saints of the Catholic faith.

Submissions and Payment
Guidelines available at website. Query with clips. Accepts
photocopies, disk submissions (MicrosoftWord), and email to
spedward@paulinemedia.com. SASE. Responds in 2–3
months. Publication in 2–3 years. Royalty; 5–10% based on
wholesale price. Advance; $200–$500.

Editor's Comments
We're looking for nonfiction books about the lives of saints
for ages 4–6, 7–9, 9–12; prayer books for ages 9–12; and
religious Easter stories for ages 4–7 and 8–12. New writers
have a better chance with children's books, ages 4–7.

Paulist Press

997 Macarthur Boulevard
Mahwah, NJ 07430

Managing Editor: Paul McMahon

Publisher's Interests

This Catholic publishing house features quality books on Christian and Catholic themes. It produces preschool picture books, prayer books, chapter books, guidebooks, and gift books, as well as young adult biographies.
Website: www.paulistpress.com

Freelance Potential

Published 95 titles (12 juvenile) in 2005: 1 was developed from an unsolicited submission and 2 were by agented authors. Receives 750 unsolicited mss yearly.

- **Fiction:** Publishes picture books, 2–5 years; chapter books, 8–12 years; and young adult books, 12–18 years. Features contemporary and religious fiction dealing with Catholic and Christian themes.
- **Nonfiction:** Publishes prayer books and books of blessings, 5–8 years; and Catholic guide books, 5+ years. Also offers Catholic gift books and titles on Roman Catholic activities, traditions, and rituals.
- **Representative Titles:** *My Catholic School Holiday Activity Book* by Jennifer Galvin (5–10 years) incorporates word finds, puzzles, and fun activities that enable children to learn the religion behind certain holidays. *What Is My Song?* by Dennis, Sheila, & Matthew Linn (2–5 years) tells the story of how every child comes into this world knowing his or her special purpose in life.

Submissions and Payment

Guidelines available at website. Send complete ms with résumé. Accepts photocopies. SASE. Response time varies. Publication in 2–3 years. Royalty, 8%; advance, $500.

Editor's Comments

We are seeking children's nonfiction chapter books for middle-grade readers on Christian themes and historical biographies on the saints and modern-day heroes.

Peachtree Publishers

1700 Chattahoochee Avenue
Atlanta, GA 30318-2112

Submissions Editor: Helen Harriss

Publisher's Interests

Peachtree Publishers offers children's fiction and nonfiction picture books, as well as chapter books, middle-grade readers, and young adult novels.
Website: www.peachtree-online.com

Freelance Potential

Published 32 titles (13 juvenile) in 2005: 3 were developed from unsolicited submissions, 6 were by agented authors, and 10 were reprint/licensed properties. Of the 32 titles, 2 were by unpublished writers and 8 were by new authors. Receives 20,000 queries and unsolicited mss yearly.

- **Fiction:** Published 3 early picture books, 0–4 years; 3 chapter books, 5–10 years; 4 middle-grade titles, 8–12 years; and 3 young adult books, 12–18 years. Genres include historical, regional, and multicultural fiction.
- **Nonfiction:** Publishes early picture books, 0–4 years; story picture books, 4–10 years; chapter books, 5–10 years; and middle-grade titles, 8–12 years. Topics include travel, recreation, nature, and the outdoors.
- **Representative Titles:** *Dad, Jackie, and Me* by Myron Uhlberg (4–8 years) is the story of a young boy who shares the excitement of Jackie Robinson's first Major League baseball season with his deaf father. *My Mother Talks to Trees* by Doris Gove (4–8 years) follows a girl and her mother as they walk through the neighborhood, learning about nature.

Submissions and Payment

Guidelines available. Send complete ms for works under 5,000 words. Query with résumé, outline, and 2–3 sample chapters for longer works. Accepts photocopies and computer printouts. SASE. Responds in 4–6 months. Publication period varies. Payment policy varies.

Editor's Comments

We are interested in fiction and nonfiction titles for children.

Peartree

P.O. Box 14533
Clearwater, FL 33766

Submissions Editor: Barbara Birenbaum

Publisher's Interests

Children's fiction and nonfiction books, as well as educational parenting books, and books of interest to the general public can be found in this independent publisher's catalogue. 30% subsidy-published.

Freelance Potential

Published 3–4 titles (1–2 juvenile) in 2005: all were developed from unsolicited submissions. Receives 30–50 queries, 25 unsolicited mss yearly.

- **Fiction:** Publishes early picture books, 0–4 years; story picture books, 4–10 years; chapter books, 5–10 years; middle-grade books, 8–12 years; and young adult novels, 12–18 years. Genres include adventure, animal stories, and contemporary and historical fiction.
- **Nonfiction:** Publishes early picture books, 0–4 years; story picture books, 4–10 years; middle-grade books, 8–12 years; and young adult books, 12–18 years. Topics include nature and natural history. Also publishes parenting and educational titles, self-help books, and travel and recreational guides.
- **Representative Titles:** *Amazing Bald Eaglet* by Barbara Birenbaum (8+ years) follows the life of a bald eagle including hatching, its habitat, parenting skills, and growth and development. *Og and His Frogs* by Gabriel Simon (0–4 years) is an early reader rhyming story about a boy named Og who collects all kinds of frogs.

Submissions and Payment

Guidelines available. Query or send complete ms. Accepts photocopies and computer printouts. SASE. Responds in 6–8 weeks. Publication in 1 year. Payment policy varies.

Editor's Comments

We're looking for short-run limited edition poetry books for readers ages 8–12. In addition, areas of interest include humor, and interactions of children of all ages with parents.

Pelican Publishing Company

1000 Burmaster Street
Gretna, LA 70053

Editorial Department

Publisher's Interests

Regional, holiday, and historical topics are the specialty of Pelican Publishing Company. Its list consists of easy-to-read books, middle-grade fiction and nonfiction, and traditional folktales from around the world.
Website: www.pelicanpub.com

Freelance Potential

Published 75 titles (18 juvenile) in 2005: 20 were developed from unsolicited submissions and 7 were by agented authors. Of the 75 titles, 20 were by unpublished writers and 30 were by authors new to the publishing house. Receives 6,500 queries, 3,500 unsolicited mss each year.

- **Fiction:** Publishes easy-to-read books, 4–7 years; middle-grade books, 8–12 years; and young adult books, 12–18 years. Genres include historical, regional, and holiday fiction.
- **Nonfiction:** Publishes easy-to-read books, 4–7 years. Topics include regional history and social commentary. Also publishes travel guides, cookbooks, biographies, and self-help books.
- **Representative Titles:** *The Honest-to-Goodness Story of Raggedy Andy* by Patricia Hall (5–8 years) relates the true account of how artist Johnny Gruelle came to create a companion for this famous doll. *Irish Legends for Children* by Yvonne Carroll (5–8 years) presents a collection of traditional folktales from the Emerald Isle that have been passed down for generations.

Submissions and Payment

Guidelines available. Query with synopsis. Send complete ms, easy-to-read children's books only. Accepts photocopies. No simultaneous submissions. SASE. Responds in 3 months. Publication in 9–18 months. Royalty.

Editor's Comments

We're looking for Jewish nonfiction for ages 5–8 and fiction and nonfiction about Texas.

Pembroke Publishers

538 Hood Road
Markham, Ontario, L3R 3K9
Canada

Submissions Editor: Mary Macchiusi

Publisher's Interests

This Canadian publisher of award-winning books offers educational titles for teachers, parents, and other educators. It provides strategies that are motivational and interesting on topics such as reading and writing, thinking and drama, grammar, and classroom management.
Website: www.pembrokepublishers.com

Freelance Potential

Published 15 titles (1 juvenile) in 2005. Of the 15 titles, 3 were by unpublished writers and 3 were by authors who were new to the publishing house. Receives 50 queries each year.

- **Nonfiction:** Publishes chapter books, 5–10 years; and middle-grade titles, 8–12 years. Topics include history, science, and writing. Also publishes titles for educators about literacy, spelling, grammar, educational assessment, and school safety, as well as titles on homeschool partnerships.
- **Representative Titles:** *Starting with Comprehension* by Andie Cunningham & Ruth Shagoury (teachers) offers a reading program and strategies to nurture and strengthen comprehension skills for children in preschool and kindergarten. *Writing through the Tween Years* by Bruce Morgan & Deb Odom (teachers) offers strategies for teachers to reach their tween readers, and get back the joy of teaching writing.

Submissions and Payment

Guidelines available. Query with résumé, outline, and sample chapters. Accepts photocopies and simultaneous submissions if identified. SAE/IRC. Responds in 1 month. Publication in 6–24 months. Royalty.

Editor's Comments

Send us something new and innovative that can be easily applied to the classroom. We look for strategies that get kids reading, thinking, and communicating.

Perigee Books

Penguin Group (USA), Inc.
375 Hudson Street
New York, NY 10014

Publisher: John Duff

Publisher's Interests
This imprint of Penguin Group does not publish fiction or
children's books. It is dedicated to how-to and reference
titles dealing with a wide array of topics. Perigee is interested
in informative topics that will spark a reader's interest.
Website: www.penguin.com

Freelance Potential
Published 60 titles in 2005: 30 were developed from unso-
licited submissions and 54 were by agented authors.
Receives 300–400 queries, 30 unsolicited mss each year.

- **Nonfiction:** Publishes young adult books, 12–18 years. Topics
  include sexuality, health, and spirituality. Also publishes parenting, childcare, and informational and reference books for
  parents.
- **Representative Titles:** *A World of Baby Names* by Teresa Norman (parents) is a comprehensive guide of baby names from
  around the world. *Growing and Changing* by Kathy McCoy,
  Ph.D. & Charles Wibbelsman, M.D. (8–12) offers tweens advice
  on how to transition from childhood to adulthood. *TeenVestor*
  by Emmanuel & Andrea Walker presents easy-to-read basics
  about investing.

Submissions and Payment
Query. Accepts photocopies and computer printouts. SASE.
Responds in 3–4 weeks. Does not accept proposals via
email. Publication in 18 months. Royalty; advance.

Editor's Comments
We are interested in hearing from authors who can present
self-help and how-to information on a wide range of topics.
While children's books are not a part of our publishing
program, we will consider prescriptive nonfiction and material
dealing with parenting and childcare.

Peter Pauper Press, Inc.

Suite 400
202 Mamaroneck Avenue
White Plains, NY 10601

Editorial Director: Barbara Paulding

Publisher's Interests

Female-oriented, gift books, journals, organizers, and activity books are the hallmark of this specialty publisher that has been around since 1928. Material should lend itself to holidays, special occasions, or relationships centering around friends, mothers, sisters, grandparents, or teachers.
Website: www.peterpauper.com

Freelance Potential

Published 50 titles (8 juvenile) in 2005: 2 were developed from unsolicited submissions and 4 were by agented authors. Receives 250 queries, 200 unsolicited mss yearly.

- **Nonfiction:** Publishes gift books, 4–10 years. Topics include animals, holidays, and humor.
- **Representative Titles:** *Princess Bella* (4+ years) is a scratch and sketch art activity book about the adventures of a little princess. *Sheep Thrills* by Ewegenie R. Woolsey (YA) combines humorous photographs of these wild and woolly creatures together with life lessons that everyone can live by.

Submissions and Payment

Guidelines available with a 9x12 SASE. Send complete manuscript or proposal. Accepts photocopies, computer printouts. SASE. Responds in 2–3 months. Publication period varies. Flat fee.

Editor's Comments

Send us original work. You must certify that you have the right to use any material or quotes that you submit. We do not accept poetry, short stories, novels, how-to manuscripts, or other narrative nonfiction. If sending photographs or artwork, please make sure they are color copies or duplicates—never send originals. Browse through our catalogue to get an in-depth look at what type of material we publish before you pitch your idea to us.

Philomel Books

Penguin Young Readers Group
345 Hudson Street
New York, NY 10014

Editorial Assistant: Bryan Saunders

Publisher's Interests

Philomel is an imprint dedicated to producing quality fiction and nonfiction books for young readers through young adults. It publishes books that stretch the limits of reality whether culturally, imaginatively, historically, or artistically. **Website:** www.penguingroup.com

Freelance Potential

Published 42 titles in 2005: 34 were by agented authors. Receives 800 queries yearly.

- **Fiction:** Publishes early picture books, 0–4 years; story picture books, 4–10 years; chapter books, 5–10 years; middle-grade books, 8–12 years; and young adult books, 12–18 years. Genres include fantasy; and contemporary, historical, multicultural, and science fiction. Also publishes poetry.
- **Nonfiction:** Publishes story picture books, 4–10 years; and young adult books, 12–18 years. Features biographies and first-person narratives.
- **Representative Titles:** *The Pirate Meets the Queen* by Matt Faulkner (5+ years) is an adventure between a young, red-headed pirate and Red Liz, the Queen of England. *Travel Team* by Mike Lupica (10+ years) depicts what a group of 12-year-old children do after they are cut from their local basketball team.

Submissions and Payment

Guidelines available with SASE. Query with outline/synopsis. No unsolicited mss. SASE. Responds in 1–2 months. Publication in 1–2 years. Royalty.

Editor's Comments

We'd like to see mysteries, sports books, and historically-themed picture books. Stories that contain cultural diversity are high on our wish list. Send a query letter; we do not accept unsolicited manuscripts. Include the length, the intended audience, and a brief description.

Phoenix Learning Resources

Suite 210
25 3rd Street
Stamford, CT 06902

Executive Vice President: John A. Rothermich

Publisher's Interests

With a wide range of subjects for students in kindergarten through high school, this educational publisher is known for its textbooks that serve the school market. It also publishes reference books and biographies, as well as materials for special education students and those in English-as-a-Second-Language programs.

Website: www.phoenixlearninggroup.com

Freelance Potential

Published 12 titles in 2005. Receives 40–50 queries, 30–40 unsolicited mss yearly.

- **Nonfiction:** Publishes textbooks and educational materials for pre-K–post grade 12. Also publishes books for special and gifted education students, materials for use with ESL students, reference books, and biographies. Topics include language skills, integrated language arts, reading, comprehension, math, study skills, and social studies.
- **Representative Titles:** *Guidebook to Better English* (grades 4–7) is a series of basic English skills that emphasizes vocabulary building. *Spelling 2,100* (grades 1–6) is a phonetically based spelling program for the direct teaching of 2,100 words that are most needed in writing.

Submissions and Payment

Query or send complete ms with résumé. Accepts photocopies, computer printouts, and simultaneous submissions if identified. SASE. Responds in 1–4 weeks. Publication in 1–15 months. Royalty. Flat fee.

Editor's Comments

We are in the market for textbooks dealing with reading and math skills for students in kindergarten through grade twelve. We also want to see age-appropriate study skills textbooks for students in grades four through eight; and manuscripts for grades one through twelve that address writing skills.

The Pilgrim Press

700 Prospect Avenue East
Cleveland, OH 44115-1100

Editorial Director: Kim M. Sadler

Publisher's Interests

Targeting scholars, students, laypersons, and church professionals, this publisher strives to discern how God is disclosed in various Christian and world religions through its nonfiction titles for adults and children of all ages.
Website: www.pilgrimpress.com

Freelance Potential

Published 54 titles in 2005: 23 were developed from unsolicited submissions and 1 was by an agented author. Of the 54 titles, 1 was by an unpublished writer and 12 were by authors who were new to the publishing house. Receives 200+ queries and mss yearly.

- **Nonfiction:** Publishes educational titles of interest to religious educators, clergy, parents, and caregivers. Also publishes informational titles on religion, social issues, and multicultural and ethnic subjects.
- **Representative Titles:** *Helping Others* by Carol Wehrheim (0–4 years) is a colorful Bible story picture book with bright illustrations. *Come to Jesus* by Carol Wehrheim (0–4 years) offers an ideal introduction to Jesus.

Submissions and Payment

Guidelines available at website. Query with table of contents and sample chapters; or send complete ms. Accepts photocopies. SASE. Responds to queries in 6–8 weeks, to unsolicited mss in 2–3 months. Publication in 9–12 months. Flat fee for work-for-hire.

Editor's Comments

We look for material that addresses difficult and complex social issues in the context of faith. In order for your material to be considered, you must follow our acquisitions process, which includes sending a sample chapter, highlighting compelling unique features, and showing usefulness for the intended readership. See guidelines for information.

Piñata Books

Arte Público Press
452 Cullen Performance Hall
University of Houston
Houston, TX 77204-2004

Submissions Department

Publisher's Interests

Piñata Books, the children's imprint launched in 1994 by Arte Público Press, is devoted to providing enriching and entertaining literature to children and young adults on Hispanic culture.

Website: www.artepublicopress.com

Freelance Potential

Published 28 titles (8 juvenile) in 2005: 9 were developed from unsolicited submissions and 3 were by agented authors. Receives 3,000 queries yearly.

- **Fiction:** Publishes story picture books, 4–10 years; middle-grade books, 8–12 years; and young adult books, 12–18 years. Genres include contemporary fiction, drama, poetry, and anthologies.
- **Nonfiction:** Publishes story picture books, 4–10 years; and young adult books, 12–18 years. Publishes biographies and autobiographies.
- **Representative Titles:** *The Empanadas that Abuela Made* by Diane Gonzales Bertrand (3–7 years) combines family and fun in a whimsical look at making empanadas. *Lorenzo's Secret Mission* by Lila & Rick Guzmán (11+ years) is the story of 15-year-old Lorenzo Bannister who joins a secret flatboat operation delivering much-needed medicine and gunpowder to George Washington's army.

Submissions and Payment

Guidelines and catalogue available at website. Query with sample chapter. Accepts complete ms for easy-to-read books. Accepts photocopies and computer printouts. SASE. Responds to queries in 2–4 months, to mss in 3–6 months. Publication in 2 years. Royalty.

Editor's Comments

We're looking for realistic stories that authentically portray characters and customs unique to U.S. Hispanic culture.

Pineapple Press

P.O. Box 3889
Sarasota, FL 34230

Executive Editor: June Cussen

Publisher's Interests
Specializing in nonfiction books about Florida, Pineapple Press also publishes some literary novels that feature Florida settings. Its children's books, which are marketed to the state's schools, cover topics related to Florida.
Website: www.pineapplepress.com

Freelance Potential
Published 19 titles (4 juvenile) in 2005: 18 were developed from unsolicited submissions and 1 was a reprint/licensed property. Of the 19 titles, 5 were by unpublished writers and 7 were by authors who were new to the publishing house. Receives 800 queries yearly.

- **Fiction:** Published 1 middle-grade novel, 8–12 years; and 1 young adult book, 12–18 years. Genres include folklore, mystery, science fiction, mythology, and historical fiction related to Florida.
- **Nonfiction:** Published 1 easy-to-read book, 4–7 years; and 1 middle-grade book, 8–12 years. Topics include sports, wildlife, nature, and environment of Florida.
- **Representative Titles:** *Those Funny Flamingos* by Jan Lee Wicker (5–9 years) introduces readers to this big, pink bird. *Florida Lighthouses for Kids* by Elinor De Wire (9+ years) details the history and lore of Florida's 33 lighthouses.

Submissions and Payment
Guidelines available at website. Query with clips, synopsis, and sample chapters for fiction. Query with table of contents and sample chapters for nonfiction. Accepts photocopies, computer printouts, and simultaneous submissions if identified. SASE. Responds in 2 months. Publication in 12–18 months. Royalty.

Editor's Comments
Fiction and nonfiction for all age groups is welcome here, as long as the work concentrates on some aspect of our state.

Pioneer Drama Service

P.O. Box 4267
Englewood, CO 80155-4267

Assistant Editor: Lori Conary

Publisher's Interests

This well-established publisher offers a complete selection of theatrical material for performing groups. Its roster includes children's plays and musicals, one-act and full-length plays, holiday plays, and melodramas.
Website: www.pioneerdrama.com

Freelance Potential

Published 25+ titles in 2005: 10–15 were developed from unsolicited submissions and 10+ were by agented authors. Receives 400–500 queries, 400 unsolicited mss yearly.

- **Fiction:** Publishes plays, 4–18 years. Genres include comedy, mystery, fantasy, adventure, folktales, and musicals.
- **Representative Titles:** *Twinderella* by Charlie Lovett introduces Bob, Cinderella's long lost brother, in a humorous send-up of the classic Cinderella story. *The Lady Pirates of Captain Bree* by Martin A. Follose (with music and lyrics by Bill Francoeur) is a zesty musical about female pirates.

Submissions and Payment

Guidelines available. Query. If accepted, submit play with synopsis and 9x12 SASE. Accepts photocopies, computer printouts, and simultaneous submissions if identified. SASE. Responds to queries in 1 month, to mss in 3 months. Publication in 3–6 months. Royalty.

Editor's Comments

We're on the lookout for new plays, specifically large cast comedies featuring many female roles. We prefer "ensemble" casts and plays must be family-friendly. Writers are encouraged to go to our website, where you can view the kind of plays we've previously published. You may query us with an idea, or email us at playwrights@pioneerdrama.com. All plays must be unpublished but we ask that you submit proof of production (programs or reviews) as a fundamental "field test" before we consider them.

Pipers' Ash Ltd.

Church Road, Christian Malford
Chippenham, Wiltshire SN15 4BW
United Kingdom

Manuscript Evaluation Desk

Publisher's Interests
General fiction and nonfiction for children ages four through eighteen can be found in the catalogue of this British publisher. Its list includes titles by new and established authors.
Website: www.supamasu.com

Freelance Potential
Published 12 titles in 2005: all were developed from unsolicited submissions and 1 was from a reprint/licensed property. Of the 12 titles, 7 were by unpublished writers and 9 were by authors who were new to the publishing house. Receives 1,500 queries yearly.

- **Fiction:** Publishes chapter books, 5–10 years; middle-grade books, 8–12 years; and young adult books, 12–18 years. Genres include contemporary and historical fiction, fairy tales, fantasy, folklore, mystery, and science fiction.
- **Nonfiction:** Publishes young adult books, 12–18 years. Topics include animals, crafts, hobbies, and history. Also publishes biographies.
- **Representative Titles:** *The Cockatoos of Kelly's Place* by Prue Mason (7+ years) is a series of bright, breezy stories of an Australian family farming in Kelly country. *Northern Lights* by Anne Colledge (8+ years) is a story of a young boy who is deaf, but still has big adventures along the rugged coastline of northeast England.

Submissions and Payment
Guidelines available. Short, 25-word query. Accepts email queries to pipersash@supamasu.com. Response time and publication period vary. Royalty, 10%.

Editor's Comments
We look for inspiring books that will introduce new worlds, warts and all, provide realistic stories to broaden a child's understanding, and offer science fiction that will give a glimpse of the far and not-so-far-off future.

Pitspopany Press

Suite 16D
40 East 78th Street
New York, NY 10021

Publisher

Publisher's Interests
Books for children ages three and up that explore the Jewish heritage appear in this publisher's catalogue. Among its offerings are books that teach about the Bible, the Holocaust, Israel, Jewish holidays, and Jewish values.
Website: www.pitspopany.com

Freelance Potential
Published 20 titles (10 juvenile) in 2005. Receives 30 unsolicited mss yearly.

- **Fiction:** Publishes toddler books and early picture books, 0–4 years; easy-to-read books, 4–7 years; story picture books, 4–10 years; chapter books, 5–10 years; middle-grade books, 8–12 years; and young adult books, 12–18 years. Genres include historical, multicultural, religious, and science fiction; mystery; adventure; and humor.
- **Nonfiction:** Publishes easy-to-read books, 4–7 years; story picture books, 4–10 years; chapter books, 5–10 years; middle-grade books, 8–12 years; and young adult books, 12–18 years. Topics include multicultural and ethnic issues, religion, fitness, sports, and history.
- **Representative Titles:** *God's World* by Sylvia Rouss is a story that shows what young children can do to fight pollution. *And Then There Were Dinosaurs* by Sari Steinberg (3–6 years) is based on a Jewish legend that says six worlds were created before our world—and the sixth was the dinosaur world.

Submissions and Payment
Catalogue and guidelines available at website. Send complete ms. Accepts photocopies and email submissions to pitspop@netvision.net.il. SASE. Responds in 3 months. Publication in 4–6 months. Royalty; advance.

Editor's Comments
We accept very few unsolicited manuscripts. Previously published authors stand a better chance of acceptance, however.

The Place in the Woods

3900 Glenwood Avenue
Golden Valley, MN 55422-5302

Editor & Publisher: Roger Hammer

Publisher's Interests

The books from A Place in the Woods spotlight diversity.
People of all cultures are portrayed in their titles, and
persons with disabilities play prominent roles as well. Its
editorial emphasis is on uplifting stories of triumph over
adversity; many of the titles on its juvenile list are adventure
stories about children learning and sharing together.

Freelance Potential

Published 4 titles in 2005: all were developed from unsolicited submissions. Of the 4 titles, 1 was by an unpublished
writer and 3 were by authors who were new to the publishing house. Receives 300–500 queries.

- **Fiction:** Published 2 story picture books, 4–10 years; and
  2 middle-grade books, 8–12 years. Genres include inspirational and multicultural fiction, humor, mystery, suspense,
  folktales, and fairy tales.
- **Nonfiction:** Publishes middle-grade books, 8–12 years. Topics
  include history and multicultural and ethnic issues. Also publishes biographies and books about special education.
- **Representative Titles:** *African America: Heralding a Heritage*
  looks at 20 contributions to medicine, engineering, science,
  business, and other fields made by African Americans. *Hispanic
  America* features new perspectives on the roles people of Hispanic heritage have played in American history.

Submissions and Payment

Guidelines available. Query. Accepts computer printouts. No
simultaneous submissions. SASE. Responds in 1–4 weeks.
Publication in 18 months. Royalty; Flat fee.

Editor's Comments

We look for stories that spotlight contributions made by
minorities, particularly those submitted by authors who are
members of minority communities.

Platypus Media

627 A Street NE
Washington, DC 20002

Editor: Dia L. Michels

Publisher's Interests
Families, teachers, and parenting professionals read the creative books produced by this small press publisher. Its catalogue includes children's books and nonfiction focusing on family closeness and child development, science related material, birth, and lactation.
Website: www.platypusmedia.com

Freelance Potential
Published 5 titles (3 juvenile) in 2005: 1 was developed from an unsolicited submission. Of the 5 titles, 3 were by unpublished writers and 1 was by an author who was new to the publishing house. Receives 240 queries.

- **Nonfiction:** Published 2 middle-grade books, 8–12 years. Topics include animals, health, fitness, mathematics, multicultural issues, nature, the environment, science and technology, and social concerns.
- **Representative Titles:** *Look What I See! Where Can I Be? At the Synagogue* by Dia L. Michels (0–7 years) introduces children to the richness of Jewish celebrations. *I Was Born To Be a Sister* by Akaela S. Michels-Gualtieri (3–5 years) explains how for an older sibling, having a new baby at home can be a fun, frustrating, and rewarding experience.

Submissions and Payment
Catalogue available. Query. Accepts photocopies and simultaneous submissions if identified. SASE. Response time varies. Publication in 9–12 months. Royalty. Flat fee.

Editor's Comments
This year we are looking for upper elementary science topics. We look for books that parents love, children enjoy, teachers appreciate, and parenting professionals value in their work. We do not publish fiction, poetry, or plays. Please note that we are a small press with a small staff and publish very few new authors so make sure you send your very best.

Players Press

P.O. Box 1132
Studio City, CA 91614

Editor: David Cole

Publisher's Interests
Books for aspiring actors of all ages are featured in the catalogue of Players Press. In addition to full-length dramas and
musicals, it publishes titles on acting techniques, directing,
drama education, and theater history.

Freelance Potential
Published 122 titles (72 juvenile) in 2005: 9 were developed
from unsolicited submissions and 2 were reprint/licensed
properties. Of the 122 titles, 10 were by unpublished writers
and 19 were by authors who were new to the publishing
house. Receives 1,000–1,500 queries yearly.

- **Fiction:** Published 40 middle-grade plays, 8–12 years; and 20
  young adult plays, 12–18 years. Genres include musicals,
  drama, and humor.
- **Nonfiction:** Published 8 middle-grade books, 8–12 years; and
  4 young adult books, 12–18 years. Topics include audition
  techniques, stage management, mime, makeup, clowning, acting methods, and costume design. Also publishes education
  titles for drama teachers.
- **Representative Titles:** *A Frog King's Daughter Is Nothing to
  Sneeze At* by Cheryl Thurston is a musical fairy tale about a
  prince with terrible allergies. *The Magic Swap Shop* by Fay
  Welch is a suspense-comedy about a good witch who runs a
  magic shop and the evil witch who plagues her.

Submissions and Payment
Guidelines available. Query with résumé, outline, synopsis,
production flyer, program, tape of music for musicals, and
reviews if available. Accepts photocopies. SASE. Responds
in 3–6 weeks. Publication in 3–24 months. Royalty, 10%;
advance.

Editor's Comments
Plays will be considered for publication only if they have had
at least one professional or two amateur productions.

Playwrights Canada Press

Suite 230
215 Spadina Avenue
Toronto, Ontario M5T 2C7
Canada

Editorial Coordinator: Betony Main

Publisher's Interests

Playwrights Canada Press is the largest publisher of Canadian drama. Its titles include drama collections as well as new plays that have been professionally produced and written by Canadian citizens. Its Theatre for Young Audiences list features titles for students in kindergarten through high school.
Website: www.playwrightscanada.com

Freelance Potential

Published 25 titles (2 juvenile) in 2005: 1 was developed from an unsolicited submission. Receives 10–15 queries each year.

- **Fiction:** Publishes plays for elementary, middle-grade, middle school, and high school students. Also publishes resources for teachers of drama.
- **Representative Titles:** *Danny, King of the Basement* by David S. Craig (grades 7–10) is a drama that tackles the issues of child poverty and homelessness. *Two for the Show: Scenes for Young Actors* by Brian Kennedy, ed. (grades 7–10) takes first-time actors from simple scenes and roles to those that are more complex using characters and situations young people can relate to.

Submissions and Payment

Canadian authors only. Guidelines available. Query with synopsis. Accepts computer printouts and simultaneous submissions if identified. SASE. Responds in 6–12 months. Publication in 5 months. Royalty.

Editor's Comments

Our editorial committee reviews submissions from Canadian citizens or landed immigrants only. A play submitted for publication must include proof that it has had at least one professional production within the past ten years. Cast and crew lists must be enclosed. Theatrical arts material from teachers who feel others may benefit from their experience is welcome.

Pleasant Company Publications

8400 Fairway Place
Middletown, WI 53562

Submissions Editor

Publisher's Interests
Fiction and nonfiction for middle-grade readers can be found in the catalogue of this publisher. In addition to its popular American Girl dolls and books, it also produces activity books, contemporary fiction, and other titles that explore pre-teen issues.
Website: www.americangirl.com

Freelance Potential
Published 40 titles in 2005: 2 were developed from unsolicited submissions.

- **Fiction:** Publishes middle-grade novels, 10+ years. Genres include mystery; and contemporary and historical fiction.
- **Nonfiction:** Publishes middle-grade books, 8–12 years. Features advice books, activity books, and interactive CD-ROMS.
- **Representative Titles:** *Angelina, Star of the Show* by Katherine Holabird follows Angelina and her grandmother on a boat trip to a dance festival where Angelina runs into some costume trouble after disobeying her grandmother. *Lindy's Happy Ending* by Valerie Tripp tells of a young girl who forgets to put the lid back on a box of ducklings, and lets trouble loose in her classroom.

Submissions and Payment
Guidelines available. Prefers query with first chapter for fiction. Accepts complete ms. Accepts photocopies and simultaneous submissions if identified. SASE. Responds in 3–4 months. Publication period and payment policy vary.

Editor's Comments
We are seeking advice books for pre-teens that address social issues, as well as submissions of contemporary fiction. Make sure your writing style is geared towards our audience of middle-grade readers. Please note that we are not accepting submissions for our American Girl Collection.

Plexus Publishing, Inc.

143 Old Marlton Pike
Medford, NJ 08055

Publisher: John B. Bryans

Publisher's Interests
This regional publisher focuses on the history, culture, and natural history of southern New Jersey. Although its titles are written for adults, they are usually suitable for young adults and middle-grade readers.
Website: www.plexuspublishing.com

Freelance Potential
Published 5 titles in 2005: 3 were developed from unsolicited submissions. Of the 5 titles, 1 was by an unpublished writer and 3 were by authors who were new to the publishing house. Receives 144 queries yearly.

- **Fiction:** Publishes historical and regional fiction for young adults and adults.
- **Nonfiction:** Publishes history and reference titles for young adults and adults. Topics include regional history, nature, hiking, flora and fauna, and natural history.
- **Representative Titles:** *Patriots, Pirates, and Pineys: Sixty Who Shaped New Jersey* by Robert A. Peterson (13+ years) is a collection of biographies about New Jersey men and women who helped make America what it is today. *Whitman's Tomb: Stories from the Pines* by Robert Bateman (13+ years) is a book of short stories of the mysteries of New Jersey's Pine Barrens.

Submissions and Payment
Guidelines available. Catalogue available with 9x12 SASE ($.67 postage). Query with synopsis, table of contents, and biography. Accepts photocopies and computer printouts. SASE. Responds in 60 days. Publication in 10 months. Royalty, 12%.

Editor's Comments
We are interested in proposals for material with a regional emphasis on southern New Jersey, especially the Pine Barrens. We like to see titles about tourist and vacation spots, such as Atlantic City, Cape May, and Long Beach Island.

Polychrome Publishing Corporation

4509 North Francisco Avenue
Chicago, IL 60625-3808

Editorial Department

Publisher's Interests

An independent press founded in 1990, Polychrome produces children's books for a multicultural market. Children of all ages and colors can identify with the characters and themes they seek to portray.
Website: www.polychromebooks.com

Freelance Potential

Published 3 titles in 2005: all were developed from unsolicited submissions. Of the 3 titles, all were by unpublished writers. Receives 1,000 unsolicited mss yearly.

- **Fiction:** Publishes toddler books, 0–4 years; early picture books, 0–4 years; story picture books, 4–10 years; chapter books, 5–10 years; middle-grade books, 8–12 years; and young adult books, 12–18 years. Genres include adventure, contemporary, and historical fiction.
- **Nonfiction:** Publishes books about Asian American culture for families and educators.
- **Representative Titles:** *The Lobster and the Sea* by Esther Chiu (7–11 years) is the reassuring tale of a child faced with the departure of a loved one who discovers that separation will not undermine the infinite nature of love. *Stella: On the Edge of Popularity* by Lauren Lee (9–13 years) describes a Korean American preteen caught between two cultures.

Submissions and Payment

Guidelines available at website. Send complete ms with résumé. Accepts photocopies, computer printouts, and simultaneous submissions if identified. SASE. Responds in 3–6 months. Publication in 1–2 years. Royalty; advance.

Editor's Comments

In keeping with our policy on diversity and multiculturalism, we are seeking children's books dealing with biracial adoption and stories that promote tolerance. We are not interested in fables, folktales, fairy tales or animal stories.

Portage & Main Press

100-318 McDermont Avenue
Winnipeg, Manitoba R3A 0A2
Canada

Submissions Editor: Jill Condra

Publisher's Interests

Offering up-to-date resources and new ideas for educators, this Canadian publisher's catalogue includes materials for teaching science, math, language arts, social studies, and English-as-a-Second-Language to students of all ages. It also includes assessment tools.

Website: www.portageandmainpress.com

Freelance Potential

Published 18 titles in 2005: 1 was developed from an unsolicited submission. Of the 18 titles, 2 were by unpublished writers. Receives 20 queries, 10 unsolicited mss yearly.

- **Nonfiction:** Publishes curriculum-based education books for teachers, grades K–8. Topics include reading, spelling, math, assessment, literacy, ESL, school safety, social studies, peer mediation, and theater.
- **Representative Titles:** *For the Love of Language* by Nancy Lee Cecil (grades K–6) provides activities that explore poetry including haiku, free verse, nonsense, shape poems, and many more. *Thinking Strategies* by Celia Baron (grades 1–6) provides easy-to-follow, comprehensive strategies for teaching basic mathematics.

Submissions and Payment

Guidelines available with SAE/IRC ($.50 postage). Query with table of contents and 1 sample chapter; or send complete ms. Accepts photocopies and IBM disk submissions. SAE/IRC. Responds in 1–2 months. Publication in 6 months. Royalty, 8–12%.

Editor's Comments

We seek high-quality educational materials that are new and motivating including hands-on, easy-to-read resources that contain engaging lessons. Also, we would like to see more English-as-a-Second-Language programs, and materials that will encourage and assess the learning process.

PowerKids Press

29 East 21st Street
New York, NY 10010

Editorial Director: Joanne Randolph

Publisher's Interests

PowerKids Press publishes juvenile nonfiction titles in six-book series for sale to school and public libraries. Its titles cover a range of educational topics that supplement the curriculum of students in kindergarten through grade four.
Website: www.powerkidspress.com

Freelance Potential

Published 130 titles in 2005. Of the 130 titles, 15 were by unpublished writers and 15 were by authors who were new to the publishing house. Receives 800 queries yearly.

- **Nonfiction:** Publishes educational materials, pre-K–grade 8. Topics include art, social studies, science, geography, health, fitness, sports, math, social issues, Native Americans, ancient history, natural history, politics and government, special education, and multicultural and ethnic subjects. Also publishes biographies and bilingual titles.
- **Representative Titles:** *Community Needs* by Angela Catalano (grades K–5) explains the difference between needs and wants, and shows how both can be met. *Thomas Becket: English Saint and Martyr* by David Hilliam (grades 5–8) discusses the struggle for power between church and state in twelfth-century England.

Submissions and Payment

Guidelines available. Query with outline and sample chapter. Accepts photocopies, computer printouts, and simultaneous submissions if identified. SASE. Responds in 3 months. Publication in 9–18 months. Flat fee.

Editor's Comments

All of our titles are written at the third-grade reading level, and cover high-interest, extracurricular, age-appropriate topics. We are currently seeking material that deals with history, the community, science, animals, and how to cope with various social, personal, and health problems.

Prometheus Books

59 John Glenn Drive
Amherst, NY 14228-2197

Editor-in-Chief: Steven L. Mitchell

Publisher's Interests
This leading publisher in philosophy, popular science, and critical thinking offers books, journals, and audio tapes. Targeting educational, scientific, library, professional, and popular markets, its catalogue includes fiction, nonfiction, social science and religious studies, as well as children's books on contemporary issues.
Website: www.prometheusbooks.com

Freelance Potential
Published 90–105 titles in 2005: 15–20 were developed from unsolicited submissions. Receives 300 queries, 400 unsolicited mss yearly.

- **Nonfiction:** Publishes easy-to-read books, 4–7 years and middle-grade books, 8–12 years. Topics include social issues, health, sexuality, religion, critical thinking, and decision making.
- **Representative Titles:** *The Tree of Life* by Ellen Jackson (4–9 years) captures the excitement and sweep of Darwin's famous theory in an easy-to-read, fun manner. *Humanism, What's That?* by Helen Bennett (10+ years) offers an innovative approach to presenting humanism to young adults. It includes suggestions for activities and a bibliography.

Submissions and Payment
Guidelines available. Query or send complete ms with résumé and bibliography. Accepts photocopies, computer printouts, and simultaneous submissions if identified. SASE. Responds in 2–3 months. Publication in 12–18 months. Payment policy varies.

Editor's Comments
We look for thoughtful and authoritative works on topics such as science and evolution. Send us something fresh and thought-provoking that will encourage children to use their minds and explore issues and the world around them.

Puffin Books

Penguin Putnam Books for Young Readers
345 Hudson Street
New York, NY 10014

Manuscript Submissions

Publisher's Interests

This division of the well-known Penguin Putnam Books publishes reprint paperback editions of popular hardcover books. Its list includes a few original fiction and nonfiction titles.
Website: www.penguinputnam.com

Freelance Potential

Published 217 titles in 2005: 195 were reprint/licensed properties. Receives 100+ queries yearly.

- **Fiction:** Publishes early picture books, 0–4 years; easy-to-read books, 4–7 years; story picture books, 4–10 years; chapter books, 5–10 years; middle-grade titles, 8–12 years; and young adult books, 12–18 years. Genres include historical fiction, science fiction, mystery, adventure, and romance.
- **Nonfiction:** Publishes story picture books, 4–10 years; and middle-grade titles, 8–12 years. Topics include social issues and science.
- **Representative Titles:** *An Ellis Island Christmas* by Maxinne Rhea Leighton (5+ years) is a richly illustrated story about a young girl who undergoes the long ocean voyage to America, arriving at the Statue of Liberty on Christmas Eve. *So You Want To Be an Inventor?* by Judith St. George (all ages) is an introduction to some of the world's best-known inventors, as well as some of the lesser-known geniuses.

Submissions and Payment

Guidelines available. Query with outline/synopsis. Accepts computer printouts. SASE. Responds in 4–5 months. Publication in 12–18 months. Royalty, 2–6%.

Editor's Comments

Our list ranges from picture books to high school level titles, in both fiction and nonfiction. Most titles are paperback reprints. We do publish several paperback originals, such as young chapter books and easy to read titles, and lift-the-flap books. We are always interested in the work of new writers.

G. P. Putnam's Sons

345 Hudson Street
New York, NY 10014

Manuscript Editor

Publisher's Interests

From bedtime stories to daring adventures and mysteries, this publisher's catalogue includes fiction and nonfiction for children of all ages. It is an imprint of Penguin Group, USA. **Website:** www.penguin.com

Freelance Potential

Published 45 titles in 2005: 2 were developed from unsolicited submissions. Of the 45 titles, 2 were by unpublished writers and 18 were by authors who were new to the publishing house. Receives 1,500 queries, 8,000 unsolicited mss yearly.

- **Fiction:** Publishes toddler books and early picture books, 0–4 years; story picture books, 4–10 years; chapter books, 5–10 years; middle-grade books, 8–12 years and young adult books, 12–18 years. Also publishes novelty books. Genres include contemporary and multicultural fiction.
- **Nonfiction:** Publishes early picture books, 0–4 years; story picture books, 4–10 years; chapter books, 5–10 years; and middle-grade books, 8–12 books.
- **Representative Titles:** *Show Way* by Jacqueline Woodson (5+ years) is an intergenerational story about the quilts that showed slaves the way to freedom. *The Liberation of Gabriel King* by K. L. Going (8+ years) is a story about the summer Gabriel's best friend helped him overcome his fears.

Submissions and Payment

Guidelines available. Send complete ms for picture books. Query with outline/synopsis and 3 sample chapters for chapter books. Accepts photocopies, computer printouts, and simultaneous submissions if identified. SASE. Responds in 2 months. Publication in 18–36 months. Royalty; advance.

Editor's Comments

We're looking for young adult fiction with unusual plotlines that will excite readers and keep them turning the pages.

Quest Books

P.O. Box 270
Wheaton, IL 60189

Assistant Editor: Nancy Grace

Publisher's Interests
An affiliate of the Theosophical Society in America, this publisher of nonfiction targets adults and young adults. Its catalogue includes books that cover topics related to spirituality, religion, women's studies, social issues, self-help, and animals. It strives to present material that allows readers to better understand themselves and their place in the universe.
Website: www.questbooks.net

Freelance Potential
Published 5 titles in 2005. Of the 5 titles, 1 was by an unpublished writer and 2 were by authors who were new to the publishing house. Receives 5,000 queries yearly.

- **Nonfiction:** Publishes young adult books, 12–18 years. Topics include alternative healing, development of creativity, transpersonal psychology, deep ecology, mythology, comparative religion, consciousness, spiritual evolution, ancient wisdom, mysticism, esoteric studies, and perennial philosophy.
- **Representative Titles:** *The Boundless Circle* by Michael W. Fox examines religion's attitude, especially Christianity, toward the treatment of animals and nature. *Beyond Religion* by David Elkins tells how authentic, soul-nurturing spirituality can be found in unlikely places, and explores how to be spiritual without being religious.

Submissions and Payment
Guidelines available at website. Query with author biography, table of contents, introduction, and sample chapter. Prefers email submissions (no attachments) to olcott@ theosmail.net. No unsolicited mss. SASE. Responds in 4–6 weeks. Publication period varies. Royalty; advance.

Editor's Comments
We demand high standards of writing quality. Currently, we would like to see queries for nonfiction books for young adults on astrology and theosophy.

Quixote Press

1854 345th Avenue
Wever, IA 52658

President: Bruce Carlson

Publisher's Interests

Children's books are among the titles published each year by Quixote Press. Cookbooks for adult readers and books about the Midwestern region of the U.S., especially regional folklore, are major components of its list. 20% self-, subsidy-, co-venture, or co-op published material.

Freelance Potential

Published 40 titles in 2005: 20 were developed from unsolicited submissions and 8–10 were by agented authors. Of the 40 titles, 12 were by unpublished writers and 15 were by authors who were new to the publishing house. Receives 200 queries, 250 unsolicited mss yearly.

- **Fiction:** Published 12 chapter books, 5–10 years; and 14 young adult books, 12–18 years. Genres include regional folklore and humor. Also publishes activity books, educational and how-to books, and informational titles.
- **Nonfiction:** Publishes cookbooks, craft and hobby books, and books on regional subjects for adults.
- **Representative Titles:** *Keepers of the River* by Keith Schulz is a tale of terror, mystery, and intrigue set on the Mississippi River. *My Very First . . .* is a collection of stories written by children who describe "firsts" in their lives, such as their first sleigh ride, first fight, and first day of kindergarten.

Submissions and Payment

Query or send complete ms. Accepts photocopies, computer printouts, and simultaneous submissions if identified. SASE. Responds in 1 week. Publication in 2–24 months. Royalty.

Editor's Comments

Regional topics are of particular interest to us, including historical fiction set in the Midwest. We're also interested in submissions of regional folklore, ghost stories, and cookbooks. Most of our titles target a general audience, but children's books are welcome.

Rainbow Publishers

P.O. Box 261129
San Diego, CA 92196

Editorial Director: Christy Scannell

Publisher's Interests
Reproducible classroom resource books using crafts, puzzles, and games to teach the Bible can be found in this publisher's catalogue. It offers creative, hands-on learning tools for Christian educators to use with children of all ages.
Website: www.rainbowpublishers.com

Freelance Potential
Published 16 titles in 2005. Receives 100 queries, 500 unsolicited mss yearly.

- **Fiction:** Publishes middle-grade books, 8–12 years. Genres include inspirational and religious fiction.
- **Nonfiction:** Publishes Christian education resource materials, pre-K–grade 6. Topics include the Bible, religion, crafts, and hobbies. Also offers titles in series, 8+ years; and activity books, 2–12 years.
- **Representative Titles:** *Walking with Jesus* (5–10 years), part of the Instant Bible Lessons series, provides teachers with interactive, flexible lessons to teach biblical messages. *Bible Outreach Activities* (pre-K–grade 4) helps kids share the good news of the Gospel through crafts and cards.

Submissions and Payment
Guidelines and catalogue available with 9x12 SASE (2 first-class stamps). Query with résumé, table of contents, first 3 chapters, and a market analysis. Accepts photocopies. SASE. Responds in 3 months. Publication in 1–3 years. Flat fee.

Editor's Comments
We are especially seeking reproducible classroom resource books that include games for ages two through twelve. We only publish teacher-friendly books that utilize crafts, games, puzzles and other activities to creatively teach the Bible. We don't accept children's picture books, fiction, poetry; nor do we publish academic books. Since we are a niche market, it is best to study our titles for a better understanding.

Raven Tree Press, LLC

Suite 306
200 South Washington Street
Green Bay, WI 54301

Publisher: Dawn Jeffers

Publisher's Interests

Established in 2001, this publisher offers universally appealing dual-language picture books. Its list also includes innovative story books and chapter books that enhance reading enjoyment for bilingual families. 10% self-published.
Website: www.raventreepress.com

Freelance Potential

Published 10 titles in 2005: 9 were developed from unsolicited submissions. Of the 10 titles, 2 were by unpublished writers. Receives 1,200 unsolicited mss yearly.

- **Fiction:** Publishes early picture books, 0–4 years; easy-to-read books, 4–7 years; and story picture books, 4–10 years. Genres include contemporary and multicultural fiction, drama, fairy tales, fantasy, folklore and folktales, humor, nature, and the environment.
- **Representative Titles:** *Polar Slumber* by Dennis Rockhill (grades 2 and up) is a bilingual tale about the surprising power of a young girl's imagination. *Counting Coconuts* by Wendi Silvano (grades 3 and up) engages a silly monkey and a variety of rainforest creatures to teach readers to count in both English and Spanish.

Submissions and Payment

Guidelines and catalogue available at website. Send complete ms. Accepts photocopies and simultaneous submissions if identified. SASE. Responds in 2–4 months. Publication in 18–24 months. Royalty; advance.

Editor's Comments

Bilingual English and Spanish picture books of 500 to 700 words are needed. We like to see entertaining, insightful stories brought to life for readers learning a new language or for bilingual families sharing the reading experience together. Check our website before you send material; submissions are periodically closed.

Rayve Productions Inc.

P.O. Box 726
Windsor, CA 95492

Editor: Barbara Ray

Publisher's Interests

This publisher offers a range of books, from illustrated children's titles that encourage young readers to step-by-step guides for adults that enrich body and soul.
Website: www.rayveproductions.com

Freelance Potential

Published 4 titles (1 juvenile) in 2005: 1 was developed from an unsolicited submission. Of the 4 titles, 1 was by an author who was new to the publishing house. Receives 100+ queries, 75 unsolicited mss yearly.

- **Fiction:** Publishes easy-to-read books, 4–7 years; story picture books, 4–10 years; and chapter books, 5–10 years. Genres include historical, multicultural, and ethnic fiction; folktales; and adventure stories.
- **Nonfiction:** Publishes history books and biographies, 5 years–adult. Also publishes educational and multicultural titles for teachers, children's counselors, and parents; cookbooks; and how-to books.
- **Representative Titles:** *Buffalo Jones: The Man Who Saved America's Bison* by Carol A. Winn (10–14 years) tells the true story of Charles Jesse Jones, who risked his life to save America's bison from extinction. *Link Across America* by Mary Elizabeth Anderson (7–13 years) highlights the historic Lincoln Highway, which runs from New York to San Francisco.

Submissions and Payment

Guidelines available. Query with résumé for adult books. Send complete ms for children's books. Accepts photocopies and computer printouts. SASE. Responds in 6 weeks. Publication in 1 year. Royalty, 10%; advance, varies.

Editor's Comments

We are looking for new and established writers to give us ideas for award-winning titles. We believe that every project is a team effort.

Razorbill

Penguin Young Readers Group
15th Floor
345 Hudson Street
New York, NY 10014

Editorial Assistant: Margaret Wright

Publisher's Interests
This imprint of the Penguin Young Readers Group is devoted to publishing contemporary fiction and nonfiction titles for tween and teen readers.
Website: www.penguinputnam.com

Freelance Potential
Published 30 titles (27 juvenile) in 2005: 2 were developed from unsolicited submissions; 10 were by agented authors, and 3 were reprint/licensed properties. Of the 30 titles, 6 were by unpublished writers and 11 were by authors who were new to the publishing house. Receives 200 queries, 100 unsolicited mss yearly.

- **Fiction:** Published 5 middle-grade books, 8–12 years; and 20 young adult books, 12–18 years. Genres include contemporary fiction, suspense, and science fiction.
- **Nonfiction:** Published 1 middle-grade book, 8–12 years; and 1 young adult book, 12–18 years. Topics include popular culture, media trends, and film and television.
- **Representative Titles:** *Watching Alice* by Daniel Parker (12+ years) is the story about Tom, a teenager who's in love with Alice. When Alice disappears, Tom follows the clues. *The Bermudez Triangle* by Maureen Johnson (14+ years) is a novel about a love and friendship triangle.

Submissions and Payment
Query. SASE. Response time and publication period vary. Advance. Flat fee.

Editor's Comments
We're interested in contemporary material that is of interest to middle-grade and young adult readers. We are seeking stand-alone titles and series, especially about movie and television series, as well as coming-of-age, mysteries, and science fiction.

Red Deer Press

MacKimmie Library Tower, Room 813
2500 University Drive NW
Calgary, Alberta T2N 1N4
Canada

Children's Editor: Peter Carver

Publisher's Interests

Canadian authors and illustrators create the books published by Red Deer Press. Some juvenile literature appears on its list. All of its titles are about Canadians or deal with topics of special interest to Canadians.
Website: www.reddeerpress.com

Freelance Potential

Published 18 titles (7–8 juvenile) in 2005: 1 was developed from an unsolicited submission and 3 were by agented authors. Of the 18 titles, 1–3 were by authors who were new to the publishing house.

- **Fiction:** Publishes story picture books, 4–10 years; middle-grade books, 8–12 years; and young adult books, 12–18 years. Genres include regional and contemporary fiction, adventure, fantasy, mystery, suspense, drama, and multicultural and ethnic fiction.
- **Nonfiction:** Publishes family activity books, 4+ years. Features nature series, field guides, biographies, and anthologies for adults.
- **Representative Titles:** *When Night Eats the Moon* by Joanne Findon (9–14 years) follows a young girl as she steps back and forth in time. *The Leftover Kid* by Joanne Stanbridge (8–14 years) is a novel about a young girl who becomes world famous when her mother marries the Prime Minister.

Submissions and Payment

Canadian authors only. Guidelines and catalogue available with 9x12 SASE. Query with outline and 2 sample chapters. Accepts photocopies. SASE. Responds in 4–6 months. Publication in 2–3 years. Royalty.

Editor's Comments

Our program is full for the next three years in the picture book, juvenile fiction, and teen fiction categories. We will only review children's submissions that show exceptional potential.

Redleaf Press

10 Yorkton Court
St. Paul, MN 55117

Acquisitions Department

Publisher's Interests
A division of Resources for Child Caring, Redleaf Press provides early childhood educational resources for professionals who work with young children. Its catalogue includes titles on early literacy and math, anti-bias education, and bilingual programs and curricula for children from birth to eight years.
Website: www.redleafpress.org

Freelance Potential
Published 18 titles in 2005: 6 were developed from unsolicited submissions and 1 was by an agented author. Of the 18 titles, 1 was by an author who was new to the publishing house. Receives 24 queries yearly.

- **Nonfiction:** Publishes curriculum, management, and business resources for early childhood professionals. Topics include math, science, language and literacy, cultural diversity, music and movement, health, safety, nutrition, child development, special needs children, and teacher training and assessment.
- **Representative Titles:** *Creative Resources for the Anti-Bias Classroom* by Nadia Saderman Hall (teachers) offers activities designed to integrate the anti-bias approach into all curriculum areas. *The Power of Relaxation* by Patrice Thomas (teachers) explains how to teach children stress management techniques such as tai chi, yoga, and visualization.

Submissions and Payment
Guidelines available. Query with résumé, outline, table of contents, and sample chapters. SASE. Responds in 3 months. Publication in 18–24 months. Payment policy varies.

Editor's Comments
In addition to submissions on early literacy and math, anti-bias education, and bilingual curricula, we're also interested in material that discusses how to meet early childhood educational standards. Manuscripts that focus on development of program policies and procedures are also welcome.

Renaissance House

9400 Lloydcrest Drive
Beverly Hills, CA 90210

Editor: Raquel Benatar

Publisher's Interests

Renaissance House is a packager representing authors and illustrators dedicated to creating educational books and multicultural materials that captivate young audiences.
Website: www.renaissancehouse.net

Freelance Potential

Published 12 titles in 2005: 1 was developed from an unsolicited submission. Of the 12 titles, 2 were by unpublished writers and 2 were by authors who were new to the publishing house. Receives 200 queries, 150 unsolicited mss yearly.

- **Fiction:** Publishes story picture books, 4–10 years; and middle-grade titles, 8–12 years. Genres include folklore, folktales, and stories with multicultural and ethnic themes.
- **Nonfiction:** Publishes middle-grade titles, 8–12 years. Topics include animals, pets, and multicultural themes. Also publishes biographies.
- **Representative Titles:** *Gray Feather and the Big Dog* by Cesar Vidal is a captivating Native American legend about the Great Spirit who comes to the aid of his people. *Gigi and the Birthday Ring* by Giselle Fernandez is a hip story about a girl empowered by her grandmother's magical ring.

Submissions and Payment

Guidelines and catalogue available at website. Query or send complete ms. Accepts email submissions to info@renaissancehouse.net (include synopsis in body of text or make a link to your site). Response time and publication period vary. Royalty.

Editor's Comments

As last year, we continue to need multicultural titles aimed at a Spanish readers. If we are interested in marketing your manuscript around to the publishers we work with, or in representing you, we will go over the details of getting your work published.

Resource Publications, Inc.

Suite 290
160 East Virginia Street
San Jose, CA 95112

Publisher: William Burns

Publisher's Interests

Resource materials for ministry, worship, and education are offered by this Christian publisher. Its books, workbooks, and activity books are designed to help readers achieve their full spiritual potential.
Website: www.resourcepublications.com

Freelance Potential

Published 5 titles in 2005: 1 was developed from an unsolicited submission. Of the 5 titles, 2 were by unpublished writers and 2 were by authors who were new to the publishing house. Receives 100+ queries yearly.

- **Fiction:** Publishes young adult books, 12–18 years. Genres include religious and spiritual fiction.
- **Nonfiction:** Published 2–5 young adult books, 12–18 years. Publishes middle-grade books, 8–12 years. Topics include religion, prayer, faith, catechism, meditations, the sacraments, and spirituality. Also publishes books on prayer, pastoral ministry, liturgy, and personal growth.
- **Representative Titles:** *Heroes, Rebels, and Survivors* by Larry Castagnola compiles 21 stories that highlight the bravery and enthusiasm of young people. *Your Will Be Done on Earth* by Christie L. Jenkins (12–18 years) is an activity book that integrates theology and science.

Submissions and Payment

Guidelines and catalogue available with 9x12 SASE ($1.03 postage). Query with clips. SASE. Responds in 6–8 weeks. Publication in 9–18 months. Royalty, 8% of net.

Editor's Comments

We want to lead, rather than follow, and pursue solutions to core issues in the church, in schools, in our society, and in the world at large. Following the golden rule and other principles from our Judeo-Christian heritage, universal values such as truth, justice, charity, and growth are important.

Rising Moon

P.O. Box 1389
2900 N. Fort Valley Road
Flagstaff, AZ 86001

Children's Editor: Theresa Howell

Publisher's Interests
The goal of Rising Moon is to provide children with entertaining and informative books that follow the heart and tickle the funny bone.
Website: www.risingmoonbooks.com

Freelance Potential
Published 6 titles in 2005: 3 were developed from unsolicited submissions and 3 were by agented authors. Of the 6 titles, 1 was by an unpublished writer and 2 were by authors who were new to the publishing house. Receives 100 queries, 1,800 unsolicited mss yearly.

- **Fiction:** Publishes concept books, 0–4 years; and easy-to-read books, 4–8. Genres include fairy tales, folklore, humor, and inspirational and multicultural fiction about the American Southwest. Also publishes activity books, novelty and board books, and bilingual Spanish/English books, 4–8 years.
- **Representative Titles:** *Phoebe and Chub* by Matthew Henry Hall (4–8 years) is the story of a tree frog who learns that dreams can come true. *Kissing Coyotes* by Marcia Vaughan (5–8 years) captures the true spirit of adventure as the conniving Jack Rabbit makes good on a dare.

Submissions and Payment
Guidelines available. Accepts picture book submissions from agented and previously published authors only. Accepts queries and unsolicited mss for books with Southwestern themes. SASE. Responds in 3 months. Publication in 1–2 years. Royalty, varies; advance, varies.

Editor's Comments
We are returning to our roots by considering manuscripts that relate to the Western and Southwestern United States. We are looking for exceptional bilingual stories, original stories with Southwest flavor, and traditional fairy tales with a Southwestern twist.

River City Publishing

1719 Mulberry Street
Montgomery, AL 36106

Assistant Editor: Gail Waller

Publisher's Interests

Fiction and narrative nonfiction that focus on the American South appear in the catalogue of River City Publishing. A publisher of adult titles, its list typically features one illustrated children's book each year. This title reflects some aspect of the South and is characterized by text and artwork that appeal to adults as well as to children.

Website: www.rivercitypublishing.com

Freelance Potential

Published 9 titles (1 juvenile) in 2005: 2 were developed from unsolicited submissions and 4 were by agented authors. Of the 9 titles, 2 were by unpublished writers and 3 were by authors who were new to the publishing house. Receives 1,000 unsolicited mss yearly.

- **Fiction:** Published 1 early picture book, 0–4 years. Genres include regional, historical, and multicultural fiction; humor; and adventure. Also publishes literary fiction for adults.
- **Nonfiction:** Publishes narrative nonfiction for adults. Topics include travel, history, and biography related to the South.
- **Representative Titles:** *Moon of the Wishing Night* by Gail Renfroe Lamar tells the story of a bored and lonely moon that slips away to have an adventure. *The Alphabet Parade* by Charles Cthinga is a colorful combination of animals and the letters of the alphabet.

Submissions and Payment

Guidelines available at website or with SASE. Send complete ms for children's books; include reproductions of illustrations. Accepts photocopies, computer printouts, and simultaneous submissions. SASE. Responds in 1–6 months. Publication in 1 year. Royalty; advance, $1,000–$5,000.

Editor's Comments

Text-only submissions of children's books are acceptable, but not encouraged. It's best to include copies of artwork.

Robins Lane Press

10726 Tucker Street
Beltsville, MD 20704

Acquisitions Editor

Publisher's Interests

A publisher of parenting titles, Robins Lane Press specializes in books that acknowledge that today's lifestyles have changed the way parents have traditionally raised their children. Its publications address questions contemporary parents ask and offer advice on how to deal with the unique situations they face.

Website: www.robinslane.com

Freelance Potential

Published 1 title in 2005. Receives 100+ queries, 40+ unsolicited mss yearly.

- **Nonfiction:** Publishes parenting titles that offer information and guidance for parents confronting complex issues of society, home, and self; easy, practical parenting ideas; and activities that engender curiosity and creative play in children.
- **Representative Titles:** *Snacktivities!* by MaryAnn F. Kohl & Jean Potter offers 50 easy activities for turning everyday food items into works of art such as dinosaur eggs, tomato towers, and alphabet sandwiches. *The Business Traveling Parent* by Dan Verdick contains over 100 tips, games, and ideas that business travelers can use to stay involved in their children's lives.

Submissions and Payment

Guidelines available. Query or send complete ms. SASE. Responds to queries in 4–6 weeks, to mss in 6–8 weeks. Publication in 9–12 months. Royalty; advance.

Editor's Comments

Before you submit your book, identify your market. Who are the people who will read your book? Is there a need for a book such as yours? Why? What, specifically, qualifies you to write this book? Include this information with your submission or query, along with the titles of similar books already on the bookstore shelves.

Rocky River Publishers

P.O. Box 1679
Shepherdstown, WV 25443

Acquisitions Editor

Publisher's Interests
This publisher produces high-quality books with creative approaches to help children deal with problems they face from infancy to adulthood. Its list includes both fiction and nonfiction titles.
Website: www.rockyriver.com

Freelance Potential
Published 10 titles in 2005. Receives 240 queries, 720 unsolicited mss yearly.

- **Fiction:** Publishes toddler books, 0–4 years; easy-to-read books, 4–7 years; story picture books, 4–10 years; and young adult books, 12–18 years. Genres include contemporary, inspirational, and educational fiction.
- **Nonfiction:** Publishes middle-grade books, 8–12 years; and young adult books, 12–18 years. Topics include drug education, self-esteem, stress avoidance, youth safety, abuse, health, disabilities, and addiction. Also offers parenting resources.
- **Representative Titles:** *Eglin Long-Horn of Nightshade County* by Debra Wert is about a grasshopper whose story helps people understand the short- and long-term consequences of using tobacco. *Henrietta* by Wayne Walker has a powerful message to teach children the importance of dealing with their fears rather than pretending that they don't exit.

Submissions and Payment
Guidelines available. Query or send complete ms. Accepts photocopies. Availability of artwork improves chance of acceptance. SASE. Response time and publication period vary. Royalty; advance. Flat fee.

Editor's Comments
We look for stories that provide important messages for children to help them deal with issues they may face in life. Material should be inspirational and age appropriate.

Ronsdale Press

3350 West 21st Avenue
Vancouver, British Columbia V6S 1G7
Canada

Submissions Editor: Veronica Hatch

Publisher's Interests
Each year, Ronsdale Press publishes a small number of
books for children between the ages of 8 and 15. A literary
publisher, its special focus is on historical novels for young
adults. Ronsdale Press welcomes submissions from Canadian
authors only.
Website: www.ronsdalepress.com

Freelance Potential
Published 10 titles (3 juvenile) in 2005: 3 were developed
from unsolicited submissions and 1 was by an agented
author. Of the 10 titles, 3 were by unpublished writers and
8 were by authors who were new to the publishing house.
Receives 500 queries, 2,000 unsolicited mss yearly.

- **Fiction:** Published 1 early picture book, 0–4 years; 1 middle-
  grade book, 8–12 years; and 1 young adult book, 12–18
  years. Genres include Canadian historical fiction.
- **Nonfiction:** Publishes adult titles. Topics include economics,
  politics, and language. Also publishes biographies.
- **Representative Titles:** *Ten Mondays for Lots of Boxes* by Sue
  Ann Alderson (3–8 years) is a story about moving to a new
  neighborhood and discovering that change is not always a bad
  thing. *Chaos in Halifax* by Cathy Beveridge (YA) is a novel that
  uses time travel as a device for exploring the 1917 Halifax
  Explosion.

Submissions and Payment
Canadian authors only. Guidelines available at website.
Query with sample chapter; or send complete ms. Accepts
photocopies and computer printouts. SASE. Responds in
1–2 months. Publication in 1 year. Royalty, 10%.

Editor's Comments
We are no longer publishing 32-page picture books, but
Canadian historical fiction for young adults continues to be
of particular interest to us.

The Rosen Publishing Group

29 East 21st Street
New York, NY 10010

Editorial Director, YA Division: Iris Rosoff

Publisher's Interests

Empowering nonfiction for teens on issues such as eating disorders, violence prevention, and divorce are produced by this publisher. Its list also includes books that supplement classroom learning on subjects such as science and history.
Website: www.rosenpublishing.com

Freelance Potential

Published 200 titles in 2005: 20 were by unpublished writers and 20 were by authors who were new to the publishing house. Receives 75 queries yearly.

- **Nonfiction:** Publishes middle-grade books, 8–12 years; and young adult books, 12–18 years. Topics include history, health, science, the arts, sports, safety, guidance, and careers.
- **Representative Titles:** *How Do We Know the Age of the Earth?* by Charles J. Caes (YA) offers a straightforward presentation that gives a good sense of the process and sequence of discovery of the origin and age of the earth. *Cool Careers Without College for Animal Lovers* by Chris Hayhurst offers information on careers that do not require years of advanced schooling, for people who love to work with animals including trainers, groomers, breeders, and veterinary assistants.

Submissions and Payment

Query with outline and sample chapter. Accepts photocopies, computer printouts, and simultaneous submissions if identified. SASE. Responds in 3 months. Publication in 9 months. Royalty. Flat fee.

Editor's Comments

We are looking for queries for interesting, educational books for our middle-school imprint, Rosen Central on topics such as science, guidance, and drug-abuse prevention. We also look for captivating books for reluctant readers on high-interest subjects such as extreme sports, computers, and the Internet. Please note that we do not publish fiction.

RP Books

P.O. Box 362
East Olympia, WA 98540-0362

Vice President & Publisher: Thomas Green

Publisher's Interests
Originally an e-book publisher known as Virtual Press, it launched its first print books in 2002 under its present name. RP Books publishes children's fiction and nonfiction in the realm of science fiction and fantasy.
Website: www.reagentpress.com

Freelance Potential
Published 40 titles in 2005: 20 were developed from unsolicited submissions and 20 were by agented authors. Of the 40 titles, 20 were by authors new to the publishing house. Receives 1,200 queries, 200 mss yearly.

- **Fiction:** Publishes chapter books, 5–10 years; middle-grade books, 8–12 years; and young adult books, 12–18 years. Genres include adventure, fantasy, mystery, and science fiction.
- **Nonfiction:** Publishes young adult books, 12–18 years. Publishes educational, reference, and series books.
- **Representative Titles:** *The Elf Queen and the King II* by Robert Stanek (YA) is the second volume featuring Princess Adrina and how she and others set out to save the Great Kingdom; part of the Ruin Mist Tales series. *The Kingdom & the Elves of the Reaches* by Robert Stanek (YA) follows three heroes on an epic journey of discovery; part of the Ruin Mist series.

Submissions and Payment
Guidelines and catalogue available at website. Query with writing samples to reagentpress@aol.com. Accepts photocopies and computer printouts. SASE. Responds to queries in 1 month, to mss in 1–3 months. Publication in 9–12 months. Royalty; advance.

Editor's Comments
Writers experienced in writing game rule books and roleplaying game guides and who have a strong background in gaming are needed. You must be able to demonstrate an extensive working knowledge of Ruin Mist and its characters.

Running Press Kids

125 South 22nd Street
Philadelphia, PA 19103-4399

Senior Editor: Elizabeth Encarnacion

Publisher's Interests
The catalogue of this publisher includes fiction and nonfiction books and activity kits for children of all ages. It strives to present material that is interactive as well as educational.
Website: www.runningpress.com

Freelance Potential
Published 63 titles in 2005: 3 were developed from unsolicited submissions and 15 were reprint/licensed properties. Of the 63 titles, 2 were by unpublished writers and 5 were by authors who were new to the publishing house. Receives 800 queries, 700 unsolicited mss yearly.

- **Fiction:** Published 5 story picture books, 4–10 years; 10 chapter books, 5–10 years; 5 middle-grade books, 8–12 years; and 3 young adult books, 12–18 years. Genres include historical fiction, folklore, and suspense.
- **Nonfiction:** Published 10 concept books; 10 toddler books; and 5 early picture books, 0–4 years; 5 easy-to-read books, 4–7 years; and 10 activity kits. Features activity and discovery books. Topics include geography, biography, fairy tales, science, and arts and crafts. Also publishes parenting titles.
- **Representative Titles:** *Goodnight Baxter* by Nicola Edwards (4–8 years) is the story of an irrepressible puppy, filled with humorous moments and phrases children will enjoy repeating. *Explorers* by Charlie Watson (8–12 years) takes a look at explorers of the past; part of the Atlas in the Round series.

Submissions and Payment
Catalogue available. Send ms for picture books. Query with outline, table of contents, and synopsis for all other material. SASE. Responds in 2–3 months. Publication in 1–2 years. Advance, varies.

Editor's Comments
We look for books that promote a love of learning. We are publishing more for middle-grade and young adult readers.

St. Anthony Messenger Press

28 West Liberty Street
Cincinnati, OH 45202

Editorial Director: Lisa Biedenbach

Publisher's Interests
Striving to support the church in its spread of the gospel, this publisher offers inspirational books that explore the Catholic faith and identify the trends surfacing in the Catholic world. In addition to adult books, it offers catechetical materials, and Franciscan resources.
Website: www.americancatholic.org

Freelance Potential
Published 39 titles (3 juvenile) in 2005: 7 were by reprint/licensed properties. Of the 39 titles, 4 were by unpublished writers and 15 were by authors who were new to the publishing house. Receives 375 queries yearly.

- **Nonfiction:** Publishes middle-grade books, 8–12 years; and young adult books, 12–18 years. Topics include the Christian community, prayer, scripture, spirituality, spiritual heroes, personal growth, faith, and the sacraments. Also publishes titles for adults.
- **Representative Titles:** *Taming the Media Monster: A Family Guide to Television, Internet, and All the Rest* by Dan Andriacco (Parents) offers practical suggestions to help families become media literate and begin to cope with the overwhelming presence and influence of mass media in today's world. *The Blessing Cup: Prayer-Rituals for Families and Groups* by Rock Travnikar, O.F.M. (Parents) offers prayer rituals for families, which center on sharing the cup of blessing.

Submissions and Payment
Guidelines available. Query with outline/synopsis. Accepts photocopies. No simultaneous submissions. SASE. Responds in 6–8 weeks. Publication in 1–2 years. Royalty, 10%; advance, $1,000.

Editor's Comments
We're looking for books that are practical and inspirational. Please note that we do not publish books for young children.

Saint Mary's Press

702 Terrace Heights
Winona, MN 55987-1320

Submissions Coordinator

Publisher's Interests

Striving to share God's word with children between the ages of ten and nineteen, this Catholic publisher offers nonfiction titles on topics such as spirituality and Christianity. It also offers materials for adults who minister to youth in schools, parishes, and home.
Website: www.smp.org

Freelance Potential

Published 25–30 titles in 2005: 2 were developed from unsolicited submissions and 5 were reprint/licensed properties. Receives 360 queries, 100+ unsolicited mss yearly.

- **Nonfiction:** Publishes middle-grade books, 8–12 years; and young adult books, 12–18 years. Topics include spirituality, Christianity, and the Catholic faith. Also publishes titles for adults who minister to youth.
- **Representative Titles:** *Celebrating Sacraments* by Joseph Stoutzenberger (YA) is designed to help students in tenth grade cultivate awareness of the seven sacraments. *Growing in Christian Morality* by Julia Ahlers, Barbara Allaire & Carol Koch (YA) offers a Christian vision for answering questions related to decision making, wise judgment, justice, wholeness, honesty, and respect.

Submissions and Payment

Guidelines available. Query with outline and sample chapter; or send complete ms. Accepts computer printouts, disk submissions (RFT files), and simultaneous submissions if identified. SASE. Responds to queries in 2 months, to mss in 2–3 months. Publication in 18 months. Royalty; 10%.

Editor's Comments

We are currently looking for unique material that is fresh and will meet the needs of our readers. Keep in mind that your writing must reach our target audience of Catholic middle and high school students. We do not publish fiction.

Salina Bookshelf

Suite 130
1254 West University Avenue
Flagstaff, AZ 86001

Editor: Jessie Ruffenach

Publisher's Interests
Salina Bookshelf publishes Navajo/English picture books
for children, all of which focus on the Navajo people, culture, or
language. Also included in its publishing program are Navajo
language workbooks intended for classroom use.
Website: www.salinabookshelf.com

Freelance Potential
Published 12 titles in 2005: 6 were developed from unsolicited
submissions. Of the 12 titles, 6 were by unpublished writers
and 6 were by authors who were new to the publishing
house. Receives 75 unsolicited mss yearly.

- **Fiction:** Published 4 concept books, 0–4 years; 4 early picture
  books, 0–4 years; and 4 story picture books, 4–10 years. Genres
  include folklore, folktales, multicultural and ethnic fiction, and
  stories about nature and the environment. Also publishes
  bilingual Navajo/English books, 4–7 years.
- **Representative Titles:** *Little Prankster Girl* by Martha Blue
  tells of a young girl who tries to prove to her family that she is
  grown up enough to learn to weave. *Day and Night* by Nedra
  Emery is a traditional Navajo folktale about a moccasin game
  played by the animals of the day and the animals of the night,
  the outcome of which will determine the length of the days
  and nights.

Submissions and Payment
Guidelines available. Send complete ms. Accepts photo-
copies, computer printouts, and disk submissions (Adobe
Acrobat). SASE. Responds in 3 weeks. Publication in 1 year.
Royalty, varies; advance, varies.

Editor's Comments
The only unsolicited submissions we typically review are
children's picture books. As yet, we have not published poetry
or novels, but we will consider submissions of that type if
the focus is on the Navajo culture.

Sandcastle Publishing

1723 Hill Drive
P.O. Box 3070
South Pasadena, CA 91030

Acquisitions Editor

Publisher's Interests

This company produces high-quality materials designed to develop the skills of young people interested in the performing arts. Its goal is to encourage youth to improve themselves through participation in the performing arts and to enhance their opportunities for growth. Sandcastle also publishes early reader fiction.

Website: www.childrenactingbooks.com

Freelance Potential

Published 2 titles in 2005: 1 was developed from an unsolicited submission and 1 was by an agented author. Receives 500 queries, 400 unsolicited mss yearly.

- **Fiction:** Publishes story picture books, 3–8 years. Features 32-page read-aloud stories that include parts for children to act out. Also publishes collections of monologues and dramatic scenes.
- **Nonfiction:** Published 1 middle-grade book, 8–12 years; and 1 young adult book, 12–18 years. Topics include acting and the dramatic arts.
- **Representative Titles:** *Magnificent Monologues for Kids* by Chambers Stevens presents basic information and secret tips for successful auditions. *Sensational Scenes for Kids* by Chambers Stevens includes comedy scenes, dramatic scenes, advice on character motivation, and an introduction to script formatting.

Submissions and Payment

Guidelines available. Query with résumé. Send complete ms for early reader fiction. SASE. Responds in 2–3 months. Publication period and payment vary.

Editor's Comments

We're committed to literacy as well as to youth achievement in the arts, and we take pride in the quality of our materials. We welcome the chance to review your ideas and stories.

Sandlapper Publishing

P.O. Box 730
Orangeburg, SC 29116

Managing Editor: Amanda Gallman

Publisher's Interests
Celebrating South Carolina's rich heritage, this publisher offers regional nonfiction in the areas of history, cooking, travel, recreation, photography, natural history, and folklore. Its books for young readers include nonfiction books on regional topics.
Website: www.sandlapperpublishing.com

Freelance Potential
Published 4 titles (2 juvenile) in 2005: 4 were developed from unsolicited submissions. Of the 4 titles, 1 was by an unpublished writer and 3 were by authors who were new to the publishing house. Receives 200 queries yearly.

- **Nonfiction:** Publishes easy-to-read books, 4–7 years; story picture books, 4–10 years; chapter books, 5–10 years; middle-grade books, 8–12 years; and young adult titles, 12–18 years. Also publishes biographies. Topics include history, travel, nature, culture, and photography. All books focus on South Carolina and the American Southeast.
- **Representative Titles:** *Amadeus the Leghorn Rooster* by Delores B. Nevils (4–10 years) is the true story of a leghorn rooster who becomes the pride of the neighborhood until one day things start to go wrong. *Come to the Cow Pens!* by Christine R. Swager (12–18 years) presents the story and illustrations of the Battle of Cowpens, Janaury 17, 1781.

Submissions and Payment
Guidelines available. Query with résumé, outline/synopsis, 3 sample chapters, and bibliography. Accepts photocopies and computer printouts. SASE. Responds in 2 months. Publication in 2 years. Royalty.

Editor's Comments
We're looking for nonfiction books on South Carolina history. Subjects of special interest are Gullah, plantations, lighthouses, the American Revolution, and the Civil War.

Sasquatch Books

Suite 400
119 South Main Street
Seattle, WA 98104

The Editors

Publisher's Interests

This publisher offers titles that explore the lifestyle, landscape, and world view of the Pacific Northwest, Alaska, and California. Its catalogue includes adult fiction and nonfiction books on travel, food, wine, gardening, and history, as well as children's books on topics that celebrate the region.
Website: www.sasquatchbooks.com

Freelance Potential

Published 32 titles (5 juvenile) in 2005: all were by agented authors. Receives 200+ unsolicited mss yearly.

- **Fiction:** Publishes early picture books, 0–4 years, easy-to-read books, 4–7 years; and story picture books, 4–10 years. Genres include regional history, multicultural and ethnic fiction, and stories about animals and nature.
- **Nonfiction:** Publishes activity books, 6–12 years. Topics include regional history, nature, the environment, and multicultural issues.
- **Representative Titles:** *Under Alaska's Midnight Sun* by Deb Vanasse (3–6 years) is a poetic narrative that follows a young Alaskan girl who plans to stay up and play all day and night. *Out & About with Kids: Seattle* by Ann Bergman & Virginia Smith (parents) offers a candid and comprehensive all-around guide for family fun and learning in Seattle, Washington.

Submissions and Payment

Guidelines available at website. Send complete ms. Accepts photocopies and computer printouts. No electronic submissions. SASE. Responds in 1–3 months. Publication period and payment policy vary.

Editor's Comments

We are looking for queries and proposals for new projects that fit into our publishing program. Remember, we want to know about you and your project, along with a sense of who will want to read your book.

Scarecrow Press

Suite 200
4501 Forbes Boulevard
Lanham, MD 20706

Acquisitions Editor

Publisher's Interests
Known for its scholarly biographies, historical dictionaries, and reference works in the humanities, this publisher targets librarians serving children and young adults.
Website: www.scarecrowpress.com

Freelance Potential
Published 141 titles (20 juvenile) in 2005: Of the 141 titles, 60–80 were by authors who were new to the publishing house. Receives a large number of queries and mss yearly.

- **Nonfiction:** Publishes handbooks and reference tools, bibliographies, historical dictionaries, library science monographs, and reference works. Topics include the humanities, history, social issues, music, and science.
- **Representative Titles:** *Hard Facts on Smart Classroom Design: Ideas, Guidelines, and Layouts* by Daniel Niemeyer provides thought-provoking models of imaginative, successful, and mainstream college classrooms. *Colonial America in Literature for Youth: A Guide and Resource Book* by Joy Lowe & Kathryn I. Matthew provides librarians and teachers with a collection of resources that capture the excitement, danger, and wonder of colonial America.

Submissions and Payment
Guidelines available. Prefers query with résumé, table of contents, introduction, chapter summaries, and sample chapter. Accepts complete ms with curriculum vitae. Accepts photocopies, computer printouts, and simultaneous submissions if identified. SASE. Responds in 2 months. Publication in 6–12 months. Royalty; 8–15%.

Editor's Comments
We have broadened our list to include textbooks in library and information science, and a greater scope of materials in music. We look for fresh and innovative ideas that will be useful to librarians, educators, and media specialists.

Scholastic Canada Ltd.

175 Hillmount Road
Markham, Ontario L6C 1Z7
Canada

Editors

Publisher's Interests
This well-known publisher offers a list of award-winning children's titles by Canadian authors.
Website: www.scholastic.ca

Freelance Potential
Published 70 titles (69 juvenile) in 2005: 25 by agented authors, and 10 were reprint/licensed properties. Receives 1,500+ queries yearly.

- **Fiction:** Publishes story picture books, 4–10 years; chapter books, 5–10 years; middle-grade titles, 8–12 years; and young adult books, 12–18 years. Genres include adventure, mystery, suspense, humor, drama, contemporary and historical fiction, and stories about sports.
- **Nonfiction:** Publishes concept books and toddler books, 0–4 years; easy-to-read books, and middle-grade titles, 8–12 years. Topics include Canadian history, animals, technology, and sports. Also publishes activity books and biographies.
- **Representative Titles:** *Shipwreck on the Pirate Islands* by Geronimo Stilton is a humorous tale about an adventurous rat, pirates, and secret treasure; part of the Geronimo Stilton series. *The Magic School Bus in the Rainforest* (5–7 years) continues the adventures of Ms. Frizzle and her class as they search the rain forest for clues about cocoa beans.

Submissions and Payment
Accepts queries from Canadian authors only. Query with outline and table of contents; include résumé for nonfiction. Accepts photocopies and computer printouts. No simultaneous submissions. SASE. Responds in 3 months. Publication in 2 years. Payment policy varies.

Editor's Comments
We take pride in our titles, which introduces young people to to the joys of reading and enlarges their understanding of Canada and the world.

Scholastic Children's Books (UK)

Commonwealth House
1-19 New Oxford Street
London, WC1A 1NU
United Kingdom

Editorial Department

Publisher's Interests
Scholastic Children's Books is committed to developing reading and literacy in children while supporting parents and teachers. Its list of titles covers fiction and nonfiction for children through young adults.
Website: www.scholastic.co.uk

Freelance Potential
Receives 1,200 queries, 1,200 unsolicited mss yearly.

- **Fiction:** Publishes concept books, 0–4 years; toddler books, 0–4 years; early picture books, 0–4 years; easy-to-read books, 4–7 years; story picture books, 4–10 years; chapter books, 5–10 years; middle-grade books, 8–12 years; and young adult books, 12–18 years. Genres include adventure, drama, fantasy, and contemporary and historical fiction.
- **Nonfiction:** Publishes early picture and toddler books, 0–4 years; easy-to-read books, 4–7 years; story picture books, 4–10 years; chapter books, 5–10 years; middle-grade books, 8–12 years; and young adult books, 12–18 years. Topics include geography, history, math, and sports.
- **Representative Titles:** *Looking for JJ* by Anne Cassidy (YA) is the story of a young girl who can't forget what happened to a childhood friend six years ago. *Blood, Bones and Body Bits & Chemical Chaos* by Nick Arnold gives fact files, quizzes, and cartoons to answer questions about diagnosing deadly diseases; part of the Horrible Science series.

Submissions and Payment
Catalogue available at website. Query with synopsis and 3 sample chapters. Accepts photocopies. SAE/IRC. Response time and publication period vary.

Editor's Comments
We publish a wide range of fiction and nonfiction for all ages so writers with a good, strong concept and believable story line should query us.

Scholastic Inc./Trade Paperback Division

555 Broadway
New York, NY 10012

Editorial Director/Trade Paperbacks: Craig Walker

Publisher's Interests

This well-known publisher features original fiction and non-fiction children's books in paperback format. Its products support its mission to instill a love of reading and learning in children for lifelong pleasure.
Website: www.scholastic.com

Freelance Potential

Published 350–400 titles in 2005: all were by agented authors. Of the 350–400 titles, 52 were by authors who were new to the publishing house. Receives 250 queries, 150 unsolicited mss yearly.

- **Fiction:** Publishes picture books, all ages; and middle-grade titles, 8–11 years. Genres include science fiction, fantasy, adventure, mystery, suspense, Westerns, and sports and animal stories.
- **Nonfiction:** Publishes books for all ages. Topics include science, nature, and multicultural issues. Also publishes photo essays and parenting titles.
- **Representative Titles:** *The Young Man and the Sea* by Rodman Philbrick is about a twelve-year-old boy who must keep more things in his life afloat than just his father's boat. *The Fire Within* by Chris D'Lacey combines two children and a collection of hand-crafted clay dragons that come to life and have magical power.

Submissions and Payment

Accepts submissions through literary agents and from authors who have previously published with Scholastic Trade. SASE. Response time, publication period, and payment policy vary.

Editor's Comments

We continue to need middle-grade fiction series titles. We look for strong characters, exciting plots, and contemporary topics. Agented submissions only, please.

Scholastic Press

557 Broadway
New York, NY 10012

Associate Editor: Jennifer Rees

Publisher's Interests
This division of the well-known publisher Scholastic Inc. offers fiction and nonfiction on a wide range of topics. It will consider submissions from agented or previously published authors only.
Website: www.scholastic.com

Freelance Potential
Published 30 titles in 2005: 27 were by agented authors. Receives 3,600 queries yearly.

- **Fiction:** Publishes toddler books and early picture books, 0–4; easy-to-read books, 4–7 years; story picture books, 4–10 years; chapter books, 5–10 years; middle-grade books, 8–12 years; and young adult books, 12–18 years. Genres include contemporary and multicultural fiction, adventure, fantasy, humor, mystery, and sports.
- **Nonfiction:** Publishes early picture books, 0–4 years; easy-to-read books, 4–7 years; story picture books, 4–10 years; chapter books, 5–10 years; middle-grade books, 8–12 years; and young adult books, 12–18 years. Topics include history, nature, the environment, and multicultural and ethnic subjects. Also offers biographies.
- **Representative Titles:** *The Bumpy Little Pumpkin* by Margery Cuyler (4–8 years) tells the story of an imperfect pumpkin's journey to becoming a jack-o-lantern. *Learning the Game* by Kevin Waltman (12+ years) is a story about loyalty and being a part of a team.

Submissions and Payment
Guidelines available upon request and with SASE. Query only. SASE. Responds in 2–3 weeks. Publication in 12–24 months. Royalty; advance.

Editor's Comments
We are always looking for material that spices up typically dry topics such as biography, history, math, or science. We also like to see material regarding children's relationships.

Scholastic Professional Books

557 Broadway
New York, NY 10012-3999

Editorial/Production Coordinator

Publisher's Interests

The publishing program of this division of Scholastic provides resources for teachers working with students at the elementary through middle-school levels.
Website: www.scholastic.com/professional

Freelance Potential

Published 120 titles in 2005: 8–10 were developed from unsolicited submissions. Receives 300–400 queries, 150–200 unsolicited mss yearly.

- **Nonfiction:** Publishes titles for educators, pre-K–grade 8. Topics include teaching strategies, curriculum development, assessment, evaluation, cooperative learning, and classroom management. Also offers cross-curriculum and literature-based materials for teaching reading, language arts, literature, mathematics, science, social studies, and art. Also publishes dictionaries and encyclopedias.
- **Representative Titles:** *Every Child Can Read* by Jane Baskwill & Paulette Whitman (teachers, grades K–6) offers strategies for helping struggling readers. *Easy Make & Learn Projects: Penguins* by Donald M. Silver & Patricia J. Wynne (teachers, grades 1–3) shows how to make 15 models and manipulatives that teach penguin facts, including life cycles, anatomy, and feeding habits.

Submissions and Payment

Guidelines available. Query with outline and 2 sample chapters; or send complete ms. Accepts photocopies, computer printouts, and simultaneous submissions if identified. SASE. Responds in 4 months. Publication in 12–14 months. Flat fee.

Editor's Comments

Most of our titles are written by teachers who can offer original, useful ideas to their colleagues working in mainstream settings. Successful submissions cite specific teaching approaches and strategies.

School Specialty Children's Publishing

2nd Floor
8720 Orion Place
Columbus, OH 43240

Submissions Editor

Publisher's Interests
This publisher offers educational, curriculum-based fiction for pre-K through young adult readers. Its list includes material for gifted and talented students, as well as workbooks for children who need extra help.
Website: www.childrensspecialty.com

Freelance Potential
Published 420 titles (416 juvenile) in 2005: 1 was by an agented author. Receives 400 unsolicited mss yearly.

- **Fiction:** Publishes early picture books, 0–4 years; easy-to-read books, 4–7 years; story picture books, 4–10 years; chapter books, 5–10 years; young adult books, 12–18 years. Genres include contemporary fiction, fairy tales, folklore, and folktales. Also publishes board books, novelty books, activity books, series titles, and educational workbooks.
- **Representative Titles:** *Sweet America* by Steven Kroll (grades 5–7) tells the story of a young immigrant boy in America; part of the Jamestown's American Portraits series. *Predator Attack* (pre-K–grade 2) is a book about animals that emphasizes reading comprehension; part of the Extreme Readers series.

Submissions and Payment
Guidelines available. Send complete ms with list of published works. SASE. Response time varies. Publication period and payment policy vary.

Editor's Comments
We offer imaginative and inspiring literature for young children, and we invite published authors to submit proposals for picture books that meet our standards. At this time, we are interested in proposals for high-interest, fact-based educational fiction that focuses on expanding reading comprehension. We ask that you give us exclusive right of review for two months before submitting to another publisher.

Scobre Press

2255 Calle Clara
La Jolla, CA 92037

Editor: Scott Blumenthal

Publisher's Interests
High-interest, low-level sports books for middle-grade readers can be found in this publisher's catalogue. All of its material centers around character education.
Website: www.scobre.com

Freelance Potential
Published 9 titles (all juvenile) in 2005: 2 were developed from unsolicited submissions and 2 were by agented authors. Of the 9 titles, 3 were by unpublished writers and 6 were by authors who were new to the publishing house. Receives 24–60 queries yearly.

- **Fiction:** Published 7 middle-grade books, 8–12 years. Genres include sports-related stories.
- **Nonfiction:** Published 2 middle-grade books, 8–12 years. All topics focus on sports-related issues.
- **Representative Titles:** *The Long Way Around* by Jimmie Hand (9–16 years) is a story of redemption and second chances for a high school quarterback. *Teacher's Resource Guide* (teachers) offers a step-by-step program that effectively teaches a variety of reading comprehension strategies; part of the Dream Series.

Submissions and Payment
Guidelines available. Catalogue available at website. Query. Accepts photocopies and email queries to info@scobre.com. SASE ($.83 postage). Responds in 1 week. Publication in 6 months. Royalty, 12%.

Editor's Comments
We offer more than simple, fluffy sports stories. We are looking for authors to create works for our "sports series." These sports books will help to create educational books that actually interest young adults. Multicultural books will continue to be a focus for our series as well. Authors should have a passion for and/or a history of creating young adult books.

Seal Press

Suite 250
1400 65th Street
Emeryville, CA 94608

Acquisitions Editor: Brooke Warner

Publisher's Interests

Seal Press publishes nonfiction *from* women, *by* women.
Some of its publications directly target young adults. It is
known for providing the literary world with original, lively,
radical, empowering, and culturally diverse works that
address contemporary issues from a woman's perspective.
Website: www.sealpress.com

Freelance Potential

Published 22 titles (2 juvenile) in 2005: 1 was developed
from an unsolicited submission, 18 were by agented
authors, and 1 was a reprint/licensed property. Of the 22
titles, 1 was by an unpublished writer and 8 were by authors
who were new to the publishing house. Receives 1,000
queries yearly.

- **Nonfiction:** Published 2 young adult books, 12–18 years.
  Topics include parenting, politics, health, domestic violence,
  sexual abuse, travel, and women's issues.
- **Representative Titles:** *I Wanna Be Sedated* by Faith Conlon
  & Gail Hudson, Eds. is an anthology of essays on the topic of
  parenting teenagers. *Invisible Girls* by Dr. Patti Feuereisen with
  Caroline Pincus (YA) offers guidance for girls and young women
  who are trying to overcome the trauma of abuse.

Submissions and Payment

Guidelines available. Query with résumé, project overview,
writing sample, description of target audience, and marketing strategy. SASE. Responds in 6–8 months. Publication
period and payment policy vary.

Editor's Comments

We're always interested in connecting with qualified writers
and hearing about new projects. Tell us about yourself when
you send your query. Provide detailed information about
your previous publications, and tell us why you are particularly qualified to write about your proposed subject.

Second Story Press

Suite 401
20 Maud Street
Toronto, Ontario M5V 2M5
Canada

Submissions Editor

Publisher's Interests
Books by Canadian authors that inform, enlighten, and entertain young readers, as well as adults, are the specialty of this small press.
Website: www.secondstorypress.ca

Freelance Potential
Published 10 titles (7 juvenile) in 2005: 2 were developed from unsolicited submissions. Of the 10 titles, 2 were by unpublished writers and 6 were by authors who were new to the publishing house. Receives 50 queries, 750 unsolicited mss yearly.

- **Fiction:** Published 2 story picture books, 4–10 years; and 2 young adult books, 12–18 years. Genres include historical, contemporary, and multicultural fiction; and mystery.
- **Nonfiction:** Published 3 young adult books, 12–18 years. Topics include history, nature, the environment, contemporary social issues, family life, and ethnic issues.
- **Representative Titles:** *Where's Mom's Hair?* by Debbie Watters (6+ years) chronicles a family's journey through cancer and helps children understand the treatment process. *Extraordinary Women Explorers* by Frances Rooney (9–13 years) takes readers across four continents to highlight the lives of 12 courageous women.

Submissions and Payment
Guidelines available at website. Canadian authors only. Query or send complete ms for children's books. Query with outline and sample chapter for adult titles. Accepts photocopies and computer printouts. SAE/IRC. Responds in 4–6 months. Publication period varies. Royalty; advance.

Editor's Comments
We're looking for diverse material that can help children, especially girls, understand life's challenges.

Seedling Publications

20 West Kanawha Avenue
Columbus, OH 43214-1432

Submissions Editor: Lynn Salem

Publisher's Interests
This educational publisher produces high-quality, early literacy books for the beginning reader. It produces both fiction and nonfiction titles using natural language and supportive text. Some of its books are also available in Spanish.
Website: www.seedlingpub.com

Freelance Potential
Published 20–25 titles in 2005. Receives 400 unsolicited mss yearly.

- **Fiction:** Publishes easy-to-read books, 4–7 years. Genres include fairy tales, adventure, stories about sports and nature, and humor.
- **Nonfiction:** Publishes easy-to-read books, 4–7 years. Topics include nature, science, technology, mathematics, animals, and multicultural subjects.
- **Representative Titles:** *A Whistle Tour* by Josie Stewart & Lynn Salem gives the reader a tour of America's only metal whistle factory and shows how whistles are made; part of the Treetop Books series. *Duck and Goose and the Perfect Puddle* by Wendi Silvano is for the emergent reader who will enjoy and benefit from the high-frequency words in the story.

Submissions and Payment
Send complete ms. Accepts photocopies, computer printouts, and simultaneous submissions if identified. SASE. Responds in 4–6 months. Publication in 1 year. Payment policy varies.

Editor's Comments
We have very specific guidelines for writers. Manuscripts must be for beginning readers; maximum word length is 150–200 words; we only accept an 8-, 12-, or 16-page format, including the title page. It must have a strong story line that is unique or that includes a twist at the end. Do not send us poetry books or manuscripts in rhyme.

Shen's Books

40951 Fremont Boulevard
Fremont, CA 94538

Owner: Renee Ting

Publisher's Interests

Children experience the cultures of Asian and Latin American countries through the illustrated titles available from Shen's Books.
Website: www.shens.com

Freelance Potential

Published 2 titles in 2005: 1 was developed from an unsolicited submission and 1 was by an agented author. Of the 2 titles, 1 was by an unpublished writer and both were by authors who were new to the publishing house. Receives 50 unsolicited mss yearly.

- **Fiction:** Published 2 story picture books, 4–10 years. Genres include fairy tales, folklore, and historical and multicultural fiction related to Asia and Latin America.
- **Representative Titles:** *The Wishing Tree* by Roseanne Thong (4–10 years) is the story of Ming, his grandmother, and the banyan tree they wish on every lunar new year. *Anklet for a Princess* by Lila Mehta (6–12 years) is a Cinderella story from India that depicts how Cinduri won the heart of a prince.

Submissions and Payment

Send complete ms. Accepts computer printouts, disk submissions (Microsoft Word), and simultaneous submissions if identified. SASE. Responds in 6–12 months. Publication in 18 months. Payment policy varies.

Editor's Comments

We believe that, in these times, it's more important than ever to help children learn about other places in the world and other cultures. This is the focus of our publishing program. We're highly selective in what we publish, but all our books are chosen to inspire children to look beyond their immediate world toward distant horizons. Stories about the immigrant experience in America are also welcome.

Silver Moon Press

Suite 622
160 5th Avenue
New York, NY 10010

Managing Editor: Hope Killcoyne

Publisher's Interests

This publisher features curriculum-based fiction and nonfiction material for grades two through eight, with a focus on social studies and history. It also publishes ELA workbooks that follow New York State core curriculum guidelines.
Website: www.silvermoonpress.com

Freelance Potential

Published 4 titles in 2005: 2 were developed from unsolicited submissions. Of the 4 titles, 2 were by authors who were new to the publishing house. Receives 250+ queries yearly.

- **Fiction:** Publishes chapter books, 5–10 years; and middle-grade titles, 8–12 years. Genres include historical fiction and adventure stories.
- **Nonfiction:** Publishes test preparation workbooks for grades 2–8; and biographical nonfiction, 8–12 years. Topics include New York State history, the Revolutionary War, and colonial times.
- **Representative Titles:** *Word for Word* by Inda Schaenen (grades 4–7) is a step-by-step introduction to prose composition. *Brothers of the Falls* by Joanna Emery (grades 4–6) follows orphaned Irish immigrant James Doyle as he makes his way through nineteenth-century New York.

Submissions and Payment

Guidelines available. Send complete ms with word count, chapter outlines, and brief synopsis for first book of series. Query for stand-alone titles. Accepts computer printouts and simultaneous submissions if identified. SASE. Responds in 6–12 months. Publication period and payment policy vary.

Editor's Comments

We publish one or two novels annually, focusing almost exclusively on educational material that can be used in the classroom. Our largest market is in New York State, so we look for books that fit New York curriculum requirements.

Simon & Schuster Books for Young Readers

1230 Avenue of the Americas
New York, NY 10020

Submissions Editor

Publisher's Interests
This well-known imprint of Simon & Schuster offers a broad list that includes fiction and nonfiction picture books for young children, as well as titles for middle-grade and young adult readers.
Website: www.simonsayskids.com

Freelance Potential
Published 75 titles in 2005: 60 were by agented authors. Receives 10,000 queries yearly.

- **Fiction:** Publishes toddler books and early picture books, 0–4 years; easy-to-read books, 4–7 years; story picture books, 4–10 years; chapter books, 5–10 years; middle-grade titles, 8–12 years; and young adult books, 12–18 years. Genres include contemporary, historical, and multicultural fiction; mystery; fantasy; folklore; and fairy tales.
- **Nonfiction:** Publishes story picture books, 4–10 years; and middle-grade titles, 8–12 years. Topics include social issues, science, nature, math, and history. Also publishes anthologies and biographies.
- **Representative Titles:** *Lunch Money* by Andrew Clements (8–12 years) finds a middle-grade boy in the middle of a hot new business. *And Tango Makes Three* by Justin Richardson & Peter Parnell (4–8 years) is based on the true story of two male penguins who built a nest and hatched a chick together.

Submissions and Payment
Guidelines available. Query. No unsolicited mss. SASE. Responds in 2 months. Publication in 2–4 years. Royalty; advance.

Editor's Comments
We continue to consider queries for original picture books with fresh ideas, and for middle-grade fiction that readers can relate to. Topic of interest include contemporary school and family concerns, peer issues, and history.

Simon Pulse

Simon & Schuster
1230 Avenue of the Americas
New York, NY 10020

Submissions Editor

Publisher's Interests
Paperback books for teens in various categories and formats
including reprints, original paperbacks, and original series
are produced by this publisher. An imprint of Simon &
Schuster, it offers both fiction and nonfiction titles.
Website: www.simonsays.com

Freelance Potential
Published 50 titles in 2005: all were developed from unsolicited submissions. Of the 50 titles, 1 was by an unpublished writer and 3 were by authors who were new to the
publishing house. Receives 1,000+ queries and mss yearly.

- **Fiction:** Publishes middle-grade books, 8–12 years; and young
  adult books, 12–18 years. Genres include adventure; mystery;
  suspense; romance; fantasy; folktales; drama; horror; humor;
  and contemporary, inspirational, ethnic, and multicultural fiction.
- **Nonfiction:** Publishes middle-grade books, 8–12 years; and
  young adult books, 12–18 years. Topics include animals, pets,
  current events, entertainment, multicultural and ethnic subjects, technology, science, sports, and social issues. Also publishes biographies and self-help books.
- **Representative Titles:** *Mates, Dates, and Chocolate Cheats*
  by Cathy Hopkins (12+ years) tells about a girl who tries loos-
  ing weight and forgets about the things that matter. *Can't Get
  There from Here* by Todd Strasser (12+ years) shares the story
  of a homeless teen and the realities of living on the street.

Submissions and Payment
Guidelines available. Only accepts queries from agents.
SASE. Response time varies. Publication in 6–24 months.
Payment varies.

Editor's Comments
Due to the large volume of material we receive, at this time
we can only accept queries from agented authors.

Small Horizons

34 Church Street
Liberty Corner, NJ 07938

Publisher: Dr. Joan S. Dunphy

Publisher's Interests
Self-help books that aid educators, parents, and mental health professionals who help children deal with issues such as self-esteem, depression, stress, anger, and divorce can be found in this publisher's catalogue. It is an imprint of New Horizon Press.
Website: www.newhorizonpressbooks.com

Freelance Potential
Published 12 titles (2 juvenile) in 2005: 5 were developed from unsolicited submissions and 5 were by agented authors. Receives 100+ queries yearly.

- **Fiction:** Publishes story picture books, 4–10 years. Features books about psychological and social concerns, coping skills, tolerance, and services.
- **Nonfiction:** Published 2 easy-to-read books, 4–7 years. Also publishes self-help titles for children and adults. Topics include parenting, family issues, women's rights, politics, ethnic issues, relationships, careers, and teaching children.
- **Representative Titles:** *I Don't Want to Go to School* by Nancy J. Pando offers children ways to cope with separation from loved ones. *Why Can't Jimmy Sit Still?* by Sandra L. Tunis teaches children and educators about hyperactivity, and reassures youngsters with ADHD that they are not to blame for their "racing motors."

Submissions and Payment
Guidelines available. Query with résumé, outline, 2 sample chapters, and market comparison. Accepts photocopies and computer printouts. Availability of artwork improves chance of acceptance. SASE. Responds in 3 months. Publication period varies. Royalty; 7.5% of net; advance.

Editor's Comments
We're looking for children's picture books on topics related to self-esteem, and school and personal problems.

Smith and Kraus

P.O. Box 127
Lyme, NH 03768

Submissions

Publisher's Interests
Although it focuses on plays and resource materials on theater arts, this publisher also offers a small list of fiction titles
for young readers.
Website: www.smithandkraus.com

Freelance Potential
Published 40 titles (20 juvenile) in 2005: 4–5 were developed from unsolicited submissions, and 10 were by agented
authors. Of the 40 titles, 7 were by unpublished writers and
10 were by authors who were new to the publishing house.
Receives 50 queries yearly.

- **Fiction:** Publishes story picture books, 4–10 years; and middle-grade titles, 8–12 years. Genres include animal stories,
  and contemporary and historical fiction.
- **Nonfiction:** Publishes collections of plays, scenes, and monologues, grades K–12. Also publishes instructional books for
  teachers, anthologies, collections of work by contemporary
  playwrights, translations, and books on career development.
- **Representative Titles:** *The Ultimate Monologue Book for Middle
  School Actors* by Kristen Dabrowski (grades 7–12) includes
  111 one-minute monologues ranging from highly serious to
  seriously funny. *Blue Creek Farm* by Carroll Thomas (grades
  5–8) is the story of a young wife struggling for acceptance as a
  woman doctor in a small Kansas town.

Submissions and Payment
Catalogue available. Query with résumé. Accepts photocopies,
computer printouts, and simultaneous submissions if identified. SASE. Responds in 1 month. Publication in 1 year. Royalty; advance. Flat fee.

Editor's Comments
Queries will be considered for monologues and our new
anthologies on women playwrights and new playwriters. We
are not interested in single plays at this time.

Smooch

Suite 2000
200 Madison Avenue
New York, NY 10016

Editor: Kate Seaver

Publisher's Interests

Focusing on titles for young adult girls, this publisher's list includes contemporary fiction and paranormal titles. Its stories mix romance with humor, and focus on the issues relevant to today's teens. It is an imprint of Dorchester Publishing.
Website: www.smoochya.com

Freelance Potential

Published 12 titles in 2005: 6 were developed from unsolicited submissions, 6 were by agented authors, and 8 were reprint/licensed properties. Of the 12 titles, 2 were by unpublished writers and 8 were by authors who were new to the publishing house.

- **Fiction:** Publishes young adult books, 12–18 years. Genres include contemporary fiction, horror, humor, fantasy, the paranormal, and romance.
- **Representative Titles:** *A Bird, a Bloke, and a Boyfriend* by Sally Odgers (YA) is a romance novel that tells what happens when you mix one girl with two totally different boys on a tropical sun-soaked paradise. *Who Needs Boys?* (YA) by Stephie Davis is the story of a teenage girl that only wants to date older boys, but finds herself attracted to a younger boy at work who doesn't like her.

Submissions and Payment

Guidelines and catalogue available at website. Query with synopsis and 2 chapters. Accepts photocopies. SASE. Responds in 3–8 months. Publication in 9–12 months. Payment policy varies.

Editor's Comments

We continue to seek contemporary novels and paranormals (ghosts, werewolves, vampires) set in the present-day. Make sure your writing targets our primary audience of girls ages 12–16, and contains no erotic scenes. Material should focus on the challenges teens face in today's world.

Soundprints

353 Main Avenue
Norwalk, CT 06851-1552

Submissions Editor

Publisher's Interests

To entertain and educate young minds is the focus of this publisher. Soundprints produces storybooks on wildlife, natural science, and social science that are based on facts for children through the age of ten.
Website: www.soundprints.com

Freelance Potential

Published 25 titles in 2005: Of the 25 titles, 1 was by an unpublished writer and 2 were by authors who were new to the publishing house. Receives 200 queries, 100 unsolicited mss yearly.

- **Nonfiction:** Publishes concept books, 0–4 years; toddler books, 0–4 years; early picture books, 0–4 years; and chapter books, 5–10 years. Also publishes books in series about nature, the environment, and animals.
- **Representative Titles:** *Dolphin's First Day* (pre-K–grade 2) follows a newborn dolphin during his first 24 hours of life as he learns to swim and take his first breath above water; part of the Smithsonian Oceanic Collection series. *Monarch Butterfly of Aster Way* by Elizabeth Ring (pre-K–grade 2) describes a butterfly's 5,000 mile voyage to reach a warm winter home; part of Smithsonian's Backyard series.

Submissions and Payment

Query with clips or writing samples. Accepts photocopies and computer printouts. SASE. Responds in 1 month. Publication period varies. Flat fee.

Editor's Comments

We would like to see rhyming educational titles that fit in with our series. We are also in the market for nature-based picture books of the type that we currently publish. Writers should review our books to get a good understanding of our storylines and the type of research that goes into our Smithsonian Institution series.

Sourcebooks

Suite 139
1935 Brookdale Road
Naperville, IL 60563

Editorial Submissions

Publisher's Interests

This publisher's stated mission is "to reach as many people as possible with books that will enlighten their lives." To achieve that end, it fills its catalogue with books that impart practical information; books that simply entertain; and books that expand understanding of people, history, and the world. Sourcebooks has been in business since 1987.
Website: www.sourcebooks.com

Freelance Potential

Published 130 titles in 2005: 10 were developed from unsolicited submissions, 70 were by agented authors, and 5 were reprint/licensed properties. Receives 1,000 queries, 1,000 unsolicited mss yearly.

- **Nonfiction:** Publishes self-help and how-to books. Topics include parenting, single parenting, family issues, childbirth, multicultural issues, history, business, marketing, management, entertainment, sports, psychology, stress management, and lifestyles.
- **Representative Titles:** *Your Children Are Under Attack* by Jim Taylor (parents) discusses the ways kids are exposed to greed, sexuality, and violence in today's culture. *The Amazing Mom Book* by John MacIntyre compiles facts and quotes that recognize the role mothers have played throughout history.

Submissions and Payment

Guidelines and catalogue available. Query with résumé, synopsis, table of contents, 2 sample chapters, and market analysis. Accepts photocopies, computer printouts, and simultaneous submissions if identified. SASE. Responds in 4–6 weeks. Publication in 1 year. Royalty, 6–15%.

Editor's Comments

We're interested in books that will establish a unique standard in their subject area, and we look for authors who are as committed to success as we are.

Southern Early Childhood Association

P.O. Box 55930
Little Rock, AR 72215-5930

Executive Director: Glenda Bean

Publisher's Interests
This educational publisher targets early childhood professionals with books that focus on emerging issues and ideas in the field. Its list includes titles on education strategies, theory and research, program administration, resource and referral systems, and public policy.
Website: www.southernearlychildhood.org

Freelance Potential
Published 2 titles in 2005. Receives 4 unsolicited mss each year.

- **Nonfiction:** Publishes resource guides, educational materials and books for educators and parents. Topics include assessment, guidance, behavior, education, child development, family involvement, cognitive development, accountability standards, and mathematics.
- **Representative Titles:** *Mathematics for Young Children* by Jean Shaw (teachers) is designed to help educators bring the principles of mathematics into their early childhood curriculum in a developmentally appropriate way. *Powerful, Positive, and Practical Practices: Behavior Guidance Strategies* by Jeanette C. Nunnelley (teachers) provides a review of direct and indirect guidance techniques and exercises for early childhood behavior programs.

Submissions and Payment
Guidelines available at website. Send 4 copies of complete ms. Accepts disk submissions (WordPerfect or Microsoft Word). SASE. Responds in 4 months. Publication in 9–12 months. No payment.

Editor's Comments
Our publications support constructivist approaches to learning, and we will consider material that advances the cause of developmentally appropriate practice in early childhood care and education—especially timely, critical issues and topics.

The Speech Bin, Inc.

1965 25th Avenue
Vero Beach, FL 32960

Senior Editor: Jan J. Binney

Publisher's Interests
Since 1984, The Speech Bin has provided resource books
and materials for professionals who work with children and
adults who have verbal communication disorders.
Website: www.speechbin.com

Freelance Potential
Published 10 titles in 2005: all were developed from unsolicited submissions. Receives 500+ queries yearly.

- **Fiction:** Publishes picture books, 4–10 years. Features stories
  dealing with stuttering, articulation, phonology, conversation,
  communication, and language skills.
- **Nonfiction:** Publishes concept books and early picture books,
  0–4 years; story picture books, 4–10 years; and middle-grade
  books, 8–12 years. Topics include stuttering, articulation,
  phonology, and language skills. Also publishes textbooks and
  how-to titles for speech pathologists, occupational therapists,
  and parents.
- **Representative Titles:** *Talkable Tales: Read a Rebus* by
  Lois Muehl contains different tales each targeting a different
  phoneme. *Lollipop Lunch and Other Fantastic Phonemic Stories*
  by Patricia A. Hoon present illustrated stories that are just
  right for articulation, phonology, and language.

Submissions and Payment
Guidelines available with #10 SASE ($.37 postage); catalogue
available with 9x12 SASE ($1.47 postage). Query with résumé
and outline/synopsis. Accepts photocopies. No email
queries. SASE. Responds in 1–2 months. Publication in
1 year. Royalty.

Editor's Comments
In your proposal, mention the book's goals and describe the
setting in which it can be used. Don't forget to specify who
will read it and give the targeted age range. We are open to
new ideas and want to hear from you.

Sports Publishing Inc.

804 North Nell
Champaign, IL 61820

Acquisitions Editor: Mike Pearson

Publisher's Interests

Covering a wealth of information on the sports scene, this publisher offers titles that inform and entertain readers on topics such as auto racing, football, baseball, hockey, and golf. In addition to covering college and pro sports, it produces fiction and nonfiction for middle-grade readers.
Website: www.sportspublishinginc.com

Freelance Potential

Published 150 titles in 2005. Receives 50 queries yearly.

- **Fiction:** Publishes middle-grade novels, 8–14 years. Feature stories about sports and athletics.
- **Nonfiction:** Publishes middle-grade books, 8–14 years. Topics include auto racing, baseball, basketball, football, golf, and hockey. Also publishes biographies.
- **Representative Titles:** *Life Lessons from Little League Revisited* by Dr. Vincent M. Fortanasce (Parents) offers advice and observations to parents, players, and others involved in children's baseball. *The Wallace Brothers* by Amy Rosewater (3–5 years) is the story about auto racing's most successful racing trio who are brothers.

Submissions and Payment

Guidelines available. Query with outline, synopsis, 2–3 sample chapters, competition analysis, and résumé. Accepts photocopies, computer printouts, and email submissions to mpearson@sagamore.com. SASE. Response time varies. Publication period and payment policy vary.

Editor's Comments

We have expanded to cover every part of the country, and are always looking for material to add to our list of ultimate sports books. Writers who are dedicated, creative, and ambitious about their work should send a query for a unique idea that will stand out among the rest. When submitting, make sure your outline is complete and detailed.

Square One Publishers

115 Herricks Road
Garden City Park, NY 11040

Publisher: Rudy Shur

Publisher's Interests

Specializing in adult nonfiction, Square One Publishers offers books on a wide range of topics. Parenting titles, books that deal with health issues, and how-to guides for writers are some of the highlights of its catalogue.
Website: www.squareonepublishers.com

Freelance Potential

Published 30 titles in 2005: 20 were developed from unsolicited submissions and 5 were by agented authors. Receives 1,200 queries yearly.

- **Nonfiction:** Publishes self-help and how-to books for adults. Topics include parenting, alternative health, collectibles, cooking, personal finance, and writing.
- **Representative Titles:** *How to Give Your Baby Encyclopedic Knowledge* by Glenn Doman et al. (parents) explains how to teach young children about the arts, science, and nature to fully develop their learning abilities. *How to Maximize Your Child's Learning Ability* by Lauren Bradway & Barbara Albers Hill (parents) lists hundreds of practical things parents can do every day to influence, encourage, and maximize their child's learning ability.

Submissions and Payment

Guidelines available. Query with overview, table of contents, and brief author bio. SASE. Responds in 2 weeks. Publication period varies. Royalty.

Editor's Comments

We look for interesting manuscript proposals with a fresh point of view, written by authors who truly know their topic. Our books provide information that is designed to meet the needs of specific audiences. We're interested in receiving queries for parenting titles at this time. In your query, tell us why you believe there is a need for a book such as yours, and describe its intended audience.

Standard Publishing

8121 Hamilton Avenue
Cincinnati, OH 45231

Editorial Director, Family Resources: Diane Stortz

Publisher's Interests

Biblically sound books that carry a Christian message are available from this evangelical Christian publisher. Its juvenile list includes board books, picture books, and Bible story books for preschool children; middle-grade titles; and young adult books that are challenging, authentic, culturally relevant, and biblically spiritual.

Website: www.standardpub.com

Freelance Potential

Published 110 titles (10 juvenile) in 2005: 10 were developed from unsolicited submissions and 6 were by agented authors. Of the 110 titles, 12 were by authors who were new to the publishing house. Receives 500 queries, 1,500 unsolicited mss yearly.

- **Fiction:** Publishes early picture books, 0–4 years; middle-grade books, 5–10 years; and young adult books, 12–18 years.
- **Nonfiction:** Publishes concept books and early picture books, 0–4 years; middle-grade books, 8–12 years; and young adult books, 12–18 years. Also publishes board books, devotionals, and Bible study guides.
- **Representative Titles:** *In God We Trust* by Larry Burkett (5–9 years) teaches kids the value of money. *Burnt Cookies* by Lois Walfrid Johnson (8–12 years) is a book of devotions for preteen girls.

Submissions and Payment

Guidelines available. Query with outline/synopsis and 1–2 sample chapters. Send complete ms for picture books only. Accepts photocopies, computer printouts, and simultaneous submissions if identified. SASE. Responds in 2–3 months. Publication in 18 months. Royalty. Flat fee.

Editor's Comments

Many of our titles are developed with packagers who specialize in novelty formats, but we still seek freelance material as well.

Star Bright Books

Suite 2B
42-26 28th Street
Long Island City, NY 11101

Director of Marketing: Marie Bernard

Publisher's Interests
Founded in 1994 on the belief that children who learn to read at the earliest possible age will enjoy a love of books all their lives, Star Bright Books offers pre-reader and beginning-reader titles. Its books for older children feature outstanding illustrations and writing designed to encourage kids in their reading habit.
Website: www.starbrightbooks.com

Freelance Potential
Published 15–20 titles (13 juvenile) in 2005: 2 were developed from unsolicited submissions and 1 was by an agented author. Receives 360–480 queries, 240–360 mss yearly.

- **Fiction:** Publishes concept books, toddler books, and early picture books, 0–4 years; easy-to-read books, 4–7 years; story picture books, 4–10 years; chapter books, 5–10 years; and middle-grade books, 8–12 years. Features multicultural and educational books. Also publishes board books.
- **Representative Titles:** *Disabled Fables* by L. A. Goal (all ages) is a collection of Aesop's fables as seen through the eyes of artists with developmental disabilities. *The Aminal* by Lorna Balian (4–8 years) tells of an "aminal" that Patrick finds and carries home in his lunch bag; when he describes it to his friends, they try to save him from the terrible creature they imagine it to be.

Submissions and Payment
Guidelines available. Query or send complete ms. SASE. Response time and publication period vary. Royalty; advance.

Editor's Comments
Our books embrace children of all races, nationalities, and abilities. Because we're trying to instill a love of reading in very young children, we publish board books in thirteen languages. We look for books that are both stimulating and fun.

Starscape Books

175 5th Avenue
New York, NY 10016

Editor: Susan Chang

Publisher's Interests

Devoted exclusively to the best in science fiction and fantasy for young readers, this imprint of Tor Books engages readers with its award-winning stories.
Website: www.starscapebooks.com

Freelance Potential

Published 25 titles in 2005: 3 were developed from unsolicited submissions and 22 were by agented authors. Of the 25 titles, 2 were by unpublished writers and 3 were by authors who were new to the publishing house. Receives 1,200 unsolicited mss yearly.

- **Fiction:** Publishes middle grade books, 8–12 years; and young adult books, 12–18 years. Genres include science fiction and fantasy.
- **Representative Titles:** *Mairelon the Magician* by Patricia Wrede (YA) is the story of a girl whose promise to her dying grandmother leads her on a remarkable journey. *The Garden Behind the Moon* (YA) by Howard Pyle follows the adventures of a boy as he discovers a glimmering moonlit path that leads to a magical world behind the moon.

Submissions and Payment

Guidelines available at website. Query with synopsis and first 3 chapters. Accepts photocopies, computer printouts, and email submissions to torquery@panix.com. SASE. Responds in 4–6 months. Publication in 18–24 months. Royalty; advance.

Editor's Comments

We look for unique stories that will take readers on magical heroic adventures, or transform the real world into a realm of fantasy. A healthy percentage of our most eager and enthusiastic readers have been—and continue to be—young readers. Send a query for a story that will provide a compelling journey into a magical, mystical world.

Starseed Press

P.O. Box 1082
Tiburon, CA 94920

Acquisitions: Jan Phillips

Publisher's Interests

Children's books promoting nonviolence and positive self-esteem for young readers are produced by this publisher. An imprint of New World Library, it also offers books related to personal growth and inspiration.
Website: www.newworldlibrary.com

Freelance Potential

Published 5 titles in 2005: Receives 1,500 queries yearly.

- **Fiction:** Publishes toddler and early picture books, 0–4 years; story picture books, 4–10 years; and young adult books, 12–18 years. Genres include inspirational fiction and books about nature, personal growth, and self-esteem.
- **Nonfiction:** Publishes parenting titles.
- **Representative Titles:** *A Song for Cecilia Fantini* by Cynthia Astor (YA) is the story about a child struggling with her feelings of disloyalty as the memories of her teacher who died fade. *Welcoming Spirit Home* by Sobonfu Somé (parents) is a book that offers ancient African teachings to celebrate children and community.

Submissions and Payment

Query with sample chapter. Accepts photocopies and computer printouts. No submissions via fax or email. SASE. Responds in 8–10 months. Publication in 6–18 months.

Editor's Comments

For the upcoming year we are interested in titles on topics related to parenting and women's studies. We publish books that focus on growth of the whole person, including the body, mind, and spirit. Although we provide material that is inspirational, we do not convey any specific religious affiliation. We also do not publish fantasy, fairytales, parables, or Christian material. If you have an idea for a book that will promote positive values and self-esteem in youngsters, send us a query and and tell us why.

Stemmer House Publishers

4 White Brook Road
Gilsum, NH 03448

Submissions: Craig Thorn

Publisher's Interests
Nonfiction picture books, particularly those that explore the
world of nature and feature timeless themes, appear on this
publisher's children's list.
Website: www.stemmerhousepublishers.com

Freelance Potential
Published 7 titles in 2005: 1 was a reprint/licensed property.
Of the 7 titles, 2 were by unpublished writers and 3 were by
authors who were new to the publishing house. Receives
1,000+ queries, 950+ unsolicited mss yearly.

- **Nonfiction:** Publishes story picture books, 4–10 years; easy-to-
  read books, 4–7 years; chapter books, 5–10 years; middle-
  grade books, 8–12 years; and young adult books, 12–18
  years. Topics include natural history, art, music, and geography. Also publishes biographies, cookbooks, design books,
  and gardening books for adults.
- **Representative Titles:** *Tales from the South Pacific Islands*
  by Anne Grittins (8+ years) is a collection of authentic tales
  with characters that include crabs, mosquitoes, squids,
  demons, and serpents. *Why the Possum's Tail Is Bare* by
  James E. Connolly (3–5 years) presents tales of nature from
  eight Native American cultures.

Submissions and Payment
Guidelines and catalogue available with 9x12 SASE ($.77
postage). Send complete ms for picture books. Query with
outline/synopsis and 2 sample chapters for longer works.
Accepts photocopies, computer printouts, and simultaneous
submissions if identified. SASE. Responds in 2 weeks. Publication in 1–3 years. Royalty; advance.

Editor's Comments
For the coming year, we're looking for arts and crafts books
for young adults and illustrated books about nature, animals,
or the environment for children ages four through twelve.

Sterling Publishing Company

387 Park Avenue South
New York, NY 10016-8810

Editor-in-Chief of Children's Publishing: Frances Gilbert

Publisher's Interests

Sterling Publishing concentrates heavily on producing nonfiction titles for children, particularly on the topics of science and nature. Recently, it has expanded its focus and now offers fiction in the form of picture books for readers ages three to eight.
Website: www.sterlingpub.com

Freelance Potential

Published 250 titles in 2005: 10 were developed from unsolicited submissions, 3 were by agented authors, and 125 were reprint/licensed properties. Receives 1,000 queries each year.

- **Fiction:** Published 10 early picture books, 0–4 years; 20 easy-to-read books, 4–7 years; and 10 story picture books, 4–10 years. Genres include contemporary fiction.
- **Nonfiction:** Published 5 concept books and 5 toddler books, 0–4 years; 50 chapter books, 5–10 years; and 50 middle-grade books, 8–12 years. Topics include animals, nature, science, and history. Also published 100 craft and puzzle books.
- **Representative Titles:** *ABC USA* by Martin Jarrie is a picture book that takes the reader on an alphabetical tour of the U.S. *My Closet Threw a Party* by Robyn Parnell & Jimmy Pickering is the story of a young girl's rebellious closet and the party it throws while she's away.

Submissions and Payment

Guidelines available. Query with outline. Accepts photocopies, computer printouts, and simultaneous submissions if identified. SASE. Response time varies. Publication in 1 year. Royalty; advance.

Editor's Comments

We will now review picture book submissions for ages three to eight, as well as nonfiction on science and nature, craft books, and puzzle and activity books for ages five to twelve.

Storytellers Ink Publishing Co.

P.O. Box 33398
Seattle, WA 98133-0398

Editor-in-chief: Quinn Currie

Publisher's Interests

Storytellers Ink is a small publishing house that specializes in titles that teach children to love reading. Its list includes titles on animals, nature, and the environment.
Website: www.storytellers-ink.com

Freelance Potential

Published 1–3 titles in 2005. Receives 120 queries yearly.

- **Fiction:** Publishes story picture books, 2–12 years. Genres include adventure, folktales, fantasy, and multicultural and ethnic fiction. Also publishes stories about animals, nature, and the environment.
- **Nonfiction:** Publishes story picture books, 2–12 years. Topics include animals, nature, the environment, and social issues. Also publishes biographies and bilingual titles.
- **Representative Titles:** *J. G. Cougar's Great Adventure* by Virginia Bishop Tawresey (grade 2) is the true story of a curious wild cougar who strayed from his habitat and ends up in a Seattle park. *Father Goose and His Goslings* by Bill Lishman (grade 5) is a true story about a man who must teach a gaggle of goslings to fly.

Submissions and Payment

Guidelines available. Send complete ms. Accepts photocopies and simultaneous submissions if identified. SASE. Response time, publication period, and payment policy vary.

Editor's Comments

Our goal is straightforward: to teach children to read and instill a sense of compassion, justice, responsibility, and love for all things living. To this end, our editors would like to see manuscripts for informational, educational books that help young readers learn about the world. Keep the idea simple, and you will keep your audience. All of our books are distributed free of charge through Operation Literacy, a program for promoting literacy.

Sword of the Lord

P.O. Box 1099
Murfreesboro, TN 37133-1099

Editorial Department Supervisor: Dr. Terry Frala

Publisher's Interests
Books for children, teens, and adults, parenting titles, Sunday school teaching materials, and resources for music ministers appear in this conservative Christian organization's catalogue. With a mission to win souls for Christ, it publishes only material that is scripturally sound.
Website: www.swordofthelord.com

Freelance Potential
Published 32 titles (3–4 juvenile) in 2005: 2 were developed from unsolicited submissions. Of the 32 titles, 3 were by unpublished writers and 4 were by authors who were new to the publishing house. Receives 120 queries, 50 unsolicited mss yearly.

- **Fiction:** Publishes story picture books, 4–10 years; middle-grade books, 8–12 years; and young adult books, 12–18 years. Genres include adventure; humor; and inspirational, religious, and Western fiction. Also publishes educational fiction, 6–10 years; and books in series, 6–17 years.
- **Nonfiction:** Publishes biographies, humor, and religious titles for adults.
- **Representative Titles:** *Big Ideas for a Better Sunday School* by Clarence Sexton includes teaching plans and programs for Sunday school teachers. *The Chattering Bones* by Ruth Scarff teaches children about a "people puzzle" that only God can put together.

Submissions and Payment
Guidelines available at website. Query or send complete ms. Accepts photocopies, computer printouts, and email to terryfrala@swordofthelord.com. SASE. Responds in 2–3 months. Publication period varies. Royalty, 10%.

Editor's Comments
All material submitted undergoes a rigorous review process to be certain that it is compatible with the Scriptures.

Tanglewood Press, LLC

P.O. Box 3009
Terre Haute, IN 47803

Acquisitions Editor

Publisher's Interests

Striving to excite and motivate children into reading, this fiction publisher offers historical, mystery, adventure, and humor titles for children in its catalogue. Its list includes story picture books, chapter books, middle-grade books, and young adult books.
Website: www.tanglewoodbooks.com

Freelance Potential

Published 3 titles in 2005: 1 was from an unsolicited submission and 2 were by agented authors. Receives 575 unsolicited mss yearly.

- **Fiction:** Publishes story picture books, 4–10 years; middle-grade books, 8–12 years; and young adult books, 12–18 years. Genres include adventure, historical, humor, and mystery.
- **Representative Titles:** *You Can't Milk a Dancing Cow* by Tom Dunsmuir (4–8 years) tells what happens on a farm when the farmer's wife begins making the animals clothes. *It All Began with a Bean* by Katie McKy (4–8 years) is the story of what happens when everyone farts at the same time.

Submissions and Payment

Send complete ms. Accepts photocopies. SASE. Responds in 3–6 months. Publication in 2–3 years. Royalty; 6% of retail price.

Editor's Comments

We love nothing more than to discover an unpublished, talented author with a wonderful manuscript begging to be published, or a published author whose latest work has brilliance not recognized by other publishers. We want books we think kids will love, will make them want to read, and will help them realize that books can be one of the greatest sources of entertainment. Send us something that will spark their imaginations and make them voracious readers.

Teacher Created Resources

6421 Industry Way
Westminster, CA 92683

Managing Editor: Ina Levin

Publisher's Interests

All of the material produced by this company is intended to
be used with students in preschool through grade six. The
books featured in its catalogue are created by teachers for
teachers and parents to supplement all areas of the curriculum, and all have been successfully used in classrooms
before being submitted for publication.
Website: www.teachercreated.com

Freelance Potential

Published 20+ titles in 2005.

- **Nonfiction:** Publishes workbooks and activity books, pre-
  K–grade 6. Topics include art, geography, history, social
  studies, science, mathematics, reading, phonics, spelling,
  writing, language arts, and technology. Also publishes teacher
  resource materials on student testing, gifted education, multiple intelligences, reading plans, assessment techniques, classroom management, and professional development.
- **Representative Titles:** *Newspaper Reporters* (grades 3–6)
  includes hands-on activities that help students learn the basics
  of reporting, writing headlines, interviewing, and proofreading;
  also serves as a resource for setting up a school newspaper.
  Stock Market Simulations (grades 6–8) introduces students to
  the history, terminology, and structure of the stock market
  and allows them to make imaginary investments in real stocks.

Submissions and Payment

Guidelines available. Query with table of contents and 10–
12 manuscript pages. Accepts photocopies. SASE. Responds
in 3 months. Publication in 3–12 months. Flat fee.

Editor's Comments

For students in preschool through grade six, we're currently
looking for submissions in the curriculum areas of science,
reading, and writing.

Teaching & Learning Company

P.O. Box 10
1204 Buchanan Street
Carthage, IL 62321

Vice President of Production: Jill Day

Publisher's Interests
Targeting teachers and parents, this publisher offers creative and motivational educational materials to teach science, math, social studies, language arts, and arts and crafts to children in preschool through middle school. It also includes classroom decorations and resources for teachers.
Website: www.TeachingLearning.com

Freelance Potential
Published 35–40 titles in 2005: 20 were developed from unsolicited submissions and 1 was by an agented author. Receives 350 unsolicited mss yearly.

- **Nonfiction:** Publishes educational teacher resource materials for pre-K–grade 8. Topics include language arts, social studies, current events, biography, mathematics, computers, science, nature, the environment, animals, pets, holidays, arts and crafts, hobbies, multicultural and ethnic issues, and responsibility. It also offers materials for gifted and special education classrooms.
- **Representative Titles:** *Aesop's Opposites* (grades 1–3) offers stories that concentrate on one pair of opposites and includes instructions for interaction by the class as a whole. *Two Sides to Every Story* (grades 5–9) offers unusual stories carefully chosen to provide interesting examples of human behavior, as well as questions to help students analyze what they read.

Submissions and Payment
Guidelines available. Send complete ms. Accepts photocopies and computer printouts. SASE. Responds in 6–9 months. Publication in 1–3 years. Payment policy varies.

Editor's Comments
We are looking for new and exciting resources for teachers, as well as materials covering math, science, arts and crafts, and preschool. Keep in mind that we publish ideas that motivate children to actively participate in the learning process.

TEACH Services, Inc.

254 Donovan Road
Brushton, NY 12916

Editor: Wayne Reid

Publisher's Interests
TEACH Services publishes and distributes Christian books, study guides, and resource materials for Seventh-day Adventists. 20% self-, subsidy, co-venture, or co-op published material.
Website: www.teachservices.com

Freelance Potential
Published 50 titles (37 juvenile) in 2005: 14 were developed from unsolicited submissions, 1 was by an agented author, and 35 were reprint/licensed properties. Of the 50 titles, 10 were by unpublished writers and 26 were by authors who were new to the publishing house. Receives 150 queries each year.

- **Nonfiction:** Published 6 easy-to-read books, 4–7 years; 2 chapter books, 5–10 years; 25 middle-grade titles, 8–12 years; and 4 young adult books, 12–18 years. Topics include Christian living, Bible study, church doctrine and history, prayer, youth and children's ministry, and spiritual growth. Also publishes adult titles and ministerial resources.
- **Representative Titles:** *Children's Bible Lessons* by Bessie White contains a series of illustrated children's Bible lessons for use in children's evangelism programs. *Studies in Christian Education* by Edward A. Sutherland, M.D. discusses the history of educational reform as it relates to the Seventh-day Adventist church.

Submissions and Payment
Guidelines and catalogue available at website or with 9x12 SASE ($2 postage). Query. Accepts photocopies, IBM disk submissions, and simultaneous submissions if identified. SASE. Responds in 1 week. Publication in 6 months. Royalty; advance.

Editor's Comments
We are interested in nonfiction Christian materials for children ages ten to thirteen.

Texas Tech University Press

P.O. Box 41037
Lubbock, TX 79409-1037

Editor-in-Chief: Judith Keeling

Publisher's Interests

Enlightening and entertaining books for children and adults on topics related to the American West including books on history and natural history, travel, and the Southwest are produced by this publisher.
Website: www.ttup.ttu.edu

Freelance Potential

Published 25 titles (8 juvenile) in 2005: 15 were developed from unsolicited submissions. Of the 25 titles, 7 were by unpublished writers and 16 were by authors who were new to the publishing house. Receives 300 queries yearly.

- **Fiction:** Publishes middle-grade books, 8–12 years. Genres include historical and contemporary fiction, mystery, and suspense. Also publishes poetry and stories about the environment.
- **Nonfiction:** Publishes middle-grade books, 8–12 years. Topics include the natural sciences, history, natural history, and the American West. Also publishes biographies and memoirs.
- **Representative Titles:** *The Roadrunner* by Wyman Meinzer provides a personal account of years the author spent observing the daily routine of several roadrunner families. *Butterflies of West Texas Parks and Preserves* by Roland H. Wauer describes and illustrates butterflies found in the region including details on each species and facts about its habits.

Submissions and Payment

Guidelines available at website. Query with clips. Accepts photocopies. SASE. Responds in 1–2 months. Publication in 1 year. Royalty; 10%.

Editor's Comments

We look for material that is well written and focused on specific subjects as well as carefully researched and substantiated. Writing must not become too deeply entrenched in theory and analysis or jargon. Regional novels with national appeal continue to be of interest to us.

Third World Press

P.O. Box 19730
7822 South Dobson
Chicago, IL 60619

Editorial Director

Publisher's Interests
This publishing company offers high-quality fiction, nonfiction, and poetry that focuses on African American issues and themes. Several children's books are among the titles published each year by Third World Press.
Website: www.thirdworldpressinc.com

Freelance Potential
Published 16 titles in 2005: Of the 16 titles, several were by authors who were new to the publishing house. Receives 200 queries, 400 unsolicited mss yearly.

- **Fiction:** Publishes concept, toddler, and early picture books, 0–4 years; easy-to-read books, 4–7 years; story picture books, 4–10 years; chapter books, 5–10 years; middle-grade novels, 8–12 years; and young adult novels, 12–18 years. Features stories and novels about African, African American, and Caribbean life, and the Diaspora.
- **Nonfiction:** Publishes easy-to-read books, 4–7 years; story picture books, 4–10 years; chapter books, 5–10 years; middle-grade books, 8–12 years; and young adult books, 12–18 years. Topics include history, culture, and multicultural and ethnic issues.
- **Representative Titles:** *I Look at Me* by Mari Evans is a beginning reader that introduces children to African-centered concepts. *The Tiger Who Wore White Gloves* by Gwendolyn Brooks teaches young children tolerance and self-definition.

Submissions and Payment
Guidelines available. Prefers query with synopsis. Accepts complete ms in July only. Accepts photocopies, computer printouts, and simultaneous submissions if identified. SASE. Response time varies. Publication in 1 year. Royalty.

Editor's Comments
Our goal is to reach a broader readership, especially the very young, to help them gain insight into African American culture.

Charles C. Thomas, Publisher

2600 South First Street
Springfield, IL 62704

Editor: Michael P. Thomas

Publisher's Interests

This publisher serves the needs of of professionals in the biological, social, and behavioral sciences, and in the areas of education, special education, and rehabilitation. The titles from Charles C. Thomas are frequently used as texts in preschool through high school classrooms, and many are considered classics in their fields.
Website: www.ccthomas.com

Freelance Potential

Published 800+ titles in 2005: 600 were developed from unsolicited submissions. Receives 600 queries and unsolicited mss yearly.

- **Nonfiction:** Publishes titles for educators, pre-K–grade 12. Topics include early childhood, elementary, secondary, and higher education; reading research and statistics; physical education and sports; special education; the learning disabled; teaching the blind and visually impaired; gifted and talented education; and speech and language pathology. Also offers parenting titles.
- **Representative Titles:** *A Self-Regulated Learning Approach for Children with Learning/Behavior Disorders* by Joan A. Benevento describes an approach that helps children with these disorders participate in a fuller integration of their information processing skills. *Music Therapy in Principle and Practice* by Donald E. Michel & Joseph Pinson approaches therapy from the position of assessing developmental skills.

Submissions and Payment

Guidelines and catalogue available at website. Query or send ms. Accepts disk submissions. SASE. Responds in 1 week. Publication in 6–8 months. Royalty.

Editor's Comments

Our goal is to publish significant titles, and authors with the appropriate education and experience are welcome to submit.

Thompson Educational Publishing

Suite 200
6 Ripley Avenue
Toronto, Ontario M6S 3N9
Canada

Submissions Editor: Keith Thompson

Publisher's Interests
Textbooks and supplementary materials for the social sciences and humanities for use in colleges and universities are included in the catalogue of this educational publisher. Its audience includes both Canadian and U.S. students.
Website: www.thompsonbooks.com

Freelance Potential
Published 7 titles in 2005: 1 was developed from an unsolicited submission. Of the 7 titles, 1 was by an unpublished writer. Receives 20 queries yearly.

- **Nonfiction:** Publishes undergraduate textbooks and single-author monographs for use in undergraduate education. Topics include social studies, sociology, social work, economics, communications, native studies, labor studies, and sports.
- **Representative Titles:** *Canadian Politics: An Introduction* by Tom Chambers is a comprehensive text that covers the parliamentary system, the ideals of parties, electoral procedures, and domestic and foreign policy. *Child-Rearing, Personality Development & Deviant Behavior* by Huub Angenent & Anton De Man offers an introduction to parental child-rearing practices and their influence on children's personality formation and behavior.

Submissions and Payment
Writers' guidelines available. Query with curriculum vitae and market analysis. Accepts email submissions to publisher@thompsonbooks.com. SAE/IRC. Response time, publication period, and payment policy vary.

Editor's Comments
When submitting your proposal, please supply the information asked for in our guidelines. This will give us an idea as to how you see the proposed textbook fitting into courses at the college and university level. The more information you can provide about your project, the better.

Tilbury House Publishers

2 Mechanic Street
Gardiner, ME 04345

Children's Submissions: Audrey Maynard

Publisher's Interests
Each year, this regional publisher includes a small number of children's picture books on its list. Aimed at readers ages seven through twelve, the books include enough learning content to generate interest from the educational market.
Website: www.tilburyhouse.com

Freelance Potential
Published 7 titles (4 juvenile) in 2005: 6 were developed from unsolicited submissions. Of the 7 titles, 2 were by unpublished writers and 6 were by authors who were new to the publishing house. Receives 300 queries, 300 mss yearly.

- **Fiction:** Published 2 story picture books, 4–10 years. Genres include multicultural and ethnic fiction, and stories about nature and the environment. Also publishes story picture books, 7–10 years.
- **Nonfiction:** Published 2 story picture books, 4–10 years. Also publishes middle-grade books, 8–12 years. Topics include cultural diversity, ethnic issues, nature, the environment, history, and social studies.
- **Representative Titles:** *Thanks to the Animals* by Allen Sockabasin (pre-K–grade 2) is the story of a baby who is protected by the animals of the forest. *The Carpet Boy's Gift* by Pegi Deitz Shea (grades 3–6) tackles the issue of child labor.

Submissions and Payment
Guidelines available. Prefers query with outline/synopsis and sample chapters. Accepts complete ms or partial ms with outline. Accepts photocopies and computer printouts. SASE. Responds in 1 month. Publication in 1 year. Royalty; advance, negotiable.

Editor's Comments
We're interested in books that offer the potential to be accompanied by teacher's guides. Written by educators, these guides expand the focus of our books and include learning activities.

Megan Tingley Books

Little, Brown and Company
1271 Avenue of the Americas
New York, NY 10020

Editor-in-Chief: Megan Tingley

Publisher's Interests

This imprint offers children's literature of many genres and on a variety of topics. Its list ranges from board books for infants to novels and nonfiction for teens.
Website: www.lb-kids.com

Freelance Potential

Published 150 titles in 2005: all were by agented authors and 12 were reprint/licensed properties. Of the 150 titles, 1 was by an unpublished writer and 1 was by an author who was new to the publishing house. Receives 2,000 unsolicited mss yearly.

- **Fiction:** Publishes concept books, toddler books, and early picture books, 0–4 years; story picture books, 4–10 years; chapter books, 5–10 years; middle-grade books, 8–12 years; and young adult books, 12–18 years. Genres include contemporary and multicultural fiction, adventure, humor, mystery, suspense, and chick lit. Also publishes poetry.
- **Nonfiction:** Publishes concept books, toddler books, and early picture books, 0–4 years; story picture books, 4–10 years; chapter books, 5–10 years; middle-grade books, 8–12 years; and young adult books, 12–18 years. Topics include family and social issues, nature, the environment, and crafts.
- **Representative Titles:** *The Family Book* by Todd Parr (3–6 years) celebrates the many different kinds of families. *The Code* by Mawi Asgedom (YA) explains five secrets of teen success.

Submissions and Payment

Accepts submissions through literary agents only. Send complete ms with author qualifications and publishing credits. Response time and publication period vary. Royalty, 5–10%.

Editor's Comments

We're now considering agented submissions of picture books and middle-grade and young adult novels. Material must have high literary merit on subjects currently relevant.

Torah Aura Productions

4423 Fruitland Avenue
Los Angeles, CA 90058

Submissions Editor: Jane Golub

Publisher's Interests

Torah Aura is a religious publisher that is devoted to producing high-quality, educational material for students and teachers. It offers textbooks for students and educational guides for teachers in Jewish schools.
Website: www.torahaura.com

Freelance Potential

Published 10 titles in 2005. Receives 60 queries each year.

- **Nonfiction:** Publishes story picture books, 4–10 years; chapter books, 5–10 years; middle-grade books, 8–12 years; and young adult books, 12–18 years. Topics include religious values, the Bible, Hebrew topics, prayer, history, and God.
- **Representative Titles:** *Because Nothing Looks Like God* by Lawrence and Karen Kushner (4–10 years) introduces children to the concept of a spiritual life through real-life examples of happiness and sadness. *Being Your Best* by Barbara A. Lewis (7–10 years) is a character building guide for kids and teens. *Bully Free Classroom* (teachers) by Allan L. Beane, Ph.D promotes tolerance by offering strategies to stop bullying in the classroom; it includes reproducible handouts.

Submissions and Payment

Guidelines available. Query. No unsolicited mss. Accepts photocopies. SASE. Responds in 6 months. Publication in 18 months. Royalty; 10%.

Editor's Comments

Please note that we only accept material that meets our philosophical understanding that textbooks should bring students as close to the true meaning of the text as possible. We do not publish fiction, or children's chapter or picture books, but instead focus on textbooks for grades K through adult. Material that provides reproducible handouts and/or teaching aids are sought.

Tor Books

175 5th Avenue
New York, NY 10010

Senior Editor: Children/Young Adults: Susan Chang

Publisher's Interests

This award-winning publisher produces a diverse line of science fiction and fantasy for readers of all ages, as well as nonfiction books on science and crafts.
Website: www.tor.com

Freelance Potential

Published 25 titles in 2005: 3 were developed from unsolicited submissions, 22 were by agented authors, and 10 were reprint/licensed properties. Of the 25 titles, 2 were by unpublished writers and 3 were by authors who were new to the publishing house. Receives 1,200 queries yearly.

- **Fiction:** Publishes middle-grade books, 8–12 years; and young adult books, 12–18 years. Genres include fantasy and science fiction.
- **Nonfiction:** Publishes middle-grade books, 8–12 years; and young adult books, 12–18 years. Features general interest and how-to titles, as well as books about science and crafts.
- **Representative Titles:** *Dragon Soup* by Arlene Williams (YA) teaches children about conflict resolution and cooperation through the story of a young girl and her encounter with a dragon. *Bless Your Heart* by Holly Bea (3–5 years) reminds readers that all of life is a blessing and a gift from the Creator.

Submissions and Payment

Guidelines available at website. Query with synopsis and first 3 chapters. Accepts photocopies, computer printouts, and email submissions to torquery@panix.com. SASE. Responds in 4–6 months. Publication in 18–24 months. Royalty; advance.

Editor's Comments

We continue to seek fantasy and science fiction for middle grade and young adults. Send us an idea for something fresh and unique that will spark our readers' imaginations, and provide them with an adventure they will remember.

Toy Box Productions

Division of CRT, Custom Products, Inc.
7532 Hickory Hills Court
Whites Creek, TN 37189

President: Cheryl J. Hutchinson

Publisher's Interests
Established in 1995, Toy Box Productions, a division of CRT Custom Products, Inc., creates read-along and audio-interactive storybooks for children up to the age of twelve. It produces fiction and nonfiction on religious, educational, and historical subjects.
Website: www.crttoybox.com

Freelance Potential
Published 4 titles in 2005: all were by agented authors.

- **Fiction:** Publishes story picture books, 4–10 years; chapter books, 5–10 years; and middle-grade books, 8–12 years. Genres include Western, historical, and religious fiction.
- **Nonfiction:** Publishes story picture books, 4–10 years; and chapter books, 5–10 years. Topics include history and religion.
- **Representative Titles:** *The Tuskegee Airmen: Raiders of the Skies* by Joe Loesch teaches children about these heroic African American pilots of the 99th Pursuit Squadron; part of the Time Traveler Adventures series. *Lions, Lions Everywhere: The Story of Daniel* by Joe Loesch describes the amazing Bible adventures of Daniel, who was captured in his youth by the Babylonians and was able to interpret dreams; part of the Bible Stories for Kids series.

Submissions and Payment
Query with résumé and clips. All work is done on assignment. Accepts photocopies. SASE. Response time, publication period, and payment policy vary.

Editor's Comments
We assign writers to work on our specialized materials. Our books offer great resources for children to strengthen their reading skills, memorization, and timing coordination. We feature the Time Traveler Adventures series and Bible Stories for Kids. It is best for writers to view the titles in these series to gain a better understanding of what we publish.

Tricycle Press

P.O. Box 7123
Berkeley, CA 94707

Project Editor: Abigail Samoun

Publisher's Interests
A division of Ten Speed Press, Tricycle's catalogue includes titles dealing with history, diversity, tolerance, math, nature, and multicultural themes. Its books feature fiction and nonfiction for preschool through middle-grade readers.
Website: www.tenspeed.com

Freelance Potential
Published 24 titles in 2005: 5 were developed from unsolicited submissions and 10 were by agented authors. Of the 24 titles, 5 were by unpublished writers and 8 were by authors who were new to the publishing house. Receives 20,000 unsolicited mss yearly.

- **Fiction:** Publishes concept books and toddler books, 0–4 years; story picture books, 4–10 years; and middle-grade books, 8–12 years. Topics include humor, nature, tolerance, and contemporary issues.
- **Nonfiction:** Publishes story picture books, 4–10 years; and middle-grade books, 8–12 years; and board books. Topics include gardening, cooking, mathematics, and real-life issues.
- **Representative Titles:** *My Secret Bully* by Trudy Ludwig (5–8 years) describes how one girl deals with a bully disguised as her friend. *Pet's Revenge* by Charles Ogden (9+ years) concerns the strange behavior of the twins' cyclopic companion; part of the Edgar & Ellen series.

Submissions and Payment
Guidelines and catalogue available with 9x12 SASE ($1.11 postage). Send complete ms for picture books; 2–3 sample chapters for longer mss. Accepts photocopies, computer printouts, and simultaneous submissions. SASE. Responds in 2–6 months. Publication period varies. Royalty; advance.

Editor's Comments
We are currently seeking historical picture books. For novels and real-life books, include table of contents or outline.

Turtle Books

Suite 525
866 United Nations Plaza
New York, NY 10017

Publisher: John Whitman

Publisher's Interests
An independent publisher specializing in children's picture books in English and Spanish editions, Turtle Books produces a small, select list of titles for children ages two through ten.
Website: www.turtlebooks.com

Freelance Potential
Published 4 titles in 2005: 1 was developed from an unsolicited submission and 1 was from an agented author. Receives 1,000+ unsolicited mss yearly.

- **Fiction:** Published 4 story picture books, 4–10 years. Also publishes early picture books, 0–4 years. Genres include stories with multicultural and ethnic themes; Westerns; folklore; and regional, historical, and contemporary fiction.
- **Representative Titles:** *Alphabet Fiesta* by Anne Miranda is an English/Spanish alphabet book using English and Spanish words that start with the same letter. *Prairie Dog Pioneers* by Jo & Josephine Harper relates the timeless story of a young girl in 1870's Texas who doesn't want to move from her family's home.

Submissions and Payment
Guidelines and catalogue available at website. Send complete ms. Accepts photocopies and computer printouts. SASE. Response time varies. Publication in 1 year. Royalty; advance.

Editor's Comments
We only publish children's picture books and our age range is two through ten. We want to see a good story, one that children can relate to, and one that lends itself to publication in both English and Spanish. Please don't send us concept books or series titles for we do not publish these. We prefer to see the complete manuscript so it isn't necessary to query us.

Turtle Press

91 Holmes Road
Newington, CT 06111

Editor: Cynthia Kim

Publisher's Interests

A leader in the martial arts field, Turtle Press publishes books that combine tradition with innovation. Its strives to bring readers the best in martial arts educational material and to celebrate the diversity of the martial arts heritage. **Website:** www.turtlepress.com

Freelance Potential

Published 6 titles (1 juvenile) in 2005: 4 were developed from unsolicited submissions. Of the 6 titles, 1 was by an unpublished writer and 1 was by an author who was new to the publishing house. Receives 400–500 queries yearly.

- **Fiction:** Published 1 middle-grade novel, 8–12 years. Also publishes chapter books, 5–10 years. Features stories about the martial arts, including adventure stories.
- **Nonfiction:** Publishes chapter books, 5–10 years. Topics include martial arts, self-improvement, fitness, health, sports, and Eastern philosophy. Also publishes books for adults.
- **Representative Titles:** *A Part of the Ribbon* by Ruth Hunter & Debra Fritsch (9+ years) is an action adventure story that traces the history of the martial arts in Korea. *A Bundle of Sticks* by Pat Mauser McCord (9+ years) is the story of a timid boy who finally finds the strength to overcome his fears and stand up to the schoolyard bully.

Submissions and Payment

Guidelines available. Query. SASE. Responds in 2–3 weeks. Publication period and payment policy vary.

Editor's Comments

We're open to submissions in the areas of martial arts, Eastern philosophy, and self-improvement. Your query should demonstrate that your work will be tightly focused, and your subject thoroughly covered. Please tell us about your qualifications, and then, if we feel your idea and your background are right for us, we'll invite you to submit a full proposal.

Twenty-First Century Books

2 Old New Milford Road
Brookfield, CT 06804

Editorial Director: Jean Reynolds

Publisher's Interests

Supplementary, curriculum-oriented nonfiction series and stand-alone books for young adult readers and libraries are offered by this division of Lerner Publishing Group. It has resumed its publishing program after a year of temporary suspension.
Website: www.millbrookpress.com

Freelance Potential

Published 1+ titles in 2005. Receives 100 queries yearly.

- **Nonfiction:** Publishes middle-grade titles, 8–12 years; and young adult books, 12–18 years. Topics include science, technology, health, medicine, history, social studies, contemporary issues, language arts, government, politics, and sports. Also publishes biographies and multicultural titles.
- **Representative Titles:** *Gettysburg* (grades 5–8) combines clear narrative, detailed battle maps, and an abundance of primary-source material to bring this major American battle to life; part of the Battlefields Across America series. *Earth's Fiery Fury* (grades 5–8) looks at Earth from a scientist's point of view; includes information on volcanos and earthquakes; part of the *Exploring Planet Earth* series.

Submissions and Payment

Query with outline, sample chapter, and publishing history. Accepts simultaneous submissions if identified. SASE. Responds in 2 months. Publication in 1–2 years. Royalty; advance.

Editor's Comments

Now that we are considering queries for manuscripts again, we are interested in titles that have strong ties to fifth- through twelfth-grade curriculums. We are once again accepting material from non-agented writers, as well as those with literary agents. All material should be suitable for students, not parents or teachers.

Tyndale House Publishers

351 Executive Drive
Carol Stream, IL 60188

Manuscript Review Committee

Publisher's Interests
This publisher's children division, Tyndale Kids, offers books that present the truth of Scripture in a simple and easy to understand language. It strives to minister to children in the form of Bibles, Bible storybooks, and devotionals.
Website: www.tyndale.com

Freelance Potential
Published 300 titles (45 juvenile) in 2005: 1 was developed from an unsolicited submission and 44+ were by agented authors. Receives 500 queries yearly.

- **Fiction:** Publishes middle-grade novels, 8–12 years; and young adult books, 12–18 years. Features fiction on general interest topics written from a Christian perspective.
- **Nonfiction:** Publishes concept books and toddler books, 0–4 years; easy-to-read titles, 4–7 years; story picture books, 4–10 years; middle-grade books, 8–12 years; and young adult books, 12–18 years. Features books about Christian faith. Also publishes parenting titles.
- **Representative Titles:** *Haunted Waters* by Jerry B. Jenkins & Chris Fabry (YA) follows the adventures of twin tweens as they search for truth without stopping; part of the Timberline Twins series. *Along for the Ride* explores themes such as dishonesty, consequences of sin, heroes, worship, fear, trusting in God, and pride; part of the Adventures in Odyssey series.

Submissions and Payment
Guidelines and catalogue available at website. Accepts work from agented authors, Tyndale authors, and authors introduced through other publishes only. Accepts email submissions to manuscripts@tyndale.com. SASE. Responds in 3 months. Publication period varies. Royalty; advance. Flat fee.

Editor's Comments
We look for authors that uphold moral standards, but do not preach. Make sure your writing is age appropriate.

Upstart Books

P.O. Box 800
Fort Atkinson, WI 53538-0800

Publications Director: Matt Mulder

Publisher's Interests

Teachers and librarians find materials for developing their students' library and Internet research skills in the catalogue from Upstart Books. This publisher also offers a small number of educational titles for children.
Website: www.highsmith.com

Freelance Potential

Published 15 titles in 2005: all were developed from unsolicited submissions. Of the 15 titles, 5 were by unpublished writers and 5 were by authors who were new to the publishing house. Receives 150 queries, 150 unsolicited mss yearly.

- **Fiction:** Publishes story picture books, 4–10 years; and chapter books, 5–10 years. Features stories that teach library skills.
- **Nonfiction:** Publishes elementary and middle-grade books, 6–12 years. Also publishes educational resource materials for teachers and librarians, pre-K–grade 12. Topics include library skills, storytime, reading activities, and literature.
- **Representative Titles:** *The Shelf Elf* by Jackie Mims Hopkins (pre-K–grade 2) is the story of an elf who goes to work in a library and discovers the age-old practices of proper library behavior and book care. *The Mysteries of Internet Research* by Sharron Cohen (grades 4–12) offers crimes for young research detectives to solve.

Submissions and Payment

Prefers query with outline or sample chapters for manuscripts longer than 100 pages. Prefers complete ms for shorter works. Accepts photocopies and computer printouts. SASE. Responds in 2 months. Publication period varies. Royalty, 10–12%; advance.

Editor's Comments

For our children's list, we're interested in submissions of educational picture books and chapter books. Stories that teach library skills in a fictional format are acceptable.

URJ Press

633 Third Avenue
New York, NY 10017

Editor-in-Chief: Rabbi Hara Person

Publisher's Interests
Educational materials on Jewish topics are available from
URJ Press. Its children's list consists of picture books for
preschool children, chapter books for intermediate readers,
and nonfiction titles for young adults.
Website: www.urjpress.com

Freelance Potential
Published 25 titles (10 juvenile) in 2005: 2 were developed
from unsolicited submissions. Receives 200 queries, 600
unsolicited mss yearly.

- **Fiction:** Publishes early picture books, 0–4 years; and story
  picture books, 4–10 years. Genres include religious and historical fiction. Also publishes stories based on Judaism and
  the Bible.
- **Nonfiction:** Publishes toddler books and early picture books,
  0–4 years; chapter books, 5–10 years; and young adult books,
  12–18 years. Topics include Jewish history and holidays, the
  Holocaust, and Hebrew.
- **Representative Titles:** *The Alef-Bet of Blessing* by Paul M.
  Yedwab is an illustrated Hebrew primer that guides beginners
  through the Hebrew alphabet. *Drugs, Sex, and Integrity: What
  Does Judaism Say?* by Daniel F. Polish et al. (YA–adult) helps
  readers who are encountering Jewish law for the first time deal
  with issues such as alcoholism, sex, and Jewish religious values.

Submissions and Payment
Guidelines available. Query with résumé, outline, and 2 sample
chapters. Send complete ms for picture books. Accepts
photocopies, computer printouts, and email queries to
editor@urjpress.com. SASE. Response time and publication
period vary. Royalty; advance.

Editor's Comments
Our books are intended primarily for Reform Jewish readers.
Textbooks for Jewish religious classes are a continuing need.

UXL

27500 Drake Road
Farmington Hills, MI 48331-3535

Editorial Coordinator: Julia Furtaw

Publisher's Interests
Offered in both print and electronic format, this imprint of
Gale Group offers reference materials to be used in schools,
libraries, and on the Internet. Targeting middle school and
high school students, it covers topics such as science, history,
social studies, literature, sports, the arts, and careers.
Website: www.gale.com

Freelance Potential
Published 50 titles (all juvenile) in 2005.

- **Nonfiction:** Publishes young adult books, 12–18 years. Topics
  include science, medicine, history, social studies, current
  events, multicultural issues, the arts, sports, and careers. Also
  publishes curriculum-based reference titles, encyclopedias,
  and biographies.
- **Representative Titles:** *Activists, Rebels and Reformers* by
  Phillis Engelbert is a three-volume set that examines the lives
  of prominent movers and shakers as well as lesser-known agi-
  tators, from all times and places. *Alternative Energy* is a three-
  volume set that introduces researchers to issues surrounding
  both current energy sources and alternative energy options.

Submissions and Payment
Catalogue available on website. Query with résumé and writing samples. Accepts photocopies, computer printouts, and
simultaneous submissions if identified. SASE. Response time
and publication period vary. Flat fee.

Editor's Comments
Our publishing company is best known for the accuracy,
breadth and convenience of its data, addressing all types of
information needs. We look for writers that are educational
experts that can provide materials to meet the needs of students. We're open to all areas of curriculum topics. Send us
a query first, and if we have a project that matches your
experience, we will contact you.

VanderWyk & Burnham

P.O. Box 2789
Acton, MA 01720

Publisher: Meredith Rutter

Publisher's Interests

Books that promote learning, compassion, and self-reliance, and those that make a difference in people's lives are the core of this small nonfiction publisher. Its major topics include aging and social concerns. 5% self-, subsidy-, co-venture, or co-op published.
Website: www.VandB.com

Freelance Potential

Published 3 titles in 2005: 1 was developed from an unsolicited submission and 1 was by an agented author. Of the 3 titles, 1 was by an unpublished writer and 2 were by authors who were new to the publishing house. Receives 48–120 queries, 15 unsolicited mss yearly.

- **Nonfiction:** Publishes books that provide insight into living life to the fullest and overcoming difficulties. Topics include health and fitness, self-help, social issues, aging, women's studies, and mental and emotional health. Also publishes biographies.
- **Representative Titles:** *Something's Not Right* by Nancy Lelewer (parents) is a compelling story about one mother's determination to get her family a good education despite their learning disabilities. *For the Love of Teaching* by Ira D. Shull (teachers) presents interviews with teachers across the nation on why they are so committed to their profession.

Submissions and Payment

Catalogue available at website. Query with clips and résumé. Accepts photocopies, computer printouts, and simultaneous submissions if identified. SASE. Response time varies. Publication in 1–2 years. Royalty; advance, to $2,000.

Editor's Comments

Our needs are for books that promote learning, compassion, and self-reliance. We do not publish books for children but are interested in books for parents and educators.

Viking Children's Books

Penguin Young Readers Group
345 Hudson Street
New York, NY 10014

Executive Editor: Tracy Gates
Senior Editor: Jill Davis

Publisher's Interests

Award-winning fiction and nonfiction for children of all ages can be found in the catalogue of this publisher.
Website: www.penguingroup.com

Freelance Potential

Published 60 titles (40 juvenile) in 2005: 2 were developed from unsolicited submissions and 58 were by agented authors. Of the 60 titles, 5 were by unpublished writers and 10 were by authors who are new to the publishing house. Receives 500 queries, 3,000 unsolicited mss yearly.

- **Fiction:** Published 5 early picture books, 0–4 years; 3 easy-to-read books, 4–7 years; 15 story picture books, 4–10 years; 10 chapter books, 5–10 years; 7 middle grade books, 8–12 years; and 5 young adult books, 12–18 years. Genres include adventure; mystery; contemporary, mainstream, multicultural, and science fiction.
- **Nonfiction:** Published 4 middle-grade books, 8–12 years; and 6 young adult books, 12–18 years. Topics include animals, history, biographies, geography, sports, and science.
- **Representative Titles:** *Silly Chicken* by Rukhsana Khan (4+ years) offers an original take on sibling rivalry that is hilarious and poignant at the same time. *Caught in the Act* by Peter Moore (12+ years) is a dark and funny novel about the drana of high school.

Submissions and Payment

Submit complete ms for picture books to Tracy Gates, Executive Editor. For longer works, submit outline with 3 sample chapters. Query with outline and 1 sample chapter for nonfiction to Senior Editor, Jill Davis. SASE. Responds in 6 months. Publication period varies. Royalty, 2–10%; advance, negotiable. Flat fee.

Editor's Comments

We look for top-notch material that children will love to read.

J. Weston Walch, Publisher

P.O. Box 658
40 Walch Drive
Portland, ME 04104-0658

Editor-in-Chief: Susan Blair

Publisher's Interests

Devoted to remaining a fresh and innovative publisher of educational products for teachers and students, this family-owned corporation offers high-quality materials for grades 6 through adult. Its list includes classroom activities, workbooks, and teacher books on various topics.
Website: www.walch.com

Freelance Potential

Published 130+ titles (20 juvenile) in 2005: 13 were developed from unsolicited submissions. Of the 130 titles, 33 were by unpublished writers and 33 were by authors who were new to the publishing house. Receives 200 queries each year.

- **Nonfiction:** Publishes middle-grade books, 8–12 years. Also publishes young adult books, 12–18 years. Topics include reading, writing, vocabulary, grammar, geometry, algebra, critical thinking, world history, social science, chemistry, physics, money management, careers, and special education. Also offers resource materials for teachers and guidance counselors.
- **Representative Titles:** *Art Lessons for the Middle School: A DBAE Curriculum* (grades 6–8) combines art production, history, criticism and aesthetics for middle school classes. *Short Lessons in Art History* (grades 6–adult) enriches the study of art history with art-making projects.

Submissions and Payment

Guidelines available. Query with résumé, outline, table of contents, and sample chapter. Accepts photocopies and simultaneous submissions if identified. SASE. Responds in 2–4 months. Publication period varies. Royalty. Flat fee.

Editor's Comments

We look for material that meets the educational needs of an ever-evolving market and are interested in teaching tools that can be easily implemented in classrooms.

Walker & Company

104 Fifth Avenue
New York, NY 10011

Submissions Editor

Publisher's Interests

The children's titles from this publisher include fiction and nonfiction for toddlers to teens. Among its offerings are middle-grade and young adult novels and well-paced picture books for preschool and early-elementary age readers.
Website: www.walkeryoungreaders.com

Freelance Potential

Published 26 titles in 2005. Receives 8,000 queries, 6 unsolicited mss yearly.

- **Fiction:** Publishes toddler books and early picture books, 0–4 years; easy-to-read books, 4–7 years; story picture books, 4–10 years; middle-grade books, 8–12 years; and young adult books, 12–18 years. Genres include historical and contemporary fiction.
- **Nonfiction:** Publishes story picture books, 4–10 years. Topics include nature, history, biography, and social issues.
- **Representative Titles:** *All's Fair in Love, War, and High School* by Janette Rallison (YA) is a romantic comedy about a 16-year-old girl who finds that life is suddenly not going her way. *Miss Malarkey Doesn't Live in Room 10* by Judy Finchler is a picture book that looks at the misunderstandings kids have about their teachers' private lives.

Submissions and Payment

Guidelines available. Query with outline and 3–5 sample chapters. Send complete ms for picture books. Accepts photocopies, computer printouts, and simultaneous submissions if identified. SASE. Responds in 3–4 months. Publication in 18–24 months. Royalty; advance.

Editor's Comments

We're open to works from new writers and will accept submissions from authors without agents. However, we do not publish folktales, fairy tales, textbooks, myths, legends, books in series, novelties, science fiction, fantasy, or horror.

Warner Press

P.O. Box 2499
1201 East Fifth Street
Anderson, IN 46018-9988

Senior Editor: Karen Rhodes

Publisher's Interests
The goal of this publishing house is to evangelize, educate, nurture, inspire, and unite the people of God. It is committed to developing products based on Scriptural truths. A small number of books for children appear on its list.
Website: www.warnerpress.com

Freelance Potential
Published 1 title in 2005: it was developed from an unsolicited submission. Receives 50+ queries yearly.

- **Fiction:** Publishes easy-to-read books, 4–7 years; and story picture books, 4–12 years. Features religious fiction.
- **Nonfiction:** Published 1 easy-to-read book, 4–7 years. Also publishes story picture books, 4–12 years. Also publishes activity books and coloring books.
- **Representative Titles:** *The Little Boy's Lunch* is a reproducible activity book that retells the biblical story of the loaves and the fishes. *All About Jesus* (10+ years) contains 24 crossword puzzles that highlight various events in the life of Jesus.

Submissions and Payment
Guidelines available. Query. Prefers email queries to krhodes@warnerpress.org. SASE. Responds in 3–6 months. Publication in 12–18 months. Flat fee.

Editor's Comments
Our vision is to communicate the message of Jesus Christ and to produce material that reflects the Word of God. Our children's list consists primarily of coloring and activity books for readers ages 6 to 16. These should be biblically sound and written in an easy-to-read style. Acceptable topics include exploration of various aspects of the Christian life and discussions of who God is. Avoid preachiness and negative tones in your writing—strive instead to convey the love of God.

WaterBrook Press

Suite 200
12265 Oracle Boulevard
Colorado Springs, CO 80921

Senior Editor: Ron Lee

Publisher's Interests

Launched in 1996, this evangelical publisher is a division of
Random House, Inc. Its list includes books on Christian living
and spiritual growth, inspirational fiction, and resources for
Bible study.
Website: www.waterbrookpress.com

Freelance Potential

Published 70 titles (2 juvenile) in 2005: 1 was developed
from an unsolicited submission, 55 were by agented
authors, and 1 was a reprint/licensed property. Receives
1,000+ queries yearly.

- **Fiction:** Published 2 toddler books, 0–4 years. Also publishes
  easy-to-read books, 4–7 years; story picture books, 4–10
  years; and middle-grade titles, 8–12 years. Genres include
  inspirational, religious, and contemporary fiction; and fantasy.
- **Nonfiction:** Publishes young adult books, 12–18 years. Topics
  include religion, Christianity, and personal faith.
- **Representative Titles:** *God Gave Us You* by Lisa Tawn
  Bergren offers a lesson in self-esteem as children learn they
  are treasured gifts of the the Lord. *Dragonspell* by Donita K.
  Paul weaves memorable characters, daring adventure, and a
  core of eternal truth in a story of fantasy.

Submissions and Payment

Catalogue available at website. Accepts queries through literary agents only. No unsolicited mss. SASE. Responds in
6–10 weeks. Publication in 1 year. Royalty; advance. Payment policy varies.

Editor's Comments

We seek projects that will help bring readers face to face
with God, and provide a deep well of spiritual refreshment.
We want titles that intensify and satisfy the elemental thirst
for a relationship with God. We welcome queries, but only
those from literary agents.

Watson-Guptill

770 Broadway
New York, NY 10003

Senior Acquisitions Editor: Julie Mazur

Publisher's Interests
This publisher offers illustrated art and art instruction titles and reference books for all ages. Its list includes titles that provide information and inspiration to readers at all skill levels and interests.
Website: www.watsonguptill.com

Freelance Potential
Published 100 titles (15 juvenile) in 2005: 25 were by agented authors. Of the 100 titles, 50 were by new authors.

- **Fiction:** Publishes young adult books, 12–18 years. Genres include historical fiction.
- **Nonfiction:** Publishes easy-to-read books, 4–7 years; story picture books, 4–10 years; middle-grade titles, 8–12 years; and young adult books, 12–18 years. Topics include crafts, fine art, drawing, painting, sculpture, cartooning, animation, graphic design, and pop culture.
- **Representative Titles:** *The Crocodiles' True Colors* by Eve Montanari has a captivating, yet simple plot to draw children into learning about perception and art. *Kids Draw Knights, Kings, Queens & Dragons* by Christopher Hart contains lessons for drawing all of Camelot's dashing figures.

Submissions and Payment
Guidelines and catalogue available at website. Query with table of contents and sample chapters for nonfiction and YA fiction; send complete ms for picture books. All material must be accompanied by a brief author biography and list of marketing considerations. Accepts photocopies and computer printouts. SASE. Response time and publication period vary. Royalty; advance.

Editor's Comments
We look for titles that can bring art alive to children and young adults. Even our fiction titles have a connection to the world of art.

Wayne State University Press

The Leonard N. Simons Building
4809 Woodward Avenue
Detroit, MI 48201-1309

Acquisitions Assistant: Annie Martin

Publisher's Interests
Established in 1941, Wayne State University Press publishes approximately 40 nonfiction titles each year. Its books target a diverse audience of readers that includes scholars as well as the general public.
Website: http://wsupress.wayne.edu/

Freelance Potential
Published 40 titles (3–5 juvenile) in 2005: Of the 40 titles, 4–5 were by unpublished writers and 20 were by authors new to the publishing house. Receives 300 queries yearly.

- **Nonfiction:** Publishes middle-grade books, 8–12 years. Topics include the art, architecture, and culture of Michigan; the history of the Upper Peninsula and the Great Lakes region; and historical Detroit personalities. Also publishes titles on Africana, art and culture, film and television, Judaica, labor, literature, automotive history, politics, women's studies, economics, and speech pathology for adults.
- **Representative Titles:** *Gettin' Our Groove On* by Kermit E. Campbell shows the persistence of hip hop and African American vernacular in spite of increasing criticism from the American mainstream. *Mystical Bodies, Mystical Meals* by Joel Hecker examines the role of ritual performance in Jewish mysticism with a focus on the medieval kabbalah.

Submissions and Payment
Guidelines available. Query with résumé, clips, table of contents, and chapter-by-chapter outline. Accepts photocopies, computer printouts, and email queries to annie.martin@wayne.edu. SASE. Responds in 2–3 weeks. Publication in 15 months. Royalty, 7.5–10%.

Editor's Comments
For children ages 10 and up, we publish biographies of the men and women who contributed to development of the Detroit area, as well as titles on other regional subjects.

Weigl Educational Publishers Limited

6325 10th Street SE
Calgary, Alberta T2H 2Z9
Canada

Managing Editor

Publisher's Interests

A nonfiction publisher, Weigl engages the minds of young readers by producing books with strong visual appeal and well-researched, trustworthy content. Its books are created for use with students in grades one through nine and cover all curriculum areas. They are found in classrooms throughout Canada, as well as in the United States.
Website: www.weigl.com

Freelance Potential

Published several titles in 2005.

* **Nonfiction:** Publishes chapter books, 5–10 years; middle-grade books, 8–12 years; and young adult books, 12–18 years. Topics include social studies, history, science, nature, art, career guidance, and multicultural and ethnic issues.
* **Representative Titles:** *Marine Mammals* (grades 3 and up) introduces readers to various mammals of the sea by providing facts about their habitats, diets, and life cycles; part of the Animal Facts series. *Volcanoes* (grades 2 and up) explains volcanic science and offers readers a look inside a volcano; part of the Science Matters series.

Submissions and Payment

Send résumé only. No queries or unsolicited mss. Accepts photocopies, computer printouts, and email to orders@weigl.com. SAE/IRC. Responds in 6 months. Publication in 2 years. Work-for-hire fee paid on acceptance of ms.

Editor's Comments

We're committed to bringing education to life for young readers by publishing books that captivate and enrich their imaginations. Our books encourage students to shape their own questions and seek their own answers while preparing them for the challenges of life in the information age. If you'd like to be considered for a writing assignment, send us your résumé indicating your subject area of expertise.

Whitecap Books Ltd.

351 Lynn Avenue
North Vancouver, British Columbia V7J 2C4
Canada

Editorial Assistant: Helen Stortini

Publisher's Interests

Fiction and nonfiction for children and young adults are
among the titles produced by Whitecap Books. Natural history,
Canadian history, and regional subjects are prominent features of both its adult and juvenile publishing programs.
Website: www.whitecap.ca

Freelance Potential

Published 101 titles (6 juvenile) in 2005: 2 were developed
from unsolicited submissions, 3 were by agented authors, and
76 were reprint/licensed properties. Of the 101 titles, 5 were
by unpublished writers and 6 were by authors who were new
to the publishing house. Receives 1,000 queries yearly.

- **Fiction:** Published 2 easy-to-read books, 4–7 years; 2 middle-
  grade books, 8–12 years; and 4 young adult novels, 12–18
  years. Genres include contemporary fiction, adventure, and
  fantasy. Also publishes stories about wildlife and sports stories.
- **Nonfiction:** Published 2 easy-to-read books, 4–7 years; and 2
  story picture books, 4–10 years. Topics include Canadian and
  natural history, science, the environment, tradition and folklore, and regional subjects.
- **Representative Titles:** *Eleven Lazy Llamas* by Dianna Bonder
  (4–7 years) follows the farmyard antics of a group of llamas.
  Swift Horse by Sharon Siamon (YA) is a story about the obstacles a girl faces in her quest for a new horse.

Submissions and Payment

Guidelines available. Query with outline/synopsis, table of
contents, and sample chapters. Accepts photocopies, computer printouts, and simultaneous submissions if identified.
SAE/IRC. Responds in 2–3 months. Publication in 1 year.
Royalty, negotiable; advance.

Editor's Comments

Carefully review our catalogue listings and guidelines, both
posted at our website, before sending us your query.

White Mane Publishing Company

P.O. Box 708
73 West Burd Street
Shippensburg, PA 17257

Acquisitions Department

Publisher's Interests
Captivating historical-based children's fiction for middle-grade and young readers can be found in the catalogue of White Mane. This publisher's main focus is on the American Civil War, but it also includes topics about slavery and the American Revolution. 10% self-, subsidy-, or co-op published material.

Freelance Potential
Published 14 titles in 2005: all were developed from unsolicited submissions. Receives 360 queries yearly.

- **Fiction:** Publishes middle-grade books, 8–12 years; and young adult books, 12–18 years. Main focus is historical fiction on the American Civil War, but topics also include slavery and the American Revolution.
- **Nonfiction:** Publishes middle-grade books, 8–12 years; and young adult books, 12–18 years. Also historical topics.
- **Representative Titles:** *Anybody's Hero: The Battle of Old Men and Young Boys* by Phyllis Hall Haislip is based on memoirs and records. *No Girls Allowed* by Alan Kay focuses on the roles of women during the Battle of Antietam. It is the fifth book of the Young Heroes of History series.

Submissions and Payment
Guidelines available. Query. Accepts photocopies. SASE. Responds in 2–3 months. Publication in 12–18 months. Payment policy varies. Royalty.

Editor's Comments
We are interested in powerful stories that will engross children and foster their love of reading. We strive to provide children's titles that are historically accurate, and are entertaining as well as educational. We request that all book ideas are in a standard format, which includes completion of our proposal guidelines form. Request a copy of our guidelines for details.

Albert Whitman & Company

6340 Oakton Street
Morton Grove, IL 60053-2723

Editor-in-Chief: Kathleen Tucker

Publisher's Interests

Award-winning titles and highly praised books for children ages 2–12 can be found in the catalogue of this independent publisher. Its list includes middle-grade readers, picture books, and nonfiction titles.

Website: www.albertwhitman.com

Freelance Potential

Published 30 titles in 2005: 3 were developed from unsolicited submissions, 3 were by agented authors, and 2 were reprint/licensed properties. Of the 30 titles, 2 were by unpublished writers and 2 were by new authors. Receives 300 queries, 4,500 unsolicited mss yearly.

- **Fiction:** Publishes early picture books, 0–4 years; chapter books, 5–10 years; and middle-grade books, 8–12 years. Genres include historical fiction, mystery, and humor.
- **Nonfiction:** Publishes early picture books, 0–4 years. Topics include family, ethnic and multicultural issues, and social issues.
- **Representative Titles:** *Grandma Lena's Big Ol' Turnip* by Denia Lewis Hester (3–8 years) is the story of a family that pulls together to get an enormous turnip in Grandma's garden out of the ground. *The Cat Who Came for Tacos* by Diana Star Helmer (6–8 years) is a story about a stray cat that is invited to lunch and must follow the house etiquette rules.

Submissions and Payment

Guidelines available. Send complete ms for picture books. Send query and 3 sample chapters for novels and nonfiction. Indicate if package is query or ms. Accepts simultaneous submissions if identified. SASE. Responds to queries in 6 weeks, to mss in 3–4 months. Publication in 18–24 months. Royalty; advance.

Editor's Comments

We seek books that will continue to reflect the diversity, creativity, and fine quality of our publishing program.

Wiley Children's Books

John Wiley & Sons
111 River Street
Hoboken, NJ 07030

Senior Editor: Kate Bradford

Publisher's Interests

Wiley Children's Books is a division of John Wiley & Sons, a publishing house whose tradition of excellence dates back to the Jefferson Administration. Nonfiction titles for students in the middle grades and up appear on its list, all of them created with the desire to making learning fun.
Website: www.wiley.com/children

Freelance Potential

Published 15–18 titles (13–14 juvenile) in 2005: 12–14 were by agented authors and 2 were reprint/licensed properties. Receives 300 queries yearly.

- **Nonfiction:** Publishes middle-grade books, 8–12 years; and 2 young adult books, 12–18 years. Topics include history, nature, science, arts and crafts, mathematics, multicultural issues, and sports. Also publishes biographies, activity books, parenting books, and educational resources for teachers.
- **Representative Titles:** *Janice VanCleave's Help! My Science Project Is Due Tomorrow!* by Janice VanCleave presents easy experiments that can be completed overnight with materials found around the house. *African American Entrepreneurs* by Jim Haskins profiles 30 African Americans whose contributions helped shape the American dream.

Submissions and Payment

Guidelines available. Query with résumé, outline, sample chapter, artwork if applicable, and summary of primary market and competition. Accepts photocopies, computer printouts, and simultaneous submissions if identified. SASE. Responds in 1–3 months. Publication in 18 months. Royalty; advance.

Editor's Comments

Along with parenting titles, we're looking for educational resources for teachers and material for language arts, social studies, math, and science classes.

Williamson Publishing

P.O. Box 185
Charlotte, VT 05445

Editorial Director: Susan Williamson

Publisher's Interests

Learning and how-to activity books that make a difference in the lives of children between the ages of two through fourteen are offered by Williamson Publishing. Its list includes secular, educational nonfiction titles.
Website: www.williamsonbooks.com

Freelance Potential

Published 8 titles in 2005: 5 were developed from unsolicited submissions and 1 was by an agented author. Of the 8 titles, 4 were by unpublished writers and 4 were by authors who were new to the publishing house. Receives 1,000 queries each year.

- **Nonfiction:** Publishes active learning titles, pre-K and up. Topics include arts and crafts, math, science, geology, history, natural history, and multicultural subjects.
- **Representative Titles:** *The Secret Life of Math* by Ann McCallum (7–14 years) traces its roots (and routes) around the world. *Wordplay Cafe* by Michael Kline (3--7 years) combines vocabulary building with word games, codes, puzzles, and phonetics.

Submissions and Payment

Guidelines available. Query with outline, table of contents, and 2--3 sample chapters. Accepts photocopies, computer printouts, and simultaneous submissions if identified. SASE. Responds in 3--4 months. Publication in 12--24 months. Royalty; advance; flat fee.

Editor's Comments

We want to see the following topics: historical fiction, events, or biographies; science books; works on countries such as India, Japan, and others; and subjects dealing with the abolitionists. These should be written for readers eight through fourteen. Look at our website to determine if your proposal is appropriate for us.

Windward Publishing

3943 Meadowbrook Road
Minneapolis, MN 55426-4505

President: Alan E. Krysan

Publisher's Interests
This imprint of Finney Company offers books on popular natural history of interest to children and adults that are fun to read, colorful, and informative.
Website: www.finney-hobar.com

Freelance Potential
Published 10 titles (6 juvenile) in 2005: 8 were developed from unsolicited submissions, and 1 was a reprint/licensed property. Of the 10 titles, 2 were by unpublished writers and 9 were by authors who were new to the publishing house. Receives 200+ queries, 90+ unsolicited mss yearly.

- **Nonfiction:** Publishes easy-to-read books, 4–7 years; story picture books, 4–10 years; chapter books, 5–10 years; middle-grade titles, 8–12 years; and young adult books, 12–18 years. Topics include space, seashells, nature, fishing, mammals, sharks, birds, and sports.
- **Representative Titles:** *Nightlight* by Jeannine Anderson tells the tale of two little bears who discover something amazing is happening in the sky. *Space Station Science* by Marianne Dyson explains all the systems needed to keep the International Space Station up and running.

Submissions and Payment
Query with publishing credits, synopsis, table of contents, introduction, and up to 3 chapters; or send complete ms. Accepts photocopies, computer printouts, and simultaneous submissions if identified. No electronic submissions. Availability of artwork improves chance of acceptance. Accepts 8x10 or 35mm B/W or color prints or transparencies, line art, and drawings. SASE. Responds in 8–10 weeks. Publication in 6–8 months. Royalty, 10% of net.

Editor's Comments
We welcome submissions of books that combine educational details with stories about natural history and science.

Wizards of the Coast

P.O. Box 707
Renton, WA 98057-0707

Editor: Susan Morris

Publisher's Interests

Quality fantasy and science-fiction literature for young adults and adults are the focus of this popular publisher. Its list includes games and role-playing guides.
Website: www.wizards.com

Freelance Potential

Published 65–70 titles (11 juvenile) in 2005: 6 were developed from unsolicited submissions and 32 were by agented authors. Of the 65–70 titles, 16 were by unpublished writers and 19 were by authors who were new to the publishing house. Receives 500 queries yearly.

- **Fiction:** Publishes middle-grade books, 8–12 years. Genres include adventure; science fiction; and medieval, mystical, heroic, and epic fantasy.
- **Nonfiction:** Publishes role-playing games and guidebooks for young adults and adults.
- **Representative Titles:** *Elminster's Daughter* by Ed Greenwood (8+ years) tells the story of a girl who finds out her father is a powerful wizard; part of The Elminster series. *Nova Rocks!* by Tea Emesse (8+ years) is a story about a girl that follows her dreams of playing the electric guitar; part of the Star Sisterz series.

Submissions and Payment

Guidelines available at website. Query. Check website for submission periods. Accepts photocopies and simultaneous submissions if identified. SASE. Responds in 4 months. Publication in 1 year. Payment policy varies.

Editor's Comments

First-time authors are often asked to submit short story anthologies before being considered for a full-length novel. If you want to show your writing ability, write about anything. We will be evaluating your writing, not your story proposal at this stage. We will contact you if we feel your style, tone, and standards match our needs. Only send your very best.

Woodbine House

6510 Bells Mill Road
Bethesda, MD 20817

Acquisitions Editor: Nancy Gray Paul

Publisher's Interests

Informational, how-to books for parents on developmental disability issues relating to children are the primary focus of Woodbine House. It publishes parents' guides and reference books on disability-related topics.
Website: www.woodbinehouse.com

Freelance Potential

Published 8 titles in 2005: 2 were developed from unsolicited submissions. Of the 8 titles, 1 was by an unpublished writer and 2 were by authors new to the publishing house. Receives 800 queries, 500 unsolicited mss yearly.

- **Fiction:** Published 1 early picture book, 0–4 years; and 1 story picture book, 4–10 years. All stories feature children with disabilities.
- **Nonfiction:** Publishes chapter books, 5–10 years. Topics include developmental disabilities such as autism, Tourette syndrome, and epilepsy; and mental health issues.
- **Representative Titles:** *The Best Worst Brother* by Stephanie Stuve-Bodeen (4–8 years) is a realistic look at how a sibling relationship between an older sister and younger brother with Down syndrome evolves. *Meaningful Exchanges for People with Autism* by Joanne M. Cafiero, Ph.D., (parents) presents tools and techniques that make communication possible for people with autism spectrum disorders.

Submissions and Payment

Guidelines available. Query with outline, sample chapters, and résumé. Accepts complete ms for picture books only. SASE. Accepts photocopies, computer printouts, and simultaneous submissions if identified. SASE. Responds in 1–3 months. Publication in 1–2 years. Payment varies.

Editor's Comments

We're especially receptive to books written from the point-of-view of a young child with a disability or a sibling or peer.

Workman Publishing Company

708 Broadway
New York, NY 10003-9555

Submissions Editor

Publisher's Interests
Passionate about the materials they produce, this independent publisher offers books, calendars, and activity books for adults and children of all ages.
Website: www.workman.com

Freelance Potential
Published 42 titles (14 juvenile) in 2005: all were developed by agented authors. Of the 42 titles, 5 were by authors who were new to the publishing house. Receives 1,000 queries, 2,000 unsolicited mss yearly.

- **Fiction:** Publishes toddler books, 0–4 years; story picture books, 4–10 years; and board and novelty books. Features humor and books about nature.
- **Nonfiction:** Publishes concept and early picture books, 0–4 years; story picture books, 4–10 years; middle-grade books, 8–12 years; and young adult books, 12–18 years.
- **Representative Titles:** *101 African-American Read-Aloud Stories* by Susan Kantor offers diverse tales and drawings that offer the perfect activities for parents, grandparents, siblings, or babysitters to read to children; part of the Read-Aloud series. *The 60-Second Encyclopedia & Minute Glass* by Michael J. Rosen is filled with hundreds of incredible facts and statistics, as well as interactive activities.

Submissions and Payment
Guidelines available. Query with clips; or send complete ms with illustrations. Query with table of contents, outline/synopsis, sample chapters, and clips for nonfiction. Accepts photocopies and computer printouts. No email submissions. SASE. Responds in 3 months. Publication period varies. Royalty; advance.

Editor's Comments
We're still growing and evolving and are committed to publishing material with a mixture of care and innovation.

World Book

Suite 2000
233 North Michigan Avenue
Chicago, IL 60601

Managing Editor: Maureen M. Leibenfon

Publisher's Interests
This well-known leading publisher of award-winning encyclopedias and reference books features titles that keep pace
with the current discoveries, research, and technological
developments of today's world.
Website: www.worldbook.com

Freelance Potential
Published 30 titles (15 juvenile) in 2005: 2 were reprint/
licensed properties.

- **Nonfiction:** Publishes easy-to-read books, 4–7 years; middle-
  grade titles, 8–12 years; and young adult books, 12–18 years.
  Topics include social studies, cultural studies, science, nature,
  health, geography, history, and language. Also publishes Span-
  ish/bilingual encyclopedias, professional development titles
  for educators, and multimedia educational resources.
- **Representative Titles:** *My World* includes stories about the
  lives of youngsters in ancient Egypt, Rome, the Middle Ages,
  and even the Plains Indians. *Christmas in Ukraine* offers a fascinating look at old-world traditions for the winter holiday,
  including songs, recipes, and crafts.

Submissions and Payment
Catalogue available with 9x12 SASE. Query with outline or
synopsis. No unsolicited mss. Accepts simultaneous submissions if identified. SASE. Responds in 1–2 months. Publication in 18 months. Payment and policies vary.

Editor's Comments
We are committed to publishing encyclopedias and reference
books for home and schools. Designed for students, teachers,
librarians, researchers, and families, our materials are written
and produced to meet the highest quality standards in education. We continue to need multimedia material for adults,
children, and educators. We also continue to need authoritative, up-to-date, and innovative pieces.

Zephyr Press

814 North Franklin Avenue
Chicago, IL 60610

Acquisitions Editor: Jerome Pohlen

Publisher's Interests

Resources for educators are available through Zephyr Press.
Its publications help teachers better understand how their
students learn and show them how they can be more effective in the classroom. Major focuses of the publishing program include gifted education, multiple intelligences, and
brain-compatible learning.
Website: www.zephyrpress.com

Freelance Potential

Published 10 titles in 2005: 4 were developed from unsolicited submissions and 3 were reprint/licensed properties.
Receives 250 queries yearly.

- **Nonfiction:** Publishes educational titles for use in grades
  K–12. Topics include gifted education, multiple intelligences,
  brain-based learning, thinking skills, science, technology,
  history, mathematics, social studies, literacy, and character
  education.
- **Representative Titles:** *Passport to Learn* by Jacque Melin
  (teachers, grades 3–6) targets teachers of gifted children with
  activities that emphasize creativity, problem solving, inquiry,
  and critical thinking. *Rights to Responsibility* by Alanda Greene
  (teachers, grades 4–9) offers activities that help students gain
  an understanding of the relationship between rights and
  responsibilities.

Submissions and Payment

Guidelines and submissions packet available. Send completed
packet, detailed outline, and sample chapter. Accepts photocopies and computer printouts. Availability of artwork
improves chance of acceptance. SASE. Responds in 3–6
months. Publication in 1–2 years. Royalty, varies.

Editor's Comments

We're always looking for innovative approaches to teaching
all children any of the curriculum subjects.

Additional Listings

We have selected the following publishers to offer you additional marketing opportunities. Most of these publishers have special submissions requirements or they purchase a limited number of juvenile titles each year.

For published authors, we include information about houses that produce reprints of previously published works. For writers who are proficient in foreign languages, we list publishers of foreign-language material. You will also find publishers who accept résumés only; who work with agented authors; or who usually accept unsolicited submissions, but due to a backlog, are not accepting material at this time.

As you survey these listings, you may find that a small regional press is a more appropriate market for your submission than a larger publisher. Also, if you are involved in education or are a specialist in a certain field, consider sending your résumé to one of the educational publishers—you may have the qualifications they are looking for.

Publishers who usually accept unsolicited submissions but were not accepting unsolicited material at our press time are designated with an ⊗. *Be sure to contact the publisher before submitting material to determine the current submissions policy.*

As you review the listings that follow, use the Publisher's Interests section as your guide to the particular focus of each house.

A & B Publishers Group

223 Duffield Street
Brooklyn, NY 11201

Managing Editor: Wendy Gift

Publisher's Interests
Helping young readers embrace different cultures is the mission
of this children's publisher. This year it seeks young adult novels
that promote self-esteem.

Freelance Potential
Published 16 titles (6 juvenile) in 2005: 8 were developed
from unsolicited submissions, and 2 were by agented authors.
Of the16 titles,12 were by unpublished writers and 6 were by
authors who were new to the publishing house. Receives 200
queries yearly.
Submissions and Payment: Query with sample chapters and
table of contents. Accepts computer printouts, and simultaneous
submissions if identified. SASE. Responds in 2–3 months.
Publication period varies. Royalty 4–5%; advance, $500.

Abbeville Kids

Suite 500
116 West 23rd Street
New York, NY 10011

Editor: Susan Costello

Publisher's Interests
The focus of Abbeville Kids is teaching young readers about
art. It offers children under the age of twelve a selection of
quality, illustrated fiction and nonfiction. An imprint of
Abbeville Press, the company was founded in 1977.
50% self-, subsidy-, co-venture, or co-op published material.
Website: www.abbeville.com

Freelance Potential
Published 20–25 titles in 2005. Receives 120 unsolicited mss
each year.
Submissions and Payment: Send complete ms with illustrations. Prefers agented authors. Accepts photocopies and computer printouts. SASE. Responds in 5 weeks. Publication in
18–24 months. Royalty; advance. Flat fee.

Abdo Publishing Company

Suite 622
4940 Viking Drive
Edina, MN 55435

Editor-in-Chief: Paul Abdo

Publisher's Interests
This leading educational publisher has provided pre-K- through
eighth-grade readers with nonfiction titles offered in school and
public libraries since 1985. Its imprints include Sandcastle,
Buddy Books, Checkerboard, Library, and Abdo & Daughters.
Website: www.abdopub.com

Freelance Potential
Published 300 titles (all juvenile) in 2005: 23 were developed
from unsolicited submissions. Of the 300 titles, 2 were by
unpublished writers and 5 were by authors who were new to
the publishing house. Receives 120 queries yearly.
Submissions and Payment: Guidelines and catalogue available at website. Query with résumé. No unsolicited mss.
Response time varies. Publication in 1 year. Flat fee.

Abingdon Press

P.O. Box 801
201 8th Avenue South
Nashville, TN 37203

Editor: Judy Newman-St. John

Publisher's Interests
In business since the early 1920s, Abingdon Press is firmly
entrenched in religious publishing. Its list of titles for children
three to twelve includes picture books and easy-to-read stories. It also offers computer software and audio and video cassettes. 50% co-op published material.
Website: www.abingdonpress.com

Freelance Potential
Published 10 titles in 2005: 2–3 were developed from unso-
licited submissions. Receives 600 queries yearly.
Submissions and Payment: Guidelines available. Query with
outline. Accepts photocopies and email submissions. SASE.
Responds in 3 months. Publication in 2 years. Royalty; 5–10%.
Flat fee, $1,000+.

Achievement Publishing

P.O. Box 1357
New York, NY 10013-0877

Submissions: Kurt Trentman

Publisher's Interests
This educational publisher provides study guides with examples of exam questions and short cuts for the mathematics portion of the SAT college entrance exam. It looks for guides that offer what other study guides do not, and presents math test preparation in a simple and understandable manner. It favors material that is clear and user friendly.
Website: www.apluspublishing.com

Freelance Potential
Published 2 titles (all juvenile) in 2005: 2 were developed from unsolicited submissions. Receives 24 queries yearly.
Submissions and Payment: Query. Accepts photocopies and computer printouts. SASE. Response time varies. Publication period and payment rate varies.

Activity Resources Company

20655 Hathaway Avenue
Hayward, CA 94541

Editor: Mary Laycock

Publisher's Interests
To develop mathematical thinking through books, manipulatives, investigation, and games is the goal of Activity Resources Company. Created by a mathematics educator over 25 years ago, its titles are geared towards teachers working in kindergarten through grade nine.
Website: www.activityresources.com

Freelance Potential
Published 4 titles in 2005. Receives 25–30 queries yearly.
Submissions and Payment: Guidelines available. Query with résumé, sample chapters, and bibliography. Accepts photocopies, computer printouts, and simultaneous submissions if identified. SASE. Responds in 2–4 weeks. Publication in 1 year. Royalty, varies.

Alef Design Group

4423 Fruitland Avenue
Los Angeles, CA 90058

Submissions Editor: Jane Golub

Publisher's Interests
Alef Design Group, a sister company of Torah Aura
Productions, produces Jewish fiction and nonfiction material
for the trade market and educational settings. It is currently
looking for juvenile nonfiction material.
Website: www.torahaura.com

Freelance Potential
Published 1 title in 2005: it was a reprint/licensed property.
Receives 50 queries, 50 unsolicited mss yearly.
Submissions and Payment: Prefers query with sample
chapters. Accepts complete ms. Accepts photocopies and
computer printouts. SASE. Responds to queries in 1–2 weeks;
to mss in 3–6 months. Publication in 1–2 years. Royalty,
5–10%.

Aquila Communications Ltd.

2642 Diab Street
St. Laurent, Quebec H4S 1E8
Canada

President: Sami Kelada

Publisher's Interests
This publisher's focus is on French-as-a-Second-Language reading materials for grades four through college. Genres include
humor, fantasy, mystery, and adventure; most feature end-of-
book exercises and many also feature audio cassettes, supplementary exercises, and teacher's guides. All submitted
materials must be written in French.
Website: www.aquilacommunications.com

Freelance Potential
Published 12 titles in 2005. Receives 100 queries yearly.
Submissions and Payment: Guidelines available at website.
Query with synopsis. Accepts photocopies. SAE/IRC. Responds
in 1 month. Publication in 2–6 months. Royalty, 5%. Flat fee,
$50–$500+.

Association for Childhood Education International

Suite 215, 17904 Georgia Avenue
Olney, MD 20832-2277

Director, Editorial Department: Anne Bauer

Publisher's Interests
This educational publisher offers resource and reference books, videotapes, and audio cassettes that promote, support, and value the education and development of children. It seeks manuscripts that describe programs for children from infancy through early adolescence.
Website: www.acei.org

Freelance Potential
Published 3 titles in 2005. Receives 120 unsolicited mss yearly.
Submissions and Payment: Guidelines available. Send complete ms. Accepts photocopies, computer printouts, and disk submissions (ASCII or Microsoft Word 5.0). SASE. Responds in 2 weeks. Publication in 1–3 years. Provides author's copies in lieu of payment.

Avocet Press

19 Paul Court
Pearl River, NY 10965

Editor

Publisher's Interests
Avocet Press is a small, independent publisher that offers a "wide variety of titles that range from contemporary poetry to mysteries and suspense to historical fiction. It looks for unique work that offers readers a different perspective of the world."
Website: www.avocetpress.com

Freelance Potential
Published 6 titles in 2005: 2 were developed from unsolicited submissions; and 2 were by agented authors. Receives 1,440 queries and 960 unsolicited mss yearly.
Submissions and Payment: Writers' guidelines available at website. Query. SASE. Responds in 2 months. Response time and publication period vary. Royalty; advance.

Azro Press

PMB 342
1704 Llano Street B
Santa Fe, NM 87505

Publisher: Gae Eisenhardt

Publisher's Interests
This publisher offers early picture books and easy readers, all written or illustrated by residents of the Southwestern U.S.
Website: www.azropress.com

Freelance Potential
Published 5 titles in 2005: 3 were developed from unsolicited submissions and 1 was a reprint/licensed property. Of the 5 titles, 3 were by unpublished writers and all were by authors who were new to the publishing house. Receives 1,000 queries yearly.
Submissions and Payment: Guidelines available. Query with résumé. Accepts photocopies and simultaneous submissions if identified. SASE. Responds to queries in 1 week, to mss in 3–4 months. Publication in 2 years. Royalty, 5%.

Ballyhoo Bookworks, Inc.

P.O. Box 534
Shoreham, NY 11786

Executive Editor: Liam Gerrity

Publisher's Interests
Activity-based, craft, and how-to books for children ages 4 through 10 are published by Ballyhoo Bookworks, Inc. It is currently seeking nonfiction books for young readers about nature and will begin reading manuscripts in the fall of 2006.

Freelance Potential
Published 2 titles in 2005: both were reprint/licensed properties. Receives 100 queries, 200 unsolicited mss yearly.
Submissions and Payment: Guidelines available. Query with outline and 3 sample chapters for long works. Accepts photocopies, computer printouts, and simultaneous submissions if identified. SASE. Responds in 1 month. Publication in 12–18 months. Royalty; advance. Flat fee.

Bancroft Press

P.O. Box 65360
Baltimore, MD 21209

Editor: Bruce Bortz

Publisher's Interests
Bancroft Press publishes fiction and nonfiction for readers in the middle grades through high school. For the coming year it seeks interesting nonfiction, particularly biographies.
Website: www.bancroftpress.com

Freelance Potential
Published 6 titles (5 juvenile) in 2005: 1 was by an agented author. Of the 6 titles, 3 were by authors who were new to the publishing house. Receives 5,000 queries yearly.
Submissions and Payment: Guidelines and catalogue available at website. Query with 4 or 5 chapters; or send complete ms. Accepts photocopies and computer printouts. SASE. Responds in 6 months. Publication period varies. Royalty, 8%; advance.

Bantam Books for Young Readers

1745 Broadway
New York, NY 10019

Editor

Publisher's Interests
This imprint of Random House features fiction and nonfiction titles for children through young adults on subjects including contemporary fiction and mysteries. Board books and picture books are also included on its list.
Website: www.randomhouse.com/kids

Freelance Potential
Published 275–300 titles in 2005: most were by agented authors, and 90 were reprint/licensed properties. Receives 2,000 queries yearly.
Submissions and Payment: Queries accepted through agents only. No simultaneous submissions. SASE. Response time varies. Publication in 2 years. Royalty; advance.

Barron's Educational Series

250 Wireless Boulevard
Hauppauge, NY 11788

Acquisitions Editor: Wayne Barr

Publisher's Interests
Test preparation manuals and school directories are Barron's specialty. It also has a line of children's fiction and nonfiction. 50% self-, subsidy-, co-venture, or co-op published material.
Website: www.barronseduc.com

Freelance Potential
Published 400 titles (100 juvenile) in 2005. Receives 1,000 queries, 600 unsolicited mss yearly.
Submissions and Payment: Guidelines available. Send complete ms with résumé for fiction. Query with résumé, table of contents, outline/synopsis, 2 sample chapters, and description of audience for nonfiction. SASE. Responds to queries in 1–3 months, to mss in 6–8 months. Publication in 2 years. Royalty; advance. Flat fee.

Bay Light Publishing

P.O. Box 3032
Mooresville, NC 28117

Publisher: Charlotte Soutullo

Publisher's Interests
Since 1998 this Christian publisher has been dedicated to publishing books that "inspire, motivate, and educate children about the Bible." Its latest series, Thank You, targets children between the ages of four and twelve and has won numerous awards.
Website: www.baylightpub.com

Freelance Potential
Published 4 titles in 2005. Of the 4 titles, 1 was by an unpublished writer. Receives 25 queries, 30 unsolicited mss yearly.
Submissions and Payment: Query. Accepts photocopies and simulaneous submissions. SASE. Responds in 3–6 weeks. Publication in 1 year. Payment policy varies.

Baylor University Press

One Bear Place #97363
Waco, TX 76798-7363

Director: Carey C. Newman

Publisher's Interests
This publisher presents scholarly works on subjects such as sociology, Judaism, Christianity, ethics, and the arts, particularly as they relate to Texas and the Southwest. Its purpose is to advance knowledge to scholars beyond campus limits.
Website: www.baylorpress.com

Freelance Potential
Published 14 titles in 2005. Of the 14 titles, 12 were by authors who were new to the publishing house. Receives 120–180 queries yearly.
Submissions and Payment: Guidelines and catalogue available with 9x12 SASE or at website. Query. Accepts photocopies and IBM disk submissions. SASE. Responds in 1 month. Publication in 9 months. Royalty, 10%.

Alexander Graham Bell Association for the Deaf and Hard of Hearing

3417 Volta Place NW
Washington DC 20007-2778

Chief Development Officer: Corrinne Abbott

Publisher's Interests
Striving to educate parents and professionals about hearing loss and the auditory approach, this publisher offers instructional materials, brochures, books, videos, and cassettes. Its nonfiction books include titles on cochlear implants and hearing aids. It also produces inspirational biographies and fiction titles for children with hearing loss. It is looking for material that supports the use of hearing aids to promote speech.
Website: www.agbell.org

Freelance Potential
Published 6 titles in 2005. Receives 10–15 mss yearly.
Submissions and Payment: Guidelines available. Send up to 15 ms pages. Accepts computer printouts. SASE. Responds in 3 months. Publication in 9–16 months. Royalty, to 10%.

The Benefactory

P.O. Box 128
Cohasset, MA 02025

Creative Director: Richard Bly

Publisher's Interests
This publisher strives to motivate children to read and
become proactive with regards to animal welfare. It offers
books based on true stories about real animals that are
accompanied by plush toys, audiotapes, or video cassettes.
It targets children ages four through ten.
Website: www.readplay.com

Freelance Potential
No titles were published in 2005; publishing program will
resume in 2006.
Submissions and Payment: Guidelines available. Most work
is done on assignment. Query only. No unsolicited mss.
Accepts computer printouts. SASE. Responds in 6–8 weeks.
Publication in 2 years. Royalty; advance, 5%.

BePuzzled

University Games Corporation
2030 Harrison Street
San Francisco, CA 94110

General Manager: Connie Gee

Publisher's Interests
Acquired in 1999 by University Games Corporation, BePuzzled's
products, for children ages seven to nine, offer mystery stories
of 2,500 and 3,000 words paired with jigsaw puzzles that provide clues to solving the mystery. It does not accept stories containing sex, violence, drugs, profanity, or terrorism.
Website: www.areyougame.com

Freelance Potential
Published 15 titles (10 juvenile) in 2005: all were developed
from unsolicited submissions. Receives 500 queries yearly.
Submissions and Payment: Guidelines available. Query with
short mystery sample. Accepts computer printouts. SASE.
Responds in 2 weeks. Publication in 1 year. Buys world rights.
Flat fee.

Bick Publishing House

307 Neck Road
Madison, CT 06443

President: Dale Carlson

Publisher's Interests
This small publishing house offers both fiction and nonfiction, and is currently seeking material for young adults that deals with positive communication.
Website: www.bickpubhouse.com

Freelance Potential
Published 2 titles in 2005: 6 were developed from unsolicited submissions, 1 was by an agented author. Of the 2 titles, 1 was by an author who was new to the publishing house. Receives 200–300 queries yearly.
Submissions and Payment: Guidelines and catalogue available. Query with 3 chapters, outline/synopsis, table of contents, and author biography. Accepts photocopies. SASE. Responds in 2 weeks. Publication in 1 year. Royalty, 10% net; advance.

Birdsong Books

1322 Bayview Road
Middletown, DE 19709

Acquisitions Editor: Nancy Carol Willis

Publisher's Interests
This independent publisher offers natural science picture books and educational activity books about North American animals and their habitats. All of its titles promote a knowledge and understanding of nature that fosters caring and a desire to protect the Earth and all living creatures.
Website: www.birdsongbooks.com

Freelance Potential
Published 1 title in 2005.
Submissions and Payment: Guidelines available. Send complete manuscript with résumé. Accepts photocopies and computer printouts. SASE. Responds in 3 months. Publication in 3 years. Payment policy varies.

Bollix Books

1609 West Callender Avenue
Peoria, IL 61606

Submissions Editor

Publisher's Interests
A fiction only publisher, Bollix Books offers early picture
books for children up to the age of four, story picture books
for children ages four to ten, middle-grade novels, and young
adult books. Its editors look for unique titles that encourage
enthusiam in children. Contemporary, multicultural, and ethnic
fiction are also on its list.
Website: www.bollixbooks.com

Freelance Potential
Published 4 titles in 2005.
Submissions and Payment: Writers' guidelines and catalogue
available at website. Query. Accepts email to editor@
bollixbooks.com. SASE. Responds in 3 weeks. Publication
period varies. Royalty; advance.

Books of Wonder

18 West 18th Street
New York, NY 10011

President: Peter Glassman

Publisher's Interests
Books of Wonder seeks to stimulate and encourage young
imaginations by publishing stories written in the tradition of
L. Frank Baum, author of *The Wizard of Oz*. Each manuscript
submitted is carefully reviewed by the publisher's staff of children's book lovers, who also look for nonfiction that encourages a love of learning and knowledge.
Website: www.booksofwonder.com

Freelance Potential
Published 1–4 titles in 2005. Receives 15 unsolicited mss yearly.
Submissions and Payment: Guidelines available at website.
Send complete ms. Accepts photocopies and computer print-
outs. SASE. Responds in 6 months. Publication period varies.
Royalty; advance.

Breakwater Books

P.O. Box 2188
St. John's, New Foundland A1C 636
Canada

General Manager: Wade Foote

Publisher's Interests
Breakwater Books publishes resource materials and educational
books for all ages that preserve the unique culture of New
Foundland, Labrador, and the Maritime provinces.
Website: www.breakwater.nf.net

Freelance Potential
Published 12 titles (4 juvenile) in 2005: 6 were developed
from unsolicited submissions. Of the 12 titles, 1 was by an
unpublished writer and 5 were by authors who were new to
the publishing house. Receives 600+ queries yearly.
Submissions and Payment: Guidelines available at website.
Query with résumé and clips. No unsolicited mss. Artwork
improves the chance of acceptance. SAE/IRC. Responds in 8
months. Publication in 1 year. Royalty; 10%.

Caddo Gap Press

PMB 275
3145 Geary Boulevard
San Francisco, CA 94118

Publisher: Alan H. Jones

Publisher's Interests
Since 1987, Caddo Gap Press has been gearing its titles
towards teachers and teacher educators. Topics it covers
include multicultural education, curriculum, science and
museum education, international education, women in education, social foundations of education, and teacher education.
Parenting titles appear also on its list.
Website: www.caddogap.com

Freelance Potential
Published 45 titles in 2005: all were developed from unsolicited
submissions. Receives 15–20 unsolicited mss yearly.
Submissions and Payment: Query or send complete ms.
Accepts photocopies. SASE. Response time and publication
period vary. Royalty, 10%.

Calkins Creek Books

815 Church Street
Honesdale, PA 18431

Submissions Editor: Jeanna DeLuca

Publisher's Interests
Calkins Creek Books, a new imprint of Boyds Mills Press, published its first title in 2005 and plans to greatly expand its list in 2006. U.S. history is the specialty of this imprint, and it welcomes historical fiction, as well as nonfiction for readers between the ages of 8 and 14.
Website: www.boydsmillspress.com

Freelance Potential
Published 1 title in 2005: it was developed from an unsolicited submission by an unpublished writer. Receives 700 unsolicited mss yearly.
Submissions and Payment: Guidelines available. Send complete ms with detailed biography. Accepts photocopies. SASE. Response time and publication period vary. Royalty.

Carolina Wren Press

120 Morris Street
Durham, NC 27701

Manuscript Acquisitions

Publisher's Interests
With its imprint Lollipop Power Books, Carolina Wren Press publishes health and mental health topics in children's literature, as well as fiction and nonfiction for adults.
Website: www.carolinawrenpress.org

Freelance Potential
Published 1–3 titles in 2005.
Submissions and Payment: Guidelines available at website. Query with outline, synopsis, and sample chapters. Accepts photocopies, computer printouts, email queries to carolina@ carolinawrenpress.org and simultaneous submissions if identified. SASE. Responds in 3 months. Publication in 2 years. Royalty or flat fee.

Carousel Press

P.O. Box 6038
Berkeley, CA 94706-0038

Publisher: Carole T. Meyers

Publisher's Interests
Carousel Press concentrates on books that deal with traveling across the U.S. and throughout Europe. Travel guides for all ages, travel-related games and activities, and guides to family-friendly destinations and attractions are among the material it produces. Freelancers whose work fits this publisher's focus are invited to submit a query.
Website: www.carousel-press.com

Freelance Potential
Published 1 title in 2005. Receives 50 queries yearly.
Submissions and Payment: Query with table of contents and sample chapter. Accepts photocopies and computer printouts. SASE. Responds in 1 month. Publication in 1 year. Royalty; advance.

Chaosium

895 B Street #423
Hayward, CA 94541

Editor-in-Chief: Lynn Willis

Publisher's Interests
For 30 years, Chaosium has been publishing horror anthologies, adventure stories, and award-winning role-playing and card games, as well as related resource guides for both young adults and adults alike. It is not in the market for fiction submissions. This publisher is a member of the Adventure Gaming Industry.
Website: www.chaosium.com

Freelance Potential
Published 12 titles in 2005. Receives 40 queries yearly.
Submissions and Payment: Guidelines available. Query with summary and writing samples. Accepts photocopies and Macintosh disk submissions. SASE. Responds in 1–2 weeks. Publication in 1–2 years. Flat fee, $.03–$.05 per word.

Children's Story Scripts

2219 West Olive Avenue
PMB 130
Burbank, CA 91506

Editor: Deedra Bébout

Publisher's Interests
Theater-style scripts intended for use in kindergarten through eighth-grade classrooms are available from this publisher. Curriculum-based, the scripts promote learning, stimulate the imagination, and develop reading skills. Each script presents a positive story and includes activities that reinforce key concepts. The publisher is not seeking submissions this year.

Freelance Potential
Published 4 titles in 2005: all were developed from unsolicited submissions. Receives 500 unsolicited mss yearly.
Submissions and Payment: Writers' guidelines available. Accepts computer printouts and simultaneous submissions if identified. SASE. Responds in 2–4 weeks. Publication period varies. Royalty, 10–15%.

Child Welfare League of America

3rd Floor
440 1st Street NW
Washington, DC 20001

Assistant Direct of Publications: Tegan Culler

Publisher's Interests
CWLA publishes titles that reach all segments of child welfare and related fields. Its readership includes professionals in the fields of social work and child care, librarians, educators, pediatricians, and parents.
Website: www.cwla.org/pubs

Freelance Potential
Published 6 titles in 2005: Of the 5 titles, 3 were by unpublished writers and all were by authors who were new to the publishing house. Receives 500+ unsolicited mss yearly.
Submissions and Payment: Send complete ms. Accepts photocopies, computer printouts, email submissions to tculler@cwla.org, and simultaneous submissions if identified. SASE. Responds in 6–7 months. Publication in 2 years. Royalty.

Chivalry Bookshelf

3305 Mayfair Lane
Highvillage, TX 75077

Editorial Staff

Publisher's Interests
Chivalry Bookshelf produces books that go beyond the interest of specialists and capture the imagination of those interested in history and the ideals of chivalry. It publishes titles on Western martial arts, medieval arts and crafts, armour and weaponry, and philosophy for ages 14 and up.
Website: www.chivalrybookshelf.com

Freelance Potential
Published 8 titles in 2005.
Submissions and Payment: Guidelines available at website. Query with synopsis and current market analysis. Accepts photocopies and computer printouts. No electronic submissions. SASE. Responds in 1 month. Royalty; advance.

Clark City Press

P.O. Box 1358
Livingston, MT 59047

Submissions Editor

Publisher's Interests
Clark City Press strives for excellence in the writing, design, and production of the books it publishes. Its goal is to have each book bear its own clear vision and be capable of translating that vision to its readers. Some children's titles appear on this publisher's list. Clark City Press does not review unsolicited manuscripts but will consider queries that may result in a freelance assignment.
Website: www.clarkcitypress.com

Freelance Potential
Published 4–6 titles in 2005. Receives 5 queries yearly.
Submissions and Payment: All work is assigned. Query. No unsolicited mss. SASE. Responds in 2–3 weeks. Publication in 6 months. Payment policy varies.

Consortium Publishing

640 Weaver Hill Road
West Greenwich, RI 02817-2261

Chief of Publications: John M. Carlevale

Publisher's Interests
This publisher offers books to teachers and educators on
counseling, health and safety, child abuse, and early education. 5% self-, subsidy-, co-venture, or co-op published.

Freelance Potential
Published 20 titles in 2005: 2 were developed from unsolicited
submissions and 1 was by an agented author. Of the 20 titles,
2 were by unpublished writers and 1 was by an author new to
the publishing house. Receives 150 queries yearly.
Submissions and Payment: Guidelines available. Query or
send complete ms with résumé. Accepts photocopies, computer printouts, and Macintosh disk submissions (Microsoft
Word). SASE. Responds in 1–2 months. Publication in 3
months. Royalty.

Continental Press

520 East Bainbridge Street
Elizabethtown, PA 17022

Vice President, Publications: Beth Spencer

Publisher's Interests
Continental Press was established in 1937 as an educational
publisher. Providing textbooks for use in kindergarten through
high school classrooms and for adult education programs, it
welcomes manuscripts and proposals for programs that have
been used successfully in classrooms and that fit specific
educational purposes.
Website: www.continentalpress.com

Freelance Potential
Published 50 titles in 2005: 2 were by authors who were new
to the publishing house. Receives 50 unsolicited mss yearly.
Submissions and Payment: Guidelines available. Query or
send complete ms. SASE. Responds in 6 months. Publication
period and payment policy vary.

Cornerstone Press Chicago

939 West Wilson Avenue
Chicago, IL 60640

Submissions Editor

Publisher's Interests
This Christian publisher of fiction and nonfiction for adults also welcomes submissions of children's fiction.
Website: www.cornerstonepress.com

Freelance Potential
Published 1 title in 2005: it was developed from an unsolicited submission and it was by an author who was new to the publishing house. Receives 100+ proposals yearly.
Submissions and Payment: Guidelines available. Send proposal that includes author biography, synopsis, 3–5 sample chapters, description of book's audience, and estimated length. Accepts disk submissions and email to cspress@jpusa.org. SASE. Responds in 2 weeks. Publication period varies. Royalty, 10%.

Cottonwood Press

109-B Cameron Drive
Fort Collins, CO 80525

President: Cheryl Thurston

Publisher's Interests
Cottonwood Press specializes in clever, thought-provoking, and ready-to-use material for English language and language arts teachers of grades five through twelve.
Website: www.cottonwoodpress.com

Freelance Potential
Published 4 titles in 2005: 2 were developed from unsolicited submissions. Of the 4 titles, 2 were by authors who were new to the publishing house. Receives 50 queries, 60 unsolicited mss yearly.
Submissions and Payment: Guidelines available. Query with sample pages; or send complete ms. Accepts computer printouts and simultaneous submissions if identified. SASE. Responds in 1–4 weeks. Publication in 6–12 months. Royalty; 10%.

Course Crafters

3 Washington Square
Haverhill, MA 01830

Editor: Kristin Bair

Publisher's Interests
This niche publisher focuses on high-quality educational materials for students in English-as-a-Second-Language classes in kindergarten through high school. For teachers, this publisher offers student texts, supplementary materials, teacher's editions, and multimedia learning materials. It welcomes freelance submissions. Check the website for details.
Website: www.coursecrafters.com

Freelance Potential
Published 12 titles in 2005. Of the 12 titles, 3 were by authors who were new to the publishing house.
Submissions and Payment: Guidelines available. Query with clips. Accepts photocopies. SASE. Responds in 1 month. Publication in 1–2 years. Flat fee.

Creative Editions

123 South Broad Street
Mankato, MN 56001

Managing Editor: Aaron Frisch

Publisher's Interests
Each year, Creative Editions publishes a small number of high-quality, distinctive titles. These may include illustrated story books, fairy tales, folktales, poetry, and nonfiction about nature, the environment, animals, and sports. Many of its titles are intended for young children; others are more appropriate for young adults and adults.

Freelance Potential
Published 5 titles (4 juvenile) in 2005: 3 were by agented authors. Receives 50 queries yearly.
Submissions and Payment: Query with 500-word sample from manuscript. Accepts photocopies and computer printouts. No simultaneous submissions. SASE. Responds in 4–6 months. Publication in 4 years. Royalty; advance.

Creative Education

123 South Broad Street
Mankato, MN 56001

Managing Editor: Aaron Frisch

Publisher's Interests
Books for the school and library markets are available from
Creative Education. Its titles, which cover areas such as
humanities, literature, the arts, and science, correlate with the
curricula of grades one through nine and are used as supplemental classroom resources.

Freelance Potential
Published 55 titles (all juvenile) in 2005. Of the 55 titles,
3 were by authors who were new to the publishing house.
Receives 100–150 queries yearly.
Submissions and Payment: Guidelines available. Query with
manuscript sample. Accepts photocopies and computer printouts. No simultaneous submissions. SASE. Responds in 4–6
months. Publication in 4 years. Payment policy varies.

Creative Paperbacks

123 South Broad Street
Mankato, MN 56001

Managing Editor: Aaron Frisch

Publisher's Interests
Creative Paperbacks publishes fiction and nonfiction for elementary school children in kindergarten through sixth grade. Its list
features biographies, historical and contemporary fiction, fantasies, and nonfiction on educational subjects such as history,
geography, science, and technology. Creative Paperbacks seeks
books of the finest quality for its young readers.

Freelance Potential
Published 10–12 titles in 2005. Receives 1,200–1,800 queries
each year.
Submissions and Payment: Guidelines available. Query with
manuscript sample. Accepts photocopies and computer printouts.
SASE. Responds in 4–6 months. Publication in 2–4 years.
Payment policy varies.

Creative With Words Publications

P.O. Box 223226
Carmel, CA 93922

Editor & Publisher: Brigitta Geltrich

Publisher's Interests
Fiction and nonfiction to 800 words and poetry to 20 lines are included in the anthologies produced by this publisher. Works for all age groups are welcome.
Website: http://members.tripod.com/CreativeWithWords

Freelance Potential
Published 12 titles (11 juvenile) in 2005: all were developed from unsolicited submissions. Of the 12 titles, 6 were by unpublished writers. Receives 1,000 queries and mss yearly.
Submissions and Payment: Guidelines available. Query or send complete ms. Accepts photocopies and computer print-outs. SASE. Responds to queries in 1–4 weeks, to mss 1 month after anthology deadline. Publication period varies. No payment; 20–40% discount on 10+ copies purchased.

Crossquarter Publishing Group

P.O. Box 23749
Santa Fe, NM 87502

Submissions Editor: Anthony Ravenscroft

Publisher's Interests
Mysteries, science fiction, and books on metaphysical topics for young adults and adults are available from Crossquarter.
Website: www.crossquarter.com

Freelance Potential
Published 12 titles (2 juvenile) in 2005: 11 were developed from unsolicited submissions and 1 was by an agented author. Of the 12 titles, 9 were by unpublished writers and 11 were by authors who were new to the publishing house. Receives 1,500 queries each year.
Submissions and Payment: Guidelines available at website. Query. Accepts photocopies and simultaneous submissions if identified. SASE. Responds in 2–3 months. Publication in 9 months. Royalty, 5–10%.

Displays for Schools, Inc.

1825 NW 22nd Terrace
Gainesville, FL 32605

Manager: Sherry DuPree

Publisher's Interests
An educational publisher with a list of nonfiction books for
kindergarten through high school students, Displays for
Schools produces instructive materials that promote learning
for students and their teachers.
Website: www.displaysforschools.com

Freelance Potential
Published 2 titles (1 juvenile) in 2005. Of the 2 titles, 1 was
by an author who was new to the publishing house. Receives
180 queries yearly.
Submissions and Payment: Guidelines available. Query with
outline/synopsis, sample chapters, and a brief biography.
SASE. Responds in 2 months. Publication in 4–24 months.
Royalty, 10%.

Dog-Eared Publications

P.O. Box 620863
Middleton, WI 53562-0863

Publisher: Nancy Field

Publisher's Interests
Because of its desire to instill environmental awareness in young
people, Dog-Eared Publications specializes in producing nature
books for children. It has published interactive games, mysteries,
puzzles, and stories for middle-grade readers, all of which were
written to foster a love for science and nature. Few books are
scheduled for publication each year, and at this time, the publisher is not reviewing queries or manuscripts. Freelancers may
check for changes to this policy at a future date.
Website: www.dog-eared.com

Freelance Potential
Published no titles in 2005. Receives 100 queries yearly.
Submissions and Payment: Not accepting queries or unso-
licited mss at this time.

Domhan Books

Suite 514
9511 Shore Road
Brooklyn, NY 11209

Young Adult Editor

Publisher's Interests
This publisher offers a wide variety of middle-grade and young adult fiction and nonfiction, including e-books.
Website: www.domhanbooks.com

Freelance Potential
Published 50 titles (20 juvenile) in 2005: 48 were developed from unsolicited submissions and 12 were by agented authors. Of the 50 titles, 25 were by unpublished writers and 25 were by authors who were new to the publishing house. Receives 500+ queries, 1,500+ unsolicited mss yearly.
Submissions and Payment: Guidelines and catalogue at website. Query with clips. Accepts disk submission (RTF or ASCII). SASE. Responds to queries in 1–2 weeks, to mss in 4–6 weeks. Publication in 6 months. Royalty, 30–50% net.

Doral Publishing

P.O. Box 9068
Suryrise, AZ 85374

Senior Consultant: Dr. Alvin Grossman

Publisher's Interests
This publisher is known for its high-quality dog titles, which include breed specific information, training, and healthcare. It also produces a small amount of dog stories for children.
Website: www.doralpub.com

Freelance Potential
Published 5 titles in 2005: 2 were developed from unsolicited submissions and 3 were by agented authors. Of the 5 titles, 2 were by unpublished writers and 3 were by authors who were new to the publishing house. Receives 240 queries yearly.
Submissions and Payment: Guidelines available. Query with clips and artwork. Accepts photocopies and disk submissions. SASE. Responds in 3 weeks. Publication in 18 months. Royalty; 10% of net.

Dundurn Press

Suite 200, 8 Market Street
Toronto, Ontario M5E 1M6
Canada

Acquisitions Editor

Publisher's Interests
This publisher strives to offer quality Canadian books in a
wide variety of genres. Its list includes popular nonfiction on
history and music, literary fiction, and young adult titles. It
does not accept romance or experimental fiction.
Website: www.dundurn.com

Freelance Potential
Published several titles in 2005.
Submissions and Payment: Guidelines available at website.
Prefers query with résumé, sample chapters, and a 1-page synopsis. Accepts complete manuscripts with résumé and at least
3 sample chapters. No email submissions. Accepts photocopies and computer printouts. SAE/IRC. Responds in 1–2
months. Publication in 1 year. Royalty; 10%.

Earthkids Publishing

1974 Palo Alto Avenue
Lady Lake, FL 32159

Submissions

Publisher's Interests
This publisher offers "down-to-earth books for parents, kids,
and teachers" including easy-to-read and story picture books,
as well as educational materials for pre-K through sixth grade
students. It publishes fun and interesting materials to prompt
children to love learning and develop their curiosity.
Website: www.earthkidspublishing.com

Freelance Potential
Published 3 titles (1 juvenile) in 2005.
Submissions and Payment: Guidelines available. Query.
Accepts computer printouts. SASE. Response time varies.
Publication period varies. Payment policy varies.

Eastgate Systems

134 Main Street
Watertown, MA 02472

Acquisitions Editor: Elin Sjursen

Publisher's Interests
The world of literature beyond the confines of paper is the
goal of this online publishing house. Its interactive material
includes online pictures, sound, and video.
Website: www.eastgate.com

Freelance Potential
Published 10 titles (5 juvenile) in 2005: all were developed
from unsolicited submissions. Receives 25 unsolicited
mss yearly.
Submissions and Payment: Guidelines available at website.
Send complete ms. Accepts disk submissions, CD-ROMs,
email submissions to elins@eastgate.com, and simultaneous
submissions if identified. SASE. Responds in 4–6 weeks.
Publication in 1 year. Royalty, 15%; advance.

Ebooksonthe.net

Write Words, Inc.
2934 Old Route 50
Cambridge, MD 21613

Publisher: Arline Chase

Publisher's Interests
This electronic publisher is currently phasing out of its children's
list. Books for young adults, however, continue to be of interest,
especially mysteries, romance novels, and how-to titles.
Website: www.ebooksonthe.net

Freelance Potential
Published 30 titles in 2005: 3 were developed from unsolicited
submissions, 3 were by agented authors, and 5 were
reprint/licensed properties. Of the 30 titles, 2 were by unpublished writers and 5 were by authors who were new to the
publishing house. Receives 25–30 queries, 30 unsolicited mss
each year.
Submissions and Payment: Guidelines available. Currently
not reviewing submissions; check website for updates.

Encounter Books

Suite 330
665 3rd Street
San Francisco, CA 94107-1951

Acquisitions Editor

Publisher's Interests
Books that make a difference in the world is the focus of this nonfiction publisher. It produces titles for young adults and adults on public policy, politics, religion, history, and education. Submissions are accepted through literary agents only.
Website: www.encounterbooks.com

Freelance Potential
Published 20–25 titles in 2005: 16 were by agented authors, and 1 was a reprint/licensed property. Receives 300–500 unsolicited mss yearly.
Submissions and Payment: Guidelines available. Accepts manuscripts through literary agents only. No email submissions. SASE. Response time and publication period vary. Advance: one-third at signing, one-third when received, one-third at publication.

Excelsior Cee Publishing

P.O. Box 5861
Norman, OK 73070

Publisher: J. C. Marshall

Publisher's Interests
Publishing nonfiction exclusively, Excelsior Cee Publishing offers biographies, inspirational books, humor, writing texts, self-help books, poetry, and titles on family history and personal philosophy for young adults and adults.
Website: www.excelsiorcee.com

Freelance Potential
Published 6–8 titles in 2005: 6 were developed from unsolicited submissions. Receives 1,500+ queries yearly.
Submissions and Payment: Query with synopsis; include sample chapter for longer works. Accepts photocopies, computer printouts and simultaneous submissions if identified. SASE. Responds in 6 weeks. Publication in 6 months. Payment policy varies.

Exclamation! Publishers

P.O. Box 664
Phoenixville, PA 19460

President & Publisher: Denise E. Heap

Publisher's Interests
This publisher is interested in world historical fiction and non-fiction for adults and children that is thoroughly researched.
Website: www.deheap.com

Freelance Potential
Published 5 titles (2 juvenile) in 2005: 2 were developed from unsolicited submissions. Of the 5 titles, 1 was by an unpublished writer and 2 were by authors who were new to the publishing house. Receives 250 queries yearly.
Submissions and Payment: Writers' guidelines available at website. Query with author biography or résumé. No unsolicited mss. Accepts email queries to dheap@deheap.com (no attachments). Responds in 4–6 weeks. Publication period varies. Royalty, 15%.

Family Learning Association & ERIC/REC Press

Suite 103
853 Broadway
New York, NY 10003

Director: Carl B. Smith

Publisher's Interests
This publisher provides parents and educators with resource materials, reference books, and research titles with a focus on English, reading, and communication. Family Learning Association & ERIC/REC Press have temporarily suspended publication, but are still accepting queries for future projects.
Website: www.kidscanlearn.com

Freelance Potential
Publication was suspended in 2005. Receives 200 queries each year.
Submissions and Payment: Query with table of contents, sample chapter, and market analysis. Accepts photocopies and computer printouts. SASE. Responds in 1 month. Publication in 1–2 years. Royalty, 6–10%. Flat fee.

The Feminist Press

The Graduate Center
365 5th Avenue
New York, NY 10016

Publisher: Jean Casella

Publisher's Interests
Multicultural and ethnic fiction featuring strong female characters along with women's history, politics, sociology, and educational resources comprise this publisher's list. Until recently The Feminist Press published children's material, but they have since decided to cease publication of their children's line.
Website: www.feministpress.org

Freelance Potential
Published 15 titles: 2 were by agented authors, and 2 were reprint/licensed properties. Receives 800 queries yearly.
Submissions and Payment: Guidelines available at website. Query via email (200 words or less) with "submission" in subject line to jcasella@gc.cuny.edu. Responds in 3–4 months. Publication period varies. Royalty; advance.

Fiesta City Publishers

P.O. Box 5861
Santa Barbara, CA 93150-5861

President: Frank E. Cooke

Publisher's Interests
This small publisher produces a limited number of titles each year. It publishes music and songs, and also offers musical plays for middle school and high school students, nonfiction (particularly how-to books and musical instruction books), and fiction. Music or song submissions must be accompanied by a lead sheet or the complete keyboard score, as well as a cassette or CD.

Freelance Potential
Published 2 titles in 2005. Receives 80–100 queries yearly.
Submissions and Payment: Guidelines available. Query with clips or writing samples. Accepts photocopies and simultaneous submissions if identified. SASE. Responds in 1–2 months. Publication period varies. Royalty.

Fondo de Cultura Economica USA

2293 Verus Street
San Diego, CA 92154

Submissions Editor: Ignacio de Echevarria

Publisher's Interests
Targeting Latin Americans in pre-K through high school, this
publisher supplies Spanish-language fiction and nonfiction to
schools, libraries, and bookstores in the United States.
Website: www.fceusa.com

Freelance Potential
Published 5,000 titles (2,000 juvenile) in 2005: 5 were developed from unsolicited submissions and 35 were by agented
authors. Of the 5,000 titles, 10 were by authors who were
new to the publishing house. Receives 300 queries yearly.
Submissions and Payment: Query with résumé. Accepts
photocopies, computer printouts, and disk submissions.
SASE. Responds in 6 months. Publication in 6 months.
Royalty; advance. Flat fee.

Franklin Watts

Scholastic Inc.
90 Sherman Turnpike
Danbury, CT 06816

Acquisitions Editor

Publisher's Interests
Franklin Watts provides curriculum-based titles for students
in middle grades through high school. It does not publish
fiction and all titles target the school and library markets.
Website: www.scholastic.com/librarypublishing

Freelance Potential
Published 300 titles in 2005: 5 were developed from unsolicited submissions and 20 were by agented authors. Of the
300 titles, 8 were by unpublished writers and 13 were by
authors who were new to the publishing house. Receives
1,000+ queries yearly.
Submissions and Payment: Query with résumé, outline,
and sample chapters. No unsolicited mss. SASE. Responds
in 3–5 weeks. Publication period and payment policy vary.

Gefen Publishing House

600 Broadway
Lynbrook, NY 11563

Editor: Ilan Greenfield

Publisher's Interests
Children's books on Jewish culture, holidays, folklore, and Israel are published by Gefen Publishing House, which has its headquarters in Jerusalem.
Website: www.israelbooks.com

Freelance Potential
Published 20 titles (4 juvenile) in 2005: most were developed from unsolicited submissions. Of the 20 titles, most were by authors who were new to the publishing house. Receives 240 queries, 100+ unsolicited mss yearly.
Submissions and Payment: Guidelines available. Query or send complete ms. Accepts photocopies, computer printouts, and simultaneous submissions if identified. SASE. Response time, publication period, and payment policy vary.

David R. Godine, Publisher

9 Hamilton Place
Boston, MA 02108

Editorial Department

Publisher's Interests
David R. Godine is a small, independent publisher that offers fiction and nonfiction books for young readers of all ages. It is interested in picture books, chapter books, and young adult novels. Genres include history, poetry, fables, folktales, mystery, literature, humor, art, nature, travel, gardening, and fiction.
Website: www.godine.com

Freelance Potential
Published 30 titles (2 juvenile) in 2005: 10 were by agented authors, and 20 were reprint/licensed properties. Receives 1,000 queries yearly.
Submissions and Payment: Guidelines available at website. Query. No unsolicited mss. Publication period and payment policy vary.

Great Potential Press

P.O. Box 5057
Scottsdale, AZ 85261

Editor

Publisher's Interests
This publisher features books for parents, educators, and children. Its list includes biography, humor, and self-help books. It is currently seeking material on the social and emotional needs of the gifted child.
Website: www.giftedbooks.com

Freelance Potential
Published 5 titles (1 juvenile) in 2005. Receives 120 queries each year.
Submissions and Payment: Guidelines and catalogue available at website. Query with introduction, table of contents, 3 sample chapters, and market analysis. Accepts photocopies, computer printouts, or submissions through website. SASE. Responds in 2 months. Publication period varies. Royalty.

Greenwillow Books

HarperCollins Children's Books
1350 Avenue of the Americas
New York, NY 10019

Editorial Department

Publisher's Interests
An imprint of HarperCollins Children's Books, Greenwillow Books features picture books, fiction for young readers of all ages, and nonfiction for children under seven years of age. Its list includes contemporary fiction, animal stories, and nonfiction books on nature and animals.
Website: www.harperchildrens.com

Freelance Potential
Published 60 titles in 2005: 11 were developed from unsolicited submissions. Of the 60 titles, 12 were by authors who were new to the publishing house. Receives 5,500 queries, 8,000+ unsolicited mss yearly.
Submissions and Payment: Not accepting queries or unsolicited mss at this time. Check website for updates.

Group Publishing

1515 Cascade Avenue
Loveland, CO 80538

Editorial Assistant: Kerri Loesche

Publisher's Interests
This religious publisher provides life-changing resources for churches in its adult and children's titles for Christian educators. It does not publish children's fiction or picture books. At this time, Group Publishing is only accepting queries.
Website: www.group.com

Freelance Potential
Published 15 titles in 2005. Receives 500+ queries, 500+ mss each year.
Submissions and Payment: Guidelines available. Query with outline, book introduction, 2–3 chapters, and sample activites. Accepts photocopies, computer printouts, and simultaneous submissions if identified. SASE. Responds in 3–6 months. Publication period varies. Royalty, to 10%. Flat fee, varies.

Harvard Common Press

535 Albany Street
Boston, MA 02118

Editor: Valerie Cimino

Publisher's Interests
Books for parents, educators, and young adults that offer useful information and advice are published by Harvard Common Press. This year it seeks books on pregnancy and childbirth.
Website: www.harvardcommonpress.com

Freelance Potential
Published 15 titles (4 juvenile) in 2005. Receives 240 queries and 120 unsolicited mss yearly.
Submissions and Payment: Writers' guidelines and catalogue available at website. Query with résumé, outline, 1–2 sample chapters, and market analysis. Accepts photocopies, computer printouts, and simultaneous submissions if identified. SASE. Responds in 1–3 months. Publication period varies. Royalty; 5%; advance, $1,500.

Harvest House Publishers

990 Owen Loop North
Eugene, OR 97402

Manuscript Coordinator

Publisher's Interests
This Christian publishing house is dedicated to featuring
books about Christian life, education, family living, and Bible
study. Its list includes fiction and nonfiction for children and
young adults ages 0–18.
Website: www.harvesthousepublishers.com

Freelance Potential
Published 150 titles (10 juvenile) in 2005: 8 were by agented
authors, and 30 were reprint/licensed properties. Of the 150
titles, 11 were by unpublished writers and 16 were by authors
who were new to the publishing house. Receives 1,500
queries yearly.
Submissions and Payment: Query. Accepts computer printouts.
Response time, publication period, and payment policy vary.

Hensley Publishing

6116 East 32nd Street
Tulsa, OK 74135

Acquisitions Editor

Publisher's Interests
This religious publisher is devoted to offering Bible study
guides for young adults and adults. They seek guides that get
the reader directly involved in studying the Bible, and that
come from tried and true programs.
Website: www.hensleypublishing.com

Freelance Potential
Published 4 titles in 2005: 2 were developed from unsolicited
submissions. Receives 100+ queries yearly.
Submissions and Payment: Writers' guidelines available at
website. Query with first 3 chapters and chapter-by-chapter
summary. Accepts simultaneous submissions if identified.
SASE. Responds in 10–12 weeks. Publication period varies.
Royalty.

Hodder Children's Books

338 Euston Road
London NW1 3BH
United Kingdom

Editorial Assistant: Sarah Gay

Publisher's Interests
Read-alone fiction for beginning readers, story books, and novels for children ages eight and up are available from Hodder, along with informational nonfiction for children and teens.
Website: www.madaboutbooks.com

Freelance Potential
Published 500 titles in 2005: 10 were developed from unsolicited submissions, 200 were by agented authors, and 20 were reprint/licensed properties. Receives 3,000 queries, 2,000 unsolicited mss yearly.
Submissions and Payment: Guidelines available. Query with synopsis; or send complete ms. Accepts photocopies and computer printouts. SAE/IRC. Responds in 3–6 months. Publication in 12–18 months. Royalty; advance. Flat fee.

Hyperion Books for Children

14th Floor
114 5th Avenue
New York, NY 10011

Vice President of Publishing: Brenda Bowen

Publisher's Interests
Hyperion Books for Children publishes board books, picture books, chapter books, and young adult and middle-grade novels. An imprint of the Walt Disney Company, its fiction and nonfiction titles have received numerous literary awards. Due to the large number of submisions received, this publisher's policy is to only accept manuscripts from authors who work with agents. It does not accept unsolicited submissions.
Website: www.hyperionbooksforchildren.com

Freelance Potential
Published 200 titles in 2005: all were by agented authors.
Submissions and Payment: Guidelines and titles available at website. Accepts manuscripts through literary agents only.

IB Publications

P.O. Box 5123
South Murwillumbah 2484
Australia

Director: Dr. David Vickers-Shand

Publisher's Interests
This specialty publisher focuses on the teachings of Rudolf
Steiner. 25% self-, subsidy, co-venture, or co-op published
material.
Website: www.immortalbooks.com.au

Freelance Potential
Published 4 titles (3 juvenile) in 2005: 2 were developed from
unsolicited submissions, and 2 were reprint/licensed properties. Receives 8–10 queries yearly.
Submissions and Payment: Catalogue available at website.
Send complete ms. Accepts email submissions to info@
immortalbooks.com.au (Microsoft Word). Artwork improves
chance of acceptance. Responds in 3–4 weeks. Publication in
3–6 months. Payment policy varies.

Innovative Kids

18 Ann Street
Norwalk, CT 06854

Editor: Don L. Curry

Publisher's Interests
Children's books that make reading fun and educational are
the mainstay of Innovative Kids. It offers a wide variety of fiction and nonfiction material for children up to the age of 12.
Website: www.innovativekids.com

Freelance Potential
Published 30 titles in 2005: 2 were developed from unsolicited
submissions. Of the 30 titles, 5 were by unpublished writers
and 6 were by authors who were new to the publishing house.
Receives 200 queries, 200 unsolicited mss yearly.
Submissions and Payment: Guidelines available at website.
Query or send complete ms with dummies. Accepts photocopies. SASE. Mss will not be returned. Response time and
publication period vary. Flat fee.

InQ Publishing Co.

P.O. Box 10
North Aurora, IL 60542

Editor: Jana Fitting

Publisher's Interests
The mission of InQ Publishing is to publish unique books that educate in fun and interesting ways. It offers titles on health, safety, and genealogy for children, as well as a special line of materials for babysitters and day care providers. This publisher is interested in young adult nonfiction and history titles, as well as books on genealogy for young readers.
Website: www.inqbooks.com

Freelance Potential
Published 3–4 titles in 2005: Receives 30 queries each year. **Submissions and Payment:** Catalogue available at website. Query with writing samples. No unsolicited mss. Accepts photocopies. SASE. Responds in 6 weeks. Publication in 18 months. Payment policy varies. Payment policy varies.

InterVarsity Press

P.O. Box 1400
Downers Grove, IL 60515

Editor: Elaine Whittenhall

Publisher's Interests
An interdenominational publisher, InterVarsity Press features books that stress Christian values for adults and young adults.
Website: www.ivpress.com

Freelance Potential
Published 100 titles (5 juvenile) in 2005: 5 were developed from unsolicited submissions, 10 were by agented authors, and 15 were reprint/licensed properties. Of the 100 titles, 5 were by unpublished writers and 5 were by authors who were new to the publishing house. Receives 2,000 queries yearly. **Submissions and Payment:** Guidelines and catalogue available at website. Query with résumé, chapter-by-chapter summary, and 2 sample chapters. SASE. Responds in 3 months. Publication in 2 years. Payment policy varies.

Iron Crown Enterprises

112 Goodman Street
Charlottesville, VA 22902

Managing Editor

Publisher's Interests
Iron Crown Enterprises has been known for over 20 years as a producer of non-electric, table top, and role-playing games for young adults and adults alike. It also features puzzles and fantasy role-playing, and miniature and collectible card games. For detailed information on submissions, check the website.
Website: www.ironcrown.com

Freelance Potential
Published 6 titles in 2005. Receives 10–20 queries yearly.
Submissions and Payment: Guidelines available at website. Query with outline/synopsis and writing samples. Accepts computer printouts and disk submissions. SASE. Responds in 6 months. Publication in 6–12 months. Payment policy varies.

Iron Gate Publishing

P.O. Box 999
Niwot, CO 80544

Editor: Dina Carson

Publisher's Interests
This specialty publisher features directories and how-to titles for family history and genealogy research. Please note that we are not interested in self-help titles.
Website: www.irongate.com

Freelance Potential
Published 12–15 titles in 2005: all were assigned. Receives 360–600 queries yearly.
Submissions and Payment: Query with brief description, outline, target audience, and preliminary marketing plan. Accepts photocopies and computer printouts. SASE. Responds in 3 months. Publication period and payment policy varies.

January Productions

116 Washington Avenue
Hawthorne, NJ 07506

Creative Director: Barbara Peller

Publisher's Interests
Since 1973, this educational publisher has been serving
libraries and schools. It provides quality educational materials for students in kindergarten through eighth grade; with
the majority being high-interest/low-reading level students.
Topics include language arts, study skills, consumerism,
and computers.
Website: www.awpeller.com

Freelance Potential
Receives 100 queries, 50 unsolicited mss yearly.
Submissions and Payment: Catalogue available at website.
Prefers query with outline/synopsis. Accepts complete ms
with résumé. Accepts photocopies. SASE. Response time
and publication period vary. Flat fee, $325–$375.

Jump at the Sun

114 5th Avenue
New York, NY 10011

Submissions

Publisher's Interests
Celebrating the African American experience and encouraging
readers to aim high in life and "jump at the sun," this imprint
of Disney Enterprises publishes novelty books, picture books,
middle-grade novels, and historical fiction that invite children
to embrace African American culture.
Website: www.jumpatthesun.com

Freelance Potential
Published 25 titles in 2005: all were by agented authors.
Receives 240 queries yearly.
Submissions and Payment: Catalogue available at website.
Accepts queries from agents only. Accepts photocopies.
SASE. Responds in 1–3 months. Publication in 2 years.
Royalty; advance.

Kingfisher Publications

Houghton Mifflin Company
222 Berkeley Street
Boston, MA 02116

Marketing Manager: Kristen McLean

Publisher's Interests
An imprint of Houghton Mifflin Company, Kingfisher
Publications is known for its illustrated nonfiction books for
children ages two and older. It also publishes a select number
of picture books, Spanish language titles, series, and anthologies. Its list includes books about nature, science, animals,
the environment, geography, history, and holidays. All of its
titles are written on assignment.
Website: www.houghtonmifflinbooks.com

Freelance Potential
Published 80 titles in 2005: all were by agented authors.
Submissions and Payment: Catalogue available with 9x12
SASE (5 first-class stamps). All work is assigned by publisher.
Accepts agented submissions only. No unsolicited mss.

LangMarc Publishing

P.O. Box 90488
Austin, TX 78709-0488

Submissions Editor

Publisher's Interests
This publisher offers a wide range of inspirational and educational Christian nonfiction. It seeks motivational material that
offers positive solutions to everyday problems, as well
as thought-provoking scenarios with solid, Christian-based
attitudes and values. It does not publish fiction.
Website: www.langmarc.com

Freelance Potential
Published 8 titles (1 juvenile) in 2005: All were developed
from unsolicited submissions. Of the 8 titles, 5 were by
unpublished writers and 5 were by authors who were new to
the publishing house. Receives 300 queries yearly.
Submissions and Payment: Query. Response time varies.
Publication in 9 months. Payment policy varies.

Learning Links Inc.

2300 Marcus Avenue
New Hyde Park, NY 11042

Chairman: Joyce Friedland

Publisher's Interests
This publisher is a pioneer in publishing study guides for novels and picture books to help elementary and high school teachers and educators. It only works with writers who have worked on teacher's manuals and have prior experience in writing study guides.
Website: www.learninglinks.com

Freelance Potential
Published 25 titles in 2005: 6 were developed from unsolicited submissions, and 19 were assigned. Of the 25 titles, 4 were by unpublished writers and 3 were by authors who were new to the publishing house. Receives 24 queries yearly.
Submissions and Payment: Guidelines available. Query. Responds in 1 week. Publication in 3 months. Flat fee.

LifeSong Publishers

P.O. Box 183
Somis, CA 93066

Editor: Laurie Donahue

Publisher's Interests
Committed to providing materials that will aid in growth and encouragement to all ages for living a Christian life, LifeSong Publishers seeks to increase the faith of Christian followers as well as to reach out to those who have yet to accept Jesus Christ as their Savior. It is interested in Christian workbooks, manuals, and study guides for adults and children.
Website: www.lifesongpublishers.com

Freelance Potential
Published 4 titles in 2005. Receives 48 queries and 24 unsolicited mss yearly.
Submissions and Payment: Catalogue available at website. Query. SASE. Response time varies. Publication period varies. Royalty; 10% of net.

Living the Good News

Suite 400
600 Grant Street
Denver, CO 80203

Editorial Co-Director: Liz Riggleman

Publisher's Interests
In addition to religious education books, this nondenominational publisher offers titles for children and families. It is interested in seeing children's books on Christianity and Bible stories.
Website: www.livingthegoodnews.com

Freelance Potential
Published 12 titles in 2005: 2–3 were developed from unsolicited submissions. Of the 12 titles, 6 were by authors who were new to the publishing house. Receives 30 unsolicited mss yearly.
Submissions and Payment: Query with sample chapter. Accepts photocopies, computer printouts, Macintosh disk submissions, and simultaneous submissions if identified. SASE. Responds in 2 months. Publication in 2 years. Royalty.

The Love and Logic Press

2207 Jackson Street
Golden, CO 80401-2300

Publisher

Publisher's Interests
The Love and Logic products—books, audiocassettes, videotapes, and training programs—provide practical techniques that help parents and teachers achieve respectful and healthy relationships with children. The Love and Logic philosophy puts adults in control, teaches children to be responsible, and prepares them for the real world. This publisher is not accepting unsolicited queries or manuscripts. All work is assigned and mostly staff-written.
Website: www.loveandlogic.com

Freelance Potential
Published 10 titles in 2005. Receives 30 queries yearly.
Submissions and Payment: Not accepting unsolicited queries or manuscripts.

The Lutterworth Press

P.O. Box 60
Cambridge CB12 NT
United Kingdom

Managing Editor: Adrian Brink

Publisher's Interests
For more than 200 years, this British publisher has remained committed to producing high-quality books for children and adults, with a particular emphasis on moral values. It rejects many queries simply because they are not suitable in subject matter as outlined in the guidelines. Interested authors should include a detailed market analysis with each query.
Website: www.lutterworth.com

Freelance Potential
Published 10 titles in 2005.
Submissions and Payment: Guidelines available at website. Query with outline/synopsis and 1–2 sample chapters. Availability of artwork improves chance of acceptance. SAE/IRC. Responds in 2 months. Publication period varies. Royalty.

MacAdam/Cage

Suite 550
155 Sansome Street
San Francisco, CA 94104

Assistant Editor: Jason Wood

Publisher's Interests
Literary fiction and narrative nonfiction titles appear in the catalogue of this publisher. While most of its readers are adults, some of its titles appeal to young adults as well.
Website: www.macadamcage.com

Freelance Potential
Published 40 titles in 2005: 20 were developed from unsolicited submissions and 20 were by agented authors. Receives 6,000 queries yearly.
Submissions and Payment: Guidelines and catalogue available at website or with SASE. Query with synopsis, biography, and sample chapters (no more than 30 pages total). Accepts computer printouts. SASE. Responds in 4–5 months. Publication period and payment policy varies.

Mage Publishers

1032 29th Street NW
Washington, DC 20007

Submissions Editor: Amin Sepehri

Publisher's Interests
Founded in 1985, the goal of Mage Publishers is to bring the best of Persian culture to an American audience through children's tales and legends.
Website: www.mage.com

Freelance Potential
Published 3–4 titles in 2005: 1 was developed from an unsolicited submission. Of the 3–4 titles, 1 was by an author who was new to the publishing house. Receives 50 queries, 25 unsolicited mss yearly.
Submissions and Payment: Guidelines available at website. Query or send ms. Accepts photocopies and computer print outs. SASE. Responds in 1–3 months. Publication in 9–15 months. Royalty; advance.

Marlor Press

4304 Brigadoon Drive
St. Paul, MN 55126

Editorial Director: Marlin Bree

Publisher's Interests
This small publishing house produces titles about travel and boating. Its juvenile list targets readers between the ages of four and twelve and consists of travel diaries, writing journals, and activity books. Writers are asked to list the key selling points of their proposed work in their query letters, and to explain what qualifies them to write about their subject.

Freelance Potential
Published 2 titles in 2005: both were by unpublished writers. Receives 100 queries yearly.
Submissions and Payment: Query with market analysis. No unsolicited mss. Accepts photocopies and computer printouts. SASE. Response time varies. Publication in 1 year. Royalty, 8–10% of net.

Marlowe Publishing Inc.

Suite 33712
75 Tool House Road
Catskill, NY 12414

Managing Editor: Thomas Sheldon

Publisher's Interests
Marlowe Publishing provides readers with autobiographies; self-help; and how-to books for parents, educators, and children. It seeks inspirational stories, particularly about the lives of seniors.

Freelance Potential
Published 250 titles in 2005: 100 were developed from unsolicited submissions, 5 were by agented authors. Of the 250 titles, 60 were by unpublished writers and 40 were by authors who were new to the publishing house. Receives 3,500 queries and unsolicited mss yearly.
Submissions and Payment: Guidelines available with #10 SASE ($.37 postage). Query or send complete ms. Accepts photocopies and disk submissions (Word RTF). SASE. Responds in 2 weeks–2 months. Publication in 1 year. Royalty; 15%.

Miles Kelly Publishing

Bardfield Centre, Great Bardfield
Essex CM7 4SL
United Kingdom

Submissions Editor

Publisher's Interests
Miles Kelly publishes fiction and nonfiction for children between the ages of four and fourteen. It also features poetry collections, quiz books, novelty books, reference books, and activity titles. Topics covered include history, mathematics, geography, nature, the environment, science, technology, and animals. 20% co-published material.
Website: www.mileskelly.net

Freelance Potential
Published 100 titles (90 juvenile) in 2005.
Submissions and Payment: Guidelines available at website. Query with clips. SAE/IRC. Response time varies. Publication period varies. Flat fee.

Modern Publishing

155 East 55th Street
New York, NY 10022

Editorial Director: Kathy O'Hehir

Publisher's Interests
Offering high quality children's book products for 35 years, this publisher's list includes coloring and activity books, picture storybooks, puzzles, and educational workbooks.
Website: www.modernpublishing.com

Freelance Potential
Published 300 titles in 2005: 10–15 were developed from unsolicited submissions. Receives 75 queries and mss yearly.
Submissions and Payment: Guidelines available. Query with outline/synopsis; or send complete ms. Accepts photocopies and simultaneous submissions if identified. Availability of artwork improves chance of acceptance. SASE. Responds in 2 months. Publication period varies. Royalty, by arrangement. Flat fee. Work-for-hire.

Morning Glory Press

6595 San Haroldo Way
Buena Park, CA 90620-3748

President: Jeanne Lindsay

Publisher's Interests
The goal of Morning Glory Press is to provide the best possible books and resources for pregnant and parenting teens. Several of its topics include teen fathers, parenting skills, nurturing newborns, baby's first year, teen pregnancy, single parenting, discipline for children, and partner abuse. It also publishes a teen fiction series dealing with contemporary topics such as domestic violence, homosexuality, and date rape.
Website: www.morningglorypress.com

Freelance Potential
Published 3 titles in 2005. Receives 100 queries yearly.
Submissions and Payment: Query. Accepts photocopies. SASE. Responds in 1–3 months. Publication in 6–8 months. Royalty; advance, $500.

Mountain Meadow Press

P.O. Box 447
Kooskia, ID 83539

Submissions Editor

Publisher's Interests
Since 1983, Mountain Meadow Press has been publishing
books that spotlight compelling events in the history of the
Pacific Northwest. Many of its titles have been used as supplemental material in homeschooling programs. Because its
sister company sponsors road tours throughout the Pacific
Northwest, Mountain Meadow Press also publishes regional
travel books. No new titles were released in 2005, and for the
present time, the publisher is not accepting queries or unsolicited manuscripts.

Freelance Potential
Published no titles in 2005. Receives 6 queries yearly.
Submissions and Payment: Catalogue available. Not accept-
ing queries or unsolicited mss at this time.

Mount Olive College Press

634 Henderson Street
Mount Olive, NC 28365

Acquisitions Editor: Pepper Worthington

Publisher's Interests
This regional press is interested in work that relates to some
aspect of the culture, wildlife, or history of North Carolina. It is
currently looking for books on nature for middle-grade readers.

Freelance Potential
Published 2 titles (1 juvenile) in 2005: 1 was developed from
an unsolicited submission. Of the 2 titles, 1 was by an unpublished writer. Receives 500+ queries, 400 unsolicited mss
each year.
Submissions and Payment: Guidelines available. Query with
outline/synopsis and 3 sample chapters; or send complete
ms. Accepts photocopies and computer printouts. SASE.
Responds in 6–12 months. Publication in 1 year. Payment
policy varies.

National Geographic Books for Children

1145 17th Street NW
Washington DC 20036-4688

Editorial Assistant: Susan Donnelly

Publisher's Interests
Targeting readers ages four through young adult, this publisher offers educational and inspirational nonfiction titles on topics such as history, science, geography, adventure, culture, nature, animals, and exploration. It is not accepting unsolicited materials at this time.
Website: www.nationalgeographic.com/books/kids.splash

Freelance Potential
Published 25 titles in 2005: 3 were developed from unsolicited submissions, 2 were by agented authors, and 12 were assigned. Of the 25 titles, 3 were by unpublished writers and 15 were by authors who were new to the publishing house.
Submissions and Payment: Not accepting queries or unsolicited manuscripts at this time.

National Resource Center for Youth Services

College of Continuing Education, University of Oklahoma
4502 East 41st Street
Tulsa, OK 74135

Marketing Manager: Rhoda Baker

Publisher's Interests
This publisher for social service professionals and at-risk teenagers provides books that tackle sensitive issues such as self-esteem, substance abuse, depression, and sexuality.
Website: www.nrcys.ou.edu

Freelance Potential
Published 2 titles (1 juvenile) in 2005: 1 was developed from an unsolicited submission. Of the 2 titles, 1 was by an unpublished writer and 1 was by an author who was new to the publishing house. Receives 20 queries yearly.
Submissions and Payment: Guidelines available. Query with outline and 1–3 sample chapters. Accepts computer printouts and disk submissions. SASE. Responds in 1–3 months. Publication in 8–18 months. Royalty.

Natural Heritage Books

P.O. Box 95, Station O
Toronto, Ontario M4A 2M8
Canada

Editor: Jane Gibson

Publisher's Interests
Established in 1983, Natural Heritage Books publishes quality
nonfiction for middle-grade and young adult readers. Its titles
are exclusive to Canadian history, heritage, culture, and the
environment. It also publishes selected poetry.
Website: www.naturalheritagebooks.com

Freelance Potential
Published 12 titles (2 juvenile) in 2005: 1 was by an agented
author. Of the 12 titles, 5 were by authors who were new to
the publishing house. Receives 100+ queries yearly.
Submissions and Payment: Writers' guidelines available.
Query with brief synopsis and résumé to submissions@
naturalheritagebooks.com. SAE/IRC. Responds in 3–6 months.
Publication in 1–2 years. Royalty; advance.

New Canaan Publishing Company

P.O. Box 752
New Canaan, CT 06840

Editor

Publisher's Interests
This publisher offers Christian educational resources, as well
as fiction and nonfiction for children and adults. Its list
includes inspirational, theology, and Bible study titles.
Website: www.newcanaanpublishing.com

Freelance Potential
Published 3 titles (all juvenile) in 2005: 2 were by unpublished writers and 3 were by authors who were new to the
publishing house. Receives 750 queries yearly.
Submissions and Payment: Guidelines available on website.
Query with synopsis; or send complete ms. Accepts photocopies and computer printouts. SASE. Responds in 10–12
months. Publication period and policy vary. Check website for
changes in policy.

Nomad Press

2456 Christian Street
White River Junction, VT 05001

Acquisitions Editor: Lauri Berkenkamp

Publisher's Interests
An independent publisher, Nomad Press publishes children's activity books as well as books on parenting and teaching and books that relate to sports. It does not accept poetry, fiction, or cookbooks.
Website: www.nomadpress.net

Freelance Potential
Published 15 titles (6 juvenile) in 2005. Of the 15 titles, 1 was by an author who was new to the publishing house. Receives 100+ queries yearly.
Submissions and Payment: Guidelines available at website. Send complete ms, market analysis, and résumé. Accepts photocopies. SASE. Responds in 1–3 months. Publication in 6–18 months. Royalty. Flat fee.

North-South Books

Suite 1400
350 7th Avenue
New York, NY 10001

Submissions Editor

Publisher's Interests
Translating varied titles into more than 30 languages for readers from around the world, this English-language imprint of Swiss publisher Nord-Sud Verlag offers early toddler books, early picture books, easy-to-read books, and chapter books to children from birth to age 10. Genres include adventure, mystery, nature, fairy tales, folklore, fantasy, and multicultural fiction. Submissions are accepted through agented authors only.
Website: www.northsouth.com

Freelance Potential
Published 30 titles in 2005: all were by agented authors.
Submissions and Payment: Accepts submissions through literary agents only. Response time varies. Publication period varies. Royalty; advance.

Orchard Creative Group

P.O. Box 28
Port Orchard, WA 98366

Senior Editor: Ms. Cris DiMarco

Publisher's Interests
Formerly known as Little Blue Works, this publisher offers fiction in the form of early picture books, easy-to-read books, chapter books, and young adult novels.
Website: www.windstormcreative.com

Freelance Potential
Published 50 titles (48 juvenile) in 2005: 49 were developed from unsolicited submissions and 1 was by an agented author. Of the 50 titles, 20 were by unpublished writers and 40 were by new authors. Receives 10,000 queries yearly.
Submissions and Payment: Guidelines available at website. Query with 1-page synopsis. Submissions that do not indicate a website visit will be returned. SASE. Response time and publication period vary. Royalty, 10–15%.

Our Child Press

P.O. Box 4379
Philadelphia, PA 19118

President: Carol Perrott

Publisher's Interests
Our Child Press focuses solely on the subject of adoption. Books for children, teens, and adults appear on its list, all of them written to educate readers and to help them understand the emotional aspects of adoption.
Website: www.ourchildpress.com

Freelance Potential
Published 2 titles in 2005: both were developed from unsolicited submissions. Of the 2 titles, 1 was by an unpublished writer. Receives 100 queries, 95 unsolicited mss yearly.
Submissions and Payment: Guidelines available. Query with outline/synopsis; or send complete ms. Accepts photocopies and computer printouts. SASE. Responds in 1–3 months. Publication in 1 year. Royalty.

Pacific View Press

P.O. Box 2657
Berkeley, CA 94702

Acquisitions Editor: Pam Zumwalt

Publisher's Interests
Founded in 1992, Pacific View Press is best known for its multicultural nonfiction and literature that focuses on the Pacific Rim. Its children's books for ages eight to twelve are devoted to the culture and history of China, Japan, the Philippines, Mexico, and other countries on the Pacific Rim.
Website: www.pacificviewpress.com

Freelance Potential
Published 3 titles in 2005: 1 was developed from an unsolicited submission. Receives many queries yearly.
Submissions and Payment: Guidelines available. Query with outline and sample chapter. Accepts photocopies. SASE. Responds in 1 month. Publication period varies. Royalty, 8–10%; advance, $500–$1,000.

Parachute Press

Suite 302
156 5th Avenue
New York, NY 10010

Submissions Editor

Publisher's Interests
Focusing on horror fiction for middle-grade readers, Parachute Press also includes children's picture books, easy-to-read chapter books, and young adult novels in its program.
Website: www.parachutepublishing.com

Freelance Potential
Published 100 titles (80 juvenile) in 2005: 10 were developed from unsolicited submissions, and 50 were by agented authors.
Submissions and Payment: Work-for-hire guidelines available with SASE. Send résumé, and 1- to 5-page writing sample. Accepts unsolicited mss from literary agents only. No simultaneous submissions. Accepts photocopies. SASE. Response time varies. Publication in 9 months. Flat fee, $3,000–$4,000.

Paws IV Books

Suite 400
119 South Main Street
Seattle, WA 98104

Editor

Publisher's Interests
An imprint of Sasquatch Books, Paws IV Books is a regional publisher that focuses on fiction and nonfiction about the West Coast of the United States. Its list includes books for children ages four through ten about the wilderness, history, culture, and lifestyle of the region.
Website: www.sasquatchbooks.com

Freelance Potential
Published 4 titles in 2005. Of the 4 titles, 2 were by authors who were new to the publishing house. Receives 50 mss yearly.
Submissions and Payment: Send complete ms with résumé and clips. SASE. Responds in 4 months. Publication period varies. Royalty; advance.

Pearson Learning Group

135 South Mount Zion Road
P.O. Box 2500
Lebanon, IN 46052

V.P. Publisher: Celia Argiriou

Publisher's Interests
Featuring supplemental material for grades pre-K to twelve, this publisher includes bilingual products, phonics and assessment materials, and programs for special needs and ESL students. It also offers titles on math, computer technology, and literature.
Website: www.pearsonlearning.com

Freelance Potential
Published 50 titles in 2005: 1 was developed from an unsolicited submission and 1 was a reprint/licensed property. Of the 50 titles, 1 was by an unpublished writer. Receives 30 queries each year.
Submissions and Payment: Query with résumé and writing sample. SASE. Response time, publication period, and payment policy vary.

Peel Productions

P.O. Box 187
Metaline Falls, WA 99153

Editor: Susan DuBosque

Publisher's Interests
This publisher produces riddle books for beginning readers
and drawing instruction books for children ages eight and up.
At this time, Peel Productions is not reviewing freelance
queries. Writers interested in approaching this publisher are
advised to check its website for any changes to this policy.
Website: www.peelbooks.com

Freelance Potential
Published 6 titles in 2005. Of the 6 titles, 1 was by an unpublished writer and 1 was by an author who was new to the publishing house. Receives 1,500 queries yearly.
Submissions and Payment: Not accepting submissions at
this time. Check website for changes in submission policy.

Penguin Books Canada Limited

Suite 700, 90 Eglinton East
Toronto, Ontario M4P 2Y3
Canada

The Editorial Department

Publisher's Interests
Penguin Books' juvenile list includes fiction titles for middle-
grade through young adults, as well as historical nonfiction
titles. It will only consider the work of Canadian authors and
prospective authors are encouraged to look at *The Canadian
Writer's Guide* for information on the publishing process.
Website: www.penguin.ca

Freelance Potential
Published 88 titles (14 juvenile) in 2005: all were by agented
authors.
Submissions and Payment: Canadian authors only. Send com-
plete ms. Accepts submissions from literary agents only. SASE.
Responds in 1 month. Publication in 1–2 years. Royalty, 8–10%.

Perfection Learning Corporation

10520 New York Avenue
Des Moines, IA 50322

Editorial Director, Books: Sue Thies

Publisher's Interests
Curriculum materials for use in preschools through high schools
are available from this publisher, along with an extensive line
of high interest/low vocabulary books for struggling readers.
Website: www.perfectionlearning.com

Freelance Potential
Published 40 titles in 2005: 20 were developed from unso-
licited submissions and 10 were reprint/licensed properties.
Receives 500+ queries yearly.
Submissions and Payment: Guidelines available at website
or with SASE. Query with outline and 2–3 sample chapters.
Accepts photocopies, computer printouts, and simultaneous
submissions if identified. SASE. Responds in 4 months.
Publication in 1 year. Payment policy varies.

Perspectives Press, Inc.

P.O. Box 90318
Indianapolis, IN 46290-0318

Editor: Pat Johnston

Publisher's Interests
This publisher specializes in producing informative and educational books for adults on the subjects of infertility and adoption. Several of its titles are written specifically for adopted
children or the siblings of adopted children.
Website: www.perspectivespress.com

Freelance Potential
Published 2 titles (1 juvenile) in 2005. Of the 2 titles, 1 was
by an author who was new to the publishing house. Receives
300 queries yearly.
Submissions and Payment: Guidelines available at website.
Query with résumé and outline. No unsolicited mss. Accepts
photocopies and computer printouts. SASE. Responds in 1
month. Publication in 9–18 months. Royalty, 5–15%.

Piano Press

P.O. Box 85
Del Mar, CA 92014-0085

Editor: Elizabeth C. Axford

Publisher's Interests
Music-related stories, poems, essays, and children's songs for music teachers and students appear on this publisher's list.
Website: www.pianopress.com

Freelance Potential
Published 10 titles (5 juvenile) in 2005: 4 were developed from unsolicited submissions. Of the 10 titles, 5 were by unpublished writers and 5 were by authors who were new to the publishing house. Receives 150 queries, 250 mss yearly.
Submissions and Payment: Guidelines available. Query for fiction and nonfiction; send ms for poetry. Accepts photocopies, computer printouts, disk submissions (Microsoft Word), and email to pianopress@aol.com (Microsoft Word attachments). SASE. Responds in 2–4 months. Publication in 1 year. Royalty.

Pippin Press

Gracie Station, Box 1347
229 East 85th Street
New York, NY 10028

Publisher: Barbara Francis

Publisher's Interests
The titles from Pippin Press include chapter books for children ages seven to ten and novels for middle-grade readers. Historical fiction is a major interest, particularly if it features a female hero. Global autobiographical novels written as early chapter books or as middle-grade fiction are needed this year.

Freelance Potential
Published 4 titles in 2005: 2 were developed from unsolicited submissions. Of the 4 titles, 2 were by unpublished writers and 2 were by authors who were new to the publishing house. Receives 1,000 queries yearly.
Submissions and Payment: Guidelines available. Query. No unsolicited mss. SASE. Responds in 3 months. Publication in 1–2 years. Royalty; advance.

Playhouse Publishing

1566 Akron-Peninsula Road
Akron, OH 44313

Submissions Editor

Publisher's Interests
Since 1989, Playhouse Publishing has produced educational
books to inspire young minds to read. Its imprints, Picture Me
Books and Nibble Me Books, make learning and reading fun.
Currently it is not accepting unsolicited submissions.
Website: www.playhousepublishing.com

Freelance Potential
Published 20 titles in 2005: all were assigned. Of the 20 titles,
2 were by unpublished writers and 5 were by authors who
were new to the publishing house.
Submissions and Payment: Not accepting queries or unsolicited manuscripts at this time. All work is done on a work-for-
hire basis.

Polar Bear & Company

Brook Street
P.O. Box 311
Solon, ME 04979

Submissions Editor: Alex duHoux

Publisher's Interests
Children's books, novels, and philosophy that enhance cultural
diversity are produced by this publisher. It covers topics that
explore important social, environmental, and political issues.
Website: www.polarbearandco.com

Freelance Potential
Published 6 titles in 2005: all were developed from unsolicited
submissions. Of the 6 titles, 5 were by unpublished writers
and all were by authors who were new to the publishing
house. Receives 50 queries yearly.
Submissions and Payment: Guidelines available. Query for
nonfiction; include outline/synopsis and sample chapter for
fiction. Accepts photocopies and computer printouts. SASE.
Responds in 2–4 weeks. Publication in 1 year. Royalty.

Prep Publishing

1110½ Hay Street
Fayetteville, NC 28305

Submissions Editor: Frances Sweeney

Publisher's Interests
This Christian publisher features religious fiction and nonfiction titles for young adults and adults. It offers titles on Christian ethics, business, and career development, and general interest titles.
Website: www.prep-pub.com

Freelance Potential
Published 7 titles in 2005: all were developed from unsolicited submissions. Of the 7 titles, 5 were by new authors. Receives 5,000 queries, 1,000 unsolicited mss each year.
Submissions and Payment: Guidelines and catalogue available. Query with synopsis; or send complete ms with $225 reading fee. Accepts photocopies. SASE. Responds in 3 months. Publication in 18 months. Royalty, 15%.

Pruett Publishing Company

P.O. Box 2140
Boulder, CO 80306-2140

Editor: Jim Pruett

Publisher's Interests
Targeting readers in grades four through twelve, this publisher focuses on the Rocky Mountain region. This year, it seeks nonfiction titles on Western history and outdoor recreation.
Website: www.pruettpublishing.com

Freelance Potential
Published 4 titles in 2005: all were developed from unsolicited submissions. Receives 84 queries and 144 unsolicited mss each year.
Submissions and Payment: Guidelines available. Query or send complete ms. Accepts photocopies, computer printouts, and simultaneous submissions if identified. SASE. Responds to queries in 2 weeks, to mss in 1–2 months. Publication period varies. Royalty; 10–12%, to $1,000.

Prufrock Press

Suite 220
5926 Balcones Drive
Austin, TX 78731

Submissions Editor

Publisher's Interests
For more than 15 years, teachers and parents have looked to
Prufrock Press for information and resources about educating
and parenting gifted and talented children. Activity books and
lessons designed to motivate and challenge are a part of its
current list.
Website: www.prufrock.com

Freelance Potential
Published several titles in 2005.
Submissions and Payment: Guidelines available at website.
Query or send complete ms with table of contents. Accepts
CD-ROM with hard copy (Microsoft Word). SASE. Responds in
2–4 months. Publication period varies. Royalty; advance.

Publish America

P.O. Box 151
Frederick, MD 21705

Executive Editor: Miranda Prather

Publisher's Interests
Ficiton and nonfiction that deal openly with personal chal-
lenges and hardships are the specialty of this publisher.
Website: www.publishamerica.com

Freelance Potential
Published 3,000 titles (610 juvenile) in 2005: 2,000 were
developed from unsolicited submissions, and 100 were by
agented authors. Receives 17,000 queries, 3,000 unsolicited
mss yearly.
Submissions and Payment: Guidelines available. Query or
send complete ms with bio. Accepts computer printouts and
disk submissions (Microsoft Word or WordPerfect). SASE.
Responds to queries in 1–2 weeks; to mss in 1–2 months.
Publication in 10–12 months. Royalty, 8–12%; advance.

Rainbow Books

P.O. Box 430
Highland City, FL 33846-0430

Editorial Director: Betsy Lampe

Publisher's Interests
Rainbow Books is seeking submissions for dealing with pinching, kicking, and pulling hair. It does not publish picture books.
Website: www.rainbowbooksinc.com

Freelance Potential
Published 20 titles in 2005: 16 were developed from unsolicited submissions. Of the 20 titles, 10 were by unpublished writers and 20 were by authors who were new to the publishing house. Receives 200 queries, 100 unsolicited mss yearly.
Submissions and Payment: Guidelines available. Prefers complete ms with author biography. Accepts query with word count, table of contents, and author biography. Accepts photocopies and simultaneous submissions. SASE. Responds in 6 weeks. Publication in 1 year. Royalty, 6%+; advance.

Raincoast Books

9050 Shaughnessy Street
Vancouver, British Columbia V6P 6E5
Canada

Editorial Department

Publisher's Interests
The children's imprint of this publisher, Raincoast Kids, features picture books, middle-grade, and teen fiction and nonfiction. Its topics include contemporary and historical fiction as well as sports, science, and natural history.
Website: www.raincoast.com

Freelance Potential
Published 50 titles (20 juvenile) in 2005: 30 were by agented authors, and 3 were reprint/licensed properties.
Submissions and Payment: Canadian authors only. Writers' guidelines available at website. Query with outline and/or synopsis. Accepts photocopies and computer printouts. No electronic submissions. SAE/IRC. Responds in 2–4 months. Publication period varies. Royalty; advance.

Rand McNally

8255 North Central Park
Skokie, IL 60076

Editorial Director: Laurie Borman

Publisher's Interests
This well-known publisher offers activity and game books,
reference books, maps, and atlases for children and adults.
Its children's material targets readers ages 3 through 12. All
work is written on a work-for-hire basis. Interested writers are
encouraged to send a résumé for consideration.
Website: www.randmcnally.com

Freelance Potential
Published 8 titles in 2005: all were written with some freelance assistance.
Submissions and Payment: Send résumé only. All work is
done on assignment. Response time, publication period, and
payment policy vary.

Random House Children's Books

61-63 Uxbridge Road
Ealing, London W5 5SA, United Kingdom

Picture Books: Hannah Featherstone
Fiction: Naomi Wood

Publisher's Interests
The juvenile branch of well-known publisher Random House
includes The Bodley Head, Jonathon Cape, Corgi, Doubleday,
David Fickling Books, Hutchinson, and Red Fox. It publishes
children's fiction and nonfiction of the highest caliber. In addition to adventure, animal stories, mystery, and fantasy, it also
publishes joke books, activity books, and poetry for readers of
all levels.
Website: www.kidsatrandomhouse.co.uk

Freelance Potential
Published 200 titles in 2005. Receives approximately 3,000
queries yearly.
Submissions and Payment: Accepts submissions from agented
authors only. Publication in 1–2 years. Royalty; advance.

Random House Children's Publishing

1745 Broadway
New York, NY 10019

Submissions Editor

Publisher's Interests
This division of Random House produces fiction for toddlers through young adults and nonfiction in the form of chapter books for beginning readers, middle-grade titles, and young adult books. Its submissions editor will review queries submitted through literary agents only.
Website: www.randomhouse.com

Freelance Potential
Published 375 titles in 2005. Receives 5,000 queries yearly.
Submissions and Payment: Guidelines available. Accepts queries from agented authors only. Query with writing sample or partial ms. Accepts photocopies, disk submissions, and simultaneous submissions if identified. SASE. Responds in 1 month. Publication in 1 year. Royalty; advance.

Redbird Press

P.O. Box 11441
Memphis, TN 38111

Submissions Editor: Virginia McLean

Publisher's Interests
Presenting the sights, sounds, history, and culture of other countries to children from six to twelve years old, this small publisher is devoted to exposing children and adults to the wonders of the world. Although it is not currently publishing any new titles, Redbird Press plans to resume publishing sometime in 2007.

Freelance Potential
Plans to resume publishing 1 or more titles in 2007. Receives 30 queries yearly.
Submissions and Payment: Query with outline, synopsis, and clips or writing samples. Accepts photocopies, computer printouts, and simultaneous submissions if identified. SASE. Response time, publication period, and payment policy varies.

Red Rock Press

STE 114
457 Columbus Avenue
New York, NY 10024

Acquisitions Editor

Publisher's Interests
This independent publisher produces fiction and nonfiction
books for adults and children on a variety of subjects including humor, nature, fairy tales, holiday books, and craft books.
Website: www.redrockpress.com

Freelance Potential
Published 5 titles (2 juvenile) in 2005: 1 was developed from
an unsolicited submission, 2 were by agented authors, and 2
were assigned. Of the 5 titles, 2 were by unpublished writers
and 3 were by authors who were new to the publishing house.
Receives 600 queries yearly.
Submissions and Payment: Send complete ms with marketing plan. SASE. Responds in 6–10 weeks. Publication in 18–24
months. Royalty; advance. Flat fee.

Red Wheel/Weiser/Conari Press

4th Floor
368 Congress Street
Boston, MA 02210

Editorial Acquisitions: Pat Bryce

Publisher's Interests
These three imprints each publish different categories. Books
on spirituality and self-help are on Red Wheel's list. Weiser
Books is known for its magic and astrology titles; and Conari
Press produces books on women's issues and parenting.
Website: www.redwheelweiser.com

Freelance Potential
Published 100 titles in 2005: 20 were developed from unsolicited submissions, 25 were by agented authors, and 1 was a
reprint/licensed property. Receives 500 queries yearly.
Submissions and Payment: Guidelines available. Query with
outline, résumé, table of contents, and 3 sample chapters.
Accepts photocopies and simultaneous submissions if identified. SASE. Responds in 3 months. Royalty; advance.

Sandpiper Paperbacks

222 Berkeley Street
Boston, MA 02116

Editor

Publisher's Interests
Sandpiper is the reprint line of Houghton Mifflin Children's Books. All of the titles it publishes each year are paperback versions of popular hardcover books. Although in the recent past Sandpiper did consider freelance submissions of young adult fiction, as well as fiction and nonfiction for beginning readers, to publish as original paperbacks, this is no longer the case. At this time, Sandpiper publishes reprints only; its editors do not review queries or manuscripts.
Website: www.houghtonmifflinbooks.com

Freelance Potential
Published 35 titles in 2005: all were reprint/licensed properties.
Submissions and Payment: No queries or unsolicited mss are accepted.

School Zone Publishing

P.O. Box 777
1819 Industrial Drive
Grand Haven, MI 49417

Editor

Publisher's Interests
For over 20 years, School Zone Publishing has been a market leader in children's educational products for preschool through elementary grades. It produces a full line of workbooks, flashcards, software, and informational resources for parents, teachers, and children. Most materials are written by educational professionals.
Website: www.schoolzone.com

Freelance Potential
Published 5 titles in 2005: 4 were by agented authors. Receives 100 queries yearly.
Submissions and Payment: Query with résumé and writing samples. No unsolicited mss. Response time and publication period vary. Flat fee.

Servant Books

28 West Liberty Street
Cincinnati, OH 45202

Editorial Director: Lisa Biedenbach

Publisher's Interests
This Christian publisher is committed to spreading the gospel of Jesus Christ and promoting renewal and faith in the Catholic church. It publishes nonfiction for middle-grade and young adult readers, as well as adults. It does not publish poetry, drama, cartoons, short stories, or fiction.
Website: www.americancatholic.org

Freelance Potential
Published 39 titles (3 juvenile) in 2005. Receives 372 queries and 350 unsolicited mss yearly.
Submissions and Payment: Guidelines and catalogue available at website. Query with outline and synopsis. Accepts photocopies. SASE. Responds in 6–8 weeks. Publication in 1–2 years. Royalty; 10%, advance, $1,000.

Silver Dolphin Books

5880 Oberlin Drive
San Diego, CA 92121

Submissions Editor

Publisher's Interests
Activity, novelty, and educational nonfiction books for preschoolers through twelve-year-old children are the mainstay of this publishing house. Its boldly illustrated titles offer loveable characters who appeal to parents and children alike. It is an imprint of the Advantage Publishers Group.
Website: www.silverdolphinbooks.com

Freelance Potential
Published 55 titles in 2005: most were reprint/licensed properties. Receives 50+ unsolicited mss yearly.
Submissions and Payment: Writers' guidelines available. Query only. No unsolicited mss. Availability of artwork improves chance of acceptance. SASE. Responds in 1 month. Publication period and payment policy vary.

Sleeping Bear Press

Suite 300
310 North Main Street
Chelsea, MI 48118

Acquiring Editor

Publisher's Interests
This small publisher offers nonfiction, illustrated picture
books, and regional books for children up to the age of 12.
Topics include historical subjects and reading aids. It is not
currently accepting submissions.
Website: www.sleepingbearpress.com

Freelance Potential
Published 37 titles 2005: 2 were developed from unsolicited
submissions. Of the 37 titles, 14 were by unpublished writers
and 10 were by authors who were new to the publishing
house. Receives 1,500–2,000 unsolicited mss yearly.
Submissions and Payment: Guidelines available at website.
Not accepting submissions at this time. Check website for
changes to submission policy.

Smallfellow Press

Suite 320
1180 South Beverly Drive
Los Angeles, CA 90035

Manuscript Acquisitions: Claudia Sloan

Publisher's Interests
Smallfellow prides itself on an eclectic list of children's titles
that range from stories about friendship to holidays. Creative
stories with an unusual twist or wacky characters make up its
backlist. It is not currently accepting manuscripts. Previously
published material included board books for toddlers, story
picture books for children ages four to ten, young adult fiction, and humor.
Website: www.smallfellow.com

Freelance Potential
Published several titles in 2005.
Submissions and Payment: Currently not accepting submis-
sions. Check website for changes to submission policy.

Smith and Kraus Books for Kids

P.O. Box 127
Lyme, NH 03768

Publisher: Marisa Smith

Publisher's Interests
Plays, monologues, skits, acting guides, and other topics related to theater are the mainstay of Smith and Kraus Books for Kids. Its list offers plays and nonfiction material suitable for kindergarten through grade twelve. Picture books for four- to eight-year-old children, and chapter books for 10- to 14-year-old readers are also featured.
Website: www.SmithandKraus.com

Freelance Potential
Published 35 titles (11 juvenile) in 2005.
Submissions and Payment: Query with résumé for fiction. Query with outline for nonfiction. Accepts photocopies, computer printouts, and simultaneous submissions. SASE. Responds in 2 months. Publication in 1 year. Royalty; advance. Flat fee.

Soho Press

853 Broadway
New York, NY 10003

Submissions Editor: Laura Hruska

Publisher's Interests
Soho Press primarily publishes fiction, with some autobiographies and cultural historical accounts.
Website: www.sohopress.com

Freelance Potential
Published 30 titles in 2005: 2 were developed from unsolicited submissions, 6 were by agented authors, and 19 were reprint/licensed properties. Of the 30 titles, 5 were by unpublished writers and 12 were by authors who were new to the publishing house. Receives 2,400 queries yearly.
Submissions and Payment: Guidelines available. Query with first 3 chapters and outline. All mss should be 60,000+ words. Accepts complete ms. Accepts photocopies. SASE. Responds in 6 weeks. Publication in 12+ months. Royalty.

Stackpole Books

5067 Ritter Road
Mechanicsburg, PA 17055

Acquisitions Editor

Publisher's Interests
Established in 1930, Stackpole Books publishes nonfiction only. Its list includes how-to and informational books on topics such as nature, animals, crafts, hobbies, and outdoor sports.
Website: www.stackpolebooks.com

Freelance Potential
Published 70 titles in 2005: 15 were developed from unsolicited submissions, 10 were by agented authors, and 45 were assigned. Receives 360 queries yearly.
Submissions and Payment: Guidelines available. Query with clips. Accepts photocopies and simultaneous submissions if identified. Availability of artwork improves chance of acceptance. B/W prints or color transparencies. SASE. Responds in 1 month. Publication in 2 years. Royalty; advance.

Stone Arch Books

7825 Telegraph Road
Bloomington, MN 55438

Publishing Manager: Bob Temple

Publisher's Interests
This children's publisher is making its debut in 2006 with a line of 48 titles geared to the interests of 8- to 12-year-old children. It seeks high-interest fiction targeted at struggling readers in the format of chapter books and graphic novels. It also publishes humor.
Website: www.stonearchbooks.com

Freelance Potential
Publishing 48 titles (all juvenile) in 2006. Receives 120–240 queries yearly.
Submissions and Payment: Guidelines available at website. Send complete ms. Accepts photocopies and computer printouts. SASE. Response time, publication period, and payment policy vary.

Story Time Stories That Rhyme

P.O. Box 416
Denver, CO 80201

Founder: A. Doyle

Publisher's Interests
This publisher offers rhyming stories that have themes in science, math, recycling, nature, and other educational subjects. Targeting students in elementary and middle school, it provides stories that educate and entertain students, as well as assist in teaching literacy and language. It continues to seek queries on environmental topics.
Website: www.storytimestoriesthatrhyme.com

Freelance Potential
Published 3 titles in 2005. Receives 250 queries yearly.
Submissions and Payment: Writers' guidelines available. Query. No unsolicited mss. Accepts photocopies and computer printouts. SASE. Response time varies. Publication period and payment policy vary.

Success Publications

3419 Dunham Road
Warsaw, NY 14569

Submissions Editor: Dana Herbison

Publisher's Interests
This publisher's list of nonfiction titles are geared for young adults. How-to books, self-help, and topics ranging from crafts to entertainment are produced by Success Publications.

Freelance Potential
Published 6 titles (2 juvenile) in 2005: 4 were developed from unsolicited submissions and 2 were by agented authors. Of the 6 titles, 2 were by unpublished writers and 4 were by authors who were new to the publishing house. Receives 200 unsolicited mss yearly.
Submissions and Payment: Guidelines available. Send complete ms. Accepts photocopies. SASE. Availability of artwork improves chance of acceptance. Responds in 2 weeks. Publication in 3 months. Payment policy varies.

Sunburst Technology

400 Columbus Avenue
Valhalla, NY 10595

Vice President, Software: David Wolff

Publisher's Interests
Guidance and health topics for students in kindergarten through twelfth grade are this publisher's mainstay. Its list also includes titles on the subjects of social studies, the Internet, science, language arts, mathematics, creativity, and the arts.
Website: www.sunburst.com

Freelance Potential
Published 50 titles in 2005: 1 was developed from an unsolicited submission. Receives 1,500 queries yearly.
Submissions and Payment: Query with résumé and writing samples. Accepts product concept proposals and accompanying graphics. SASE. Responds in 3–6 weeks. Publication period and payment policy vary.

Teachers & Writers Collaborative

5 Union Square West
New York, NY 10003-3306

Editors: Christina Davis and Christopher Edgar

Publisher's Interests
Founded in 1967 by a group of writers and teachers who believed that writers could make a unique contribution to the teaching of writing, this impressive list includes books on oral history, creative nonfiction, and fiction writing.
Website: www.twc.org

Freelance Potential
Published 2 titles in 2005: 1 was a reprint/licensed property. Receives 224 queries yearly.
Submissions and Payment: Query with résumé, outline, market analysis, and sample chapter. Accepts photocopies, computer printouts, and email queries to editors@twc.org. SASE. Responds in 6 months. Publication in 18 months. Royalty; advance.

Thistledown Press

633 Main Street
Saskatoon, Saskatchewan S7H 0J8
Canada

Submissions Editor: Allen Forrie

Publisher's Interests
This literary publisher showcases the works of Canadian authors. Its list includes some novels and short fiction for young adults that feature quality writing and appropriate themes for young readers. It does not publish illustrated children's books.
Website: www.thistledown.sk.ca

Freelance Potential
Published 20 titles (all juvenile) in 2005. Of the 18 titles, 4 were by authors who were new to the publishing house. Receives 600 queries yearly.
Submissions and Payment: Canadian authors only. Writers' guidelines and catalogue available. Query with outline and sample chapter. SASE. Responds in 1 week. Publication in 3 months. Royalty.

Thomson Nelson

1120 Birchmount Road
Toronto, Ontario M1K 5G4
Canada

Submissions

Publisher's Interests
Thomson Nelson features educational titles in science, language arts, and mathematics. It strives to offer the most comprehensive array of elementary and secondary materials to Canadian educators and students.
Website: www.nelson.com

Freelance Potential
Published 60 titles (40 juvenile) in 2005: all were by agented authors and 10 were reprint/licensed properties. Of the 60 titles, 8 were by authors new to the publishing house. Receives 100 queries yearly.
Submissions and Payment: Query. No unsolicited mss. SAE/IRC. Responds in 6–12 months. Publication period varies. Payment policy varies.

Touchwood Editions

Suite 6, 356 Simcoe Street
Victoria, British Columbia V8V 1L1
Canada

Acquisitions Editor

Publisher's Interests
Formerly known as Horsdal & Schubart, this member of the
Heritage Group publishes fiction and nonfiction in the areas
of history, biography, nautical subjects, architecture, design,
and humor. It is interested in submissions relating to the
people, places, and culture of Western Canada for readers
of all ages.
Website: www.touchwoodeditions.com

Freelance Potential
Published 7 titles (1 juvenile) in 2005.
Submissions and Payment: Guidelines available. Query with
synopsis, table of contents, 2–3 sample chapters, and word
count. SAE/IRC. Response time varies. Publication period and
payment policy vary.

Tradewind Books Ltd.

202-1809 Maritime Mews
Vancouver, British Columbia V6H 3W7
Canada

Submissions Editor: R. David Stephens

Publisher's Interests
Quality literature that sparks the imagination of young children
can be found in the catalogue of this small publisher.
Website: www.tradewindbooks.com

Freelance Potential
Published 5 titles in 2005: 1 was developed from an unsolicited
submission. Of the 5 titles, 1 was by an unpublished writer
and 4 were by authors who were new to the publishing house.
Receives 1,000 queries, 1,500 unsolicited mss yearly.
Submissions and Payment: Guidelines available at website.
Query with résumé and sample chapter for fiction. Send com-
plete ms with résumé for nonfiction. Accepts photocopies.
SAE/IRC. Responds in 3 months. Publication in 3 years. Royalty;
advance.

Two Lives Publishing

P.O. Box 736
Ridley Park, PA 19078

Editor: Bobbie Combs

Publisher's Interests
Children's books that positively reflect the lives of gay, lesbian, bisexual, and transgendered families are the specialty of
Two Lives Publishing. Since 1999, it has published a wide
range of topics, from family planning to birth and childcare. It
is not currently accepting unsolicited manuscripts.
Website: www.twolives.com

Freelance Potential
Published 2 titles in 2005. Of the 2 titles, both were by
unpublished writers.
Submissions and Payment: Writers' guidelines available.
Query. Accepts computer printouts and email queries to
bcombs@twolives.com. Response time, publication period,
and payment policy vary.

Unity House

Unity School of Christianity
1901 NW Blue Parkway
Unity Village, MO 64065-0001

Submissions: Adrianne Ford

Publisher's Interests
Spiritual books based on Unity principles as well as inspirational books on self-help psychology and practical spirituality
make up the core of this publisher.
Website: www.unityworldhq.org

Freelance Potential
Published several titles in 2005: 1 was developed from an
unsolicited submission. Of the several titles, most were by
unpublished writers who were new to the publishing house.
Receives 450 queries yearly.
Submissions and Payment: Guidelines available by mail and
at website. Query with outline, résumé, market analysis, and
1–3 sample chapters. SASE. Responds in 6–8 weeks.
Publication in 11 months. Royalty.

Windstorm Creative

P.O. Box 28
Port Orchard, WA 98366

Senior Editor: Cris DiMarco

Publisher's Interests
An independent press, Windstorm Creative was founded in
1989. Its children's division publishes timeless picture books,
young adult novels, and role-playing games; and is very open
to publishing new writers.
Website: www.windstormcreative.com

Freelance Potential
Published 200–300 titles (100–150 juvenile) in 2005: all were
developed from unsolicited submissions. Receives 1,000-
2,000 queries yearly.
Submissions and Payment: Guidelines and required submission form and label available at website. Query with chapter
by chapter synopsis. Accepts photocopies. SASE. Responds in
1–3 months. Publication in 18 months. Royalty, 15%. Flat fee.

Windswept House Publishers

P.O. Box 159
Mt. Desert, ME 04660

Manuscript Editor

Publisher's Interests
Producing high-quality children's picture books, young adult
novels, and adult fiction, Windswept House Publishers seeks
material that transforms commonplace things into something
that young readers will appreciate and savor. Its titles promote
respect and admiration of the natural beauty of the world.
Website: www.musarts.net/windswept

Freelance Potential
Published 3 titles in 2005: Of the 3 titles, 2 were by authors
who were new to the publishing house.
Submissions and Payment: Writers' guidelines available with
SASE. Query only. Does not accept unsolicited mss. SASE.
Response time varies. Publication and payment policy vary.

Winslow Publishing

P.O. Box 38012
550 Eglington Avenue West
Toronto, Ontario M5N 3A8
Canada
President & Publisher: Michelle West

Publisher's Interests
Craft books for young readers are the mainstay of this Canadian publisher. Its titles provide easy-to-follow directions of fun and unique crafts for children ages five to twelve. Prospective writers are encouraged to query creative craft ideas with available illustrations.
Website: www.winslowpublishing.com

Freelance Potential
Published 2 titles in 2005. Receives 30–40 queries yearly.
Submissions and Payment: Query with sample illustrations. Availability of artwork improves chance of acceptance. Accepts simultaneous submissions if identified. SAE/IRC. Responds in 2 weeks. Publication in 2–3 months. Flat fee.

Wordware Publishing

Suite 200
2320 Los Rios Boulevard
Plano, TX 75074

Chief Operations Officer: Tim McEvoy

Publisher's Interests
This educational publisher seeks nonfiction books on technology and computers and professional reference works for this year.
Website: www.wordware.com

Freelance Potential
Published 20–30 titles in 2005: 5 were developed from unsolicited submissions and 2 were by agented authors. Of the 20–30 titles, 4 were by unpublished writers and 3 were by authors who were new to the publishing house. Receives 100 queries yearly.
Submissions and Payment: Guidelines available. Query with résumé. Accepts photocopies, computer printouts, disk submissions, and simultaneous submissions if identified. SASE. Responds in 6 weeks. Publication in 1 year. Royalty.

The Wright Group/McGraw Hill

Suite 400
1 Prudential Plaza
130 East Randolph Street
Chicago, IL 60601

Submissions Editor: Christine DeLuca

Publisher's Interests
The Wright Group/McGraw Hill concentrates on producing curriculum and resource materials for use in preschool settings through grade six.
Website: www.wrightgroup.com

Freelance Potential
Published 225 titles in 2005: 30 were developed from unsolicited submissions, 30 were by agented authors, and 16 were reprint/licensed properties. Of the 225 titles, 35 were by authors who were new to the publishing house.
Submissions and Payment: Not accepting queries or manuscripts at this time. Check website for changes in submission policy.

YMAA Publication Center

4354 Washington Street
Rosindale, MA 02131

Director: David Ripianzi

Publisher's Interests
Books, videos, and music on topics related to advanced martial arts and Asian health are produced by this publisher. Its titles are read by adults and young adults.
Website: www.ymaapub.com

Freelance Potential
Published 6 titles in 2005: all were developed from unsolicited submissions. Of the 6 titles, 3 were by new authors. Receives 72 queries, 240 unsolicited mss yearly.
Submissions and Payment: Guidelines and catalogue available with 6x9 SASE ($1 postage) or at website. Query with clips or send complete ms with sample chapter. Accepts computer printouts. SASE. Responds in 1–3 months. Publication in 12–18 months. Royalty, 10%.

Contests and Awards

Selected Contests & Awards

Whether you enter a contest for unpublished writers or submit your published book for an award, you will have an opportunity to have your book read by established writers and qualified editors. Participating in a competition can increase recognition of your writing and possibly open more doors for selling your work. If you don't win and the winning entry is published, try to read it to see how your work compares with its competition.

To be considered for the contests and awards that follow, your entry must fulfill all of the requirements mentioned. Most are looking for unpublished article or story manuscripts, while a few require published works. Note special entry requirements, such as whether or not you can submit the material yourself, need to be a member of an organization, or are limited in the number of entries you can send. Also, be sure to submit your article or story in the standard manuscript submission format.

For each listing, we've included the address, the contact, a description, the entry requirements, the deadline, and the prize. In some cases, the 2006 deadlines were not available at press time. We recommend that you write to the addresses provided and ask for an entry form and the contest guidelines, which usually specify the current deadline.

American Book Cooperative
Children's Picture Book Competition

11010 Hanning Lane
Houston, TX 77041-5006

Description
This competition is sponsored by the American Book Cooperative. Ten finalists are chosen by the judges and then posted on the ABC website for others to vote on the winner. The competition accepts original, unpublished manuscripts.
Website: www.americanbookcooperative.org
Length: No length limit.
Requirements: No entry fee. Limit 5 entries per competition. Critique sheets on each entry are available by request with SASE after July 1. Accepts photocopies and computer printouts. Manuscripts will not be returned. Send an SASE or visit the website for complete guidelines.
Prizes: Winner receives publication of their manuscript along with a marketing plan and initial PR launch.
Deadline: April.

Arizona Author's Association
Literary Contests

Toby Heathcotte, Contest Coordinator
P.O. Box 87857
Phoenix, AZ 85080-7857

Description
The Arizona Author's Association sponsors these contests, which accept material in several categories including short stories, unpublished novels, children's literature, and essays.
Website: www.azauthors.com/contest.html
Length: Varies for each category.
Requirements: Entry fees range from $15 to $30 depending on category. Submit first 25 pages for novel entries. Accepts photocopies and computer printouts. Visit the website for a complete list of submission guidelines.
Prizes: Winners in each category receive a cash award of $100 and possible publication.
Deadline: July 1.

Atlantic Writing Competition

Writers' Federation of Nova Scotia
1113 Marginal Road
Halifax, Nova Scotia B3H 4P7
Canada

Description

Open to writers in the Atlantic provinces of Canada, this annual competition accepts entries in the categories of novel, short story, poetry, writing for children, and magazine/article essay. It accepts previously unpublished, original work only.

Website: www.writers.ns.ca

Length: Varies for each category.

Requirements: Entry fees: novel category, $25; all other categories, $15. WFNS members receive a $5 discount on entry fees. Published authors may not enter the competition in the genre in which they have been published. Limit one entry per category. Accepts photocopies and computer printouts. Guidelines available at website.

Prizes: First- through third-place winners in each category receive cash awards ranging from $50 to $250.

The Boston Globe-Horn Book Awards

The Horn Book
Suite 200
56 Roland Street
Boston, MA 02129

Description

The Boston Globe–Horn Book Awards honor excellence in literature for children and young adults. They are considered among the most prestigious in the nation. A committee of three judges evaluates books submitted by United States publishers and selects winners on the basis of their overall creative excellence.

Website: www.hbook.com

Length: No length limits.

Requirements: No entry fee. Publishers may submit up to 8 books from each of their juvenile imprints in the following categories: fiction or poetry, nonfiction, and picture books. Visit the website for complete guidelines, or send an SASE.

Prizes: Winner receives $500 and an engraved silver bowl. Honor books may also be named.

Deadline: May 15 of each year.

Marilyn Brown Novel Award

125 Hobble Creek Canyon
Springville, UT 84663

Description
Presenting awards every other year, this competition accepts
previously unpublished novel entries about or for Mormons celebrating the religion. It is open to all writers.
Website: www.aml-online.com
Length: No length limits.
Requirements: No entry fee. Author's name should not appear
on manuscript. Include an envelope with author's name,
address, and phone number inside and title of entry written on
the outside of the envelope. Entries should be bound with
comb binding. Include an SASE for return of manuscript.
Prizes: Winner receives a cash prize of $1,000.
Deadline: July 1.

CNW/FFWA Florida State Writing Competition

CNW/FFWA
P.O. Box A
North Stratford, NH 03590

Description
This annual competition accepts entries in the divisions of nonfiction, fiction, children's literature, and poetry. Awards are presented in several categories within each division. The competition is open to all writers.
Website: www.writers-editors.com
Length: Varies for each category.
Requirements: Entry fees vary for each category. Multiple
entries are accepted. Use paper clips only; no staples. Author's
name should not appear on manuscript. Send an SASE or visit
the website for category-specific guidelines and entry forms.
Prizes: First- through third-place winners in each category will
receive cash prizes ranging from $50 to $100.
Deadline: March 15.

Delacorte Dell Yearling Contest for a First Middle Grade Novel

Random House
1745 Broadway, 9th Floor
New York, NY 10019

Description
This annual contest looks to encourage the writing of contemporary or historical fiction set in North America for readers ages 9 to 12. It is open to writers living in the U.S. and Canada who have not previously published a middle-grade novel.
Website: www.randomhouse.com/kids/writingcontests
Length: 96- to 160-typewritten pages.
Requirements: No entry fee. Accepts photocopies and computer printouts. No simultaneous submissions or foreign-language translations. Include a brief plot summary and cover letter. Include an SASE for return of manuscript.
Prizes: Winner receives a book contract including an advance of $7,500 and a cash prize of $1,500.
Deadline: Entries must be postmarked between April 1 and June 30.

Delacorte Press Contest for a First Young Adult Novel

Random House
1745 Broadway, 9th Floor
New York, NY 10019

Description
Open to writers living in the U.S. and Canada who have not yet published a novel for young adults, this annual contest accepts entries of contemporary fiction for young adults.
Website: www.randomhouse.com/kids/writingcontests
Length: 100- to 224-typewritten pages.
Requirements: No entry fee. Accepts photocopies and computer printouts. No simultaneous submissions or foreign-language translations. Include a brief plot summary and cover letter. Include an SASE for return of manuscript.
Prizes: Winner receives a book contract including an advance of $7,500 and a cash prize of $1,500.
Deadline: Entries must be postmarked between October 1 and December 31.

Paul Gillette Memorial Writing Contest

Pikes Peak Writers
P.O. Box 63114
Colorado Springs, CO 80962

Description

Encouraging emerging authors to focus on producing a marketable manuscript, this contest is held each year. It accepts manuscripts in several categories, including children's, young adult, mystery, historical fiction, and creative nonfiction.
Website: www.pikespeakwriters.org
Length: Varies for each category.
Requirements: Entry fee, $25 ($40 entry fee includes a manuscript critique). Accepts photocopies and computer printouts. All entries must be accompanied by an entry form, a cover letter, and two copies of manuscript. Guidelines available at website.
Prizes: First-place winner in each category receives $100. Second-place winner in each category receives $50.
Deadline: November 1.

The Barbara Karlin Grant

The Society of Children's Book Writers and Illustrators
8271 Beverly Boulevard
Los Angeles, CA 90048

Description

Established to recognize and reward the work of aspiring picture book writers, The Barbara Karlin Grant is available to both full and associate members of the Society of Children's Book Writers who have not yet published a picture book. Original short stories, nonfiction, or re-tellings of fairy tales, folktales, or legends are eligible.
Website: www.scbwi.org
Length: 8 pages.
Requirements: No entry fee. Requests for application may be made beginning October 1 of each year. Instructions and complete guidelines are sent with application forms.
Prizes: Cash grants of $1,500 and $500 are awarded in each of the 5 categories.
Deadline: Ongoing.

Maryland Writers Association Novel Contest

P.O. Box 142
Annapolis, MD 21404

Description
Open to all writers, this contest accepts novel-length fiction manuscripts in the categories of horror, fantasy, mystery, science fiction, romance, and historical fiction.
Website: www.marylandwriters.org
Length: 50,000 words minimum.
Requirements: Entry fee, $35. Accepts photocopies and computer printouts. Visit the website or send an SASE for complete guidelines.
Prizes: The overall contest winner receives a cash award of $100. First-place winners in each category receive a cash award of $50.
Deadline: March 31.

Mid-List Press First Series Award for the Novel

4324 12th Avenue South
Minneapolis, MN 55407-3218

Description
Open to writers who have not yet published a novel, this competition is sponsored by Mid-List Press.
Website: www.midlist.org
Length: 50,000 words minimum.
Requirements: Entry fee, $30. Limit one entry per competition. Accepts photocopies and computer printouts. Include an SASE for winners' list. Visit the website or send an SASE for complete guidelines.
Prizes: Winner receives publication by Mid-list Press and an advance against royalties.
Deadline: Entries are accepted between October 1 and February 1.

Milkweed Prize for Children's Literature

Milkweed Editions
Suite 300, 1011 Washington Ave. South
Minneapolis, MN 55415-1246

Description

Open to authors who have previously published a book of fiction or a minimum of three short stories, this competition is looking for high-quality manuscripts for readers ages 8 to 13 that embody humane values and contribute to cultural understanding.

Website: www.milkweed.org
Length: 90–200 typewritten pages.
Requirements: No entry fee. Entries must have been accepted for publication by Milkweed during the calendar year by a writer not previously published by Milkweed. Picture books and collections of stories are not eligible. All entries must follow Milkweed's usual children's manuscript guidelines.
Prizes: Winners receive a $10,000 cash advance on royalties.
Deadline: Ongoing.

National Children's Theatre Festival Competition

Actors' Playhouse at the Miracle Theatre
280 Miracle Mile
Coral Gables, FL 33134

Description

The Actor's Playhouse at the Miracle Theatre invites the submission of original scripts for musicals to be judged by a distinguished panel from both professional and academic theatre. All entries should target the 3-to-12 age group, but plays that are appealing to both children and adults are preferred.

Website: www.actorsplayhouse.org
Length: Running time, 45–60 minutes.
Requirements: Entry fee, $10 per submission. Multiple entries are accepted. Accepts photocopies and computer printouts. Include an SASE for return of manuscript. Guidelines available at website.
Prizes: Winner receives a cash prize of $500 and a full production of their play.
Deadline: June 1.

Newbery Medal Award

American Library Association
50 East Huron
Chicago, IL 60611

Description

This medal is presented annually to an author who has made a distinguished contribution to American literature for children published in the U.S. Eligible authors must be citizens or residents of the U.S.

Website: www.ala.org

Length: No length limit.

Requirements: No entry fee. Multiple submissions are accepted. All entries must have been published in the year preceding the contest. Guidelines available at website.

Prizes: The Newbery Medal is awarded to the winner. Honor books may also be named.

Deadline: December 31.

New Voices Award

Attn. New Voice Award
Lee & Low Books
95 Madison Avenue
New York, NY 10016

Description

This award is sponsored by Lee & Low Books, the award-winning publisher of multicultural books for children. It is presented annually to an author of color for a picture book manuscript. The contest is open to U.S. residents who have not published a children's picture book. All entries should target children ages 2 through 10 and may be either fiction or nonfiction.

Website: www.leeandlow.com

Length: To 1,500 words.

Requirements: No entry fee. Limit 2 entries per competition. Accepts computer printouts. Guidelines available at website.

Prizes: Winner receives a cash grant of $1,000 and a standard publishing contract from Lee & Low Books. An honor grant of $500 will also be awarded.

Deadline: December 31.

Ursula Nordstrom Fiction Contest

HarperCollins Children's Books
1350 Avenue of the Americas
New York, NY 10019

Description

This annual first-fiction contest is open to U.S. writers over the age of 21 who have not been previously published. It looks to encourage new talent in the writing of innovative and challenging middle-grade fiction. All entries must be suitable for children ages 8 to 12.
Website: www.harpercollins.com/writingcontest
Length: 100 to 300 pages.
Requirements: No entry fee. Limit one entry per competition. Accepts photocopies and computer printouts. Include an SASE for return of manuscript. Guidelines available at website.
Prizes: Winner receives a book contract for a hardcover edition, a $7,500 advance, and a $1,500 cash award.
Deadline: Entries will be accepted between March 15 and April 15 only.

NWA Novel Contest

National Writers Association
3140 S. Peoria Street #295
Aurora, CO 80014

Description

This award is presented annually by the National Writers Association. It looks to encourage the development of creative skils and recognize outstanding ability in novel writing. It accepts previously unpublished novel entries in any genre.
Website: www.nationalwriters.com
Length: To 100,000 words.
Requirements: Entry fee, $35. Accepts photocopies and computer printouts. Include an SASE for return of manuscript. If entrants would like their manuscripts critiqued, please note this on the entry form. Guidelines available at website.
Prizes: First-place winners receive $500. Second- and third-place winners receive $250 and $150, respectively. Fourth- through tenth-place winners receive a book and an honor certificate.
Deadline: April 1.

Once Upon a World Book Award

Museum of Tolerance
1399 S. Roxbury Drive
Los Angeles, CA 90035-4709

Description
The mission of this award is to support and perpetuate the values and mandate of the Simon Wiesenthal Center & Museum of Tolerance by honoring children's books targeting the 6 to 10 age group. Entries should promote acceptance, tolerance, and communication among people. It accepts entries of fiction, nonfiction, or poetry.
Website: www.wiesenthal.com/library/award.cfm
Length: No length limit.
Requirements: No entry fee. All entries must have been published in the year preceding the contest. A nomination form must accompany each submission. Guidelines and nomination form available at website.
Prizes: Winners receive a cash award of $1,000.
Deadline: April.

Pacific Northwest Writers Association Literary Contests

PNWA
P.O. Box 2016
Edmonds, WA 98020-9516

Description
Held annually, these contests are offered in several categories, including juvenile/young adult novel; nonfiction book; juvenile memoir; and short story. The competition accepts original, previously unpublished material only.
Website: www.pnwa.org
Length: Varies for each category.
Requirements: Entry fee, $35 for members; $45 for non-members. Multiple entries are accepted. Accepts photocopies and computer printouts. All entries must include an official entry form. Submit 2 copies of each entry. Guidelines and category information available at website.
Prizes: Winners receive cash awards ranging from $150 to $600.
Deadline: February.

Skipping Stones Awards

Skipping Stones Awards
P.O. Box 3939
Eugene, OR 97403

Description
These awards focus on multicultural awareness and honor exceptional contributions to ecological and multicultural education. Books, magazines, and educational videos are considered in each of the four categories: Ecology & Nature, Educational Videos, Multicultural & International, and Teaching Resources.
Website: www.efn.org/~skipping
Length: No length limits.
Requirements: Entry fee, $50. Multiple entries are accepted. Send 4 copies of each book and magazine entry; 2 copies of each video. Only entries produced in the preceding calendar year are eligible.
Prizes: Cash prizes are awarded to first- through fourth-place winners. Winning entries are reviewed in *Skipping Stones.*
Deadline: January 15.

Smart Publishing Winter Revelation Contest

11832 S. Bishop
Chicago, IL 60643

Description
Smart Publishing is currently seeking unpublished manuscripts for fiction novels, novellas, short stories, and poetry. Entries are accepted for all reading levels. All manuscripts must be original and previously unpublished.
Website: www.geocities.com/smart_suzette/ smartpublishing.html
Length: No length limits.
Requirements: Entry fee, $10. Multiple entries are accepted. Accepts photocopies and computer printouts. All manuscripts must be bound. Visit the website or send an SASE for complete guidelines.
Prizes: Winner receives a publishing contract with Smart Publishing.
Deadline: May 1.

Kay Snow Writing Contest

Willamette Writers
Suite 5A
9045 SW Barbour Blvd
Portland, OR 97219-4027

Description
This contest presents awards in several categories, including juvenile short story or article, fiction, nonfiction, and student writer. Held annually, it accepts original, unpublished material only.
Website: www.willamettewriters.com
Length: Varies for each category.
Requirements: Entry fee, $10 for members; $15 for non-members. Submit 3 copies of each entry. Author's name must not appear on manuscript. Request complete contest guidelines or visit website for additional information.
Prizes: Cash prizes ranging from $50 to $300 are awarded in each category. A Liam Callen award will also be presented to the best overall entry with a cash prize of $500.
Deadline: May 15.

Southwest Writers Contests

Southwest Writers Workshop
Suite 106
8200 Mountain Road NE
Albuquerque, NM 87110

Description
This competition looks to recognize, encourage, and honor excellence in writing. These contests present awards in several categories including middle-grade novel, young adult novel, children's picture book, and nonfiction book.
Website: www.southwestwriters.org
Length: Varies for each category.
Requirements: Entry fee, $29 for members; $39 for non-members. Submit 2 copies of each entry. Each entry must be accompanied by an official entry form. Author's name should appear on the entry form only. Multiple entries are accepted. All entries must be typed. Send an SASE for complete contest guidelines and official entry form, or visit the website.
Prizes: Cash prizes ranging from $75–$100.
Deadline: May 1.

Tall Tales Press Hidden Talents Short Story Contest

20 Tuscany Valley Park NW
Calgary, Alberta T3L 2B6
Canada

Description

Offering writers a chance to gain the experience that publishers demand, this contest accepts manuscripts in several categories from both adult and young adult writers. It accepts previously unpublished work only.

Website: www.talltalespress.com
Length: To 5,000 words.
Requirements: Entry fees, $10 for adults categories; $5 for junior categories. Multiple entries are accepted. All entries must be accompanied by an official entry form. Guidelines and entry forms available at website.
Prizes: Winners and honorable mentions receive cash prizes ranging from $10 to $500 and possible publication.
Deadline: May 31.

Peter Taylor Prize for the Novel

Knoxville Writers Guild
Suite 101
100 S. Gray Street
Knoxville, TN 37902

Description

Held annually, this competition is open to both published and unpublished writers living in the U.S. It looks to identify, promote, and publish novels of high literary quality.

Website: www.knoxvillewritersguild.org
Length: 40,000 words minimum.
Requirements: Entry fee, $25. Multiple submissions are accepted provided that each is accompanied by an entry fee. Entries must be on standard white paper. Manuscripts will not be returned. Include an SASE for contest results.
Prizes: The prize includes a $1,000 cash award, publication of the novel by the University of Tennessee Press, and a standard royalty contract.
Deadline: Entries must be postmarked between February 1 and April 30.

Work-in-Progress Grants

The Society of Children's Book Writers and Illustrators
8271 Beverly Boulevard
Los Angeles, CA 90048

Description
The Society of Childrens Book Writers and Illustrators presents
five grants annually to assist children's book writers in the completion of a project. Grants are awarded in the categories of
General Work-in-Progress; Contemporary Novel for Young People; Nonfiction Research; and Unpublished Author.
Website: www.scbwi.org
Length: 750-word synopsis and writing sample from the entry
that is no longer than 2,500 words.
Requirements: No entry fee. Requests for applications may
be made beginning October 1 of each year. Instructions and
complete guidelines are sent with application forms.
Prizes: Cash grants of $1,500 and $500 are awarded in each
of the five categories.

Paul Zindel First Novel Award

Hyperion Books for Children
P.O. Box 6000
Manhasset, NY 11030-6000

Description
The Paul Zindel First Novel Award is presented annually for the
best contemporary or historical fiction for readers ages 8 to 12
that is set in the United States and that reflects the diverse ethnic and cultural heritage of the country. The competition is open
to all writers living in the U.S. who have not yet published a
novel.
Website: www.hyperionbooksforchildren.com
Length: 100- to 240-typewritten pages.
Requirements: No entry fee. Limit two entries per competition.
Accepts photocopies and computer printouts. Include an SASE
for return of manuscript. Guidelines available at website.
Prizes: Winner receives a book contract and an advance against
royalties of $7,500 and a cash prize of $1,500.
Deadline: April 30.

Indexes

2006 Market News

New Listings ☆

Achievement Publishing
Adams Media Corporation
Andersen Press Ltd.
Archimedes Press
Arizona Author's Association
  Literary Contest
Avalon Books
Baycrest Books
Birdsong Books
Carolina Wren Press
Chivalry Bookshelf
Chronicle Books
Claire Publications
Creative Book Publishing
DaCapo Press
DNA Press
Doral Publishing
Dundurn Press
Earthkids Publishing
Fairview Press
Flashlight Press
Paul Gillette Memorial
  Writing Contest
Great Potential Press
Harvest House Publishers
Helm Publishing
Hensley Publishing
Iron Gate Publishing
Kids Can Press
Luna Rising
Marlowe Publishing

Maryland Writers Association
  Novel Contest
Medallion Press
Messianic Jewish Publishers
Mid-List Press First Series
  Awards for the Novel
Mountain Press Publishing
  Company
New Age Dimensions
Orchard Creative Group
O'Reilly Media Inc.
P & R Publishing Company
Pauline Books & Media
Platypus Media
Plexus Publishing, Inc.
Prufrock Press
Red Rock Press
RP Books
Scholastic Children's Books
  (UK)
Scobre Press
Servant Books
Smart Publishing Winter
  Revelation Contest
Square One Publishers
Stackpole Books
Stone Arch Books
Teacher Created Resources
Thomson Nelson
VanderWyk & Burhnam

2006 Market News

Deletions/Name Changes

Advocacy Press: No response
Alpha Publishing: No response
Amirah Publishing: No response
A.R.E. Publishing, Inc.: No response
Blue Marlin Publications: No response
BOW Books: No response
Branden Books: No response
Camex Books: No response
Charles River Media: No response
Childswork/Childsplay: No response
Contemporary Books: Publishing division sold
Cornell Maritime Press: No response
Dandy Lion Publications: Bought by **Prufrock Press**
Delmar Learning: No response
ESP Publishers, Inc.: No response
ETC Publications: No response
Greenwood Publishing Group: No response
Hampton Roads Publishing: No longer publishing material for children
Harcourt Canada Ltd.: K-12 products now published under **Thomson Nelson**
HarperCollins Children's Fiction: No response
Heritage House: Removed per editor's request
Key Porter Books: No response
Kodiak Media Group: No response
Marsh Media: No response
Munchweiler Press: Ceased publication
The New England Press: No response
Quartz Editions: Unable to locate
Riverfront Books: No longer publishing; see **Stone Arch Books**
Scorpius Digital Publishing: Unable to locate
Scott Foresman: All material written in-house
Seaburn Publishing: Unable to locate
Silver Whistle: No response
Siphano Picture Books: No response
Stiles-Bishop Productions Inc.: No longer in business
Teacher Created Materials: No response
TowleHouse Publishing: No response
Twenty-Third Publications: No longer publishing children's material
Visual Education Corporation: Unable to locate
XC Publishing: Ceased publication

Category Index

To help you find the appropriate market for your query or manuscript, we have compiled a selective index of publishers according to the types of books they currently publish.

If you don't find a category that exactly fits your material, try a broader term that covers your topic. For example, if you have written a middle-grade biography, look through the list of publishers for both Middle-Grade (Nonfiction) *and* Biography. If you've written a young adult mystery, look under Mystery/Suspense *and* Young Adult (Fiction). Always check the publisher's listing for explanations of specific needs.

For your convenience, we have listed all of the categories that are included in this Index.

Activity Books
Adventure
Animals/Pets
Bilingual (Fiction)
Bilingual
  (Nonfiction)
Biography
Board Books
Canadian
  Publishers
Chapter Books
  (Fiction)
Chapter Books
  (Nonfiction)
Concept Books
Contemporary
  Fiction
Crafts/Hobbies
Current Events
Drama
Early Picture Books
  (Fiction)
Early Picture Books
  (Nonfiction)
Easy-to-Read
  (Fiction)
Easy-to-Read
  (Nonfiction)
Education/Resource
  Material
Fairy Tales
Fantasy

Folklore/Folktales
Geography
Gifted Education
Health/Fitness
High-Interest/
  Low-Vocabulary
Historical Fiction
History (Nonfiction)
Horror
How-to
Humor
Inspirational Fiction
Language Arts
Mathematics
Middle-Grade
  (Fiction)
Middle-Grade
  (Nonfiction)
Multicultural/
  Ethnic (Fiction)
Multicultural/Ethnic
  (Nonfiction)
Mystery/Suspense
Nature/
  Environment
Parenting
Photo Essays
Picture Books
  (Fiction)
Picture Books
  (Nonfiction)
Plays

Reference Books
Regional (Fiction)
Regional
  (Nonfiction)
Religious (Fiction)
Religious
  (Nonfiction)
Romance
Science Fiction
Science/Technology
Self-Help
Series
Social Issues
Social Sciences
Special Education
Sports (Fiction)
Sports (Nonfiction)
Story Picture Books
  (Fiction)
Story Picture Books
  (Nonfiction)
Toddler Books
  (Fiction)
Toddler Books
  (Nonfiction)
Travel
Western
Young Adult
  (Fiction)
Young Adult
  (Nonfiction)

Horror

How-to

Humor

Inspirational Fiction

Language Arts

Mathematics

Middle-Grade (F)

Parenting

Photo Essays

Picture Books (F)

Picture Books (NF)

586

Publisher and Contest Index

If you do not find a particular publisher, turn to page 555 for a list of deletions and name changes.

★ indicates a newly listed publisher or contest